TOURNAMENT PLAYER'S REPERTOIRE OF OPENINGS
Series edited by R.G. Wade, O.B.E.

Sicilian . . . e6 and . . . d6 Systems

Gary Kasparov and
Aleksander Nikitin

American Chess Promotions, Macon, Georgia

First published 1983
Second, fully revised edition 1983
© Gary Kasparov, Alexander Nikitin, 1983
ISBN 0 7134 4627 7 (limp)

Set by Hope Services, Abingdon
and printed in Great Britain by
Dotesios Ltd
Bradford upon Avon, Wilts.
for the publishers
American Chess Promotions
3055 General Lee Road
Macon, Georgia 31204

First published 1983 in United States
for American Chess Promotions

A BATSFORD CHESS BOOK
Adviser: R.G. Wade, O.B.E.
Technical Editor: P.A. Lamford

Contents

Acknowledgements

The authors would like to thank Bob Wade for checking references and Kevin Wicker for proofreading the entire book.

Translator's Preface

This is a translation of the book "Vsyo o Scheveningenye" by Kasparov and Nikitin. It was written when the authors were engaged in updating the B8 sections of volume "B" of the *Encyclopedia of Chess Openings*, and when Kasparov was engaged in work on *Batsford Chess Openings*. It contains all relevant theoretical and practical material up to April 1982, and was expanded by Kasparov and myself to include further references up to the start of the Interzonal event in Moscow, 1982. The expanded version was checked by the authors during that event, at which time we also discussed the translation. Every attempt has been made to ensure that this translation meets the expectations aroused by the original Russian title, which means "Everything about the Scheveningen".

Eric Schiller

Symbols

+	Check
±∓	Slight advantage
± ∓	Clear advantage
±± ∓∓	Winning advantage
=	Level position
∞	Unclear position
!	Good move
!!	Outstanding
!?	Interesting move
?!	Dubious move
?	Weak move
??	Blunder
corr.	Correspondence
OL	Olympiad
IZ	Interzonal
L	League
Ch	Championship
½f	Semi-final
Δ	With the idea of

Introduction

The Sicilian Defence is one of the most popular openings of our time. The theory of the opening is enlarged and improved in almost every important competition, with evaluations of particular variations being modified all the time. Even after many years of research, analysis, and praxis there remain positions about which theoreticians and practical players cannot agree, and for which no clear cut assessments are available. Fortunately, chess is a game, and not a matter of purely mathematical calculations, and therefore these "Sicilian secrets" only help to draw more masters and amateurs into the study of the opening.

The so-called "Scheveningen" variation is one of the most strategically and tactically profound variations of the opening. It is thought that it first appeared on the tournament scene in Scheveningen, 1923, and came into fashion 10 years later. When work was taking place on the book *M. Chigorin*, however, it was discovered by one of the authors that the variation was played in the game Chigorin – Paulsen, in a Berlin event of 1882! In that game White adopted a modern strategy, reaching the variation now known as the Classical Scheveningen.

There are two special points which must be made about the Scheveningen:

1) Black has a pawn advantage in the centre: Pe6 and Pd6 against Pe4, but the so-called "small centre" is used as the basis of defence of the central squares c5, d5, e5 and f5. If Black advances his pawns in the centre, most often with e6-e5, he usually does so only to prevent e4-e5. Black usually operates on the queenside, exploiting the semi-open c-file. The knight c3 is the customary target, since it blocks the c-file and defends the e-pawn. The liquidation of the knight partially guarantees Black the successful resolution of his opening problems, and to this end he often employs the exchange sacrifice ♖c8xc3.

2) White's pieces dominate the centre and this allows him to play in various areas of the board. He customarily uses his spatial advantage for the transfer of his forces to the kingside, to which flank the Black king usually flees.

As a result, the play follows lines which are worked out with an understanding of the above-mentioned plans. Unclear positions are created, but at the same time these positions are elastic, so that success will depend not on the knowledge of lengthy variations alone. It is the understanding of the nuances of the chosen formations, the boldness and energy in the carrying out of the attack or spontaneous transfer to a counterattack which are more important. There are plenty of examples of cases in which the Black position is overrun, but some times it is White, having failed to display sufficient activity in the organization of his kingside operations, who surprisingly finds that the initiative has passed over to his opponent. In such cases there is often no stopping Black.

The theory of the openings has developed to such an extent that one can no longer be guaranteed the advantage in the opening phase of the game. The majority of opening systems and variations conclude with the evaluation "equal game", "double-edged game", or the like. Even experienced masters do not argue with such evaluations, since these evaluations by no means indicate that the game must end in a draw. Now the selection of opening is more a preparation for a game, not a feverish attempt to find "winning variations" in the numerous opening manuals. The choice of opening system must not only be in accordance with your individual style of play, but should also be influenced by the circumstances of the game. By this we mean the game which lies immediately before you, taking into account the tournament situation and other relevant considerations. At the same time, of course, you should not play into the hands of your opponent. (A careful study of Kasparov's openings in the 49th USSR Championship will help clarify the above statements — tr.) The Scheveningen system meets these requirements, providing a flexible opening system to the player of the Black side.

In the present book the authors have the following goal: to provide analysis of the state-of-the-art theory and praxis of the Scheveningen system, paying special attention to the ideas which lie behind the openings, the methods employed in the opening struggle, the plans for both sides, and the most problematic positions. On the basis of the body of practical experience, we give the most characteristic and logical continuations of the opening battle.

At times we leave the realm of praxis, when the move which contains the essential thought behind a certain plan was not adopted in tournament games. In our attempt to describe our ideas, there is sometimes contrast with praxis, but we wish to give the greatest amount of relevant material possible, while at the same time limiting ourselves to those characteristic fragments which are most interesting in relation to the games. As a result our book will hopefully prove useful to two types of players: those who are First Category players or Candidate Masters (i.e. under 2300 Elo), and those of the highest class, who have a professional relationship with the chess conflict.

To the first group we recommend that you focus your attention on the verbal material, in order to gain a deep understanding of the opening. To the second we point out the long-branched analyses and practical examples. In the course of the book we devote the most time to those variations and lines which occur most frequently in tournament practice.

The authors are also responsible for the material on the Scheveningen in the second edition of ECO B (B80-85). Nevertheless, this book is not merely a commentary on the encyclopedia. Here we have adopted a more personal approach, and this is reflected in our evaluations, which, however, are as objective as possible.

We fully understand that time will perhaps show that not all of our evaluations are 100% correct but they are well founded and thought-provoking, and that is important in a book which is aimed at players of the highest calibre.

Those who read this book in order to obtain a universal winning line in the. Scheveningen defeat its purpose. The authors demonstrate that the player who wins the opening battle is the player who plays more strongly. We think that the person who uses this book as a sort of compass in the confusing labyrinth of the Scheveningen will be satisfied.

You can have confidence in our analysis, but don't forget the maxim: "Believe it, but check it."

1 Classical Scheveningen: Introduction

1 e4 c5 2 ᗺf3 e6 3 d4 cd 4 ᗺxd4
ᗺf6 5 ᗺc3 d6 6 ♗e2

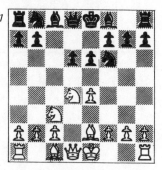

Among chessplayers who are only superficially acquainted with the theory of the Sicilian Defence, there exists the opinion that this modest move leads to less interesting play than 6 g4 or 6 ♗c4. Not so! The system with 6 ♗e2 may not be quite so direct, but it is more solid and no less exciting than other lines of the Scheveningen. Double-edged play is unavoidable, and sacrifices (or counter-sacrifices) abound, since White is gunning for the Black king.

6   ...   a6

In the Classical Scheveningen this move is considered obligatory, since it secures a safe square for the queen on c7 and prepares counterplay on the queenside with b7-b5 etc. It is played at move six according to the principle "the sooner the better". Recent theory and praxis has somewhat altered the picture. While the move a7-a6 remains useful, it is no longer considered essential in the early stages of the game.

A "modern" handling of the Scheveningen has emerged in which Black delays or omits this prophylactic move. For some time it was eclipsed by its older sister, but 6 ... a6 remains, like a sunspot, and now we have two methods of conducting the defence: Classical and Modern. The merits of these two formations are considered to be equal by connoisseurs of the Sicilian Defence.

7   0-0   ♗e7

Praxis has shown that plans which involve a delay in the development of the kingside do not bring Black success against the well-principled development of White's forces. There is not yet any real target for Black, unlike positions in which White has already castled queenside. Therefore action on that flank will take time and solid preparation, which can only occur after Black has completed both development and castling.

Here are a few examples showing the risks involved when Black delays ... ♗e7:

7 ... ♘c6   8 ♗e3 ♕c7   9 f4

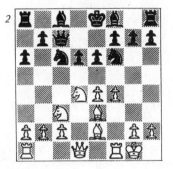

It is still not too late to play 9 ... ♗e7, but...

a) 9 ... ♘a5?!   10 f5! ♘c4   11 ♗xc4 ♕xc4   12 fe fe   13 ♖xf6! gf   14 ♕h5+ ♔d8   15 ♕f7!, Lasker − Pirc, 1935, or 10 ... e5   11 ♘b3 ♘c4   12 ♗g5! ♘xb2   13 ♕e1 ♘c4   14 ♗xf6 gf   15 ♘d5; or 10 ... ♗e7   11 ♕e1 b5?   12 ♕g3 b4   13 fe fe   14 ♕xg7 ♖g8   15 ♗h5+ ♔d8   16 ♕f7 ♖f8   17 ♘xe6+ ♗xe6   18 ♕xe6 bc   19 e5! b) 9 ... b5?   10 ♘xc6 ♕xc6   11 e5 de   12 fe ♗c5   13 ♗f3 ♗xe3+   14 ♔h1.

In each case White has a decisive attack.

Of course, these examples are a call for common sense in the opening, and not proof that Black's position is lost after 9 ... ♘a5   10 f5. Even after 10 ... ♗e7, for example, Black can meet 11 ♕e1 with 11 ... ♘c4   12 ♗xc4 ♕xc4   13 ♕g3 0-0,

i.e. 14 ♖ad1 ♔h8   15 fe fe   16 e5 de   17 ♕xe5 ♗d7 and White's initiative comes to a full stop.

Besides, Black can avoid both 9 ... ♘a5 and 9 ... b5 and find original play through 9 ... ♗d7, even though after 10 a4 Black has nothing better than transposing into the Classical variation with 10 ... ♗e7. If White declines to play 10 a4, however, Black obtains queenside counterplay.

10 ♕e1, for example, seems most logical.

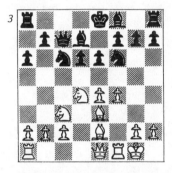

Black now has several options, other than 10 ... ♗e7.

a) 10 ... ♘xd4   11 ♗xd4 ♗c6   12 ♗f3 (or 12 ♗xf6 gf   13 ♗h5 0-0-0!?)   12 ... ♗e7   13 ♕g3 0-0   14 ♖ae1 g6, transposing to a comfortable line of the Classical, as the white bishop is misplaced on f3.

b) 10 ... b5   11 a3 (11 ♗f3 b4   12 ♘ce2 ♗e7   13 ♕g3 0-0 again leads to a double-edged position. The complications which arise after 14 e5 de   15 fe ♘xe5, or even 15 ... ♕xe5 are quite acceptable for Black.) branches off into two directions:

b1) 11 ... ♘xd4   12 ♗xd4 ♗c6

13 ♗f3 e5 14 fe de 15 ♕g3 ♗d6!?
16 ♕xg7 ed 17 e5 ♗xe5 or the
rather similar
b2) **11 ... ♗e7** 12 ♕g3 0-0 13 e5!
(All other moves lead to positions
which are thoroughly discussed in
the Classical variation, i.e. 13 ♔h1,
13 ♖ad1, 13 ♖ae1.). In the final
analysis this is a sharp tactical game
which holds danger for both sides,
and it comes about whenever Black
succeeds in getting in an early ... b5.
The subtleties of the variation will
be discussed later by comparison
with the e4-e5 thrust in the Classical
Scheveningen.

What can we conclude about
these variations? It seems that
Black must not hasten to castle, but
at the same time he can not delay
castling for too long! Timing, in
short, is everything.

8   f4   0-0

This is the most logical move,
but by no means the only one. If
Black plays carefully he can delay
castling in order to arrange his
forces on the queenside, i.e. 8 ...
♗d7 (8 ... ♘c6 9 ♘xc6 bc 10 e5
♘d5 11 ♘e4 ±) 9 ♗e3 ♘c6

Now Tukmakov-Petrosian, 1973,
continued 10 a4 ♘xd4 11 ♕xd4
♗c6 12 ♖fd1 0-0 13 a5 ♖ac8 14
♗f3 d5! 15 e5 ♘d7 16 ♘e2 ♗b5
with an excellent game for Black.

Instead, White can play along
standard lines with 10 ♕e1, practically forcing Black to transpose
into the main lines, since on 10 ...
e5 White seizes the initiative with
11 ♘xc6! ♗xc6 12 fe de (12 ...
♘xe4? loses to 13 ♖d1 ♗h4 14
♘xe4 ♗xe1 15 ♘xd6+ ♖f8 16

♖xf7+ ♔g8 17 ♗c4 b5 18 ♗b3.)
13 ♕g3 with threats on g7 and e5.
After 10 ... ♕c7 11 ♕g3

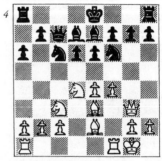

praxis has seen both 11 ... g6 12
♖ad1 ♘xd4 13 ♗xd4 ♗c6 14 e5
de 15 fe ♘d7 16 ♗f3! ±, Tsesh-
kovsky-Petkevich, 1977, and the
reckless 11 ... h5 12 ♖ad1 (12
♕xg7?! ♖g8 13 ♕h6 gives Black
the option of taking the draw with
13 ... ♖g6 14 ♕h8+ ♖g8 or continuing with 13 ... 0-0-0) 12 ... h4
13 ♕f2 0-0-0 (or 13 ... b5 14 ♗f3
b4 15 ♘ce2 e5 16 fe de 17 ♘b3
h3 18 g4 ♘d8! = Hort-Filipowicz,
1971). 14 h3 ♖dg8 15 ♘f3 ♘h5
16 ♖fe1 ♔b8 17 a3 ♘d8 18 ♗d3
f6 19 f5 g6 with a sharp game,
Suetin-Tolush, 1958.

But does it really pay to push
the h-pawn? White can force through
e4-e5 by meeting 11 ... h5 with 12
♗f3! h4 (12 ... 0-0-0 13 e5! de 14
♘xc6 ♗xc6 15 fe ±) 13 ♕f2 ♖c8
(13 ... b5? 14 e5! or 13 ... 0-0-0
14 ♘xc6) 14 ♖ae1! ♕b8 15 a4.
Black has no counterplay to neutralise the threat of e4-e5 and this
renders his position difficult.

8 ... ♕c7 9 ♗e3 ♘c6 10 ♕e1
♘xd4 11 ♗xd4 b5 also works
toward the goal of rapid deploy-

ment of forces on the queenside.

After 12 ♕g3 0-0 (but not 12 ... b4? 13 e5 de 14 fe bc 15 ♕xg7 ♖f8 16 ef with a big edge for White) the game enters the Classical mold. But White can try to exploit the location of the Black king in the centre by playing 12 e5 de 13 fe. Now there is no point to 13 ... ♗c5, as after 14 ♕f2! ♗xd4 15 ♕xd4 ♘d7 16 ♗xb5! White wins. That

leaves only 13 ... ♘d7 14 ♘e4 ♗b7, where the defence is difficult after 15 ♗d3 0-0 16 ♕g3. After 8 ... 0-0 White must decide what to do about the ♗c1. He can deploy it immediately on e3 or b2, or he can forget about it for a while and carry out the final phase of the opening, regrouping his forces with the intention of operating in one area of the board.

2 Classical Scheveningen with 9♔h1 or 9♗f3

In this chapter we examine the position after 1 e4 c5 2 ♘f3 e6 3 d4 cd 4 ♘xd4 ♘f6 5 ♘c3 d6 6 ♗e2 a6 7 0-0 ♗e7 8 f4 0-0 where White does not play 9 ♗e3. We ought to point out that it is also possible to fianchetto the queen's bishop. This plan is discussed in the introduction to the Modern Scheveningen, Chapter 10.

A 9♔h1
B 9♗f3

A

9 ♔h1

When the bishop is left on c1, this move becomes not merely a prophylactic, but a necessity, avoiding pins along the a7-g1 diagonal. Now Black has to reckon with the positional threat f4-f5 as well as the thrust e4-e5. After f4-f5, e6-e5 the d5 square becomes weak, but otherwise White threatened to capture on e6, which keeps the ♗c8 tied to the defence of that square.

9 ... ♕c7 *(6)*

On 9 ... ♘c6 10 ♘xc6 (also 10 ♘b3) 10 ... bc 11 e5 *(5)* is recommended, and now:

a) 11 ... ♘e8 12 ♗e3 ♕c7 13 ♘a4 de 14 ♗b6 ♕b8 15 ♗f2 and here instead of 15 ... ♕b4?! 16 ♘b6

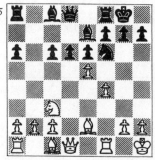

5

♖b8 17 fe! ♖xb6 18 a3! ♕a5 19 b4 ±, Romanishin–Dorfman, 1981, it is better to sacrifice the exchange with 15 ... ef 16 ♘b6 ♘f6, leading to a complicated situation.

b) 11 ... de 12 fe ♘d5 (12 ... ♘d7 13 ♗f4 ♗g5 14 ♕d6 ♖b8 15 ♘e4 with better chances for White, Ubilava–Mikhalchishin, 1979) 13 ♘e4! c5 (On 13 ... ♕c7 14 ♘d6! is powerful, threatening c2-c4-c5.) 14 ♕e1 ♗b7 15 ♕g3 ♔h8 16 ♘g5 ♗xg5 17 ♗xg5 ♕c7 and here too White stands better, Mestel–Stean, 1982.

10 a4

The intricate strategical system developed by Maroczy begins with this move. White does not yield space to his opponent by allowing ... b7-b5 and cuts down Black's

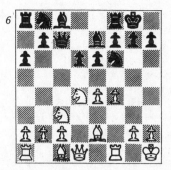

initiative on the queenside while retaining for himself the possibility of play in other parts of the board.

If White wishes to play the Maroczy system then 10 a4 is the best move. On 10 ♗f3 he must contend with 10 ... ♘c6, see variation B, and 10 ... e5.

Sometimes 10 f5 is played in order to weaken the Black's central pawn duo after the exchange 11 fe fe. We can recommend 10 ... e5 11 ♘b3 b5 12 ♗f3 ♗b7 as a method of equalisation for Black.

A cunning idea lies behind the manouvre 10 ♕e1. In this case on 10 ... b5 White can regroup his forces with 11 ♗f3 ♗b7 12 e5 de 13 fe ♘fd7 14 ♕g3 ♔h8 15 ♗f4, after which he achieves a typical Scheveningen position, but with the advantage that the bishop has reached f4 in one move and his king has already moved to safety. In the game Belyavsky–Ribli, 1977, White mounted a strong attack after 15 ... ♘b6?! 16 ♘e4 ♘8d7 17 ♗g5! ♗xg5 13 ♘xg5.

Additional subtleties of this system are considered in our analysis of 7 0-0 ♕c7 8 f4 ♗e7 9 ♔h1 0-0 10 ♕e1 b5 11 ♗f3 ♗b7. In answer to 10 ♕e1 Black can also play 10 ... ♘c6, leading to Classical Scheveningen positions which we will look at later.

   10   ...   ♘c6
   11   ♘b3!

The second important point of Maroczy's plan. White does not allow the exchange ♘c6xd4 which would give Black space for the redeployment of his forces. At the same time he strengthens his control over the d5 square and threatens to cramp his opponent even further by playing a4-a5. Black's reply is practically forced.

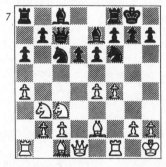

   11   ...   b6

Capablanca's recommendation 11 ... ♘a5 12 ♘xa5 ♕xa5 13 ♕e1 ♔h8 is apparently insufficient for equality. After 14 ♗d2 ♕c7 (15 ♘d5 was threatened.) 15 a5! White retains a small but solid positional edge.

   12   ♗f3

The famous game Maroczy–Euwe, 1923, reached this position via the popular system with ♔h1 and ♘b3. After 12 ... ♗b7 14 ♗e3 ♘b4?? (Black could I 'e maintained a solid position by playing

13 ... ♖fd8 14 ♕e1 ♘d7 15 ♖d1
♖ab8 16 ♕f2 ♗c8) 14 ♕e2 d5
15 e5 ♘e4 16 ♗xe4 de 17 ♕f2 b5
18 ab ab 19 ♘d4 ♗c6 20 ♕g3!
White obtained a clear advantage.
The plan involving the rapid advance d6-d5 is faulty and merely
established White's domination of
the centre. 12 ... ♗b7 is probably
premature since it renders the defence of the b-pawn more difficult.

12 ♗d3 is also occasionally encountered, and this is a more
aggressive formation, for example:
12 ... ♗b7 13 ♕e2 ♘d7 14 ♖f3
♘b4 15 ♖h3 ♖fe8 = or 13 ♕f3
♘b4 14 ♘d4 g6 ∆e5 and d5. One
can conclude that White cannot
obtain anything by playing the
time-consuming manouevre ♗f1-e2-
d3 and operating on the kingside in
conjunction with the move a2-a4.

12	...	♖d8
13	♕e1	♖ab8!
14	♗e3	♘a5!

Now the idea behind 12 ... ♖b8
becomes clear. After 15 ♘xa5 the
rook would find employment along
the b-file. It is worth noting that the
play would not be significantly
altered if White had placed his
Queen on e2.

15	♖d1	♘c4
16	♗c1	b5

Now the rook guarantees the advance of the b-pawn and Black has
a promising game, Foltys–Benko,
1948.

B

9	♗f3	♕c7
10	♔h1	

White initiates preparations for a
kingside pawn storm. In this case

White is trying to prevent possible
Black counterplay along the a7-g1
diagonal.

The immediate **10 g4** can be
countered by a counterthrust in the
centre: 10 ... ♘c6 11 g5 ♘xd4 12
♕xd4 d5! or 11 ♘xc6 bc 12 g5
♘e8 13 f5 ef 14 ef d5! The transfer of the knight after 10 g4 ♘c6
11 ♘de2 b5 12 g5 ♘d7 13 ♘g3
gives Black time to regroup with
13 ... b4 14 ♘ce2 ♗b7 15 ♗e3
♖fd8 16 c4 ♘c5 = Klovan–Platonov
1972.

10 f5?! is not at all dangerous
for Black and can be met by 10 ...
e5 11 ♘b3 b5 12 a3 ♗b7 13 ♗e3
♖d8 14 ♘d2 ♘bd7 15 ♔h1 ♖ac8
16 ♕e2 ♘b6 17 ♕f2 ♘c4! ∓,
Petrosian–Smyslov 1949.

Also innocuous is **10 ♘de2** ♘c6
11 b3 b5! 12 ♗b2 ♗b7 13 ♔h1
♖fd8 14 a3 d5! 15 ed b4! 16 ab
♘xb4 =, Suetin–Spassky, 1963.

10	...	♘c6

11	g4!?

White has no time to withdraw
the knight. **11 ♘b3** ♖d8 12 g4 d5!
13 e5 ♘e4 14 ♗xe4 de 15 ♕e2 b6
gives Black excellent counterplay.

White has some initiative after

11 ♘xc6 bc 12 e5 ♘d5 13 ed
♗xd6 14 ♘e2 △ c2-c4.

White won beautifully in the
game Geller–Sax, 1975: **11 a4** ♖b8
12 ♗e3 ♘a5 13 ♕e2 ♘c4? 14 e5!
de 15 ♘db5! ab 16 ♘xb5 ♕d7 17
♕xc4 ♘d5 18 ♗a7 ♖a8 19 ♕b3!,
but this was a consequence of the
loss of time involved in the manouvre ♘c6-a5-c4. Black has a more
solid way to develop in 11 ... ♘xd4
12 ♘xd4 e5 or 11 ... ♗d7 12 ♘b3
(On 12 g4 Black succeeds in recon-
structing his position with 12 ...
♘xd4 13 ♕xd4 ♗c6 14 g5 ♘d7
15 ♘d5?! ♗xd5 16 ed e5!∓,
Fernandez–Gufeld, 1974.) 12 ...
♘a5 13 ♘xa5 ♕xa5 14 ♕e1 (14
e5 de 15 fe ♕xe5 16 ♗xb7 ♖a7
17 ♗f4 ♕a5∓) 14 ... ♕c7 15 e5
♘e8. Both of these lines give Black
reasonable counterplay.

The gambit **11 e5!?** leads to
very confusing situations. If Black
plays 11 ... de 12 fe ♘xe5 13 ♗f4
♘fd7 14 ♖e1 he finds it difficult to
break the pin, e.g. 14 ... ♗d6 15
♘e4! Instead of accepting the pawn
Black would play 11 ... ♘xd4 12
♕xd4 de 12 fe ♗c5 13 ♕h4 ♘d7.

The solid move **11 ♗e3** usually
leads to a peaceful game, i.e. 11 ...
♗d7 12 ♕e1 ♘xd4 13 ♗xd4 e5!?
14 fe de 15 ♕g3 ♗d6 16 ♗e3 ♗e6
17 ♗h6 ♘e8 18 ♖ad1 f5, according
to analysis by Unzicker dated 1975.

With **11 g4** the play becomes
more sharp. White would like to
push the pawn to g5 and then set
up the pawn trio e4, f4, g5, but this
can lead to a weakening of his
position in the centre and even on
the kingside.

11 ...   ♘xd4
Black's position is sufficiently
solid, and he can even play the
passive 11 ... ♖e8 12 g5 ♘d7 13
a4 ♗f8 14 ♗g2 ♖b8 15 ♗e3 ♘b6,
but the exchange in the centre gives
Black space for manoeuvring and a
working diagonal for the ♗c8, and
it is therefore the most logical move.

12 ♕xd4   ♘fd7!
12 ... e5 would be a horrible
positional blunder. After 13 ♕g1!
Black loses the battle for the d5-
square, since on 13 ... ef White
plays 14 g5! (Here is where the
tempo saved by omitting ♗c1-e3
is meaningful!) and gets a firm
grip on the initiative, after 14 ...
♘d7 15 ♘d5! ±.

13 g5
The attempt to limit Black's
activity on the queenside with 13
a4 gives Black, in addition to the
straightforward 13 ... b6, the interesting possibility 13 ... ♗f6 14
♕d2 ♖fd8 (but not 14 ... ♗xc3?
15 ♕xc3 ♕xc3 16 bc ±), which is
sufficient for equality, for example
15 g5 ♗xc3 16 ♕xc3 ♕xc3 17 bc
♘c5 18 ♗e3 ♗d7 19 a5 ♗c6 or 15
♘e2 d5! 16 ed ♘b6 17 g5 ♗e7.

13 ...   b5
After 11 ... ♘xd4 the best system of defence is 13 ... ♖e8 14 a4
b6 15 ♕f2 ♗b7 16 ♗e3 ♗f8, since
the Black bishops occupy good
working positions and it is difficult for White to breach the kingside defences, for example: 17 ♖g1
g6 18 ♖g3 ♗g7 19 ♖h3 b5! 20 ab
ab 21 ♖xa8 ♖xa8 22 ♘xb5 ♖a1+
23 ♔g2 ♕c6 24 c4 ♗a6 25 ♕e2
♖a2 26 e5 d5 ∓ Tal–Andersson,

1976.

14   ♗e3   ♗b7

White cannot strengthen his position. 15 ♖f2 ♖ac8 16 ♖g1 e5! 17 ♕d2 ef 18 ♗xf4 ♘e5 and 15 ♕d2 ♘b6 16 ♗xb6 ♕xb6 17 a3 ♖ac8 are both equal, while 15 ♗g2 ♖ac8 16 a3 ♕c4! 17 ♖ad1 ♖fe8 18 h4 ♗f8 19 ♖f2 ♕xd4 20 ♗xd4 ♖c4 21 ♗f3 ♖ec8!∓, Mestel–Belyavsky, 1974–75. This leaves just the continuation of the pawn storm.

15   f5   ♘e5
16   ♗g2

This move secures the further advance of the f-pawn. Moreover, the bishop can transfer to h3 in order to increase the pressure on the e6-pawn, e.g. 16 ... ♖fc8 17 fe fe 18 ♗h3 ♕d7 19 ♖ad1 ♗c6 20 ♘d5 ♗d8 21 ♘f4.

In the game Khasin–Stein, 1965, White proposed a pawn sacrifice with 16 f6 gf 17 gf ♗xf6 18 ♗h6, but got an exchange sacrifice in return, which gave Black the initiative: 18 ... ⬦h8! 19 ♗xf8 ♖xf8 20 ♖ad1 ♖d8 21 ♗g2 ♗g7.

16   ...   ♖fe8!
17   f6   ♗f8!

White has lost the initiative. His attack on the kingside has run out of steam and black has more chances to create counterplay on the queenside.

3 Classical Scheveningen with ♗e3: Introduction

In this chapter we shall consider lines in which White places his bishop on e3, but where one of the players deviates from the so-called main lines.

First let us consider the variation where the White bishop moves to f3, without early castling. 1 e4 c5 2 ♘f3 e6 3 d4 cd 4 ♘xd4 ♘f6 5 ♘c3 d6 6 ♗e2 a6 7 f4 ♗e7 8 ♗e3 ♕c7

10

After 9 0-0 Black often delays castling, choosing 9 ... ♘c6. Now on 10 ♗f3 the lack of pressure in the centre allows him peacefully to conclude his development with either 10 ... 0-0 11 g4?! ♘xd4 12 ♗xd4 e5 13 ♗e3 ef 14 ♗xf4 ♗e6 15 ♔h1 ♖ac8 16 ♖e1 ♘d7! =, Spassov–Kozma, 1965, or 10 ...

♗d7 11 ♔h1 ♘xd4 12 ♗xd4 e5 13 ♗e3 ♗c6 14 ♕e1 0-0 15 ♕g3 ef 16 ♗xf4 ♘d7 △ ... ♘e5. In either case he has full equality.

White can also play ♗f3 before castling, e.g. 9 ♗f3 0-0 10 ♕e2 ♘c6. In this case 11 0-0 is a mere transposition of moves, but 11 0-0-0 can allow the game to take on an original (for the Classical Scheveningen) character. The game Quinteros–Diesen, 1977, continued 11 ... ♖b8! 12 g4 ♘xd4 13 ♗xd4 ♘d7 14 g5 b5 15 ♕g2 b4 16 ♘e2 ♖e8?! (16 ... ♘c5! 17 ♔b1 a5!=) 17 h4 e5 18 ♗f2 ef 19 ♗xf4 ♗b7 20 ♔b1 ♘e5 21 ♘d5 ♗xd5 22 ed ♗f8 23 h5, and White was ahead of his opponent in the attack. Even so, the scheme with long castling while the bishop is on f3 is unconvincing. Black can play 11 ... ♘xd4 12 ♗xd4 e5 13 ♗e3 ♗e6 14 f5 ♗c4 15 ♕d2, and then either 15 ... ♖fd8 16 g4 (or 16 b3) 16 ... d5!, or 15 ... b5 16 g4 b4 17 ♘a4 d5! 18 ♘b6 ♖ad8. In both cases Black has good counter-chances.

Now on to the primary focus of attention, the move 9 ♗e3. (1 e4 c5 2 ♘f3 e6 3 d4 cd 4

♘xd4 ♘f6 5 ♘c3 d6 6 ♗e2 ♘c6
7 0-0 ♗e7 8 f4 0-0)

This is the most common continuation. The bishop takes up a
comfortable position, and the queen
is freed from the necessity of defending the knight.

9   ♗e3   a6

Now White has a choice. He can
either transfer the queen to g3, in
order to include it in the attack on
the king, or he can make several
useful prophylactic moves, without
having to adjust his plans depending
on the moves of his opponent.
A 10 ♔h1
B 10 a4

A

10   ♔h1

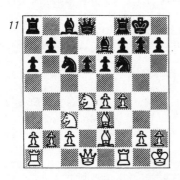

Here is a case where White,
making a "simply useful" move
does not try to place any difficult
questions before his opponent right
away, but awaits the latter's reaction
hoping that he might prematurely
disclose his plans.

If, instead of 12 ♗f3, White
risks playing 12 g4, then the play
on both flanks, with the centre un-
stabilised, can become dangerous

because of the typical counterthrust 12 ... d5! 13 ed ♘b4! (13 ...
♖d8 is weaker because of the sacrifice 14 dc! ♖xd1 15 ♖axd1.) The
game Leouw–Stean, 1973, continued 14 de ♗xe6 15 f5 ♗xb3 16
cb ♖ad8 17 ♕c1 ♘d3 18 ♕b1
♕e5! 19 ♖f3 (19 ♗xb6 ♗d6!∓) 19
... ♘xg4 when Black had a strong
attack.

Now we consider:
A1   10 ... ♘xd4
A2   10 ... ♗d7
A1

10   ...   ♘xd4
11   ♕xd4

After 11 ♗xd4 ♕c7 12 ♕e1 b5 a
typical Scheveningen tabiya is
reached, which is considered later.

The capture with the queen adds
a little originality to the game. The
queen, standing in the centre, occupies a strong and solid position,
spreading its influence all over the
board.

11   ...   ♕c7

12   ♖ad1   b5

Black can certainly play 12 ... e5
as well, since after 13 ♕d3 b5 the
weakness of the d5 square is inconsequential. After 14 fe de 15

♗g5 ♗b7 16 ♕h3 b4! 17 ♗xf6 ♗xf6 18 ♖d7 ♕c8! the chances are equal, Belyavsky-Kochiev, 1976.

13 e5 de
14 ♕xe5

The pawn capture, 14 fe, does not give Black any problems concerning the development of his pieces: 14 ... ♘d7 (14 ... ♖d8? 15 ♕f4 ±) 15 ♗f3 ♖b8 or 15 ♗f4 ♖d8 16 ♕f2?! ♗b7 17 a3 ♗c5 18 ♕h4 ♘f8 19 ♗d3 ♘g6 20 ♕h3 ♗c6∓, Hartston-Andersson, 1975. On the contrary, Black's position has become slightly more consolidated and the weakness of the Pe5 is all the more strongly felt.

The capture of the pawn with the queen frees White from the problems of a Pe5, since 14 ... ♕xe5 15 fe ♘d7 leads to the loss of the exchange after 16 ♗f3 ♖b8 17 ♗a7.

14 ... ♕b8!

Only in this manner can Black defend his queen while securing the b7 square for the bishop, solving all of his opening problems. After 15 ♕xb8 ♖xb8 16 ♗a7 ♖a8 17 ♗b6 ♗b7 18 a3 ♖fc8 19 ♗a5 g6 the game is roughly level, Vogt-Andersson, 1975, although for full equality White must play two precise moves: 20 ♗b4! ♗d8 21 ♗d6=.

A2

10 ... ♗d7 *(13)*
11 ♕e1

On 11 ♗f3 Black should play conventionally with 11 ... ♕c7, and on 12 a4, 12 ... ♘a5 is quite possible, i.e. 13 ♕d3 ♖ac8 14 ♖ae1 ♘c4. If 12 ♘de2, Black obtains excellent counterplay with 12 ... e5 13 f5 d5! 14 ♘xd5 ♘xd5 15 ♕xd5 ♖fd8.

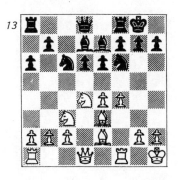

13

There is no profit in the move 11 a4 either. Black can complete his development without difficulty and can even allow the pawn to reach a5 after 11 ... ♘xd4 12 ♕xd4 ♗c6 13 ♗f3 ♖c8 14 a5, since he has central counterplay which provides full equality: 14 ... d5! 15 e5 ♘e4 16 ♘xe4 de 17 ♗e2 ♕xd4 18 ♗xd4 f5! Pritchett-Andersson, 1976. The impotence of 11 a4 is supported by the more conservative developing move 11 ... ♖c8, proposed by Polugayevsky. In the variation 12 ♘b3 ♘a5 13 e5 ♘e8 14 ♘xa5 ♕xa5 Black wins a valuable tempo and earns equality: 15 ♗f3 ♗c6! 16 ♗d4 de 17 fe ♖d8, Geller-Polugayevsky, 1978. On 12 ♕e1, besides the customary 12 ... ♘xd4 we can recommend a move which exploits the insufficiency of the move a2-a4, while at the same time takes advantage of the placement of the rook at c8: 12 ... ♘b4!, e.g. 13 ♖d1 g6 14 ♕g3 ♖xc3 15 bc ♘xe4 with sufficient compensation for the exchange.

11 ... b5

After 11 ... ♕c7 the game returns to the standard mold.

12 a3 ♕b8!

14

An original move, which is possible thanks to the inertia of 10 ♔h1. Black's queen not only takes control of the e5-square, but also supports the further advance of his b-pawn.

Black has no difficulties against some continuations:

a) 13 ♗f3 ♘xd4 14 ♗xd4 e5 15 ♘d5 (15 ♗e3 ♗c6 16 ♖d1 ♖e8=) 15 ... ♘xd5 16 ed ed! 17 ♕xe7 ♗f5 18 ♖ac1 ♖e8 19 ♕g5 ♕c8 20 c3 h6 21 ♕h5 d3!, Szabo-Larsen, 1976.

b) 13 ♕g3 b4 14 ab ♕xb4 15 ♘xc6 (15 ♖fd1 ♕xb2 16 ♘xc6 ♗xc6 17 ♗d4 ♕b7 ∓, Shibarevich-Kasparov, 1979) 15 ... ♗xc6 16 e5 ♘e4 17 ♘xe4 ♗xe4 18 ed ♗xd6 19 ♖ad1 ♗xc2 20 ♖d4 ♕b8 21 ♗f3 e5! 22 ♗xa8 ed 23 ♗xd4 g6=, Kavalek-Larsen, 1970.

c) 13 ♗d3 is somewhat more complicated since Black cannot carry out the standard plan 13 ... ♘xd4 14 ♗xd4 e5, Sznapik-Langeweg, 1981 on account of 15 ♘d5 ♘xd5 16 ed ed 17 ♕xe7, as he doesn't have the move ♗f5 available. Nor is 14 ... ♗c6 sufficient, as White stands better after 15 e5 de 16 fe ♘d7 17 b4!, Dobosz-Jansa, 1979.

Black can, however, push the b-pawn, 13 ... b4 14 ♘xc6 ♗xc6 15 ab ♕xb4, and then after 16 e5 de 17 fe the queen can go on a raid with 17 ... ♕g4! A sharp endgame arises after 16 ♘d5 ♘xd5 17 ed ♕xe1 18 ♖fxe1 ♗xd5 19 ♖xa6, while on 16 ♖a3, 16 ... ♖fb8 17 ♖b3 ♕a5 gives equal chances.

d) The move 13 ♖d1 can lead to a beautiful attack after 13 ... ♘xd4 14 ♗xd4 ♗c6 15 ♕g3 ♕b7 16 ♗f3 ♖ad8 17 ♖fe1 a5?! (17 ... g6 ∞) 18 ♘d5! ed (After 18 ... ♔h8 19 ♘xe7 ♕xe7 20 ♗c3 White also has a clear advantage, Sznapik-Adamski, 1978) 19 ed ♗e8 20 ♖xe7! ♕xe7 21 ♖e1! But instead of 14 ... ♗c6 Black should simply play 14 ... e5, and even 13 ... ♘xd4 is not obligatory. The advance of the b-pawn to b4 is even more effective here than against 13 ♗d3, since the a6 pawn remains alive.

B

10   a4

A useful move which limits Black's activity. It also shows that White's basic plan is not confined to the kingside.

10   ...   ♕c7
11   ♔h1 *(15)*

A second prophylaxis, which supports the view that White's opening strategy is viable, and which invites Black to show his hand. White awaits 11 ... ♗d7 before retreating the knight to b3.

If instead 11 ♘b3 b6, the Maroczy bind is less effective with the bishop already on e3. After 12 ♗f3 ♖b8 13 ♕e2 Black has several comfortable configurations for his

15

pieces, for example 13 ... ♘a5 14
♘xa5?! (After this exchange White
must proceed with extreme caution.
Black's pieces have great freedom of movement, which fully
compensates for the defects of his
pawn chain. Instead of 14 ♘xa5,
a more promising plan is 14 g4 ♘c4
15 g5 ♘d7 16 ♗c1 ♖e8 17 ♗g2 or
14 ♘d2 ♖d8 15 ♔h1 ♗b7 16 ♕f2
♘d7 17 ♖ae1, although even here
Black has everything under control.)
14 ... ba 15 ♖ab1 ♖b4! 16 ♖fd1
♗b7 17 ♗d2 d5 18 ed ed, Alye-
shin–Aramanovic, 1947 or 13 ...
♘d7 14 g4 ♘c5 15 g5 ♖e8 16 ♗g2
♘b4 17 ♘d4 e5! 18 fe de 19 ♘f5
♗f8   20 ♕f2 ♗e6, Dolmatov–
Palatnik, 1978.

We examine the rook moves
B1   11 ... ♖d8!
B2   11 ... ♖e8
and these lesser moves:
a) 11 ... ♗d7 12 ♘b3 b6 13 ♗f3
(13 g4 d5!? 14 ed ♘b4 15 de
♗xe6) 13 ... ♖b8 14 ♕e2 ♘a5 15
♘xa5 (If 15 ♕xa6 ♘c4! is dangerous) 15 ... ba 16 ♖ab1 ♗c8 17
g4 ♖e8 18 g5 ♘d7 19 ♕f2 ♗b7=
Vogt–Schmidt, 1976.
b) 11 ... ♘xd4 12 ♕xd4 e5 13 ♕d3
ef 14 ♗xf4 ♗e6 15 ♖ad1 ♖fd8 16

♕g3±, with White having a small
initiative,   Velimirović–Janošević,
1974.
c) 11 ... ♘a5 12 ♕e1 (12 ♕d3 e5
13 ♘f5 ♗xf5 14 ef ♖ad8=) 12 ...
♘c4 13 ♗c1 ♗d7 14 b3 ♘a5 15
♗b2 ♘c6 16 ♘xc6 ♗xc6 17 ♗d3
e5 18 ♕e2, where White has a
small spatial advantage, Karpov–
Tukmakov, 1971.
B1
   11 ...   ♖d8!
This is the logical and consequential response to White's moves.
The rook transfers to the centre,
securing counterplay there in the
event of a pawn storm by White on
the kingside. Simultaneously, the
typical advance of the e-pawn
(e6-e5xf4) will open up the e-file
and isolate the Pe4. Praxis has shown
that 11 ... ♖d8 is not the only move,
as we have already seen in our discussion of the "lesser" moves above.
   12   ♕e1
The idea behind the move 11 ...
♖d8 becomes clear in the event of
12 ♗f3 ♘e5!, when Black gets full
counterplay against any of the
following moves:
a) 13 ♕e2 ♘xf3 14 ♖xf3 b6 15
♖af1 ♗b7 16 ♖g3 ♘xe4 17 ♘xe4
♗xe4 18 ♘xe6 fe 19 ♗d4 e5,
according to analysis by Jansa.
b) 13 ♗e2 b6 (The knight can also
return to c6.) 14 ♘b3 ♘ed7 15
♗f3 ♗b7   16 ♕e2 ♖ac8, Haag–
Jansa, 1976.
c) 13 ♘db5 ab 14 ♘xb5 ♕a5
15 fe de 16 ♕e2 ♗d7 17 ♗d2,
following analysis by Honfi, dated
1977.
   Instead of 12 ♕e1 White can

avoid the central break by playing
12 ♘b3. Now it is dangerous to
continue 12 ... d5 13 e5 d4 because
of 14 ef ♗xf6 (14 ... de 15 fe±)
15 ♘e4! de 16 ♘xf6+ gf 16 ♗d3±.
Black can equalise, however, by
following the general strategy in the
Maroczy. The game Reshevsky-Ree,
1978, continued 12 ♘b3 b6 13
♕e1 ♖b8 14 ♕f2! ♘b4 15 ♗f3 e5!
16 a5 ba   17 ♘xa5 ♘c6 (The
operation 17 ... ef 18 ♗a7 ♘g4 19
♗xg4 ♗xg4 20 ♗xb8 ♖xb8 21
♕xf4 ♗e6   22 ♖f2 ♗f6 favours
White.) 18 ♘c4 and here 18 ...
♘b4! 19 b3 ♘d7, according to
Reshevsky's analysis, would have
given Black good counterplay.
In our opinion 14 ... ♘a5 would
also have equalised.

| 12 | ... | ♘xd4 |
| 13 | ♗xd4 | e5 |

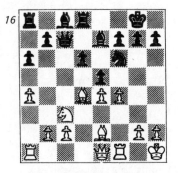

    14   ♖g1!?
Otherwise the inclusion of the
moves 11 a4 ♖d8 has only made it
easier for Black to carry out his
strategic counterthrust in the centre:
a) 14 fe de 15 ♗e3 (The move 15
♕g3 is not available.) 15 ...♗e6 16
♕g3. White does not have any concrete threats so Black can improve

his position without interference.
16 ... ♕a5! 17 ♗g5 ♔h8 18 ♗d3
♖d7 19 ♘d5?! ♗xd5 20 ed ♖xd5
21 ♗xf6 ♗xf6 22 ♕h3 e4! 23
♗xe4 ♖h5∓,   Raman-Kasparov,
1977.
b) 14 ♗e3 ef 15 ♗xf4 ♗e6 16 ♕g3
also fails to provide an advantage
for White. On the contrary, the excellent post for Black's pieces at
e5 gives him better chances in the
ensuing struggle: 16 ... ♘d7! 17
♗d3 ♘e5 18 ♘d5 ♗xd5 19 ed g6
20 c3 ♗f6! 21 ♗c2 ♗g7 22 ♕f2
♖ac8 23 ♖ad1 ♖e8 ∓, Karpov-
Ribli, 1977.
    The text is an original idea of
Efim Geller.

14	...	ef
15	a5!	♖e8
16	♗b6	♕b8
17	♖xf4	

In the game Geller-Tal, 1977,
White obtained the advantage here
after 17 ... d5 18 ♕f2 de? 19 ♗c4!
♗e6 20 ♗xe6 fe 21 ♘xe4. Black
can doubtless improve his defence.
Instead of 17 ... d5 he can regroup
with 17 ... ♗e6 18 ♕d2 ♘d7 19
♗e3 ♗g5! But Tal's fundamental
mistake was to open the centre before completing his development.
After 18 ... ♗e6 (Instead of 18 ...
de), Black would have limited the
activity of the ♗e2 and obtained a
fully satisfactory position, for example 19 ♗d3 de! 20 ♘xe4 ♘d5!
B2
    11   ...   ♖e8 *(17)*
A typical method of building up
tension in the opening. Black intends to exchange on d4 at a
propitious moment, and then ex-

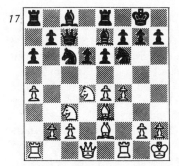

17

change on f4 after playing e6-e5, which releases the ♖e8, which in turn pressures the e4-pawn. This pressure will make up for the weakness of the Pd6.

12 ♗f3

One of the fine points of the move 11 ... ♖e8 is revealed if the Queen sets off on her usual route: 12 ♕e1! ♘xd4 13 ♗xd4 e5 14 fe de 15 ♕g3, when Black can play 15 ... ♗d8!, when the bishop simultaneously defends both queen and knight, and the central pawn is held by the ♖e8. After 16 ♗e3 ♔h8 17 ♗g5 ♗e6 18 ♖ad1! ♘g8! (The last subtlety! On 18 ... ♖c8 the exchange sacrifice 19 ♖xd8! △ 20 ♕h4 is very strong, threatening a powerful second sacrifice with 21 ♖xf6) 19 ♗e3 with equal chances, Tal-Andersson, 1976.

12 ... ♖b8

A useful waiting move, which frees the rook from the sphere of influence of the White bishop. 12 ... ♘xd4 △e6-e5 is also quite possible.

13 ♕e1

After 13 e5!? de 14 fe ♘xe5 15 ♗f4 ♗d7! 16 ♗g3 ♗d6 17 ♗e4 ♘fg4 White did not manage to exploit the pin of the heavy pieces in

Ghinda–Urzica, but the move 13 e5 deserves consideration. Other plans have been seen in this position but they all lead to positions where the chances are equal:

a) 13 ♗f2 ♗f8 14 ♖e1 ♘d7 15 ♕e2 ♘xd4 (15 ... ♘a5!?) 16 ♗xd4 b6 17 e5 de 18 fe, Razuvayev-Kasparov, 1978. Here 18 ... ♗c5! led to excellent counterplay for Black.

b) 13 ♕d2!? ♘xd4 15 ♗xd4 e5 15 ♗g1! ef 16 a5! ♗e6 17 ♗b6 ♕c8 18 ♕xf4 ♘d7 19 ♗a7 ♖a8 20 ♗d4 ♘e5 with a complicated struggle, Geller-Timoshchenko, 1980.

c) 13 ♕e2 ♘xd4 14 ♗xd4 e5 15 ♗e3 ♗e6 16 ♖fd1 ♗c4 17 ♕f2 b5 18 ab ab 19 ♖a7 ♖b7 with equal chances, Balashov-Kavalek, 1976.

By playing 13 ♕e1 White restricts his opponent's choice of plans. He must now carry out the advance and subsequent exchange of the e-pawn. In addition he can quickly remove the queen from the e-file.

13 ... e5

White retains a small positional advantage if Black plays the standard 13 ... ♘xd4 14 ♗xd4 e5 15 ♗a7 ♖a8 16 ♗e3 ♗e6 17 ♕g3 ef 18 ♗xf4 ♘d7, by continuing 19 ♗g4, as in Dolmatov-Timoshchenko, 1979.

14 ♘b3 ef
15 ♗xf4 ♗e6
16 ♕g3 *(18)*

The knight pair ♘b3/♘c6 lends a touch of originality to this position. Of course one would prefer to play the White side here, but Black's defence is quite solid. In the game Marjanović–Tringov, 1979, Black

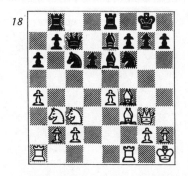

18

allowed the ♘b3 back into the game too quickly: 16 ... ♘e5?! 17 ♘d4! ♘fd7 18 ♖ad1 ♗f8 19 ♘f5! and White's initiative became dangerous: 19 ... b5 20 ab ab 21 ♖f2 b4 22 ♘d5! Instead of 16 ... ♘e5 Black could have obtained a more solid position by 16 ... ♔h8, i.e. 17 ♖ad1 ♖bd8 18 ♘d5 ♗xd5 19 ed ♘e5 20 ♘d4 ♘fd7 21 ♘f5 ♗f8.

All this just goes to show that Black has a more promising position after 11 ... ♖d8 than after 11 ... ♖e8, which is too passive.

4 Classical Scheveningen 10 ♕e1: Part 1

1 e4 c5 2 ♘f3 e6 3 d4 cd 4 ♘xd4 ♘f6 5 ♘c3 d6 6 ♗e2 a6 7 0-0 ♗e7 8 f4 0-0 9 ♗e3 ♘c6 10 ♕e1

An aggressive continuation, which is indisputably the most popular line in the Classical Scheveningen. White holds nothing back and prepares a piece attack on the Black king. The constantly shifting evaluations of the positions considered here and in the next chapter partially account for that popularity.

The move 10 ♕e1 is also encountered in the position which arises after 8 ... ♕c7 9 ♗e3 ♘c6. In this case Black must castle, since any premature activity in the centre or on the queenside could lead to serious consequences, for example: 10 ... ♘xd4 11 ♗xd4 e5? 12 fe de 13 ♕g3 ♗c5 14 ♗xc5 ♕xc5+ 15 ♔h1 ♔f8 16 ♘d5! ± Boleslavsky–Böök, 1948, or 10 ... ♘xd4 11 ♗xd4 b5? 12 e5! de 13 fe ♘d7 14 ♘e4 ♗b7 15 ♘d6+ ♗xd6 16 ed ♕xd6 17 ♖d1 ♕c7 18 ♕f2 ±, according to analysis by Tolush.

Even quite recently it was thought that it was necessary to play 10 ... ♕c7 in reply to 10 ♕e1, just as 6 ... a6 had been considered obligatory. The popularity of the Classical Scheveningen today has rejected this dogma and revealed important nuances in the formation of Black's and White's pieces. Black no longer is afraid to allow the advance e4-e5 in many variations, considering the control of the squares along the a8-h1 diagonal more important. But this brashness is the result of exact knowledge of defensive resources in positions which were previously considered to be dangerous. Now we consider:

A 10 ... ♘xd4
B 10 ... ♗d7

A

	10	...	♘xd4
	11	♗xd4	b5

By saving time on the move ♕d8-c7 Black has turned a profit. It is not easy for White to establish a pawn on e5, since after 12 e5 de there is no 13 fe, thanks to the ♕d8. But it isn't easy for White to prepare the advance, as he must contend with the danger facing the Pe4 after 12 ... b4. The prophylactic move 12 a3 solves only part of the problem, as will be seen below, leaving us with the central question: How to carry out e4-e5 with greatest effect? And is the threat of b5-b4 really all that dangerous?

A1   12 a3
A2   12 ♖d1

A1

12   a3   ♗b7
13   ♕g3

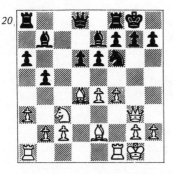

20

It becomes clear that White has set aside his aggressive intentions for just a single move, and now that the Pa3 has paralysed Black's pawn pair a6-b5, he returns to his operations on the kingside and in the centre.

On 13 ♗f3, Black can either play 13 ... ♕c7 14 e5 de 15 fe ♘d7 or the solid 13 ... ♘d7!? After 14 ♖ad1 ♕c7 15 ♔h1 ♖ad8 16 ♕f2

♗c6 White has a solid, if little-promising position, Butnorius-Magerramov, 1978.

13   ...   ♗c6

Black continues his preparation to advance the b-pawn. One must consider the plan with 13 ... ♗c6 more constructive by comparison with other plans which are sometimes encountered in tournament praxis. Later developments will show why, but before proceeding with our analysis of 13 ... ♗c6, let us consider the alternatives:

a) 13 ... g6 14 ♗f3 (14 f5 e5 leads to a sharp game.) 14 ... a5! (14 ... d5 and 14 ... ♘d7 are also sufficiently solid) 15 ♖ad1 b4 16 e5 ♗xf3 17 ef ♗xf6 18 ♗xf6 ♕xf6 19 ♖xf3 bc = Byrne-Stean, 1975. Or 14 ♗d3 ♖c8 (14 ... a5! is also quite acceptable, e.g. 15 f5 b4. Also good is 14 ... ♘h5 15 ♕e3 ♕d7 16 ♖ad1 ♘xf4 17 ♕xf4 e5 18 ♗xe5 de 19 ♕xe5 ♕d6, Suetin-Anikayev, 1974.) 15 f5 e5 16 ♗e3 ♖xc3! 17 bc ♘xe4 18 ♕g4 ♘f6 19 ♕h3 ♕c8! with sufficient compensation for the exchange, Jansa-Hartston, 1975.

b) 13 ... ♖c8 14 ♗d3 (14 ♔h1 is somewhat more precise here, as it does not block the d-file: 14 ... ♖e8 15 ♖ad1 ♗f8 16 e5. In the game Karpov-Andersson, 1977, the game continued 14 ... g6 15 ♗d3 ♘h5 16 ♕e3 ♕d7 17 ♗e2 ♘xf4?! 18 ♕xf4 e5 19 ♕g3 ed 20 ♗g4 with a sharp and approximately even game. Instead of 17 ... ♘xf4 Gligorić considers 17 ... ♘g7 or 17 ... ♘f6 as more reliable equalising methods.) 14 ... ♖e8 15 ♔h1

♗f8   16 ♕h3 e5! (Just in time!
White was about to play e4-e5 himself!) 17 fe de 18 ♘d5 ♗xd5 19
ed g6 20 ♗c3 ♗g7 21 ♖ad1 ♖c5
22 d6 ♖d5!∓, Diaz–Andersson,
1976.

14   ♗d3   ♕d7!

An important point of Black's
plan. The ♕d7, on the one hand,
helps to keep the pawn pair a6/b5
alive, and on the other hand keeps
an eye on the ♗d4, thereby interfering with the advance 15 e5 de
16 fe.

15   ♖ae1!

White has concluded the last of
his preparations. Actually, the
opening has already ended and
White, having developed his forces
harmoniously, can be satisfied with
the results. And Black? His defences
are solid enough but there does not
seem to be any counterplay which
will balance White's attacking
threats. This forces us to conclude
that White has the better chances in
the middlegame.

This is not necessarily the case if
White declines to play 15 ♖ae1:
a) **15 ♔h1** a5 16 ♖ae1 b4 17 ab ab
18 ♘d1 g6, Lanka–Ligterink, 1978.
b) **15 e5** de 16 ♗xe5 g6 17 f5
♘h5! 18 ♕g4 ef 18 ♗xf5 ♗c5+ 20
♔h1 ♕e7, Hecht–Larsen, 1972.

Neither of these alternatives
poses any great difficulties for
Black.

15   ...   a5

In the game Ostojić–Kaplan,
1975, White obtained a clear advantage after 15 ... ♖ae8 16 ♔h1
♗d8 17 e5! de 18 ♗xe5 g6 19
♕h3 ♘d5 20 ♘e4 f5 21 ♘c5, but

the rook does not accomplish anything on e8. It participates more
fully in the battle when sitting on
a8.

16   ♖f3!?

A somewhat unexpected re-
source which strengthens White's
attacking potential.

16 e5 (Not 16 ♕h3? e5!) de 17
♗xe5 leads to "somewhat quieter",
but also quite sharp play: 17 ... g6
(17 ... b4 18 ab ab 19 ♘e4! ±) 18
f5 ♘h5 19 ♕h3 ef 20 ♗xf5 ♕b7
21 ♗e4 ♖ae8!

16   ...   b4

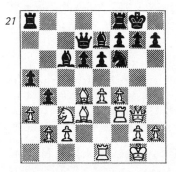

This is the critical position, and
it is quite interesting from an analytical standpoint. It seems as though
Black's attack will bear fruit first,
but by sacrificing a knight White
opens a diagonal for his ♗d3 and
a file for the ♖e1, initiating a dangerous attack of his own.

17   ♘d5!   ed

18   ed   ♗xd5

Analytical research and practical
experience of the position yields
the following results:
a) **19 ♖xe7 ♕xe7** 20 ♖e3 (20♗xh7+
♔h8!) 20 ... ♗e6 21 ♗xh7+ ♔xh7
22 ♕g5? (After 22 ♕h4+ ♔g8 23

♖g3 ♗g4! 24 ♖xg4 ♖fe8 25 ♖xg7+ White would still have been able to draw according to analysis by Minić.) 22 ... ♖h8!∓, Bellon–Larsen, 1977.

b) **19 ♗xh7+ ♔h8!** (19 ... ♔xh7 20 ♕h4+ ♔g8 21 ♖xe7 (After 21 ♖g3 ♗e6 22 ♖xg7+ there is no more than a draw.) 21 . . . ♕g4! 22 ♕xg4 ♘xg4 23 ♖g3 with better chances in the endgame, Kupreichik–Langeweg, 1975.) 20 ♕h4 (20 ♖xe7 ♕xe7 21 ♕h4 ♗xf3 22 ♗g6+ ♔g8 and White's attack has been repelled. 20 ♖fe3! – Nunn). 20 ... ♕g4! 21 ♕xg4 ♘xg4 22 ♖h3 ♗f6 with a complicated and double-edged game.

A2

12 ♖ad1 *(22)*

White brings his rook into the game and prepares to confront his opponent with the forcing advance e4-e5. The defence of the e-pawn in this case often relies on a tactic, and the advance b5-b4, as more detailed analysis shows, has its drawbacks as well as its merits. Sometimes other continuations are encountered in which White ignores his opponent's initiative on the queenside:

a) **12 ♗f3**. Tal considers this move most exact, but it seems that this is partly a matter of taste. Black is not obliged to place his queen on c7, since the threat of a4-a5 is nothing terrible. After 12 ... b4! 13 ♘a4 (13 e5 de! 14 ♗xe5 ♗b7!) 13 ... ♖b8 15 e5 de 15 ♗xe5 ♖b5 Black stands no worse, according to analysis by Magerramov, dated 1977.

b) **12 ♗d3**. This is a direct and little-investigated continuation. White tries to carry out e4-e5 after the two preparatory moves ♔h1 and a4. In reply to b5-b4 he planned to transfer his knight to c4. The game Kovacs–Ornstein, 1976, continued 12 ... ♗b7 13 ♔h1 ♗c6 14 a4 b4 15 ♘b1 ♕b8 16 ♘d2 e5 17 fe de 18 ♗e3 ♕b7 19 ♗g5 ♘e8? (19 ... ♘h5=) 20 ♗xe7 ♕xe7 21 ♘c4 a5 22 ♕e3 with a small advantage for White. But it would seem that after 12 ♗d3 Black should have time to regroup comfortably and organise counterplay which will lead to equality. Thus on the 12th and 13th moves the advance of the Pb5 seems more consequential.

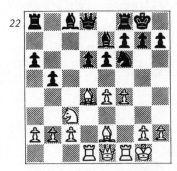

22

12 ... ♗b7

At first glance this looks risky because of the opposition ♖d1-♕d8, but it is quite playable. The solid reputation of another method of defence, **12 ... ♕c7** 13 e5 de 14 fe ♘d7 15 ♘e4 ♗b7 (15 ... ♘xe5? 16 ♕g3 ±) is based on the favourable result in the game Geller–Tal, 1976, which saw 16 ♘f6+ ♔h8! (but not 16 ... gf? 17 ♕g3+ ♔h8 18 ef ♕xg3 19 fe+ winning) 17 ♕h4 h6 18 ♕h5 ♗c5! with further analysis by Magerramov: 19 ♘xd7 ♕xd7 20 c3 ♕e7! 21 ♖f6! ♗e4!. This was blown away by a brilliant idea of A. Ivanov: 17 ♗d3! h6 18 b4!! It turns out that all that is needed for a successful attack is to take the c5 square away from black. After 18 ... ♖fd8 19 ♘h5 ♘f8 20 c3! ♗xb4 21 ♕g3 White's attack cannot be stopped, A. Ivanov–Magerramov, 1980.

In a positional sense it is dubious for Black to try for simplification by **12 ... b4?!** 13 ♘a4 (13 e5 de 14 fe ♘d7 15 ♗f3 ♖b8 16 ♗a7? bc! ∓ or 16 ♘e4 ♕a5!∓) 13 ... ♘xe4 14 ♗f3 f5 15 ♘b6 ♖b8 16 ♘xc8 ♖xc8 17 ♗xe4 fe 18 ♕xe4 ♕d7 where Black has several weak pawn islands and can only hope for a draw with exact play.

13   ♗f3 *(23)*

White's plan is clear: He wants to place the pawn on e5, chase the knight from f6, and, after exchanging the distant but dangerous ♗b7, initiate an attack on the kingside, bringing in his knight via e4.

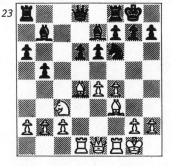

23

Black does not have any way of preventing the advance e4-e5, but with his next moves he can try to

prevent the journey of the ♘c3.

13   ...   ♕c7

Other tries:

a) **13 ... b4.** After 14 ♘a4 ♕a5 (14 ... a5 15 e5 ♘d5 is also possible) 15 e5 de 16 fe ♘d5 17 ♘b6 ♖ad8 18 ♔h1 ♘xb6 19 ♗xb7 ♗c5 leads to a level game, while 14 e5 can bring about a sharp rook ending: 14 ... ♗xf3 15 ♖xf3 bc (15 ... de? 16 fe ♘d5 17 ♘e4 ♕c7 18 ♕g3 ♖ac8 19 c3 ♕c6 20 ♘f6+ ♗xf6 21 ef, Geller–Grigorian, 1976) 16 ef ♗xf6 17 ♕xc3 ♖c8 18 ♗xf6 ♖xc3! (18 ... gf? 19 ♖xd6! ± or 18 ... ♕xf6 19 ♕xf6 gf 20 c3 d5 21 f5 ±) 19 ♗xd8 ♖xf3 20 ♗e7 ♖xf4 21 ♗xf8 ♔xf8 22 ♖xd6 ♖a4 23 a3 ♔e7 24 ♖b6 f5.

b) **13 ... ♘e8.** The temporary transition to passive defence. On 14 e5 Black can counter the transfer of the knight to e4 by playing 14 ... ♗xf3 15 ♖xf3 d5, but both the ♘e8 and ♖f8 are out of the game. In the game Diesen–Hort, 1977, Black achieved approximate equality after 14 a3 ♕c7 15 ♕f2 ♗c6 16 e5 ♗xf3 17 ♕xf3 ♖c8 18 ♔h1 ♕c6, since the Black knight will reach either d5 or f5. White can doubtless improve, however.

The text is the move which is most in accordance with the principles governing the position. Black assumes that his defence will be sufficiently solid, since the ♗f3 cannot join in the attack against his king. He therefore allows White to carry out his plan.

14	e5	de
15	fe	♘d7
16	♗xb7	♕xb7

17 ♘e4

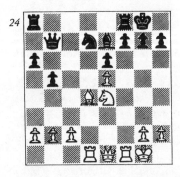

24

This is the critical position. The game Tseshkovsky-Petrushin, 1973, shows that the f7 point is the weak spot in the defences surrounding the Black king: 17 ... ♖ac8?! 18 c3 ♔h8 19 ♖f4! b4 20 ♕g3 bc 21 bc ♖c4 22 ♖df1±. Black's counterplay lies in the strengthening of pressure on the Pe5 with the aim of tying the White pieces to its defence. To this end 17 ... ♕c7 is best. After 18 ♖d3 ♘xe5 19 ♕g3 f6 20 ♘xf6+ ♗xf6 21 ♖xf6 ♖xf6 22 ♗xe5 ♕c5+ 23 ♗d4 ♕f8 or 18 ♘f6+ ♔h8 19 ♘xd7 (19 ♘h5 ♕xc2) 19 ... ♕xd7 Black has everything under control, according to analysis by Vainstein. Nor does 18 ♘f6+ ♔h8 19 ♘xd7 ♕xd7 20 ♖d3 ♖ac8 21 c3 b4 22 ♖b3 bc 23 bc ♕b7 24 ♕e3 ♕b2 25 a4 ♕c2, Olafsson-Panno, Buenos Aires, 1980, present any problems. But how can Black defend after 18 ♕g3 ♔h8 19 ♘d6!? Hartston considers that White has the better chances. In our opinion 19 ... ♔g8 will hold the balance if Black plays precisely, for example 20 ♖xf7 ♖xf7 21 ♘xf7 ♕xc2 22 ♕g4 ♕g6.

B

10 ... ♗d7

This is less popular than 10 ... ♘xd4 11 ♗xd4 b5, but it is a quite playable continuation, in which Black also delays committing his queen. The bishop will move to c6, where it will occupy a better position than on b7. After b7-b5 Black's queen can go to b7 and increase the pressure on the White e-pawn, while if the light-squared bishops are exchanged it will be placed in an active position on c6.

11 ♖ad1

After 11 ♕g3 b5 12 a3 ♘xd4 13 ♗xd4 ♗c6 Black will be free in his choice of location for the queen. In this connection Black's defence in the game Vukčević-Sigurjonsson, 1976, is quite interesting: 14 ♗d3 ♕d7 15 ♖ae1 (15 e5 de 16 ♗xe5 g6 17 f5 ♘h5 18 ♕g4 ef 19 ♗xf5 ♕a7+ 20 ♗d4 ♗c5=, Byrne-Najdorf, 1976) 15 ... a5 16 ♕h3 e5 17 fe de 18 ♗xe5 (18 ♘d5 ♗d8) 18 ... ♕xh3 19 gh b4 20 ab ab 21 ♘d1 ♗c5+ 22 ♔g2 ♖ae8! ∓.

11 ... ♘xd4
12 ♗xd4 ♗c6
13 ♗f3! ♕c7

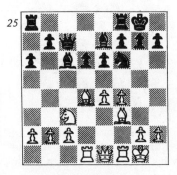

25

White's threats force the Black queen to take up a position only on c7, but this is just a small moral victory, because he really does not have a significant opening advantage. It is true that after 14 e5 ♘e8 15 ♔h1 ♖d8 16 ♖d3 de (16 ... b5!?) 17 fe g6 18 ♕f2 ♖d7 19 ♗xc6 ♕xc6 20 ♖f3 ♕c4? (Better is 20 ... ♘g7!? 21 ♖xf7 ♘f5 22 ♖xf8+ ♗xf8 with counterplay — Geller.) 21 ♗e3 ♗h4 22 ♕g1 ♗d8? 23 ♗c5! ♗e7 24 ♗xe7 White won by means of a direct attack on the king in Geller–Sigurjonsson, 1977: 24 ... ♖xe7 25 ♕e3 ♘g7 26 b3 ♕c7 27 ♘e4 ♘f5 28 ♘f6+ ♔g7 29 ♖h3!

White would have had more difficulty organising his attack if Black had played 14 ... de 15 fe ♘d7, for example 16 ♗xc6 ♕xc6 17 ♘e4. The position arose by transposition in the game Tal-–Andersson, 1976, in which White, after 17 ... b5 18 ♖d3 ♖ad8 19 ♖g3! ♕xc2 20 ♕e3 ♕c4, could have won quickly by 21 ♘f6+! ♘xf6 22 ef ♖xd4 23 ♖xg7+ ♔h8 24 fe or 21 ... ♗xf6 22 ef g6 23 ♖g4 e5 24 ♕h6 ♘xf6 25 ♖xf6 ed 26 ♖h4 ♖fe8 27 ♖xg6+ etc., according to analysis by Tal. Instead of 17 ... b5, 17 ... ♕c7! is significantly stronger, intending to meet 18 ♘f6+ with 18 ... ♔h8. Also much better is 17 ... ♖ad8 18 ♖f8 ♔h8. Besides, the exchange 14 ... de is not obligatory, and Black can play 14 ... ♘d7 15 ed (otherwise 15 ... d5 is coming) 15 ... ♗xd6 16 ♗xd6 ♕xc6 17 ♕g3 g6 18 ♔h1 ♗c5, which would give him counterplay which is sufficient for equality.

5　10 ♔e1 ♛c7

1 e4 c5　2 ♘f3 e6　3 d4 cd　4 ♘xd4 ♘f6　5 ♘c3 d6　6 ♗e2 a6　7 0-0 ♗e7 8 f4 0-0　9 ♗e3 ♘c6　10 ♕e1 ♛c7

More than 50 years have passed since the birth of the Scheveningen, during which a number of modifications have taken place, but this position is still symbolic of the Sicilian Scheveningen. With his last move White frees the d1 square for a rook, and the ♗e2 prepares to take place in the battles in the centre and on the queenside, from the f3 square, or take part in the attack on the king from the d3 square. The queen heads for the g3 square, where it will lead the operations in the centre (the advance e4-e5) or on the kingside. There is, in a word, a large choice of plans for White, and the position is full

of dynamism. In such a situation the transition to a decisive operation may take place at any moment, which means that the play requires finesse, which often depends on the character of the player. White now can force his preparations for the kingside assault, and can carry out preventative measures in the centre and on the queenside in order to limit the possibility of his opponent's counterplay. We will thoroughly examine the continuations 11 a4 (A), and 11 ♔h1 (B) in the present chapter, reserving discussion of 11 ♕g3 for the next. First let us note in passing the following alternatives: a) **11 g4** (This looks aggressive, but it is an illogical continuation which cuts down the effectiveness of a later ♕g3). 11 ... ♘xd4 12 ♗xd4 e5 13 fe de　14 ♕g3 ♗c5　15 ♗xc5 ♛xc5+ 16 ♔h1 ♗e6 17 g5 ♘d7 and Black, we feel, has a more promising position since the pawn at g5 cannot move backwards to help protect the king.
b) **11 ♗f3** ♘xd4 12 ♗xd4 e5 13 ♗e3 b5　14 ♖d1 ♗e6　15 a3 ♖b8. Here the ♗f3 only gets in the way, and Black is clearly ahead with his

operations on the queenside.

c) **11 ♘b3 b5!** 12 a3 ♗d7 13 ♗f3 ♖fd8 14 ♖f2 ♗e8 15 g4 ♘d7 16 g5 ♘c5 and the Pb5 guarantees Black the necessary space for his queenside operations.

d) **11 a3.** A little prophylactic. White keeps the b4 square out of the clutches of the Pb5 or ♘c6. But this is also a loss of time. Therefore Black does not have a difficult path to equality, for example 11 ... ♘xd4 12 ♗xd4 ♗d7 13 ♕g3 ♗c6 14 ♔h1 b5 or 12 ... e5 13 fe de 14 ♕g3 ♗c5 15 ♗xc5 ♕xc5+ 16 ♔h1 ♔h8 or 16 ... ♕e7 with equal play.

e) **11 ♖d1.** This is an interesting conception. White awaits the exchange ... ♘xd4, after which the ♕e1 will be in a position to support the advance e4-e5, in which case the White rook will be sitting usefully on d1. It is up to Black to choose one of the many known plans, which will ensure that the gain from the placement of the rook will be minimal, for example: 11 ... ♗d7 12 ♗f3 ♖ac8 (12 ... ♘xd4 13 ♖xd4! e5 14 ♖d2!±) 13 ♕g3 ♘xd4 (13 ... b5 14 e5±) 14 ♗xd4 ♗c6 15 e5 de 16 fe (16 ♗xe5 leads to an equal game.) 16 ... ♘d7 17 ♘e4 ♗xe4 18 ♗xe4 ♗c5 19 ♖fe1 ♘xe5 20 ♗xh7+ ♔xh7 21 ♖xe5 ♗xd4 22 ♖xd4 ♕xc2! ∓ Schneider-Schmidt, 1979.

A

11 a4

A blend of phrophylaxis with a waiting move. White prevents b7-b5 and besides that, expects that with his reply Black will be the first to reveal his plans. The danger is that 11 a4 may turn out to be a loss of time and allow Black to establish a solid defence on the kingside, and this can be significant. This is why 11 a4 is seen less frequently than 11 ♔h1 or 11 ♕g3.

  11   ♘xd4

In conjunction with the move 11 ... ♗d7 two original ideas should be kept in mind:

a) **12 ♘b3 ♘b4 13 ♗d1!? d5 14 e5 ♘e4 15 a5** ±, Tukmakov-Belyavsky, 1973.

b) **12 ♕g3 ♖fc8!? 13 ♖ae1 ♕d8!? 14 ♘xc6 ♗xc6 15 ♗d4 g6 16 ♗d3 d5 17 e5 ♘e4 18 ♕e3 ♗b4 19 ♗xe4 de 20 ♖d1 ♗xc3=**, Sigurjonsson-Panno, 1975.

  12 ♗xd4   e5

Only this move will give independent meaning to the move 11 a4. After 11 ... ♗d7 12 ♘b3 the game takes on the contours of the Maroczy system.

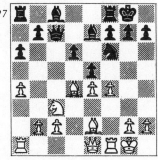

  13 ♗e3

After 13 fe de 14 ♕g3 ♖e8 15 ♔h1 ♗d8! 16 ♗e3 ♔h8 the position is level, as we are back into the game Tal-Andersson, 1976, which has already been discussed. There is, by the way, another method of defence: 16 ... ♗e6 17 ♘h6 g6 18 ♖ad1 ♖ac8 19 ♕f2 ♗e7 20 ♗g5 ♘g4!, which gave Black a good game in Tseshkovsky-Garcia, 1974.

13 ... ef
14 ♖xf4

Another equally valid continuation is 14 ♗xf4, since it is dangerous to capture the b-pawn: 14 ... ♕b6+ 15 ♔h1 ♕xb2 16 ♕g3 which carries with it a lot of threats, such as 17 ♖fb1, 17 e5 and 17 ♗h6. But even after 14 ♗xf4 Black will secure control of the e5 square, which must lead to equality, i.e. 14 ... ♗e6 15 ♕g3 ♘d7 (15 ... ♖fd8 is inferior: 16 ♗h6 g6 17 ♔h1 ♖ac8 18 ♗g5 ♘e8 19 ♖ae1 with unpleasant pressure in the centre, Dolmatov-Tal, 1979.) 16 ♗h6 ♕c5+ 17 ♔h1 ♕e5 18 ♗f4 ♕c5 19 ♘d5 (19 b4 ♕xb4 20 ♖ab1 ♕c5 21 ♖xb7 ♖fe8 leads to complicated play.) 19 ... ♗xd5 20 ♗h6! g6! (Tal considers Black's position satisfactory after 20 ... ♕d4.) 21 ♗xf8 ♗xf8 22 ed ♕xc2 23 ♕f2 ♘e5 with sufficient compensation for the exchange.

14 ... ♗e6
15 ♕g3 ♘d7
16 ♗d4

An original, but not quite effective idea of Boris Spassky was 16 ♖af1 ♘e5 17 ♖f5!? ♖fe8 18 ♖h5 g6 19 ♔h1 ♗f8 20 ♗h6 ♗xh6 21 ♖xh6 ♕e7= Spassky-Kavalek, 1977.

16 ... ♘e5

The ♘e5 paralyses both White bishops, and now in order to seize the advantage Black must find a way to take over the initiative. After 17 ♗d3 (17 ♖af1 ♖ac8 18 b3 ♕a5

19 ♗d1 ♗d8! ∓ is weaker.) 17 ... ♕a5 (17 ... ♖fe8 18 ♖af1 ♗f8 19 ♘d5 ♗xd5 20 ed g6, Georgiev-Ermenkov) 18 ♔h1 ♖ac8 19 ♘e2 ♖fe8 20 ♗c3 ♕d8 21 ♘d4 ♗g5 22 ♘f5 ♗xf5 the game did not leave the region of equality in Larsen-Andersson, 1974. A bit riskier, but also slightly more promising, is Magerramov's 22 ... g6, for example 23 ♘xd6 ♖xc3 24 ♘xe8 ♖c8 25 ♖ff1 ♘xd3 26 cd ♗e7 27 d4 ♕xe8 28 d5 ♗d7 29 e5 ♗b4∓.

B

11 ♔h1

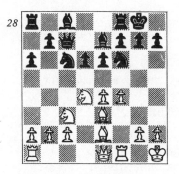

28

White removes his king from the a7-g1 diagonal in order to avoid possible Black counterplay. Furthermore, White waits for his opponent to show his hand.

It is not so easy for Black to find a plan which exploits White's last move. Thus in the scheme 11 ... ♗d7 17 ♘f3; on 12 ... ♖fd8?! there follows 13 ♕f2! ♖ab8 14 ♖ad1 ♗e8 15 g4 ♘xd4 16 ♗xd4 b5 17 g5 with an initiative for White in Zakharov-Korchnoi, 1963.

We now consider two plans for Black:

B1   11   ...   ♘xd4
B2   11   ...   ♗d7

B1

      11   ...   ♘xd4
      12   ♗xd4   b5

Black can also play 12 ... e5 13 fe de here. Although after 14 ♕g3 the prophylactic 11 ♔h1 has made 14 ... ♗c5 impossible, there is still 14 ... ♗d6!, which we have looked at earlier with the king still on g1. The position of the king on h1 does not change our assessment of the idea. Both 15 ♖xf6 ed 16 ♕xd6 ♕xd6 17 ♖xd6 dc 18 bc ♗e6 △ ♖fc8, and 15 ♗e3 ♘e8 16 ♘d5 ♕xc2! 17 ♖f2! ♗e6 18 ♗f3 ♕c6 19 ♖c1 ♕b5 give Black plenty of play.

We shall examine ideas involving ... b7-b5 and we will demonstrate the viability of Black's defences in even less favourable circumstances, in the line 11 ♕g3 ♘xd4 12 ♗xd4 b5.

It is natural to propose that if this plan is sufficently solid, even against 11 ♕g3, then it must be viable if White plays the less active 11 ♔h1.

      13   e5

After 13 ♗d3 ♗b7 14 a3 ♘d7! 15 ♕g3 it is Black who will plant a pawn on e5, not White, annihilating the activity of the white bishops. It is true that a new form of conflict arises, centering around the squares d5, e5, f5. For example 15 ... e5 16 fe ♘xe5 17 ♘d1 ♖fe8 18 ♘e3 ♗f8 19 ♖f5 g6 20 ♗xe5 ♖xe5 21 ♘g4! with the initiative, Polovodin-Adamsky, 1980. Apparently 16 ... de 17 ♗e3 ♕d6 18 ♘d5 ♗d8 △ f7-f5 will also give equality.

We will look at continuations such as 13 a3 ♗b7 14 ♕g3, that is, where the queen moves quickly to g3, in later chapters.

      13   ...   de

13 ... ♘e8 is also possible, leading to a passive but solid position. After 14 ♗f3 ♗b7 15 ♗xb7 ♕xb7 16 ♘e4 ♖c8 17 c3 ♕d5! Black has a good game, Bellon-Ungureanu, 1977. There are no particular difficulties in store for him after 15 f5, either: 15 ... ♗xf3 16 ♖xf3 de 17 ♗xe5 ♕c4 or 17 ... ♕c6.

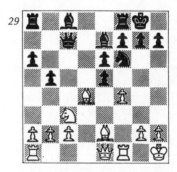

29

      14   ♗xe5

Interesting complications follow 14 fe ♘d7 15 ♗d3 (15 ♗f3 ♗b7 16 ♗xb7 ♕xb7 17 ♘e4 ♖ac8 18 c3 ♕d5 19 ♖d1, Gligoric, 1978).
15 ... ♗b7 16 ♘e4. It becomes clear that the preventative move 11 ♔h1 has made the capture of the pawn dangerous: 16 ... ♘xe5 17 ♕g3 f6 18 ♘xf6+ ♗xf6 19 ♖xf6 ♖xf6 20 ♗xe5 ♕f7 (There is no 20 ... ♕c5+!) 21 ♗xf6 ♕xf6 22 ♖f1 ♕xb2? 23 ♕c7! ±, but there is a solid way to get an equal game: 16 ... ♖ad8! 17 ♕e3 (The game is simpler after 17 ♕g3 ♗xe4 18 ♗xe4 f5! 19 ef ♕xg3 20 hg

♘xf6= or 17 c3 ♘xe5! 18 ♕g3
f6 19 ♘xf6+ ♗xf6 20 ⧄xf6
⧄xf6 21 ♗xe5 ⧄xd3=) 17 ...
♘xe5! 18 ♗b6 ♕c6 19 ♗xd8
⧄xd8 20 ♕g3 ♘xd3 21 cd ♕d5
and the two strong bishops compensate for Black's small material
disadvantage, according to 1976
analysis by Honfi.

14   ...   ♕b6
15   ♗d3   ♗b7

There is an untested idea of Tal
which is based on a trick: 15 ...
♘g4!? △ 16 ♕e4 f5! 17 ♕xa8 ♗b7
18 ♗d4 ♕c6! 19 ♗e4 fe 20 ♕a7
e5! (20 ... e3 21 ⧄f3) 21 ♗e3 (21
fe e3!) 21 ... ef! 22 ⧄xf4 ⧄xf4 23
♗xf4 e3 winning. Tal's idea has a
logical thought. If Black succeeds
in exchanging the knight for the
♗e5, then his king can feel secure.

16   ♕h4!   h6
17   ♕g3!

White has managed to force a
weakness in the defence of the Black
king, and now the Pg7 is rooted to
its spot. Now Black will have to
defend passively.

If White had played 16 ♕g3
immediately, then after 16 ... ♘h5
17 ♕h3 g6 or 16 ... g6 17 ♕g5!
♕d8! 18 ♕h6 ⧄e8 19 ⧄ad1 ♗f8
20 ♕h3 ♕e7! Black would have fortified his position.

17   ...   ♘e8
18   f5   ef
19   ⧄xf5   ♗d6

White's positional advantage and
initiative are both fading. After 20
⧄af1 ⧄d8 21 a3 ♗xe5 22 ⧄xe5
♘f6, Gufeld-Platonov, 1974, Black
should not lose. Somewhat more
active is 21 a4, but even here after

21 ... b4 22 ♘e4 ♗xe4 23 ♗xe4
Black has a viable position, although he cannot count on any
more than a draw.

B2

11   ...   ♗d7 *(30)*

Before going into this move in
detail, let us tie up a few loose ends:
a) 11 ... ♘a5?! 12 ⧄d1! b5 13 ♗f3
(The pawn sacrifice also deserves
attention: 13 e5!? de 14 fe ♕xe5
15 ♗f4 ♕c5 16 ♗f3 ♗b7 17 b4!
♕xb4 18 ♗xb7 ⧄ad8 19 ♘c6
♗xc6 20 ♗xc6 ⧄c8 ±, Bellon-
Garcia, 1976.) 13 ... ♗b7 14 e5
♘e8 15 ♕g3 ♘c4 16 ♗c1 ⧄c8
17 ♘e4! with the advantage, Lalev-
Kirov, 1981.
b) 11 ... ⧄e8 12 a4 ♘xd4 13 ♗xd4
e5 14 fe de 15 ♕g3 ♗d8! (One
move solves three problems: the
defence of the Pe5, the ♕c7, and
the ♘f6!) 16 ♗e3 ♔h8!=, Tal-
Andersson, 1976.
c) 11 ... ♔h8 (If White can wait, so
can Black. The retreat into the
corner is useful, after ♕g3, ♗h6
will no longer be threatened.) 12
♗f3 ♗d7 13 a4 ⧄ac8 14 ⧄ad1
♘xd4 14 ♗xd4 e5 with equality,
Gligorić-Najdorf, 1946. Instead of
12 ♗f3, 12 ♕g3 is doubtless more
active but we will be discussing this
idea in the next chapter.

12   a4

There are fewer problems for
Black in other continuations:
a) 12 ♘f3 d5! 13 e5 ♘g4! 14 ♗g1
f6! ∓, Matanović-Portisch, 1964.
b) 12 ♘b3 ⧄fd8 13 ♗f3 b5 14
⧄c1 b4! 15 ♘e2 e5! ∓. Vajda-
Kotov, 1948.
c) 12 ♗f3 e5! 13 ♘f5 ♗xf5 14 ef

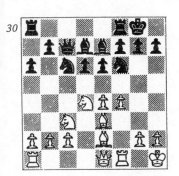

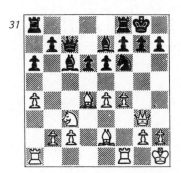

♘d4 15 ♗xd4 ed 16 ♘e2 ♕xc2
17 ♘xd4 ♕xb2 18 ♘b3 ♖ae8 19
♗xb7 ♗d8! 20 ♕g3 a5∓.

d) 12 ♖d1 b5 13 ♗d3 ♖fd8 14 a3
♖ab8 15 ♘b3 b4 16 ab ♘xb4=,
Kuijpers–Gligorić, 1967.

e) 12 ♕g3 This is probably the
most promising continuation, and
the continuation which has had the
most tournament experience up to
now, but we will put off discussion
of that move until the next chapter.

With the move 12 a4 White not
only prevents the advance of the b-
pawn, but also threatens to blockade
the queenside after a4-a5.

    12 ... ♘xd4

After 12 ... ♘a5 13 ♖d1 ♘c4
14 ♗c1 ♖ac8! 15 ♗f3 (15 b3 ♘e5!
16 ♗b2 ♘g6=) 15 ... g6 16 g4 ♘e8
17 f5?! ♕d8 18 b3 ♘e5, Diaz-
Balashov, 1975 gave Black an
excellent game. White lost the
initiative with 13 ♖d1. He should
have played 13 ♕g3 ♘c4 14 ♗c1,
trying to exploit the drawbacks of
the beautiful, if somewhat unstable, position of the ♘c4.

    13 ♗xd4 ♗c6
    14 ♕g3

White threatens to set up a
blockade with 15 a5, and on 14
... ♖ac8, 15 e5! is strong as after
15 ... de 16 ♗xe5 and the queen
has no place comfortable to
go.

If 14 ... g6 White gets a strong
initiative with 15 f5! e5 16 ♗e3,
for example 16 ... ♔h8 17 ♕h4! (or
17 fg fg 18 ♗h6±) 17 ... ♕d8 18
♗g5±, Shamkovich–Murey 1975.
16 ... ♘xe4 is no better, according
to analysis by Shamkovich: 17
♘xe4 ♗xe4 18 f6! ♗d8 19 c4! d5
20 ♕h4 ♔h8 (20 ... ♕d6 21
♖ad1!±) 21 ♕h6 ♖g8 22 ♗g5±.
Shamkovich also refuted another
attempt in his game against Grefe,
which saw 16 ... d5 17 fg hg 18
ed ♘xd5 19 ♗c4!±, and eliminated 16 ... b5 in Shamkovich–
Sherwin, from the same year: 17
♗h6 ♖fc8 18 ♗d3! ♔h8 19 ♕h3
b4 20 fg fg 21 ♕e6!±.

    14 ... b6!

A comfortable solution to all of
Black's problems. Black prevents
the blockade and finds a comfortable square for his queen, where it
will not only pressure the Pe4,

but also support the advance of the b-pawn. After 15 ♕e3 ♛b7 16 ♘f3 (16 e5 ♗xg2+!) 16 ... b5 one can hardly talk in terms of an advantage for White.

6 11 ♕g3

1 e4 c5 2 ♘f3 d6 3 d4 cd 5 ♘xd4
♘f6 5 ♘c3 e6 6 ♗e2 a6 7 0-0 ♗e7
8 f4 ♘c6 9 ♗e3 0-0 10 ♕e1 ♕c7
11 ♕g3

This is the most direct and
aggressive continuation. White
transfers his queen to an excellent
attacking position, where it not
only organizes threats to g7, but
also supports the advance of the
e-pawn.

After 11 ♕g3 Black must make
a decision, to exchange knights on
d4, which will put the white bishop
in a threatening position, or to
allow the knight to retreat to f3.

A 11 ... ♘xd4
B 11 ... ♗d7

A

11	...	♘xd4
12	♗xd4	b5

After what has already been said
about the viability of 10 ... ♘xd4
11 ♗xd4 b5 12 ♕g3 ♗b7, Black
need not fear the diagrammed
position, even though some difficult moments lie ahead.

Instead of 12 ... b5, it is premature to open up the centre before
developing the queenside. 12 ...
d5? 13 ♔h1 de 14 ♘xe4 ±. It is
also too late to transpose into
another variation — 12 ... ♗d7?!
13 e5! de 14 ♗xe5 ♕b6+ 15 ♔h1
♘e8 16 ♗d3 f6 17 ♕h4! g6 18
♘e4! ±, Hartston–Ciocaltea, 1971–
72.

13 a3

The immediate advance 13 e5
does not give White any advantage,
since Black has no weaknesses.
After 13 ... de White has a choice:
a) 14 fe ♗c5 15 ♗xc5 ♕xc5+ 16
♔h1 ♘d7 17 ♖ae1 b4 (also good is
17 ... ♗b7) 18 ♘e4 ♕xe5! 19 ♘f6+
♔h8 20 ♕h4! ♘xf6 21 ♗f3 ♕xb2!
(21 ... ♕b8 22 ♗xa8 ♕xa8 23
♖xf6! ±) 22 ♗xa8 ♗d7, according
to analysis by Altschuler in 1960.
b) 14 ♗xe5 appears dangerous but
14 ... ♕c5+ puts White into a defensive position: 15 ♔h1 ♗b7 16
♗d3 (16 ... b4 △ 17 ... ♕xc2 was

threatened) 16 ... g6!   17 ♖ae1
(The attack by 17 f5 is repulsed by
the simple 17 ... ♘h5!, and after
17 a3 ♖fd8 18 ♖ae1 ♕c6 19
♖e2 ♘h5 20 ♕h3 f5! Black stands
well.) 17 ... b4 18 ♘d1 ♘h5 19
♕h3 f6!! 20 ♕xe6+ ♖f7 21 ♗c4
♖af8 22 ♗b8 ♔h8! 23 ♘f2 ♖g7
24 ♘d3 ♕c8! 25 ♗d6 ♗xd6 26
♕xd6 ♘g3+! ∓, Reshevsky-Browne,
1977.

The idea 13 ♗f3 ♗b7 14 ♖ae1
△ e4-e5 also holds little promise.
After 14 ... ♖ad8! 15 ♔h1 b4 16
e5 ♘e8 17 ♗xb7 de! 18 ♗xa6?!
(18 ♗xe5 =) 18 ... ed 19 ♘e2
♕xc2! Black obtained the advantage in Heuer-Tal, 1977.

With the move 13 a3 White
holds up the advance of the b-pawn
and continues to strengthen his
position, before advancing his pawn
to e5.

13   ...   ♗d7

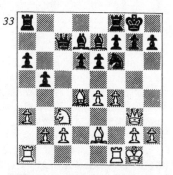

Black completes his development, not, for the moment, activating his bishop along the long
diagonal.

The move 13 ... ♗b7 seems
more natural, but most of the
time the same position will be
reached, with the bishop standing
on c6. Actually, the threat to the
e-pawn will only become real when
Black has his bishop on c6, queen
on b7, and sometimes also the
pawn on a5. These plans will be
examined below, but first let us
consider some instructive fragments
from games which concern themselves with other subtleties of the
position:
a) 14 ♖ae1 d5 (Passive play is not
advisable here — 14 ... ♗c6 15 ♗f3
♖ad8 16 e5 de 17 ♗xe5 ♕b6+ 18
♔h1, Dvoiris-Polugayevsky, 1981.
Now Black must play carefully in
order not to fall under attack, perhaps 18 ... ♖d7!?) 15 ed ♗c5!
16 ♗xc5 ♕xc5 17 ♕f2 with an
equal game, Aronson-Mascarinas,
1980.
b) 14 ♖ad1 ♗c6 15 ♗f3 ♖ac8
(weaker is 15 ... ♕b7 16 ♖fe1!?
♖fd8?! 17 ♘d5! ed 18 ed ♗e8
19 ♖xe7 ♕xe7 20 ♖e1 ♕f8 21
♗xf6 ♖d7 22 ♗e4 h6 23 ♕g4
with a strong attack, Quinones-
Fernandez, 1977) 16 e5 de 17 fe
♗xf3 18 ef ♕xg3 19 hg ♗xd1
20 fe ♖fe8 21 ♖xd1 f6 with a sharp
endgame.
c) 14 ♔h1 g6 (14 ... ♖fd8 15 ♖ae1
♘e8 16 ♗d3 ♖ac8 17 ♕f2! ♖d7
18 ♗b6 ♕b8 19 e5! ± Sax-Tompa,
1974) 15 f5 e5! 16 ♗e3 d5! 17
ed ♘xd5 18 ♘xd5 ♗xd5 19 f6?!
(19 c3!?) 19 ... ♗c5 20 ♗h6 ♖fe8
21 ♕g5 ♖ad8! 22 ♗g7 ♕c6∓,
Zuckerman-Grefe, 1977.
d) On 14 ♗d3 Black manages to
liberate his position by 14 ... e5!
(14 ... g6 15 f5! ♖ae8 16 ♕h3 ±)
15 fe ♘h5! 16 ♕e3 de and later 17

♝b6 ♛d6 18 ♖ad1 ♘f4 19 ♝e2
♛g6=, Bronstein–Kotov, 1947, or
17 ♝xe5 ♛xe5 18 ♖f5 ♛e6 19
♖xh5 g6 with sharp play. The
immediate 14 ... ♘h5!? is also a
real possibility. 15 ♛h3 ♘xf4 16
♖xf4 e5 might be followed by 17
♖g4 ed 18 ♛h6 g6 19 ♖g3 dc 20
♖h3 ♝h4! 21 ♖xh4 f6 with double-
edged play.

14　♚h1

White prevents the Black queen
from escaping with check after 15
e5 de 16 ♝xe5. The bishop on e2
controls the h5 square, hindering
the advance e6-e5.

White can also transfer the ♖a1
to the centre by 14 ♖ae1, e.g. 14
... ♝c6 15 ♖f3 b4 16 ab ♛xb4
with sharp play.

14　...　♝c6

Black has no possibility of advancing his pawn to e5. On the
contrary, the move e4-e5 is inescapable, so Black should prepare
to meet it. The most natural
manner of defence would be to
reinforce the g7 point by playing
the knight to e8, but this would
entomb the rook.

By removing the bishop to c6,
Black frees the b-file for his heavy
pieces, ensuring the advance b5-b4.
The activation of the battery ♝c6-
♛b7 cannot be felt, as yet, but all
the same White is going to have to
think about the consequences of its
creation at the appropriate time.

15　♖ae1 *(34)*

White has a wide range of plans,
leading to complicated play which
requires caution by Black.
a) 15 ♝d3 e5 (Worth analysing is

the plan 15 ... ♘h5 16 ♛h3 ♘xf4
17 ♖xf4 e5 18 ♘d5 ♝xd5 19 ed
g6 20 ♝c6 ef 21 ♛h6 f6 22
♝xg6=) 16 fe ♘h5 17 ♛h3 de 18
♝xe5 ♛xe5 19 ♖f5 ♛d4! 20 ♖xh5
g6 21 e5 ♝d7! 22 ♛g3 ♛g4!
This, of course, is just "food for
thought".
b) 15 e5 de 16 ♝xe5 ♛b7 17 f5 ef
18 ♖xf5 ♘e8 19 ♖e1 f6 20 ♝f4
♖f7 with complex play, Kuzmin-
Kochiev, 1977. From this example
it is clear that with a rook on e1 the
advance of the e-pawn would have
been more effective.
c) 15 ♝f3 ♖ac8 16 ♖ae1 ♖fd8 17
♖e2 ♘e8! 18 ♛f2 ♖b8 19 e5 ♝xf3
20 ♛xf3 b4! as Suetin-Panchenko,
USSR 1979.

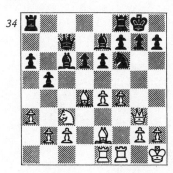

15　...　♛b7

Attempts to create counterplay
by other means are connected with
the useful deployment of the ♖a8:
a) 15 ... ♖ab8. Black would like to
play b5-b4, but White forces him
back on the defensive by the
advance of his e-pawn: 16 e5! ♘e8
17 ♝d3 (17 b4!? de 18 fe f5! 19
ef ♛xg3 20 hg is an original attempt
to play all over the board, Pan-
chenko-Osnos, 1982. But after 20

... ②xf6 21 ♗f3 ♗xf3 22 gf ♖bd8! an equal position lies on the board.) 17 ... g6 (One can, as a preliminary, exchange on e5, but it is dangerous to delay the move g7-g6 — 17 ... b4? 18 ♕h3 g6 19 ♖e3! bc 20 ed ♗xd6 21 ♕xh7+ with a mating finish.) 18 ed! ♗xd6 19 ♕h4 ♕d8 20 ♕h6 ♗xa3 21 ②e2 ♗c5 (but not 21 ... ♗e7 22 f5! ef 23 ♖xf5! ± with a very strong attack, Sznapik–Niklasson, 1978). This middlegame position is very interesting for independent analysis. White is down a pawn, but the active position of his pieces, and the coordination of his actions in response to Black's operations give him preferable chances after either 22 c3 or 22 ♗e5 ♕d5! 23 ♕h3! (but not 23 ♖f3? ♕xf3! winning) 23 ... ♖c8 24 ②c3 ♕d7 25 f5! ef 26 ♗xf5. To be honest, White can choose from many attractive moves on his 18th turn — 18 ♖e3; 18 ♕h3; 18 ②e4; 18 f5 ef 19 ♗xf5; and even 18 ②d1 de 19 fe ♕d8 20 c3 ♗h4 21 ♕h3 ♗xe1 22 ♖xe1 ②g7 23 ♕h6. Shishlov–Aronson, 1980. The method of "remote" defence with 15 ... ♖ab8 cannot really be recommended.

b) **15 ... ♖ae8.** With two ideas: After ... ♗d8 the e-pawn may be advanced to e5, and to render harmless the combinational attacks which White employs against 15 ... ♖ac8. 16 ♗d3 e5 17 fe ②h5 18 ♕h3 de 19 ♗e3 g6 20 ♗h6 ②g7 21 ②d1!, Beliavsky–Garcia, 1975, or 16 ♗f3 ♖d8 (With the bishop on f3 the advance e4-e5 is less effective, and therefore Black can improve

the position of his rook.) 17 ♕f2 ♕b7 18 e5 de 19 fe ②d7 20 ②e4 ♕c7 21 c3 ♗xe4 22 ♗xe4 ♗c5 23 ♖e3, Tal–Balashov, 1976. In each case White retains a small edge with chances for success.

c) **15 ... ♖ac8** (Black improves the position of his rooks in expectation of the White storm.) 16 ♗d3 ♖fd8. On 16 ... e5 one must carefully evaluate the consequences of the combination 17 fe ②h5 18 ♕h3 de 19 ②d5! ♗xd5 20 ♗xe5! ♕xe5 21 ed ♕g5. (We should point out that if Black had played 15 ... ♖ae8 this combination would have faltered against the simple reply 21 ... ♕xd5. Here, however, Black loses because of 22 ♗xh7! ♔xh7 23 ♖f5. In the game Karpov–Balashov, 1977, White emerged with an extra pawn after 21 ... ♕d6 22 ♕xh5 g6 23 ♕f3.) 22 ♖f5 ♕h4! (The weakness of the first rank saves Black. After 24 ♕xh4 ♗xh4 25 ♖xh5 ♗xe1 White must force a perpetual check.

16   ♗d3

On 16 ♗f3 Black can place his rook on d8 right away — 16 ... ♖ad8! 17 e5?! de 18 fe ②h5!, while on 16 e5 there follows 16 ... de and White cannot gain the advantage by either 17 fe ②e4, or 17 ♗xe5 g6.

16   ...   b4

Logical, but not Black's only plan. Praxis has demonstrated the solidity of other set-ups as well, e.g. a) **16 ... ♖ad8** 17 ♕h3 h6 18 ♖e3 b4 19 ab ♕xb4, Hartston–Larsen, 1974.

b) **16 ... g6** 17 f5 ②h5 18 ♕h3 ef

19 ♖xf5! ♗d7!   20 ♖e3 ♗f6, analysis by Barczay.

c) 16 ... a5 17 e5 de 18 ♘xe5 g6!

17   ab

It is unlikely that there is any real positional risk in 17 ♘d1 ba 18 ba. Black has no holes in his defence, and after 18 ... d5!? 19 e5 ♘e4 or 18 ... ♘h5 19 ♕g4 (19 ♕e3 ♘xf4! or 19 ♕h3 ♘xf4 20 ♖xf4 e5 21 ♖g4 ed   22 e5 g6) 19 ... ♘f6 20 ♗xf6 ♗xf6 21 e5 de 22 fe ♗e7 23 ♕h3 h6! he beats off the attack on his king and turns his attention with optimism to the other side of the board, where White's position is in ruins.

17   ...   ♕xb4
18   ♘e2   ♕b7

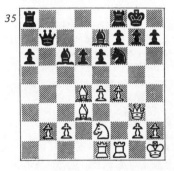

35

A dynamically balanced position has been created, with mutual counterplay, for example 19 e5 ♘h5 (inferior is 19 ... de 20 ♗xe5 ♗e4 21 ♗xe4 ♕xe4 22 ♘d4! ♕g6 23 f5! with a clear advantage, Pritchett-Sigurjonsson, 1975) 20 ♕h3 g6 21 ♘g3 de! (on 21 ... ♘xg3? 22 hg White will be able to add the h-pawn to his attack) 22 ♗xe5 ♘g7 23 ♘e4 (or 23 ♗c3 ♗b4 24 ♘e4 ♗xc3 25 bc ♕e7!) 23 ... f6

24 ♗c3 ♗d5 Ermenkov-Estevez, 1977. Besides this forced series of events, White can begin a new phase of manouvering – 19 ♔g1!? g6 20 ♕e3 a5 21 ♘g3 a4, but this does not change the evaluation of the diagrammed position.

B

11   ...   ♗d7

This is one of the ways in which Black can mark time in the given position. Black either refrains from exchanging knights entirely, or intends to follow up that exchange with ... ♗c6. It is true, though that the transfer outlined above does not always work in Black's favour.

It is worth noting that the position after 11 ... ♗d7 is often reached via different move orders, for example 6 ... ♘c6 7 ♗e3 ♗e7 8 0-0 0-0 9 f4 ♗d7 10 ♕e1 ♕c7 11 ♕g3 a6 etc.

After 11 ... ♗d7 White must decide on the proper moment for the advance e4-e5, for therein lies the essence of the conflict. Once again, the timing depends on the "taste" of the player, from his character, and how he handles the timing of the move is a good indication of his class of play.

To those who are especially impatient, we recommend that one might once again analyze a paradoxical idea of Ljubojević.

B1   12 e5
B2   12 ♘f3
B3   12 ♖ad1
B4   12 ♔h1

B1

12   e5!? *(36)*

Astounding! In more than a half-

36
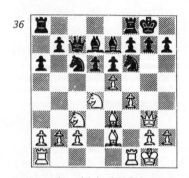

century in which the Scheveningen has been subjected to analytical and practical tests, no one seems to have seriously considered this immediate attack in the centre, which, it is said, creates all sorts of threats.

White, having just concentrated his forces in the centre, radically alters the manoeuvring nature of the struggle. He tries to exploit the fact that the ♗d7 has temporarily robbed the knight on f6 of a convenient retreat square.

    12   ...   de

It is probable that the retreat 12 ... ♘e8 gives Black a fully tenable position, i.e. 13 ♖ad1 de 14 fe f5! 15 ♗c4?! ♘xd4 16 ♖xd4 ♗c5 17 ♖h4 ♖c8, Durao–Spassov, 1977. First of all, however, White can improve his play (13 ♘f3!?) and secondly, the retreat of the knight, you must agree, is a small victory for White. We will test the acceptance of the sacrifice.

    13 fe   ♘xe5

With the king standing on g8, the capture with the queen loses immediately, 13 ... ♕xe5?? 14 ♘xc6.

    14 ♗f4   ♗d6
    15 ♖ad1!

White's rook goes gunning for the ♗d6 – this is White's basic idea. Black needs time – either to defend the ♘e5 or to defend its defender. To do this is not so simple. In the game Ljubojević–Andersson, 1976, Black was unable to stop White's attack: 15 ... ♕b8 16 ♖d3 ♘e8 17 ♘e4 ♗c7 18 ♖c3 ♘c6 19 ♗xc7 ♘xd4 20 ♗d3 ♕a7 21 ♘c5 ♗b5 22 ♗e5 ♘c6 23 ♗xh7+ ♔xh7 24 ♖f4! f6? 25 ♕h3+ ♔g8 26 ♖h4! ♘d8 27 ♗d4! etc. Later a way was found to improve the defence – 24 ... f5!? 25 ♖h4+ ♔g8 26 ♕g6 ♘xe5, or 24 ... ♘xe5 25 ♖h4+ ♔g8 26 ♕xe5 ♕b6! 27 ♖ch3 f6!. But White can also play more strongly. Exhaustive analysis is required.

Ljubovević's idea does not refute the classical construction of the Sicilian Scheveningen, but it is thought-provoking, and is a test of the solidity of all branches of this system in face of the sacrifice e4-e5.

B2

    12 ♘f3!?

37

An energetic and principled reaction to this flirting with the exchange of knights, White retreats his knight and reinforces the threat of the advance e4-e5. In fact, this move was encountered in a very similar position over 100 years ago in a game between Chigorin and Paulsen (1881). White won that game in an excellent strategical manner.

A rather similar picture of the battle arises from the move 12 ♗d3 if Black continues 12 ... ♘b4. Only in the schema 12 ... b5 13 a3! will White carry out the timely advance of the e-pawn and hang on to his initiative: 13 ... ♔h8 14 ♖ad1 (Another plan of action deserves consideration here. 14 ♔h1 ♖ab8 15 ♘xc6 ♗xc6 16 ♗d4 ♖bd8 17 ♖ae1 ♕b7 18 ♕h3, Janošević-Gligorić, 1972) 14 ... ♖ab8 15 ♘f3 b4 16 ab ♖xb4 17 e5! de 18 fe ♘h5 19 ♕h3 g6 20 ♗h6, Gligorić-Ostojić, 1965. For his part, Black may adopt the more solid route to equality, 12 ... ♘b4 13 e5 de 14 fe ♘e8 15 ♗e4 f5!, e.g. 16 ef ♕xg3 17 f7+ ♖xf7 18 hg ♘f6.

12   ...   ♘b4

Black cannot stop the White pawn from getting to e5. 12 ... e5? 13 f5! (Threatening 13 ♗g5 and 13 ♗h6) 13 ... ♘h5 14 ♕f2 with a clear advantage. Therefore Black should be prepared for this advance.

The stabilisation of the centre — 12 ... d5 13 e5 — is also in White's favour because of the poor outlook for the ♗d7. 13 ... ♘h5 14 ♕f2! g6 15 ♗b6 ♕b8 16 ♘d4 ♘g7 17 ♗d3, Trifunović-Najdorf, 1948. If he undertakes pawn operations on the flank, 12 ... b5 13 e5 ♘e8, Black will begin to feel the force of the white-squared bishop of his oppo-

nent: 14 ♗d3! f5 15 ef. Therefore the desire to eliminate this bishop is both understandable and correct. In addition, the move 12 ... ♘b4 has two more merits. The obvious goal is ♘xc2, but there is a hidden advantage as well. After the move e4-e5 by White, a knight will be able to swing into a useful position on d5. Praxis has shown that after 13 e5 (on 13 ♘d4 it is possible to offer a draw with 13 ... ♘c6) the initiative can turn in Black's favour after 13 ... ♘fd5 (Sufficiently solid, but not inconsequential is 13 ... ♘e8 14 ♖ac1 f5!, immediately grabbing the e4 square for the knight, or 14 ... ♗c6 15 a3 ♗xf3! 16 ♖xf3 ♘c6! 17 ♗d3 de 18 f5 ef 19 ♖xf5 ♖d8 20 ♖f2 g6, Gipslis-Koblenc, 1964.) 14 ♘xd5 (14 ♗d4 ♘xc3 15 bc ♘xc2 16 ed ♘xd4! ∓) 14 ... ♘xd5 15 ♗d4 ♕xc2 16 ed ♗f6 17 ♗xf6 ♘xf6, and now 18 ♕f2 ♕xb2 19 ♘e5 ♖ac8 20 ♗f3 ♖c2 ∓, Gipslis-Bokuchava, 1964.

13   ♗d3

The natural reply 13 ♖ac1 △ 14 a3, chasing away the knight, demands energetic action by Black in order to achieve equality: 13 ... d5! 14 ed ♘bxd5 15 ♘xd5 ed! 16 ♗d4 ♘h5 or 15 ... ♘xd5 16 ♗d4 f6! 17 ♘e1 ♗d6 18 ♘d3 g5!

13   ...   b5

The exchange 13 ... ♘xd3 14 cd strengthens the Pe4. Then the White knight would not return to d4, where it would not threaten anything, but White will put the ♖a1 on the c-file. Black's bishop is useless, hemmed in by pawns of both colours.

By playing 13 ... b5, Black intends to exchange the knight for
the bishop under more favourable
circumstances.

14   a3   ♘xd3
15   cd   ♕b7!

An essential move. Black threatens to play b5-b4 after which he
will be able to exploit the weakness
of the white pawn structure on the
queenside.

It is dangerous for White to play
16 b4 because of 16 ... a5, or 16 e5
because of 16 ... ♘d5 17 f5? ♘xe3
18 f6 ♘f5 ∓ A more worthwhile
method of fortifying the position
in the centre is 16 ♖ae1, but even
here after 16 ... a5 17 e5 ♘d5
Black would have a fully equal
game.

B3

12   ♖ad1 *(38)*

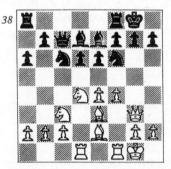

A logical decision to place the
last reserve in the centre of the
board. Still, it remains to be seen if
the rook stands better on d1 or on
e1. To this end we shall take as our
fundamental position the one with
the move 12 ♖ad1, commenting
where appropriate on the differing

possibilities offered by 12 ♖ae1.

12   ...   b5

The counterthrust 12 ... d5 is
rarely applied. It is by no means
easy for White to demonstrate an
advantage against this move, for
example 13 ed ed! or 13 e5 ♘xd4
14 ♗xd4 ♘e4 15 ♘xe4 de 16 c3
♗c6. It is worth mentioning that in
this situation there would be nothing for the rook to do on e1.

It also pays to consider the defence 12 ... ♘xd4 13 ♗xd4 ♗c6 14
♗d3 e5 15 fe ♘h5 16 ♕h3 de.
After 17 ♗e3 White has a slight
edge wherever the rooks are, but in
the case of the variation 17 ♘d5
♗xd5 18 ed ed 19 ♕xh5 g6 20
♕h6, the rook, standing on d1,
would turn out to be an empty
shell after 20 ... ♕d8! 21 ♖f3
♗g5!, while a rook on e1 would
display its full potential with the
decisive 21 ♖e5! △ 22 ♖h5!.

13   e5

The quiet 13 a3 gives Black his
usual choice: 13 ... ♘xd4 14 ♗xd4
♗c6 15 ♔h1 ♖ad8 16 ♗d3 ♕b7, or
13 ... b4 14 ab ♘xb4 15 ♔h1 ♖b8
16 e5 ♘e8, leading to well-known
positions.

Only Ljubojević's idea e4-e5 demands special consideration when
the rook is on e1. Let us consider
12 ♖ae1 b5 13 e5!? *(39)*

After 13 ... ♘e8 14 ♘f3 ♘b4 15
♗d1 Black has a strong, but cramped
position. If the sacrifice is accepted,
13 ... de 14 fe ♘xe5, White doesn't
have to waste time returning the
rook to d1, but can obtain a sharp
position with compensation for the
pawn after 15 ♗h6 ♘e8 16 ♗f4

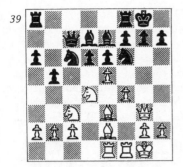

39

♗d6 17 ♘e4.

13   ...   de

After 13 ... ♘e8 14 ♘f3 b4 15 ♘e4 the exchange of pawns will prove all the more worthwhile.

14   fe   ♘e8

It is dangerous to take the pawn: 14 ... ♘xe5 15 ♗f4 ♗d6 16 ♘b3! with the unstoppable threat of ♖xd6.

After 15 ♘f3 ♘b4 16 ♖d2! ♗c6 17 ♘d4 it is possible to evaluate the position as slightly favouring White, chiefly due to the temporary unemployed status of the ♘e8 and ♖f8. Black's position is solid, though, and after 17 ... ♗b7 18 ♗f3 ♖d8 19 a3 ♘d5 Black has almost equalised, as he can activate the knight via the g7 square.

B4

12   ♔h1

A useful prophylactic move. Now, having escaped the nasty threat of checks along the g1-a7 diagonal, White has more possibilities to get in the break e4-e5. The methods of attack do not differ greatly from those discussed above, however, and we shall confine ourselves here to a discussion of the subtleties of this particular move

order. Of course the given position can be reached by a number of paths, playing ♔h1 on the 10th or 11th move, i.e. 11 ♔h1 ♗d7 12 ♕g3.

40

12   ...   b5

We consider other continuations, commenting on the relevance of the placement of the king at h1.

a) 12 ... ♘xd4 13 ♗xd4 ♗c6 14 ♖ae1 b5 15 a3 (After 15 e5 de 16 ♗xe5 Black no longer has the check at c5, which gave him such excellent counterchances in the game Reshevsky-Browne given above. Nevertheless, the inclusion of the intermediate moves ♔h1 and ♗c6 gives Black the chance to create new counterplay, using the powerful battery on the long diagonal: 16 ... ♕b7 17 f5 b4 18 ♘d1 ♗e4! 19 ♘e3 ♕c6 20 ♖f4 g6 21 fg fg, Petrienko-Balberov, 1979) 15 ... g6 (A still more solid method of play in this position is to play 15 ... ♕b7, not giving White the opportunity of breaking with f4-f5. Then the game would transpose into a well known position after 16 ♗d3 b4, or Black would obtain a fully equal game after 16

e5 de   17 ♗xe5 g6.) 16 f5 e5   17
♗e3 ♔h8 (17 ... ♗xe4 loses to 18 fg
♗xg6 19 ♖xf6 ♗xf6 20 ♘d5 ♕d8
21 ♗b6 ♗h4 22 ♗xd8 ♗xg3 23
♗f5!) 18 ♕h4 gf 19 ♗g5 ♘g8 20
♖xf5 ♗xg5 21 ♖xg5 with a complicated struggle, Schmidt-Jano-
šević, 1977.

b) 12 ... ♖fe8 13 e5! de 14 fe (It
is possible to take the pawn on e5,
as the attack on g7 is already ineffective. Nevertheless, this limits
the "Black" advantage gained from
the inclusion of the moves ♔h1 and
♖fe8) After 14 ... ♘xe5 15 ♗h6 g6
White has a choice between 16 ♗g5
♘d5 17 ♗xe7 ♖xe7 18 ♘f5! ef
19 ♘xd5 ♕c5 19 ♘xe7+ ♕xe7 20
♖ae1 ♕f6 △ ... ♗c6, and 16 ♗f4
♗d6 17 ♖ad1 with the unpleasant
threats 18 ♘db5 and 18 ♘b3, intensifying the shaky position of the
♘f6. The move 12 ... ♖fe8 brings
with it more minuses than plusses.

c) 12 ... ♔h8. Black also values the
useful waiting move, liquidating the
attack on the g7 square and stopping
for a time the breakthrough in the
centre – 13 e5?! de 14 fe ♕xe5!
15 ♘xc6 ♕xg3, as the zwischen-
schach ♘e7 is no longer available.
The most unpleasant response to
Black's counter-prophylactic is 13
♖ad1. After 13 ... b5 14 e5 de
(more resistant is 14 ... ♘e8) 15 fe
♕xe5 (or 15 ... ♘e8 16 ♘f3±,
Larsen-Hort, Bugojno 1978) 16 ♗f4
♕c5 17 ♘b3 ♕a7 18 ♗e3 ♕b8 19
♖xf6! ♕xg3 20 hg ♗xf6 21 ♖xd7
(analysis by Lepeshkin) and after
13 ... ♖ad8 14 e5 de 15 fe ♕xe5
16 ♗f4 ♕c5 17 ♘b3 ♕a7 18 ♗c7!
♖c8 19 ♖xf6 ♗xf6 20 ♖xd7 b5

21 ♘e4! (but not 21 ♕d6? ♘e5! ∓,
Kudriashov-Arbakov, 1981) White
has a clear advantage. In the last
variation instead of 18 ... ♖c8 the
sacrifice of the exchange would
have been a more stubborn defence,
18 ... b5 19 ♗xd8 ♗xd8, but even
here equality for Black lies distant.

41

13   e5!?

White can carry out this advance
a bit later, without sacrifices: 13 a3
b4 (on 13 ... ♖ab8?! the attack
with e4-e5 is employed to great
effect, since the rook falls under
the pin, as well as the queen – 14
e5 de 15 fe ♘xe5 16 ♖xf6! ♗xf6
17 ♗f4 b4 18 ♘e4 ♔h8 19 ♗d3
♕a5 20 ♘xf6 gf 21 ♕h4 ♘g6 22
♕xf6+ ♔g8 23 ♗xb8 with a decisive
advantage) 14 ab ♘xb4 15 e5 (the
inclusion of the moves 15 ♗f3
♖ab8 does not intensify the effect
of the break 16 e5 ♘e8 17 ♗e4 g6
18 ♘d1?! de 19 fe f5! 20 c3 and
Black seizes the initiative,
Taborov-Averkin, 1978) 15 ... ♘e8
16 ♖ad1 de 17 fe f5! 18 ef ♗xf6
(but not 18 ... ♕xg3 19 fe ♖xf1
20 ♖xf1 and the threat of 21 ♖xf8
mate costs Black a piece) 19 ♘e4
♕xg3   20 hg ♘d5 and Black's

chances are no worse.

13 ... de

The alternative 13 ... ♘e8 14 ♖ad1 ♔h8 15 ♘f3 f5! 16 ef ♘xf6 17 ♘g5 d5 18 ♕h4 gives the initiative to White.

14 fe ♘xe5

Attacking *à la* Ljubojević, 15 ♗h6 ♘e8 16 ♗f4 ♗d6 17 ♘e4 ♘c4 18 ♘xd6 ♘cxd6 leads to a sharp position, where White has sufficient compensation for the sacrificed pawn. But he can mess up the game even further by the sacrifice 15 ♖xf6!?, after which the ♘c3 will enter the game. We have not arrived at a definite conclusion about the correctness of this idea, there is only some analysis and

the symbol ∞. Here it is: 15 ♖xf6 ♗xf6 16 ♘f3 ♗c6 17 ♗f4 ♗xf3 (17 ... b4 18 ♗xe5 ♗xe5 19 ♕xe5 ♕xe5 20 ♘xe5 ♗xg2+ 21 ♔xg2 bc 22 b4 ♖fd8, Hoen-Øgaard, 1977 ∞) 18 ♗xf3 ♖ac8 19 ♖e1 ♘xf3! 20 ♗xc7 ♘xe1; or 16 ♗f4 b4 17 ♘e4 ♔h8 18 ♘f3 ♕xc2 19 ♘xf6 gf 20 ♘xe5 fe 21 ♗d3 ef 22 ♕h3 ♕xd3 23 ♕xd3 ♗c6 24 ♕d4+ f6!

It seems to us quite symptomatic that our discussion about the good old classical Scheveningen should end with insane complications and an unclear evaluation. As the years pass we learn more and more about this ancient variation, all the while convinced that it is almost unfathomable.

7 Systems with . . . ♘bd7

1 e4 c5 2 ♘f3 e6 3 d4 cd 4 ♘xd4 ♘f6 5 ♘c3 d6 6 ♗e2 a6

By developing the knight at d7, Black usually intends to create counterplay on the queenside as soon as possible. Meanwhile, the knight holds up the advance e4-e5, and then, when Black has basically completed his development, he can bring the knight to c4 via b6, or place it on c5 in order to attack the Pe4. With the knight on d7 the effect of the advance e6-e5 is enhanced, breaking up the White pawn chain.

The basic drawback of the system is clear. Black yields the initiative to his opponent, since the latter has an advantage in the centre and more space in which to work. As a rule, White develops either pawn or piece pressure on the kingside, and Black waits for a comfortable moment to go on to the counterattack on other fronts. The character of events is somewhat reminiscent of a bullfight, in which brute force competes with mastery and experience.

7 0-0

Other continuations will be examined in later chapters.

This is the most common move.

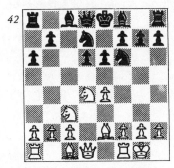

42

7 ... ♘bd7

With this move order Black intends to mobilise his queenside with b7-b5, ♗b7, and ♖c8 or ♕c7, before developing his kingside. White will try to advance his pawn to e5 and chase the knight from f6, intensifying his own attacking potential on the kingside.

That the immediate initiation of queenside activity with 7 ... b5 is premature has been accepted as a result of the game Smyslov-Kottnauer, 1946: 8 ♗f3 ♖a7 9 ♕e2 ♖c7 10 ♖d1 ♘bd7 11 a4! ba 12 ♘xa4 ♗b7 13 e5! ♘xe5 14 ♗xb7 ♖xb7 15 ♕xa6 ♕b8 16 ♘c6 ♘xc6 17 ♕xc6+ ♘d7 18 ♘c5!! dc 19 ♗f4 ♗d6 20 ♗xd6 ♖b6 21 ♕xd7+! 1-0.

White's attack makes a strong impression. Still, there is no reason why Black should lose after the rather unattractive move 8 ♗f3. In our opinion, 8 ... e5 is worth analysing, for example 9 ♘f5 d5 10 ♗g5 d4 11 ♘d5. 8 ... ♘fd7 also deserves consideration, e.g. 9 e5 ♖a7 (but not 9 ... d5 10 ♘xd5!) 10 ed ♘e5.

We will now examine the moves 8 f4 (A) and 8 a4 (B). First, however, it should be noted that the natural prophylactic move 8 ♗e3 generally transposes to level positions after 8 ... ♕c7 or 8 ... ♗e7. The bishop gets in the way of the queen and rook by occupying e3, and therefore the advance e4-e5 is more difficult to achieve. Therefore Black can try 8 ... b5, not fearing sharp play on the queenside after 9 a4 b4! 10 ♘c6 ♕c7 11 ♘xb4 d5 12 ♕d4 ♗c5 13 ♘bxd5 ed 14 ♘xd5 ♕d6 15 ♘xf6+ gf or 14 ... ♘xd5 15 ♕xg7 ♘xe3 16 ♕xh8+ ♘f8 17 fe ♗d6, as in Belyavsky-Stean, 1975.

A

	8	f4	b5
	9	♗f3	♗b7

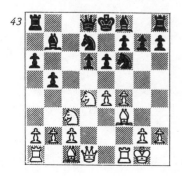

43

Once again White is faced with a dilemma: Should he play e5 immediately or first improve his position.
A1   10 a3
A2   10 e5

10 ♔h1 looks strong, since 10 ... b4 11 e5! favours White: 11 ... ♗xf3 12 ♕xf3 de 13 ♘c6 ♕c8 14 fe ♘xe5 15 ♘xe5 bc 16 b3 ♗e7 17 ♘c6 ±, Mukhin-Grushevsky, 1964. After 10 ... ♕c7, however, we would transpose into A after 11 a3.

10 ♖e1 can bring surprisingly rapid results for White, i.e. 10 ... ♘b6 11 a4 (11 a3 ♕c7 12 g4 h6!=) 11 ... b4 12 ♘d5!? ed 13 ed+ ♔d7 14 ♘c6, Lepeshkin-Yurkov, 1963. But after the natural 10 ... ♗e7 the e4-e5 break is ineffective even with the rook on e1 since Black has counterplay along the g1-a7 diagonal: 11 e5 ♗xf3 12 ♕xf3 (12 ♘xf3 de 13 fe ♘g4) 12 ... de 13 ♘c6 (13 fe ♗c5) 13 ... ♕b6+ 14 ♗e3 ♗c5! 10 ... ♖c8 can also be recommended, since the daring attack 11 a4 b4 12 ♘d5! ♖c4! 13 ♘f5 does not bring immediate success: 13 ... ♕b8 14 ♕d3 ♖c8 15 ♘xf6 ♘xf6 16 ♘d4 ♗e7 17 ♗d2 0-0 with a level game, Morović-Christiansen, 1978.

A1

10   a3

Now it is Black's turn to make a choice. He can add to his control of e5 by playing 10 ... ♕c7, or try to complete his kingside development and then consider active moves. The plan with 10 ... ♖c8 is a bit risky, since the king has not yet left the centre. In this case Black tries to create piece play in the centre and on the queenside in the hope that this will forestall a White attack on the kingside.

A11 10 ... ♛c7
A12 10 ... ♖c8!

A11

10 ... ♛c7

44

11 ♛e2

Black's last move is exclusively defensive, and this allows White to do pretty much as he wishes. The manoeuvre ♛d1-e1-g3, or 11 ♔h1 ♝e7 12 ♛e1 ♖b8 13 g4 are both good.

Since Black has not yet developed his ♝f8 he has counterplay if White chooses 11 g4: 11 ... e5 (11 ... h6 12 ♛e2 e5 is worse, because of 13 ♘f5 g6 14 ♘xh6! ♝xh6 15 g5 ♝g7 16 gf ±) 12 ♘f5 g6 13 ♘e3 ef 14 ♘ed5 ♝xd5 15 ♘xd5 (15 ed g5) 15 ... ♘xd5 16 ♛xd5 ♖c8=

11 ... ♝e7

White's intention of playing g2-g4 is obvious. Simagin proposed a radical measure to prevent this by playing 11 ... h5. It is difficult to believe that the advance of the h-pawn, which forfeits a solid escape for the king on the flank, can be

useful to him. Of course, if his opponent plays passively, then Black will have successfully solved all of his opening problems: 12 ♝e3 ♝e7 13 ♖ad1 ♖c8 14 ♝f2 ♛c4 15 ♛e1 ♘g4 16 ♝e2 ♛c7 17 ♝xg4 hg 18 ♛e2 ♘f6 19 ♖d3 ♝a8! 20 e5 ♛b7! Bobkov–Simagin, 1963. But Black hardly has any chance to equalise if White plays for the e5 break, i.e. 12 ♔h1! e5 (Otherwise White will achieve his goal: 12 ... ♝e7 13 e5! de 14 fe ♘g4 15 ♝f4 g5 16 ♝xg4 ± or 15 ♝xb7 ♛xb7 16 ♘f3±) 13 ♘f5 g6 14 ♘e3 ef 15 e5! ♘xe5 16 ♘ed5 ♘xd5 17 ♘xd5 ♝xd5 18 ♝xd5 ♖c8 19 ♝xf4 ♛xc2 20 ♛e1! ♛f5 21 ♛a5 ±.

The position of the queen on e2 gives Black a way to create counterplay with 11 ... ♖c8, for example 12 ♔h1 ♛c4 13 ♛xc4 ♖xc4 14 ♘b3 ♖c8 15 ♝d2 ♘b6 16 ♘a5 ♝a8 17 ♝e3 ♘c4 18 ♘xc4 ♖xc4 19 ♝e2 with somewhat better chances for White in a complicated middlegame, Hartston–Sigurjonsson, 1975/76.

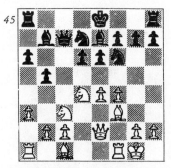

45

12 ♔h1

If White is not going to bring the ♝c1 into the game right away, then this move is not merely useful, but obligatory. White takes his king off the g1-a7 diagonal and creates threats involving the advance of the e-pawn. The immediate 12 e5 does not have much effect because of the counterplay along the afore-mentioned diagonal: 12 ... de 13 fe ♗c5! 14 ♗e3 ♘xe5 15 ♗xb7 ♕xb7 16 ♘xe6 ♗xe3+ 17 ♕xe3. The position would seem to favour White because of the dangerous-looking threats on the e-file. Black has an acceptable game, however, whether the game develops quietly with 17 ... fe 18 ♕xe5 ♕b6+ 19 ♔h1 0-0 20 ♖ae1? ♘g4!, or even if the game takes a more complex turn after 17 ... ♘eg4 18 ♘xg7+ (18 ♘c7+ ♔d7!) 18 ... ♔f8 19 ♕c5+ ♔xg7 20 ♖xf6! ♘xf6 21 ♕g5+ ♔f8 22 ♕h6+ ♔g8 23 ♕xf6 h6 24 ♖e1 ♖b8! 25 ♔f1 ♖h7 26 ♖e7 ♕c8! ∓ or 17 ... ♘fg4 18 ♘xg7+ ♔f8 19 ♘e6+ ♔e8 20 ♕g5? ♕b6+! ∓.

White can obviously play 12 g4, but sooner or later he will have to play his king to h1.

12   ...   ♖b8

Black liberates the queen from the necessity of defending the bishop and thereby increases control of e5. This only meets one of White's threats, however.

13   g4!

This position must be evaluated as favouring White. He has his king-side play underway, while there is no Black counterplay to be seen in other areas of the board.

Before moving on, we should mention the less effective plan in-volving the fianchetto of the queen

bishop. The game Tal–Smyslov, 1959, will serve to illustrate what Black can achieve against such un-energetic play (from diagram 44): 11 ♕e1 ♗e7 12 ♔h1 ♖b8 13 b3?! 0-0 14 ♗b2 ♖fe8 15 ♕g3?! ♗f8 16 ♖ae1 e5! 17 ♘f5 ♔h8 18 ♕h4 ef 19 ♕xf4 ♘e5!=

A12

10   ...   ♖c8!

As we noted above, this is a riskier move, but it is more in keeping with the logic of the Black's opening strategy. Black brings his last piece into the game and imme-diate threatens to sacrifice the ex-change, e.g. 11 ♔h1 ♖xc3!? 12 bc ♘xe4. With the king on g1 the ad-vance 11 e5 is ineffective: 11 ... ♗xf3 12 ♘xf3 de 13 fe ♘g4∓. Only the two queen moves 11 ♕e2 and 11 ♕e1 present any danger to Black. The Soviet master Mager-ramov, however, has worked out an interesting and original method of counterplay, which, in our opinion, proves the viability of 10 ... ♖c8.

11   ♕e1 *(46)*

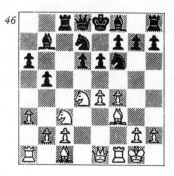

On 11 ♕e2 there follows 11 ... ♕c7 and the manouevre ♕c7-c4 is unexpectedly now possible, for example: 12 g4 ♕c4! 13 ♕f2 h5!? with sharp play.

It is considered that 11 ♕e1 forces Black to play 11 ... e5, after which 12 ♘f5 g6 13 fe ♘xe5 14 ♘h6! ♗e7 15 ♕g3 ♖c4! 16 ♗d2 ♘xf3 17 ♕xf3 secures an initiative for White in a sharp situation, as in Aronin–Smyslov, 1961.

Tal recommends 11 ... b4 instead of 11 ... ♖c4.

11   ...   ♖c4!

This is the point of Black's defence, which is based on the uninterrupted creation of concrete threats, which deflect his opponent from the preparations for the attack on Black's king.

12   ♗e3

Complications of the type 12 e5 de 13 fe ♗c5! 14 ♗xb7 ♗xd4+ 15 ♗e3 ♗xe5 16 ♗xa6 ♘g4 17 ♗xb5 ♘xe3 favour Black.

On the withdrawal of the knight with 12 ♘b3 Black can play 12 ... e5 13 ♕g3 g6 with a satisfactory game.

12   ...   ♕c7!

Black not only prevents 13 b3 but also presents the positional threat of an exchange sacrifice. After 13 ♗f2 ♗e7 it is dangerous to recommend 14 g4 to White, but both 14 ♘b3 e5 15 f5 g6! 16 ♘d2?! ♖xc3! and 14 e5?! de 15 fe ♘xe5 16 ♗xb7 ♘eg4! demonstrate the success of Black's opening strategy and evidently, the harmlessness of 10 a3.

A2

10   e5

This is the sharpest continuation, and the one which is most con-

sistent with the demands of the position. White does not waste time trying to improve his position, or defuse his opponents' threats. Instead, he uses his slight advantage in development and space and goes over to the attack immediately.

10   ...   ♗xf3

11   ♘xf3

With the king still on g1 the capture with the queen is less dangerous for Black, i.e. 11 ♕xf3 de 12 ♘c6 ♕b6+ 13 ♔h1 e4! 14 ♘xe4 ♘xe4 15 ♕xe4 ♘f6 16 ♕f3 ♖c8 17 ♘e5 ♗d6 18 ♗e3 ♕c7 19 c3 0-0, Schwarz–Simagin, 1964.

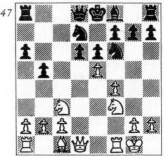

47

Black's opening strategy stands at the threshold of serious ordeals. White has completed the advance e4-e5 and has thus guaranteed himself domination in the centre, and consequently, the possibility of transferring his pieces to the attack on the king. Black does not yet have any counterplay so he must pin his hopes on the lack of control exercised by White over the a7-g1 diagonal.

11   ...   de

There is no way to avoid the early opening of lines.

a) **11 ... ♘g4** brings no relief. 12

♕e2 b4 (12 ... d5 13 f5! ± or 12
... de 13 fe ♘dxe5 14 ♘xe5 ♕d4+
15 ♔h1 ♘xe5 16 ♗f4! ±) 13 ♘a4!
(It is important to take control of
b6 and c5.) On 13 ♘e4, 13 ... d5!
is a good reply, and Black will
succeed in closing the position to
his benefit, e.g. 14 ♘eg5 h6 15
♘h3 ♗c5+ 16 ♔h1 0-0 17 ♘e1
♕h4 18 ♘d3 ♖fe8 19 ♗d2 f5! or
14 ♘g3 ♗c5+ 15 ♔h1 h5! 16 ♘g5
♕b6 17 ♘h3?! g6 18 ♖f3 a5 19
♘f1 ♕a6 ∓, Mednis–Gheorghiu,
1974.) 13 ... ♕a5 (Equality is not
provided by either 13 ... d5 14 f5!
or 13 ... de 14 fe ♘c5 15 ♕c4! or
14 ... ♘b6 15 ♕e4! ♕d5! 16 ♕xg4
♘xa4 17 a3! ±) 14 b3 ♕b5 15
♕e1 (15 c4 bc 16 ♕xb5 ab 17
♘xc3 de 18 ♘xb5 ♗c5+ 19 ♔h1
0-0! ∓) 15 ... ♘c5 16 h3!, and
Black's defence is not easy.

b) There is great risk of falling under
an attack after 11 ... b4 12 ef bc.
Simagin, who has done a lot of
analysis and frequently essayed the
Black side of this position, considers that 13 fg ♕b6+ 14 ♔h1
♗xg7 15 b3 ♘f6 is quite acceptable for Black, for example 16 f5!?
e5! 17 ♗g5 ♕c6 18 ♕e1 h6! 19
♗h4 0-0 20 ♖d1 ♖fe8, Gligorić–
Simagin, 1963. He himself pointed
out the continuation which is most
dangerous for Black: 13 f5! ♕b6+
14 ♔h1 cb 15 ♗xb2 ♕xb2 16 fe fe
17 f7+ ♔d8 18 ♘d4 ♘c5 19 ♖b1,
giving the evaluation "±" in view of
the unfortunate placement of the
Black pieces and their total lack
of coordination.

    12   fe *(48)*
    12   ...   b4

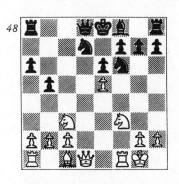

48

Here, too, the move ♘g4 has a
dubious reputation, based on the
following variations (after 12 ...
♘g4): 13 ♕e2 (13 ♕e1 b4 14 ♕g3
is considered less exact because of
14 ... h5! 15 ♘e4 ♘c5 16 ♘xc5
♗xc5+ 17 ♔h1 ♘f2+ 18 ♖xf2 h4!
19 ♕xg7 ♕d1+ 20 ♘g1 ♗xf2 21
♗e3 ♕xa1 22 ♗xf2 0-0-0 with an
advantage for Black. This beautiful
analysis by Zaitsev does, however,
require testing, and instead of 14
♕g3, 14 ♘a4 seems stronger, just
as it does after 13 ♕e2.) 13 ... ♕c7
(The move 13 ... b4 was abandoned
after the game Bykhovsky–Cheremisin, 1965, which continued 14
♘a4! ♕a5 15 b3 ♖c8 16 ♘g5! The
move 13 ... ♖c8 demands energetic
actions after 14 ♗f4, such as 14 ...
♖c4! 15 ♗g3 ♕b6+ 16 ♔h1 ♕e3)
14 ♔h1 b4 15 ♘e4 ♘gxe5 16 ♗f4
♕c4 17 ♕f2! where White has a
dangerous initiative.

    13   ef!

Here the withdrawal of the
knight to the edge of the board
allows Black to significantly improve
his position, by better deploying
his own knight with 13 ♘a4 ♘d5!
14 ♗g5 ♗e7 15 ♗xe7 ♕xe7, Nemet-

Bukić, 1975.

	13	...	bc
	14	fg	♗xg7
	15	b3	0-0
	16	♗e3	

Black has managed to complete his development, but the defects in the pawn cover of his king give White the better chances.

B

8   a4

This is not a transition to a positional struggle, but an attempt to attack on the kingside and in the centre, after first limiting his opponent's activity on the queenside. With the knight on d7 instead of c6 the move a2-a4 is significantly stronger.

	8	...	b6
	9	f4	♗b7
	10	♗f3	

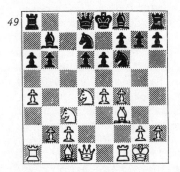

Here, as before, Black has two possibilities, and his choice is to a certain extent a matter of taste, or style.

B1 10 ... ♛c7
B2 10 ... ♖c8
B1

| | 10 | ... | ♛c7 |
| | 11 | ♛e2 | |

This is the most logical plan, although there are other moves for White which demand attention:

a) **11 g4** ♘c5?! 12 ♛e2 ♗e7 13 ♛g2! 0-0 14 g5! ♘e8 15 ♗e3 e5 16 ♘de2 ♗c6 17 f5 ♗d8 18 ♛g4! ±, Kopayev-Alatorzev, 1938. 11 ... h6 is stronger than 11 ... ♘c5. Then on 12 ♛e2 (12 g5?! hg 13 fg d5!) Black can choose between 12 ... g6 and the extremely sharp 12 ... e5 13 ♘d5 ♛c5!? 15 b4 ♛xd4+ 15 ♗e3 ♘xd5 16 ♗xd4 ♘xf4 17 ♛d2 ♘h3+ 18 ♔g2 ♘g5 19 ♗e3 ♘xf3 and it is difficult to decide whose chances are better. (Analysis by Magerramov).

b) **11 f5** e5 12 ♘b3 ♘c5?! (12 ... h6 △ ♗e7 =) 13 ♛e2 ♗e7 14 ♔h1 h6 15 ♗d2 ♖ad8 16 ♗e1±, Botvinnik-Kan, 1943.

c) **11 ♔h1** ♗e7 (11 ... ♖c8 12 ♛e2 ♛c4 deserves analysis.) 12 ♛e2 (12 e5 is premature: 12 ... de 13 fe ♘xe5 14 ♗f4 ♗xf3! 15 ♘xf3 ♗d6.) 12 ... ♖c8?! (An instructive error, which dooms the Pa6. After 12 ... 0-0 the whole battle lies ahead.) 13 e5! ♗xf3 14 ♘xf3 de 15 fe ♘g4 16 h3 h5 17 ♛xa6 with a decisive advantage, Tan-Browne, 1976.

11   ...   ♗e7

The immediate struggle for the e5 square also deserves consideration, as it fits in better with the logic of Black's opening plans. 11 ... e5!? 12 ♘d5 ♘xd5 13 ed g6 14 ♘c6 (14 ♖a3?! ♗g7 15 ♖c3 ♘c5 16 b4 e4∓) 14 ... ♗g7 15 fe ♘xe5 16 ♘xe5 ♗xe5 17 ♗h6! f6! =, Smyslov-Grigorian, 1976.

Instead of 12 ♘d5, White can

follow Grigorian's advice and fight
for the advantage by 12 ♘f5!, i.e.
12 ... g6 13 fe de (It would be interesting to test 13 ... ♘e5 14 ♘h6
♗g7 △ ♘fd7, f6 and ♔e7.) 14 ♘h6!
or 12 ... h6 13 ♘e3 ♗e7 14 ♔h1 ef
15 ♘f5.

     12   ♗e3   0-0

Besides this solid move it is
worth taking a look at the formation which was successfully defended by the Bulgarian master
Dementiev: 12 ... ♖b8!? 13 ♖d1!
g6 14 ♘b3 0-0 15 ♖fe1 e5!,
Rumiantsev-Dementiev, 1973.

After 12 ... 0-0 White usually
plays 13 ♔h1, but 13 g4 deserves
attention, leading to a complicated
and double-edged struggle i.e. 13 ...
♘c5 14 ♕g2 e5! 15 ♘f5 d5 16 ed
e4 17 ♘xe4 ♘xd5 18 ♗d2 ♘e6,
Butnorius-Platonov, 1976, or 13
♗f2 ♘c5 14 ♖ad1 ♖fd8 15 ♗g3
♗f8 16 ♗h4 Minić-Antunac, 1978.
B2

     10   ...   ♖c8

If this manoeuvre was possible
with pawns at a3 and b5, then why
shouldn't it be possible here as well?

     11   e5!

In the fight for the initiative 11
♕e1 is a useful and more solid try,
for example 11 ... ♖c4 12 e5 ♗xf3
13 ♘xf3 de 14 fe ♘g4 or 11 ...
♕c7 12 ♔h1 h5!? 13 ♗e3 ♗e7
14 ♖d1 ♘g4 15 ♗g1 g5 16 fg

♘de5 17 h4 (Geller-Barczay,
1977). In both cases White maintains his opening advantage.

     11   ...   ♗xf3
     12   ♘xf3   de
     13   fe   ♘g4
     14   ♕e2   ♕c7

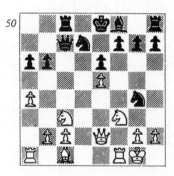

50

Now the answer to the question
posed in our remarks to 10 ... ♖c8
becomes clear. The pawn on a6 is
defenceless, since the b-pawn has
advanced to b6. With its fall the b5
square is denied to the pawn, as it is
controlled by White.

Black must seek counterchances
in the weakness of the White Pe5.
After 15 h3 ♘gxe5 16 ♘xe5 ♘xe5
17 ♕xa6 ♗c5+ the chances are
even, as is also the case after 15
♗f4 ♕c4! But Black can hardly lay
claim to equality after 15 ♕xa6
△ 15 ... ♗c5+ 16 ♔h1 ♘f2+ 17 ♖xf2!
♗xf2 18 ♘b5 (18 ♘e4 ♗c5!∓)
18 ... ♕xc2 19 ♘d6+.

8 7 0–0 ♛c7

1 e4 c5 2 ♘f3 e6 3 d4 cd 4 ♘xd4
♘f6 5 ♘c3 d6 6 ♗e2 a6 7 0-0 ♛c7

In this chapter we will examine
continuations where Black does not
hasten to commit the queen's
knight, retaining the possibility of
placing it either on d7 or c6. The
game develops more quietly, and
reckless pawn advances and thrusts
give way to more strategic plans,
which often involve complicated
manouvering.

        8 f4 *(51)*

The most energetic continuation.
To 8 ♗e3 Black can respond 8 ...
b5, i.e. 9 f3 ♗b7 10 ♛d2 ♘bd7
11 a4 b4 12 ♘a2 d5! or 9 f4 b4
10 e5 bc 11 ef gf 12 bc ♗b7 13
♛d3 ♘d7 14 ♘b3 ♖c8 15 c4
♖g8 with a quite playable game in
each case. The more active, but ineffective, 8 ♗g5 does not bring an
advantage for White after 8 ... ♗e7
9 ♛d3 ♘bd7 10 ♖ad1 b5 11 a3
♗b7, Gurgenidze–Zaichik, 1974.

        8   ...   ♗e7

The pawn has reached f4 and
made 8 ... b5 a much less attractive
proposition: 9 ♗f3 (9 e5 b4 10
♗f3 bc! leads to sharp play after 11
♗xa8 cb 12 ♗xb2 de 13 fe ♛xe5
14 ♘c6 ♛c7 15 ♘xb8 ♛a7! 16

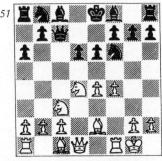

51

♗d4 ♛xa8 17 ♖b1 ♗e7, Shakhzade-
Mukhin, 1964.) 9 ... ♗b7 10 e5! de
11 fe. The Black queen cannot
simultaneously defend the bishop
and control e5, while the withdrawal 11 ... ♘fd7 leads to a large
advantage for White, i.e. 12 ♗xb7
(The alternative 12 ♗f4 ♘c6 13
♘xc6 ♗xc6 14 ♘e4 ♗xe4! 15
♗xe4 ♖d8! 16 ♛f3 ♗c5+ 17 ♔h1
0-0 is better for Black, ∓) 12 ...
♛xb7 13 ♛h5 g6 14 ♛h4 ♗g7 15
♘e4 ♗xe5 16 ♘f3 ♛b6+ 17 ♔h1
♗g7 18 ♘fg5, Riumin-Ragozin,
1934.

In reply to 8 f4 Black should
not hasten to play 8 ... ♘bd7, since
then White can choose between
playing for a clamp with 9 a4, or
continue more sharply with 9 g4!
b5 10 a3 ♗b7 11 ♗f3 ♘c5 12 ♛e2

e5   13 ♘f5! ±, Nezhmetdinov-Tal,
1961. We can, "for the sake of
knowledge", as they say, take a
look at Dementiev's idea, even
though the bishop is still on f8:
9 ♗f3 ♖b8   10 a4 g6   11 ♗e3 e5!
12 ♘de2 b6   13 ♕e1 ♗b7   14 ♖d1
♗e7   15 g4 ef!   16 ♘xf4 h6=,
Tseshkovsky-Dementiev, 1972, or
10 ♔h1 b5   11 e5! de   12 ♘c6 ♖b6
13 fe ♘xe5   14 ♘xe5 ♕xe5   15 ♗f4
♕c5   16 ♕d2± Klovan-Dementiev,
1972.

Now White must decide whether
it is worthwhile to lose time on the
generally good move 9 ♗e3, or to
exploit the lessening of pressure on
the ♘d4 by playing 9 ♗f3, preventing possible Black counterplay on
the queenside.

A 9 ♗f3!
B 9 ♔h1
C 9 ♗e3

On 9 a4 Black has a choice
between 9 ... ♘c6 and 9 ... 0-0   10
♘b3 ♘c6   11 a5 b6   12 ab ♕xb6+
13 ♔h1 ♖d8   14 ♗f3 a5 (Tringov-
Ornstein, 1974.) or 9 ... b6   10 ♗f3
♗b7   11 e5 de   12 fe ♘fd7   13
♗xb7 ♕xb7   14 ♕g4 ♗c5   15 ♔h1
♗xd4   16 ♕xd4 ♘c6   17 ♕d6 ♘dxe5
(Chiburdanidze-Platonov,   1980)
with an acceptable game in each
case.

9 g4 is premature: 9 ... d5   10 ed
♘xd5   11 ♘xd5 ed and the g-pawn
is punching at air.

A
9   ♗f3
This is a logical and useful move
whether White continues with a
positional game involving a4, or
attacks the kingside with g4. The

best location for the ♗c1 will only
be determined by future events.
Now Black, of course, can play 9
... ♘c6, transposing into lines considered previously.

9   ...   ♘bd7
Once again, 9 ... 0-0   10 ♕e2
♘c6 is possible, but it is not the
theme of the present chapter.

10   ♔h1 (52)
A passive prophylactic move,
which eliminates threats along the
g1-a7 diagonal. On 10 g4 Black can
continue 10 ... h6   11 ♕e2 g6 or 11
h4 g5!?   12 fg hg   13 ♗xg5 d5 (13
... b5!? △ ♗b7 and 0-0-0) 14 ♕d2 de
15 ♘xe4 ♘xe4   16 ♗xe4 ♗xg5   17
hg ♖h4!   18 ♕f2 ♖xg4+   19 ♗g2
♘e5 with a sharp game, Diaz-
Nikolić, 1976.

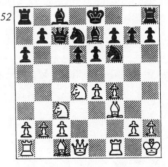

10   ...   0-0
Sometimes the curious manoeuvre 10 ... ♘f8 is met, but the profit
from the long knight tour (♘b8-d7-
f8-g6) is dubious: 11 ♕e1 ♘g6   12
♗e3 0-0   13 ♖d1 (?!) e5   14 fe de
15 ♘f5 ♗b4, Darga-Petrosian, 1961
allows Black to hope for equality,
but no more. In reply to 10 ... ♘f8
White can try two different recommended plans: 11 g4 h6   12 f5 e5

13 ♘de2 ♗d7 14 ♘g3 b5 15 a3
♗c6 16 ♔g2 ♘8d7 17 h4 ♘h7
18 ♖h1 or 11 ♘b3 ♘g6 12 g3 0-0
13 ♗e3 ♖b8 14 a4. In the latter
case the lack of the Black knight
on the queenside is felt.

Here 10 ... ♖b8 11 a4 b6?! is
refuted by 12 e5 de 13 fe ♘xe5
14 ♗f4 ♗b7 15 ♖e1 ♘fd7 16
♗xb7 ♖xb7 17 ♕e2±, Shakharov-
Kasparov, 1976.

11 g4!

11 ♕e1 promises White excellent
possibilities and is also approved,
Tseshkovsky–Cheremisin, 1964,
continued 11 ... ♖e8 12 g4 ♘f8 13
g5 ♘6d7 14 a4 b6 15 ♕g3 ♘g6 16
♘de2 ♗b7 17 h4 ♗f8 18 ♗g2±.

The immediate advance of the g-
pawn, however, forces Black to
cope with difficult problems, since
he has not yet managed to free the
d7 square for the retreat of the ♘f6.
After 11 g4 ♖fd8 12 g5 ♘e8 13
♗g2 ♘b6 14 f5 e5 15 ♘de2 White
is prepared to launch the attack on
the king, Nikitin–Nei, 1952.

B

9   ♔h1

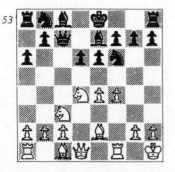

53

A cunning preventative measure.
White tries to carry out the advance

e4-e5 according to the methods of
the Classical Scheveningen. He has
in mind a more active post for the
♗c1 than e3, however, intending to
place it on f4. The necessity of the
move ♔h1 in such a strategy can be
demonstrated by taking a look at
the direct transfer 9 ♕e1 0-0 10
♕g3. In this position, besides 10 ...
b5 11 e5 ♘e8 and 10 ... ♘c6,
which lead to well known positions,
there is an original, if somewhat
risky plan: 10 ... ♕b6!? 11 ♗e3
♕xb2 12 ♗f2 ♕b4 13 ♖ab1 ♕a5.
The queen will return to c7 and
then White will have nothing to
show for the pawn, so he must act
decisively: 14 ♘f5! ef 15 ♗b6, but
even here the battle is far from over
after either 15 ... ♘xe4 16 ♘xe4
♕xa2 17 ♗d4 f6 △ ♕f7! or 15 ...
♕xb6+!? 16 ♖xb6 fe 17 f5 ♘c6△
d6-d5.

9   ...   0-0

With the king still in the centre
it is dangerous to begin operations
on the flank: 9 ... b5 10 ♗f3 ♗b7
11 e5! de (11 ... ♘fd7? 12 ed ♗xd6
13 ♘dxb5 is a rout.) 12 fe ♘fd7 13
♗xb7 (Rigo has an interesting idea
here: 13 ♗g5 ♘xe5 14 ♘dxb5 ab
15 ♘xb5 ♕b6 16 ♗xb7 ♕xb7 17
♕d6!, which meets with a reply
which is also of interest: 17 ...
♘bc6 18 ♘c7+ ♔xc7 19 ♕xc7
♗xg5 20 ♖xf7? ♗d8! 21 ♕b7 ♖b8
winning.) 13 ... ♕xb7 14 ♕g4 and
Black has nothing better than 14 ...
0-0 15 ♗h6 g6 16 ♗xf8 ♘xf8, but
even here White has a very large
advantage.

10   ♕e1

10 a4 is also quite possible here,

with the intention of continuing his game plan with less activity by Black on the queenside. In Geller–Mikhalchishin, White gained the advantage after 10 ... b6 11 ♗f3 ♗b7 12 e5! ♘e8 13 ♗e3 ♘c6 14 ♕e2 g6 15 ♖ad1. Apparently Black should develop his knight at c6, transposing to the Classical Scheveningen.

10   ...   b5

Grandmaster Andersson is quite at home in the defence of positions such as 10 ... ♘bd7 11 ♗f3 ♖e8 12 g4 ♘b6 13 a4 ♗f8 14 ♕g3. Although even Tal could not defeat him after 14 ... ♘c4 15 g5 ♘fd7 16 ♘de2 ♖b8 17 b3 ♘a5 18 ♗b2 ♘c6, you must agree that here it is much easier to attack, than to defend.

11   ♗f3   ♗b7
12   e5   ♘e8 (55)

A problematic position. Actually, 12 ... de 13 fe ♘fd7 presents us with another one. Before analysis of the position it can be stated that White has achieved a small victory — his bishop can go to either f4 or g5. So what?

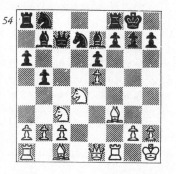

54

White has succeeded in chasing

the knight from f6 and thereby weakening the defences of the kingside, especially the squares g7 and h7. The result of the battle depends on who is faster, Black in the capture of the Pe5 or White in his transfer of pieces to the kingside. In the plan the control of the key square e4 plays an important role. Thus 14 ♗xb7 ♕xb7 15 ♕g3 ♔h8 (The exchange sacrifice 15 ... b4 16 ♗h6 g6 deserves attention.) 16 ♗f4 b4 17 ♘ce2 (This is the price of 14 ♗xb7?!) 17 ... ♘c6 gives Black the initiative, Chiburdanidze–Gufeld, 1981. After the much stronger move 14 ♕g3 Black has a choice between 14 ... ♗xf3 15 ♘xf3 ♔h8 16 ♗g5 ♘c6 17 ♘e4 h6 18 ♗f4 ♘b4 (Diaz–Macado, 1981) and 14 ... ♔h8 15 ♗f4 ♘c6 (It is possible that the preliminary exchange 15 ... ♗xf3 is more precise.) 16 ♘xc6 (16 ♘f5!? g5! 17 ♘xe7 gf leads to puzzling complications, as were seen in the game Sibarević–Antunac, 1977.) 16 ... ♗xc6 17 ♘e4. In the last variation White is a tiny bit better, but the fundamental dangers for Black are already behind him.

By retreating the knight to e8, Black defends g7 and relegates the ♖f8 to defend the f-pawn for a while. The other knight will go to d7 to attack the Pe5, without blocking the diagonal for the bishop.

13   f5!

13 ♕g3 poses difficult problems for Black, as White intends to have completed his development before the pawn storm begins, i.e. 13 ... ♘d7 14 a3 (14 ed ♗xd6

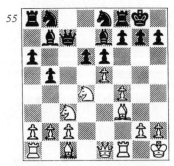

15 ♘e4 ♖c8 16 c3 ♘c5, Klovan–
Ermenkov, 1978.) 14 ... ♖c8 15
♗e3 ♘b6 16 ♖ae1 ♘c4 17 ♗xb7
♕xb7 18 ♗c1 g6 19 ♘e4 ♕d5 20
♘f3. This fragment of the game
Sznapik–Jansa well describes the
character of the fight after 13 ♕g3
and is typical of the evaluation of
the position as unclear. The immediate march of the f-pawn is an
aggressive but responsible step.
White immediately creates concrete
threats of f5-f6 and f5xe6, but seals
the fate of the Pe5.

13   ...   de
It is not easy to cope with the
threat of the advance of the white
f-pawn, for example 13 ... b4?! 14
f6 bc 15 ♗xb7 ♕xb7 16 fe ♕xe7
17 bc and the lack of an opponent
for the ♗c1 is unpleasant for Black.
Or 13 ... ♗xf3 14 ♘xf3 b4 15 f6
gf 16 ed! ♗xd6 17 ♘e4 ♔h8 18
♗d2! ♘c6. This position arose in
the game Karpov–Ermenkov, 1980.
After 19 ♕h4 ♗e7 20 ♗g5! or 19
c3 a5 20 ♖c1! White would have
had somewhat better chances, but
Black would have been able to
play on.

14   fe!   ♗xf3
The knight is untouchable: After

14 ... ed 15 ♘d5 ♗xd5 16 ♗xd5 ♘c6
17 ef+ ♔h8 18 ♗xc6 ♕xc6 19 ♕xe7
or 15 ... ♕d8   16 ♘xe7+ ♕xe7
17 ♗xb7 ♕xb7 18 e7! White is
winning.

15   ef+
15 ♘f5 is less clear after either
15 ... fe or even 15 ... f6.

15   ...   ♖xf7
16   ♘xf3
The storm which arose so sud-
denly has dissipated just as sudden-
ly, leaving material equality on the
board and presenting a new question: "Is the Pe5 a weakness?" A
glance at this problem must also
take into account the relative
strengths of the players in the
evaluation of the position which
has arisen. For the moment, Praxis
indicates the chances are roughly
level after 16 ... ♘d7 17 ♗e3 ♕c6
18 ♖d1 ♗b4 19 ♗d2 ♘d6, Jansa–
Suba, 1980. It is possible that this
is close to the truth.

C
9   ♗e3
Although this move occurs more
frequently in practice, it is perhaps
less consequential than 9 ♗f3.
Usually the bishop moves to e3
when the Black knight stands on
c6, in order to free the White queen
from the necessity of defending the
knight. With the knight on b8, first
of all it is not necessary to defend
the knight on d4, and secondly the
temporary weakening of the control
over the e5-square gives White good
chances to carry out the e4-e5
break. But in this regard the bishop,
standing on e3, only blocks the e-
file and in no way helps the advance

of the e-pawn.

9 ... 0-0

Black has a choice here. Besides 9 ... ♘bd7, which we have already examined, there is also 9 ... ♘c6 transposing into the Classical Scheveningen. But if Black plays 9 ... b5 now White can get hold of the initiative by 10 e5! de 11 fe ♘fd7 12 ♗f3 ♗b7 13 ♗xb7 ♕xb7 14 ♕g4! ♖f8 15 ♕xg7 b4 16 ♘a4, as in Popov–Balashov, 1974. It is true that such a result was a consequence of bad play by Black. He could have taken the pawn at move 11: 11 ... ♕xe5 12 ♗f4 ♕c5 13 ♗f3 ♕a7 and instead of 12 ... ♗b7 he should have decided on 12 ... ♖a7. In this case White would have retained the initiative, but Black would have had targets for his counterattack.

After 9 ... 0-0 White is at a crossroads. He can begin his pawn storm on the kingside, start to play all over the board, or concentrate his forces on the advance of the e-pawn.

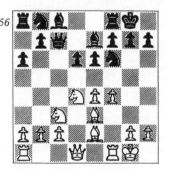

We examine four methods of play from the diagrammed position:

C1 10 g4
C2 10 a4
C3 10 ♔h1
C4 10 ♕e1

C1

10 g4

Such activity is possible because of the lack of a knight on c6, and as a result the lack of the typical counterthrust 10 ... ♘xd4 11 ♗xd4 e5.

10 ... ♘c6

This is not a transposition into the Classical Scheveningen, since the pawn immediately advances to g5.

The cold-blooded 10 ... b5 would allow White to carry out the pawn storm under more comfortable circumstances after 11 g5 ♘fd7 12 f5, while 10 ... d5 11 ed ♘xd5 12 ♘xd5 ed 13 ♗f3 ♖d8 14 ♕d2 ♘c6 leads to a position where the isolani at d5 proves to be more serious than his compensation in the form of active piece play.

11 g5 ♘d7
12 f5

White can choose a more solid continuation of his aggressive strategy by bringing his heavy pieces closer to the Black king with 12 ♗d3 △ ♕h5, ♖f1-f3-h3.

12 ... ♘de5
13 f6 ♗d8

White has accomplished much on the kingside, but the defences are still intact. After 14 fg ♔xg7 15 ♕d2 b5 it would seem that he should not lose his head and play the prophylactic move 16 a3 before carrying out the attack. In the game Sax-Stean, 1977, White attacked directly with 16 g6?! hg 17 ♗h6+ ♔g8 18 ♗xf8 ♔xf8 19 ♘xc6 ♕xc6 20 ♗d3 ♔g7 21 ♘e2 ♗b7 and there is nothing left of the formerly powerful White attacking force.

C2

10   a4

Solid positional play towards limiting Black's activity on the flank is more appropriate here since Black is not yet ready to counterattack in the centre. After 10 ... ♘c6 11 ♘b3 b6 Black can transpose into the Maroczy Attack which we considered in our first chapters. Here we will examine what might happen if Black declines the transposition.

10   ...   b6
11   ♗f3   ♗b7

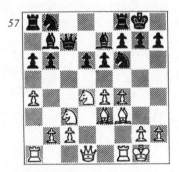

12   ♛e1

Besides this move 12 e5 de 13 ♗xb7 ♛xb7 14 fe ♘fd7 is quite playable, as are 12 g4 ♘c6 13 g5 ♘d7 14 ♘b3 ♖fe8 15 ♗g2 ♗f8 16 h4 ♘a5 and even 12 ♛e2. All of these alternatives lead to double-edged positions.

12   ...   ♘bd7

Another method of defence is 12 ... ♘c6 13 ♛g3 b5.

13   ♖ad1

It is dangerous to expose the king with 13 ♗f2 ♖fe8 14 g4?! because

of 14 ... e5! 15 ♘f5 ef 16 g5 ♘e5!, according to analysis by Magerramov.

13   ...   ♖fe8
14   ♔h1   ♗f8

The opening phase of the game has concluded to the satisfaction of both players. Black begins to threaten the advance of his e-pawn and puts pressure on the Pe4. After 15 ♛g3 ♘c5 16 e5 ♘fe4 17 ♘xe4 ♘xe4 the chances are equal.

C3

10   ♔h1

The preventative exit of the king from the a7-g1 diagonal is useful and connected with a cunning thought. Now Black can again play either 10 ... ♘c6 or 10 ... ♘bd7, leading to positions which have already been dealt with, and which are sufficiently solid.

10   ...   b5

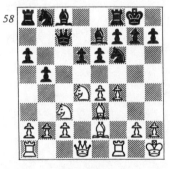

11   e5!?

White opens up the game in the centre with this advance of the e-pawn, exploiting his temporary advantage in development.

11   ...   de

Contemporary chess considers positions such as the following quite

defensible: 11 ... ♘e8 12 ♗d3 ♘d7
13 ♕f3 ♗b7 14 ♕h3 g6, for example 15 f5 ef 16 e6 ♘e5! (but
not 16 ... ♘c5 △ 17 ♘xf5! gf 18
♗xf5 with an attack, Bohm–Ree,
1980.) 17 ♗h6 ♘g7 18 ♗xg7 ♔xg7
19 ef ♕b6!, but it is more difficult
to defend than to attack.

    12   fe   ♘fd7

The threat is stronger than the
execution! After 12 ... ♕xe5 Black
loses material by force: 13 ♗f4
♕c5 14 ♗f3 ♖a7 15 ♗xb8 ♖d7
16 ♘ce2 ♖fd8 17 b4! ♕xb4 18
c3 etc.

    13   ♘f5!

This is the point of White's play.
After 13 ♗f3 ♗b7 14 ♗f4 ♘c6
15 ♘xc6 ♗xc6 16 ♕e2 ♖ac8 there
we have a complex manoeuvring
battle with equal chances.

    13   ...   ♘xe5

After 13 ... ef 14 ♘d5 ♕d8 15
♘xe7+ ♕xe7 16 ♗f3 ♘xe5 17
♗xa8 White has won the exchange
and still has active pieces.

    14   ♗f4

A typical position of the post-
opening phase of the middlegame,
of which further analysis is useful.
Black has a choice between 14 ...
♗f6 and 14 ... ef 15 ♗f3 ♖a7 16
♘d5 ♕d6 17 ♗xe5 ♕xe5 18 ♖e1,
which gave White a slight initiative
in the game Barle–Ribli, 1977.

C4

    10   **♕e1** *(59)*
    10   ...   b5

A waiting strategy with 10 ...
♘bd7 gives Black a cramped but
solid position and the choice is his
to make. It is a matter of taste and
love for defence. Here are 2 charac-

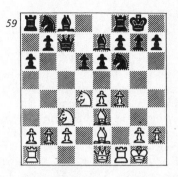

teristic examples:

a) **10 ... ♘bd7** 11 ♗f3 ♘b6 12 ♔h1
♘c4 13 ♗c1 e5 14 fe ♘xe5 15
♗g5 ♗e6 16 ♕g3 ♔h8 17 ♗e2 ♕d7
18 ♖ad1, Tseshkovsky–Bonsch,
1979.

b) **10 ... ♖e8** 11 ♕g3 ♘bd7 12 ♘f3
e5 13 ♘g5 b5 14 fe de 15 ♖ad1
♗b7, Tal–Andersson, 1976. If, instead of 12 ♘f3, White had played
12 ♗f3 ♖b8 13 a4, he would have
obtained the same small initiative
which was evident in the first
example, but no more.

    11   ♗f3

With the queen on e1 it is dangerous to sacrifice the pawn right
away: 11 e5 de 12 fe ♕xe5 13
♗f3 ♗c5! 14 ♗xa8 ♘g4!

    11   ...   ♗b7
    12   e5

White's entire opening strategy,
beginning with 10 ♕e1, is based on
just this advance of the e-pawn.
But the timing of the advance
depends to a great extent on the
style of the chessplayers. Even here
White can programmatically mar-
shall his reserve forces before advancing his e-pawn, for example
12 a3 ♘bd7 13 ♖d1 ♖fe8 14 ♕g3,

but one mustn't forget that in this case Black will have time to regroup.

| 12 | ... | de |

After 12 ... ♘e8 White manages to bring the ♖a1 into the game and thereby secure an initiative: 13 ♖d1! ♘c6 (13 ... ♘d7 doesn't change anything.) 14 ♕g3 b4 15 ♘a4! g6 16 ♘b3! (Black has everything under control after the inferior 16 f5 ♘xd4 17 ♗xd4 ef 18 ♗xb7 ♕xb7 19 ♖xf5 ♕c6.) 16 ... de 17 ♘bc5 ef 18 ♕xf4.

| 13 | fe | ♘fd7 |

If 13 ... ♘e8 14 ♕g3 ♘d7 15 ♖ad1 White will once again be able to bring his rook into the game. After 15 ... b4! 16 ♘a4 ♗xf3 17 ♘xf3 ♘c5 18 ♘xc5 ♗xc5 19 ♗f2 ♗xf2 20 ♕xf2 the accent is on the fight in the centre and the unfortunate positions of the ♘e8 and ♖f8 bother Black.

The withdrawal of the knight to the more elastic position at d7 creates pressure in the centre and thereby keeps White from directly attacking the king. The next few moves must answer the questions concerning the Pe5: What is it — a wedge which hinders Black defence, or a weakness which dooms White in the endgame?

| 14 | ♕g3! |

If White exchanges on b7 immediately he reduces the pressure on the Pe5, but he also abandons the possibility of transferring the ♘c3 to the Kingside via e4. After 14 ♗xb7 ♕xb7 15 ♘f3 b4 16 ♘e2 ♘c6 17 ♕g3 ♗c5 18 ♗xc5 ♘xc5 19 ♖ae1 ♖ad8 the chances are equal, as in Balashov–Belyavsky,

1974. There are no problems for Black after 15 ♕g3 either — 15 ... ♗c5! 16 ♔h1 ♗xd4 17 ♗xd4 ♘c6 18 ♖ad1 ♕c7 18 ♖fe1 ♔h8, when White feels the weakness of his pawn on e5 even more.

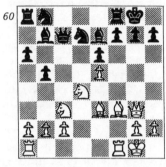

| 14 | ... | ♔h8 |

The problem of the timely exchange of bishops on the long diagonal is no less difficult than the problem of choosing the appropriate moment for the advance e6-e5. On 14 ... ♗xf3 White has a choice between 15 ♘xf3 ♗c5 16 ♗xc5 ♘xc5 17 ♖ae1 ♘c6 18 ♘g5 ♖ad8 19 ♖f6 ♘xe5 20 ♖xe5 ♘d7 and 15 ♕xf3!? ♘b6 16 ♕g4 ♕xe5 17 ♖ae1 ♗c5 18 ♔h1 f5 19 ♕h4 ♕f6 20 ♕xf6 ♖xf6 21 ♘xf5, continuations which are difficult to assess.

With the move 14 ... ♔h8 Black liquidates the threat of ♗h6 and renders the transfer of the knight from c3 to g5 via e4 more difficult. White must find a means of increasing his attacking potential, otherwise he is threatened with an endgame where he has the weakness at e5. It seems that he can fight for the advantage with 15 ♗xb7 ♕xb7 16 ♖f4!? i.e. 16 ... b4

17 ♘e4 ♘xe5 18 ♘xe6 ♘g6 19
♘xf8 ♘xf4 20 ♕xf4 ♗xf8 21 ♖f1,
but all the same the weakness of
the Pe5 should guarantee Black
plenty of counterplay and the best
way of attaining this goal is 16 ...
♘c6. Instead of the positional plan

White can play 15 ♖ad1, for example 14 ... ♘c6 16 ♗xc6 ♗xc6
17 ♘xc6 ♕xc6 19 ♘e4 ♖ad8 19
♘g5 ♔g8   20 c3, as in Ghinda-
Jansa, 1979, or 15 ♗f4, but in each
case Black has sufficient counterplay for equality.

9 7 f4 and 7 ♗e3

1 e4 c5 2 ♘f3 d6 3 d4 cd 4 ♘xd4
♘f6 5 ♘c3 e6 6 ♗e2 a6

In this chapter we will examine
continuations in which White does
not hasten to castle kingside, and
even sometimes omits castling al-
together.

A 7 f4
B 7 ♗e3

A

7   f4

This continuation is considerably
less popular than 7 0-0, but that is
a result of typically capricious
fashion. To us 7 f4 seems more promising and holding a wealth of
possibilities. In the final analysis
White can always reconsider and
rejoin the lines by playing 0-0.

7   ...   ♕c7 (61)

Now it is not so simple to advance the b-pawn. White wins a
piece after 7 ... b5? 8 e5 de 9 fe
♘d5 10 ♘xd5 ♕xd5 11 ♗f3 ♕xe5+
12 ♔f2 ♖a7 13 ♗f4. 7 ... ♘bd7
leads to a cramped position after 8
♗f3. Nor can Black try to contest
the a7-g1 diagonal by 7 ... ♕b6?!
because of 8 a3 ♗e7 9 ♗e3! and
now 9 ... ♕xb2 drops the queen
after 10 ♘a4.

8 ♗f3

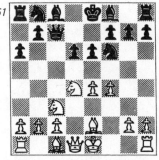

61

8 a4 b6 9 ♗f3 is also quite
possible, but more serious attention
is deserved for play in the spirit of
the Keres Attack, about which the
reader will read in later Chapters.
In Klovan–Palatnik, 1973, White
obtained a menacing attack after 8
g4!? b5 9 g5 ♘fd7 10 a3 ♘b6 11
f5 ♘c6 12 ♘xc6 ♕xc6 13 0-0
♘c4 14 fe fe 15 ♗xc4 ♕xc4 16
♕f3 ♖a7 17 ♗e3 ♖d7 18 g6!

8   ...   ♘bd7

It is still not too late to return
to the Classical Scheveningen with
8 ... ♘c6 9 ♗e3 ♗e7. But what
happens if you feel like putting the
knight on d7?

9   g4   ♘b6
10   g5   ♘fd7
11   a4

White binds his opponent on

both flanks. After 11 ... g6 12 ♕d2
♗g7 13 ♘de2 ♘c5 14 ♕e3 ♘c4 15
♕f2, Karpov–Ljubojević, 1978,
White has clearly won the opening
battle.

B

7   ♗e3

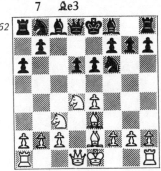

It is worth paying attention to
this position although, and because,
it can also arise from the Najdorf:
5 ... a6 6 ♗e3 e6 7 ♗e2 etc. Of
course if White chooses to castle
short the move 7 ♗e3 will have lost
its originality. Here there are three
significant branches:

B1 7 ... ♘bd7
B2 7 ... ♕c7
B3 7 ... ♗e7

7 ... b5 is considered premature,
and the proof of its inadequacy can
be made *à la* Smyslov by comparison with 7 0-0 b5. After 8 ♗f3 b4
9 e5 de 10 ♘b3 ♕xd1 11 ♖xd1 e4
12 ♘xe4 ♘d5 13 ♖xd5 ed 14
♘f6+ gf 15 ♗xd5 White has a
material advantage, Horvath–Sax,
1976.

7 ... e5 is quite playable. After 8
♘f5 (8 ♘de2 ♗b7) 8 ... d5 9 ♗g5
d4 10 ♘d5 ♕a5 11 ♗d2 ♕d8 does
White have anything better than 12
♗g5?

B1

7   ...   ♘bd7
8   a4

Besides this plan, with its intended clamp on the queenside, we
look at other possibilities, which
lead to a more lively game:
a) 8 f4 b5

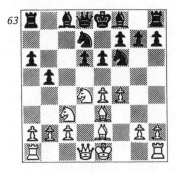

and now:
a1) 9 f5!? White tries to weaken
and then seize the d5 square. 9 ...
e5 (9 ... b4 10 fe bc!? 11 ed+ ±) 10
♘c6 ♕c7 11 ♘b4 ♗b7 12 a4 (White
keeps a small positional edge after
12 ♘bd5 ♗xd5 13 ♘xd5 ♘xd5 14
♕xd5) 12 ... ba! 13 ♖xa4 ♗e7 14
0-0 0-0 15 ♔h1 ♖fb8! 16 ♗xa6
♘c5! with a good game for Black,
Tseshkovsky–Polugayevsky, 1976.
a2) 9 ♘f3 ♗b7 10 a3 ♕c7 11 ♕e2
♗e7. Now White usually plays 12
0-0, but there is a good and aggressive plan available in 12 g4 ♘b6 13
0-0-0! ♘c4 14 g5 ♘d7 15 h4!
♘xe3 (15 ... ♘xa3 16 h5!) 16
♕xe3 0-0-0 17 f5 ±, Klovan–Petkevich, 1970.
b) 8 g4! h6. (As later developments
will show, this does not hinder
White's plans and only weakens the
defence. Therefore 8 ... ♘c5 deserves

consideration, which places White in a position of having to play a sharp line, since positional play with 9 f3 △ 0-0 seems little justified. After 9 ♗f3 h6 10 h4! both 10 ... ♕c7 11 ♕e2! ♘fd7 12 b4! ♘b3!? 13 ♘dxb5 ab 14 ♘xb5 ♕b8 15 cb d5 16 ed ♗xb4+ 17 ♔f1 0-0 18 ♕c4!, according to 1976 analysis by Minev, and 10 ... e5 11 ♘f5 g6 12 ♘g3 ♗e6 13 ♕e2! ♕a5 14 ♗d2 ♕c7 15 a4!, Tseshkovsky–Pokojowczyk, 1976, lead to an advantage for White, but Black can improve at move 9 or 10, and 10 ... g6 for example, is quite acceptable.) 9 f4.

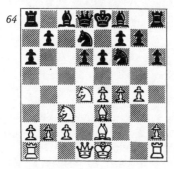

9 ... b5 (The White pawn has advanced to f4, so 9 ... ♘c5 can be well met by 10 ♗f3) 10 g5 hg 11 fg ♖h3 (After 11 ... b4 Black could still put up a fight.) 12 ♗f2! ♖xc3! 13 gf! ♖h3 (13 ... ♖c5 is a bit more resistant but even here White would have the advantage after 14 ♘xe6! ♕a5+! 15 c3 fe 16 b4 ♕a3 17 bc ♕xc3+ 18 ♔f1 ♘xc5.) 14 ♘xe6! ♕a5+ 15 c3 fe 16 fg! ♗xg7 17 ♕xd6 ♖h6 18 ♖g1! ♗f8 19 ♖g8 ♕d8 20 0-0-0! ♕e7 21 ♕c6 ♖b8 22 ♗a7! ♔f7 23 ♖g2! and White

won quickly in Tseshkovsky–Browne, 1976.

Of course, Black can still play 8 ... 0-0 transposing into lines which we have already examined.

8	...	b6
9	f4	♗b7
10	♗f3	♖ac8
11	0-0	

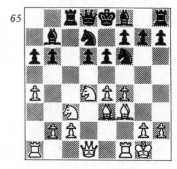

This is a critical position, which is relevant for the evaluation of Black's opening formation. He must now resolve the problem of the exchange sacrifice at c3, which must be played at the appropriate moment, but this is by no means easy to determine.

a) 11 ... ♖xc3 12 bc ♘xe4. Although the knight takes up a strong position in the centre, the lack of kingside development and the weakness of the pawns at a6 and b6 do not give Black the opportunity of developing an initiative. Of course if his opponent does not play energetically, Black can fortify his position, i.e. 13 ♘e2?! ♕c7 14 ♕e1 d5! 15 ♗d4 ♗c5 16 ♘g3?! f5! 17 ♕e3 0-0 18 ♗xc5 bc 19 a5 e5 20 ♘e2 g5!, Mednis–Browne, 1975. But White does not have to give his opponent time to consolidate: 13 c4 ♕c7 14 ♕e2 ♗e7 15 a5! ba 16 f5! e5 17 ♘b3 0-0 (17 ... a4 18 ♗xe4 ♗xe4 19 ♖xa4 is more resistant) 18 ♘xa5 ♗a8 19 ♔h1, Ostojić–Barczay, 1976. If 13 ♕e1 (Stronger is the immediate 13 f5!) 13 ... d5 14 ♗xe4 de 15 a5 b5 16 f5! e5 17 ♘e6! fe 18 fe ♘f6 19 ♖d1, Ilyin–Vaisman, 1975, 19 ... ♗d5. Apparently 11 ... ♖xc3 is not sufficient for equality.

b) White has no particular difficulty in developing an attack after **11 ...** ♕c7 12 ♕e1! ♗e7 13 ♖d1 0-0 14 g4.

c) Black successfully emerged from the opening in Tal–Browne, 1975, after **11 ...** ♗e7 12 e5 ♗xf3 13 ♕xf3 de 14 ♘c6 ♕c7 15 ♘xe7 ♔xe7 16 ♕g3 ♖he8! But if White did not try to force matters quickly, playing 12 ♕e2 instead, his position would have been preferable.

B2

| 7 | ... | ♕c7 |

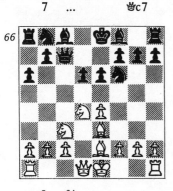

66

| 8 | f4 |

Once again White might try to play a Keres Attack with 8 g4, especially considering that 6 ... ♕c7 is not the best method of defence

against that system, just as e2 is not the most aggressive position for the bishop. In reply to 8 g4 we can recommend both 8 ... h6, i.e. 9 f4 b5 10 g5 hg 11 fg ♘fd7 12 g6 ♘e5 or 9 a4 d5 10 ed ed 11 h4 ♗b4 12 ♔f1 ♘c6 13 ♔g2 ♗xc3 14 bc ♘e4; and 8 ... b5, for example 9 g5 ♘fd7 10 a3 ♘b6 11 f4 ♘8d7 12 0-0 ♗b7 13 f3 e5 14 ♘b3 ♘a4!, Byrne–Kavalek, 1972. In each case there is a complicated position. Black has not played such bad moves in the opening that 8 g4 should be able to give White an advantage.

| 8 | ... | b5 |
| 9 | ♗f3 | ♗b7 |

Why not try 9 ... b4?

| 10 | a3 |

If White tries to force events in the centre with 10 e5, then we will reach a position which has already been studied: 10 ... de 11 ♗xb7 ♕xb7 (11 ... ed 12 ♗xa8 de deserves attention.) 12 fe ♘fd7 (12 ... ♕xg2? is dangerous – 13 ♖g1 ♕h3 14 ♕e2!) 13 0-0 ♘c6. After 14 ♘xc6 ♕xc6 15 ♔h5! g6 16 ♕h4 ♗g7 17 ♗h6 White retained a slight initiative and the Pe5 was weak in Ghinda–Ungureanu.

10	...	♘bd7
11	♕e2	e5
12	♘f5	h6

An immediate 12 ... g6 allows the typical manouevre 13 fe de 14 ♘h6, which interferes with normal development.

| 13 | 0-0 | g6 |

After 14 ♘g3 ef 15 ♗xf4 ♘e5 16 ♖ad1 ♗g7 17 ♔h1 0-0 the chances are approximately level,

Suetin–Platonov, 1977.

B3

7   ...   ♗e7

A useful waiting move, which puts off the decision of a pattern of development until the next move.

8   g4

After 8 f4 ♘c6 or 8 ... ♘bd7 the game would transpose into the usual lines of the Scheveningen. Now Black's concept is justified, since the game transposes into an unprofitable (for White) line of the Keres Attack, since White has hastened to play 6 ♗e2.

8   ...   b5
9   g5

Against 9 a3 Black has two good plans: 9 ... ♗b7 or even 9 ... d5 10 ed ♗b7, which opens up the game in the centre and exposes his opponent's weakened pawn structure.

9   ...   ♘fd7
10   f4 (67)

The "extra" move ♗e2 has brought about a situation in which the weakness of the Pg5 does not

67

give White time for a useful prophylaxis, and his knight is now exiled to the edge of the board. After 10 ... b4 11 ♘a4 ♗b7 12 ♗f3 ♘c6! 13 h4 0-0 Black has a wonderful game, i.e. 14 0-0 ♘xd4 15 ♗xd4 e5! 16 fe de 17 ♗f2 ♗c6 18 c3 ♕a5 19 b3 ♖fd8! 20 cb ♕xb4! ∓ Byrne–Polugayevsky, 1975, or 14 ♘e2 ♕a5 15 b3 ♘c5! 16 ♘b2 ♖fd8 ∓, according to 1975 analysis by Polugayevsky.

The reader should note that positions with the White bishop developing at d3 are examined in later chapters.

10 Modern Scheveningen: Introduction

1 e4 c5 2 ♘f3 d6 3 d4 cd 4 ♘xd4 ♘f6 5 ♘c3 e6 6 ♗e2 ♘c6

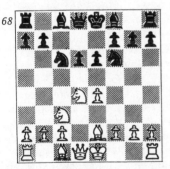

Not so long ago a Scheveningen formation without ... a6 was inconceivable. According to Tartakower, it was the Pa6 which held the Scheveningen fortress together for Black, just as a careful nanny protects a child. A more profound understanding of the fine points of the Scheveningen does not refute the contention that the move a7-a6 is useful in general, but only shakes the opinion concerning its absolute necessity. A similar re-evaluation of the need to play ... ♕c7 has been underway but to a lesser degree. Still, in the forest of the Scheveningen Variation we occasionally come across a branch or two where the

pawn is in no hurry to move from a7, and the queen does not rush to c7. Such an economy of chess time in the opening has profound significance: Black will first try a counteroperation in the centre and as will be seen from the following analysis, in a standard attack on the queenside the a-pawn will advance to a5 in one step instead of two.

Besides 6 ... ♘c6 one can play 6 ... ♗e7 in the same spirit usually transposing to the main line after 7 0-0 ♘c6. For those fond of exceptions we present a fragment from the game Adorjan–Trifunović, 1972: 6 ... ♗e7 7 0-0 ♗d7 8 ♘db5 ♗c6 (8 ... ♗xb5 9 ♗xb5+ ♘c6 also deserves consideration) 9 ♗f4 e5 10 ♗g5 ♘xe4 11 ♗xe7 ♔xe7 12 ♘xe4 ♗xe4 13 ♕d2 with a strong initiative for the sacrificed pawn. By the way, 6 ... ♘bd7 can also lead to original play, e.g. 7 g4 ♘c5 8 ♗f3 or 7 ♘bd5 ♘c5 9 ♗g5 a6 10 ♗xf6 gf 11 ♘d4.

    7   0-0   ♗e7
    8   ♗e3

While we are still in a frame of mind which is tuned to orthodox ideas, let us consider the fianchetto

of the queen's bishop. After 8 b3
0-0 9 ♗b2

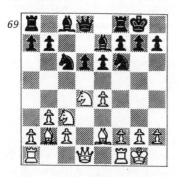

White has used up valuable time
and therefore cannot expect much.
Before attacking the Black king he
still has to remove his king from the
a7-g1 diagonal and defend or withdraw the ♘d4. This gives Black
plenty of time to create counterplay. Besides, on b2 the bishop
only aims at g7, while on e3 it
plays on both flanks. After 9 ♗b2
there are two good plans for Black:
a) 9 ... ♛a5 10 ♛d2 ♖d8 11 ♖ad1
♘xd4 12 ♛xd4 ♗d7! 13 ♔h1 ♗c6 14
f4 d5! 15 ed ♗xd5 16 ♘xd5 ♖xd5
17 ♛c3 ♛xc3 18 ♗xc3 ♖c8 =
b) 9 ... a6 10 ♔h1 ♗d7 11 f4 ♛b6!
12 ♘xc6 (12 ♘a4 ♛c7!) 12 ...
♗xc6 13 ♗d3 (13 ♗f3 ♛e3!) 13
... ♘d7 14 e5 ♘c5! 15 ed ♗xd6 =
Schwarz.

Praxis prefers to take the king
out of the centre as soon as possible,
while theory considers that 7 ♗e3
♗e7 8 f4 is more promising, since
then White retains the option of
castling on either side, for example
8 f4 a6 9 ♛d2 ♛c7 10 0-0-0 or 8
... ♗d7 9 ♘db5 ♛b8 10 g4 a6 11
♘d4 d5 12 ed ♘xd5 13 ♘xd5 ♗h4+

14 ♗f2 ♗xf2+ 15 ♔xf2 ed (The
recent game Kupreichik–Kasparov,
USSR Cup 1982 disclosed an obvious third possibility 8 ... 0-0. Now
9 ♛d2 was met by 9 ... e5!, which
exploited the unimpressive placement of the queen at d2. White's
game quickly deteriorated, and
after 10 ♘f3 ♘g4 11 f5 ♘b4 12
♗d3 d5! 13 ♘xd5 ♘xd5 14 ed e4!
15 ♗xe4 ♖e8 16 0-0-0 ♗f6 the pressure on the e-file was too great:
17 ♗g5 ♖xe4 18 h3 ♘e5 19
♗xf6 ♛xf6 20 ♘xe5 ♛xe5∓∓ —
tr.)

8   ...   0-0

One is quite accustomed to
finding this move in practice, but
if one wishes to be most precise,
then 8 ... ♗d7 is more accurate.
Since the centre is not open and
the option of castling secured, such
a supereconomy of chess time deserves attention and analysis. Black
pushes on with the development of
his pieces, which is necessary for
the creation of counterplay. At the
moment the viability of this idea
has not been disproved.

Thus after **9 ♘db5 ♛b8 10 a4
0-0** the attempt to compress the

Sicilian spring with 11 f4 (11 ♗f4 ♘e5 12 ♗g5 a6 13 ♘d4 ♘c6 is no better) 11 ... ♖d8 12 ♗f3 ♗e8 13 ♕e2 is not successful. After 13 ... a6 14 ♘d4 (14 ♘a3 d5! 15 ed ed the ♘a3 is offside.) 14 ... ♕c7 15 ♖ad1 ♘xd4 16 ♗xd4 e5 17 ♗e3 ♗c6 the spring relaxes its tension. The idea 9 ♘b3 a6 10 a4, which is usually so unpleasant for Black does not snap into action here (without the inclusion of the moves f4 0-0), since in reply to 10 ... ♘a5 there is no effect in the move 11 e5, while after 11 ♘d2 0-0 12 f4 ♕c7 13 ♕e1 b5 the initiative transfers to Black.

That leaves only 9 f4 ♘xd4 to be examined. After 10 ♗xd4 ♗c6 11 ♕d3 0-0 12 ♕g3 or 11 ♗d3 0-0 12 ♕e1 the game enters positions which are well studied and hold equal chances. Only 10 ♕xd4, with the accent on domination in the centre, presents Black with a problem to solve, but it is not very difficult: 10 ... ♗c6 11 e5 de 12 fe ♘d5 13 ♘xd5 ♕xd5 14 ♕xd5 ♗xd5 15 ♗b5+ ♗c6 16 ♗xc6 bc 17 ♖ad1 ♖b8 with an equal endgame.

9   f4 *(71)*

There is no point in White's removing the knight out of fear of a possible exchange on d4. After 9 ♘b3 a6! (Better than 9 ... ♗d7 or 9 ... ♕c7) 10 a4 the easiest road to equality is 10 ... ♘a5 11 ♘xa5 ♕xa5 12 ♕e1 ♔h8, although 10 ... b6 11 f4 ♗b7 12 ♗f3 ♘d7 or 12 ... ♕c8 is quite playable, if more complicated, leading to well-known positions.

The fashion for the reformation of the Scheveningen dogma, which we are examining in this chapter, at first only touched upon 9 ... ♗d7. Only later, during the period of "practical experience" when its dark side appeared, did its competitors arrive on the scene, also denying the absolute necessity of the move a7-a6. Let us first focus our attention on one of the rivals, saving consideration of the other moves for later chapters.

9   ...   ♕c7

The preliminary exchange 9 ... ♘xd4 10 ♗xd4 aims for manouvering space and the liberation of the diagonal after 10 ... b6, in order to place pressure on the centre. It is not sufficient for equality since it is decidedly defensive in character. By declining the standard activity on the queenside Black allows his opponent to attack the king by the most natural route: 11 ♕d3 ♗b7 12 ♖ad1 ♖c8 (12 ... g6 13 f5 e5 is somewhat better) 13 ♕g3 d5 14 ed! ed 15 ♔h1! ♖e8 16 ♗d3 ♗f8 17 ♕h3 g6 (17 ... h6 18 ♕f5! ±) 18 f5! ♗g7 19 fg hg 20 ♕f3 ♖e6 21 ♘e2±, Ostojić–Ciocaltea, 1975. There is a second possibility which provokes a crisis in the 9 ... ♘xd4 system, and that is 10 ♕xd4, which allows White to develop pressure in the centre, for example 10 ... b6 11 ♗f3 ♗b7 12 ♖ad1 (12 ♖fd1 ♕c8 13 a4?! ♖d8 14 ♔h1 d5!=) 12 ... ♕c8 (12 ... ♖c8 13 ♕a4!±) 13 e5 de 14 fe ♗c5 15 ♕f4 ♘d5 16 ♘xd5 ±.

By playing 9 ... ♕c7, Black wishes to obtain the most comfortable formation for his forces in the system with ♘d4-b3. As a matter of fact, after 10 ♘b3 he can transpose not only to the approved systems with 10 ... a6 11 a4 b6, but he can also exploit the position of the pawn at a7, comfortably completing his development with 10 ... b6 11 ♗f3 ♗a6! 12 ♖f2 ♖fd8 13 ♕e1 ♖ac8 14 ♖d1 ♗c4, Ciocaltea–Tal, 1974. The complications of 15 ♘d4 ♘xd4 16 ♗xd4 e5 17 ♗e3 d5! 18 fe ♘xe4 19 ♗xe4 de 10 ♗d4 ♗b4 21 ♕xe4 ♗xc3 11 bc ♗xa2 are in Black's favour.

In answer to the useful prophylactic move 10 ♔h1 Black has a choice between 10 ... ♘xd4 11 ♕xd4 (11 ♗xd4 e5=) 11 ... e5 12 ♕d3 ef (but not 12 ... ♗d7? 13 fe de 14 ♖xf6! ♗xf6 15 ♘d5 with an attack) 13 ♗xf4 ♗d7 14 ♖ad1 ♗c6 and the more conservative line 10 ... ♗d7 11 ♕e1 (11 ♘f3 ♖fd8 12 ♕e1 e5=) 11 ... ♘xd4 12 ♗xd4 ♗c6 13 ♕g3 ♖ad8. This position became famous as after the game Suetin–Bagirov 1963, in which White effectively sacrificed his queen with 14 e5 de 15 ♗xe5 ♕b6 16 f5 ef 17 ♖xf5 ♗d6 18 ♕xg7+!? ♔xg7 19 ♗xf6+ and won.

Later it was shown that by the bold 19 ... ♔g6 Black would have refuted the attack and instead of 14 e5, 14 ♖ae1 was adopted, after which there is a series of theoretically "best" moves – 14 ... b6 15 ♗d3 (After 15 e5 de 16 ♗xe5 ♕b7 the idea behind 14 ... b6 becomes clear: 17 ♗d3 g6 18 ♕h3 b5! 19 a3 a5) 15 ... e5 16 fe ♘h5 17 ♕h3 de – which leads to an interesting and, (this is more important) instructive middlegame Scheveningen position, exemplifying attacking and defending methods:

72

a) **18 ♘d5 ♗xd5 19 ♗xe5!** (19 ed ed 20 ♕xh5 g6) 19 ... ♕xe5 20 ed ♕g5 21 ♖f5 ♕h4 22 ♕xg4 ♗xh4 23 ♖xh5 ♗xe1 24 ♗xh7+ with a draw by perpetual check.

b) **18 ♗xe5! ♕xe5 19 ♖f5 ♘f4!** 20 ♖xe5 (20 ♕g3? loses unexpectedly to 10 ... ♕xf5! 21 ef ♗xg2+) 20 ... ♘xh3 21 ♖xe7 ♘f2+ 22 ♔g1 ♘xd3 23 cd ♖xd3 24 ♖xa7 ♖d2 25 b3 f5! 26 ♘d5 ♔h8! 27 ♖c7 ♗a8 and despite his extra pawn. White has to struggle for equality.

    10 ♕e1   ♘xd4

The immediate advance of the pawn with 10 ... e5 also appears promising: 11 ♘b3 ef! 12 ♗xf4 ♗e6 13 ♖d1 ♘e5 14 ♕d2 a6 or 11 fe de 12 ♘f5 ♗xf5 13 ef ♘b4! 14 ♖c1 ♘fd5 15 ♘xd5 ♘xd5 16 ♗f2 e4. Here Black can be satisfied with the result of the opening. On the simple exchange 11 ♘xc6!, however, Black is faced with an uneasy choice — whether to go in for a position with an isolated c-pawn: 11 ... bc 12 fe de, or to be tortured by the d5-square: 11 ... ♕xc6 12 f5 a6 (12 ... ♘xe4 13 ♗b5!) 13 ♗f3.

      11   ♗xd4   e5!

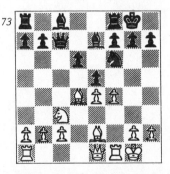

Black carries out the timely and programmatic liberating manouvre and obtains a good game. Once again it is necessary for Scheveningen players to know the fine points of the position, as they are repeated in several complicated situations.

a) 12 ♗e3 ef 13 ♗xf4 (13 ♖xf4 ♗e6 14 ♕g3 ♘d7 15 ♗d4 ♘e5 16 ♖af1 a6 17 a4 ♖ac8 18 ♔h1∞, Ermenkov–Andersson, 1980.) 13 ... ♗e6 (A dangerous line is 13 ... ♕b6+ 14 ♔h1 ♕xb2? 15 ♕g3 ♔h8 16 e5 de 17 ♗xe5 with a very strong attack in view of the threat ♘d5.) 14 ♕g3 ♖fd8 15 ♖ad1 ♕c6 16 ♗h6 g6 17 ♗g5 ♘h5 18 ♕e3 ♗xg5

19 ♕xg5 ♕b6+ 20 ♔h1 ♕xb2 with a complicated struggle, Petrushin–Espig, Berlin 1980.

b) 12 fe de 13 ♕g3

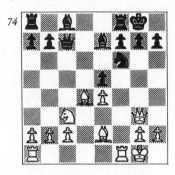

How short-sighted chess theory can sometimes be! Until recent times it was considered that with the king on g1 the only move for Black is 13 ... ♗c5!, which is sufficient for him after the almost obligatory 14 ♗xc5 ♕xc5+ 15 ♔h1 ♔h8.

The White rook on f1 is very aggressive, but if Black can manage to regroup with ♗e6 and ♘d7 then White's initiative will disappear instantaneously. White still has a draw with 16 ♖xf6 gf 17 ♕h4 ♖g8! 18 ♕xf6+ ♖g7 19 ♖d1 ♗e6 20 ♖d8+, but can he try for more? Black has a solid position in the variation 16 ♕h4 ♕b6 17 ♗d3 h6! 18 ♘d5 ♘xd5 19 ed ♕d6! 20 c4 f5 or after 16 ... ♕e7 17 ♖ad1 h6! 18 ♕g3 b6, Spassky–Tal, 1974.

This irreproachably logical construction was smashed by some women. Oh, well, *"Cherchez la femme!"* It turns out that it doesn't matter where the king stands, since Black has another paradoxical defence: 13 ... ♗d6!! White has two "winning" continuations, but they are both refuted in the same way:

a) 14 ♘b5 ed 15 ♘xd6 ♘e8

b) 14 ♖xf6 ed 15 ♕xd6 ♕xd6 16 ♖xd6 dc 17 bc ♗e6

In each case there is an even endgame. But the wonders have not ceased! White can try to win less immediately, with, for example, 14 ♗e3 ♘e8 15 ♘d5 (15 ♖ad1 ♗e6! 16 ♘b5 ♕xc2 17 ♖d2 ♕c6) and on 15 ... ♕xc2, 16 ♗h6: This looks like the end, since the g7 square is not defended after 16 ... ♗c5+ 17 ♔h1 ♕xe2 18 ♘f6+ ♔h8 19 ♘xe8. But . . . here the ladies laugh: 16 ...

f5 17 ♗h5 ♔h8 Zaitseva-Minogina, 1978 and 16 ... ♔h8 17 ♗d3 ♕xb2 18 ♗xg7+ ♘xg7 19 ♕h4 ♘h5 20 ♕xh5 ♖g8 and that is the end of White's attack. Independent analysis of similar situations is very useful since it gives a representation of the depth of chess, of the hidden possibilities of any position.

The continuation 9 ... ♕c7, in our opinion, is more flexible than 9 ... ♗d7, since it allows transposition into both the classical Scheveningen and the system with 9 ... ♗d7.

11 Modern Scheveningen: 9 . . . e5

1 e4 c5 2 ♘f3 d6 3 d4 cd 4 ♘xd4 ♘f6 5 ♘c3 e6 6 ♗e2 ♘c6 7 0-0 ♗e7 8 ♗e3 0-0 9 f4 e5

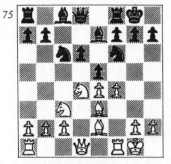

75

This system of play was worked out by a Grandmaster duo, Spassky and Bondarevsky. It is also related to a number of highly economical modifications of the Scheveningen. Black begins his operations in the centre, not wasting any time on prophylaxis, and paying no attention to the weakness of the d5 point. In return for yielding the d5 square to his opponent Black obtains a no less comfortable post at e5. After the exchange e5xf4 the weakness of the Pe4 will make up for the weakness at d6. Praxis has shown that continuations such as 10 ♘f5 ♗xf5 11 ef ef 12 ♖xf4 d5! 13 ♔h1 ♖c8 or 10 fe de 11 ♘f5 ♗xf5 12 ♖xf5 ♕a5! 13 ♔h1 ♖ad8 14 ♕g1 g6 15 ♖5f1 ♘d4, Stean-Tal, 1974, are not promising for White. 10 ♘db5 a6 11 fe is a more cunning idea which gives White a positional edge in the middle game after 11 ... de 12 ♕xd8 ♗xd8 13 ♘d6, as in the game Dolmatov-Dorfman, 1981. But instead of 11 ... de, 11 ... ♘xe5 12 ♘d4 d5!? deserves analysis, and the very author of the idea recommends another plan for equality, 10 ... ef 11 ♗xf4 ♘e5 when the knight will all the same have to go back.

Besides the fundamental variation 10 ♘b3, discussed below, we must look at the situation which arises after 10 ♘xc6 bc 11 fe de. If 12 ♗c4?! ♘g4! 13 ♕xd8 ♗xd8 14 ♗c5 ♗b6! 15 ♗xb6 (15 ♘a4? ♗xc5 16 ♘xc5 ♘e3) 15 ... ab 16 ♖fe1 b5, Black has everything under control. He may run into difficulty after 12 ♕xd8 in conjunction with the promising exchange of heavy pieces on the d-file and subsequent transition into the endgame with a defective pawn structure on the queenside. The capture with 12 ... ♗xd8 no longer has any effect, because White can play 13 ♗c5 ♗b6 16 ♘a4! ♗xc5 15 ♘xc5, so Black must slowly play for equality after 12 ... ♖xd8 13 ♖ad1 ♗e6.

10 ♘b3

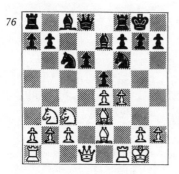

10 ... ef

Black's plan becomes clear. He wants to put his bishop on e6 and achieve the advance d6-d5.

Bondarevsky and Spassky base Black's counterplay after 10 ♘b3 on the move 10 ... a5. But the chronic weakness of the d5 and b5 squares secures a positional advantage for White after 11 a4! ♘b4 12 ♔h1! ♗d7 (An inferior formation is 12 ... ♕c7 13 ♖c1 ♗e6 14 ♘d2! ef 15 ♘b5 ♕d8 16 ♗xf4 with an obvious advantage, Geller–Spassky, 1974. Perhaps 12 ... d5 13 fe ♘xe4 gives Black more chances for equality. If 12 ... ♗e6 13 ♗f3 ♕c7 14 ♖f2 ♖fd8 15 ♖d2 ♗c4 16 ♕g1! ♘d7 17 f5 h6 18 ♗e2! Pritchett). 13 ♗f3 ♕c7 14 ♖f2 ♖fe8 15 ♖d2 b6 16 ♕g1 ♖ab8 17 h3 ♗f8, Yudovich–Razuvayev, 1977. The system 9 ... e5 began to re-emerge as a result of a re-evaluation of the position which arises after 10 ♘b3 ef.

We now examine
A 11 ♗xf4
B 11 ♖xf4

A

11 ♗xf4 ♗e6

Now White will not be able to prevent the advance 12 ... d5. Indeed, 12 ♗f3 places the bishop in a passive position and after 12 ... ♗c4 13 ♖f2 ♘e5 14 ♖d2 ♕c7 the game is equal. Against 12 ♕e1, 12 ... d5 is good and full equality is reached after either 13 e5 ♘d7 or 13 ed ♘xd5 14 ♘xd5 ♕xd5 15 ♕g3 ♕f5!, van der Wiel–Panchenko, 1981.

White allows 12 ... d5 in the most favourable circumstances available to him.

By the way, this position can also be reached via the Boleslavsky Sicilian: 1 e4 c5 2 ♘f3 ♘c6 3 d4 cd 4 ♘xd4 ♘f6 5 ♘c3 d6 6 ♗e2 e5 7 ♘b3 ♗e7 8 0-0 0-0 9 f4 ef 10 ♗xf4 ♗e6.

12 ♔h1 d5!

There is another modification of Spassky's idea which is worthy of future development: 12 ... ♕b6 13 ♕e1 (13 ♘d5 ♗xd5 14 ed ♘e5 =) 13 ... a5. At the moment this position must be considered favourable for White because of the weakness of the b5-square, i.e. 14 ♗b5! ♘b4 15 ♗e3 ♕c7 16 ♘d4.

13 e5 ♘fd7

13 ... ♘e4 14 ♗d3 leads to a complicated situation. 14 ... f5 (The plan with 14 ... ♘xc3 15 bc ♕d7 (15 ... g6 16 ♘d4 ♘xd4 17 cd ♖c8 18 ♗h6 ± Bronstein-Knaak 1977) 16 ♕h5 g6 17 ♕h6 ♖fc8, Sznapik-Knaak, 1977, △ ♕d7-d8-f8 is too pretentious and unconvincing.) 15

ef ♗xf6! 16 ♘xe4 de 17 ♘c5 ed
(17 ... ♗d5!?) 18 ♘xe6 dc   19
♕xc2 ♘d4 with equal chances,
Tseshkovsky-Tukmakov, 1981.

By withdrawing the knight to d7,
Black gives his opponent the advantage of the bishop pair, but
maintains his strong foothold in
the centre. This gives rise to a more
serious chess conflict than 13 ...
♘e4. Both sides have good chances
to prove their mastery in the fight
for the advantage.

    14   ♘xd5   ♘dxe5

Yet another problematic position
has arisen. White has a choice between improving his position in the
centre with 15 c4, or obtaining the
bishop pair with 15 ♘xe7+, and
then trying to find some way of
activating them.

    15   c4

As praxis has shown, 15 ♘xe7+
♕xe7 16 ♕e1 brings about a
position in which the Black knight
pair not only solidly defends all
objects of attack, but also refuses
to let the bishop pair into the
game, for example 16 ... ♖ad8 17
♕g3 ♘g6 18 ♗g5 f6 19 ♗e3 ♖fe8,
Klovan-Tseshkovsky, 1981, or 16

... ♘g6 17 ♗g3 f5!? 18 ♗f3 f4 19
♗f2 ♕f7 20 ♘d4 ♗c4, Marjanović-
Tarjan, 1980. 16 ♘d4 is no better:
16 ... ♖ad8 17 ♘xc6 ♘xc6 18 ♗d3
♘b4 ∓, Bielczyk-Vogt, 1977.

    15   ...   ♗g5!
    16   ♕c1

On 16 ♗g3 there follows 16 ...
♗h4, while after 16 ♘c5 ♗xf4 17
♖xf4 b6! 18 ♘e4 b5! White unexpectedly finds himself on the
defensive: 19 b3 bc 20 ♗xc4 (20
bc ♕a5!) 20 ... ♔h8! 21 ♕h5?
(White could have held on to an
equal position by 21 h3 f5 22
♘ec3) 21 ... ♗xd5 22 ♗xd5 (22
♖ad1 g6! 23 ♕h6 ♗xe4 24 ♖xd8
♖axd8 25 h3 f5 with a winning
position) 22 ... ♕xd5 23 ♖h4 h6
24 ♖d1 ♕a5! and Black won
quickly in Geller-Kasparov, 1981.

    16   ...   ♗xf4
    17   ♘xf4

A position of dynamic equality
has been created, in which once
again the Black knight pair successfully bear their great load, and
guarantee a good game, i.e. 17 ...
♕e7 18 ♕c3 ♖ad8 19 ♖ae1 ♔h8
20 a3 f6, Kuzmin-Kasparov, 1981,
or 17 ... ♗g4 18 ♗xg4 ♘xg4 19
♕e1 ♖e8 20 ♕g3 ♘f6 21 ♖ad1
♕c7, Tal-Kavalek, 1982.

B

    11   ♖xf4 *(78)*
    11   ...   ♗e6

It is worthwhile for Black to
play this useful move, even though
it reduces his chance of advancing
in the centre.

Exploiting the lack of threats on
the Pd6, Black can decline un-
loading the centre and play 11 ...

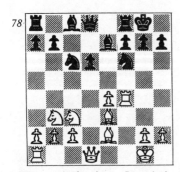

♘d7, strengthening e5 and threatening to exchange bishops in a profitable form. 12 ♖f1 ♘de5! (The ♘c6 must mark the ♘b3) 13 ♘d5 ♗g5 14 ♕d2 ♗xe3 15 ♘xe3 ♗e6 16 c3 ♕g5 17 ♖ad1 ♖ad8 18 ♘d5, Dolmatov-Stoica, 1981. The Pe4 controls squares in the enemy camp, and the Pd6 looks after home squares. All of this amounts to a minimal advantage for White, although with precise defence Black ought to be able to equalise. Another formulation of this idea is also interesting: 11 ... ♘e8 12 ♖f1 ♗f6!? △ ♗e5.

12   ♘d4

Of course after 12 ♔h1 d5! the game is equalised immediately, but 12 ♘d5 is also playable, since the rook defends the Pe4. That move gives Black a comfortable choice between 12 ... ♗xd5 13 ed ♘e5 △ ... ♘fd7 and 12 ... ♘d7 13 ♘xe7+ ♕xe7 14 ♕e1 ♘de5 15 ♘d4 ♘xd4 16 ♗xd4 ♖ac8 17 c3 a6 18 ♕g3 f6, Petrushin-Kozlov. Black has an acceptable game after 12 ♕e1 as well, i.e. 12 ... ♘d7 13 ♖f1 ♘de5 14 ♘d5 ♗g5 15 ♕d2 ♗xe3+ 16 ♘xe3 ♕g5 17 ♖ad1 g6 with equality, Tal-Vogt, 1981.

12   ...   ♘xd4

No one has looked at 12 ... d5 here, although after 13 ed ♗xd5! or 13 ♘xe6 fe 14 ed ed matters are not all that simple . . .

13   ♗xd4

White has completed a profitable operation. He has got rid of the passive knight, brought his bishop to an active position and prevented the move d6-d5.

13   ...   ♘d7
14   ♔h1   ♗g5
15   ♖f1   ♘e5

All of the Black pieces have good prospects. The game is level, i.e. 16 ♗g1 ♘c4 17 ♗xc4 ♗xc4 18 ♖f3 ♗f6.

12 Modern Scheveningen: 9 . . .&d7

1 e4 c5 2 ♘f3 d6 3 d4 cd 2 ♘xd4 ♘f6 5 ♘c3 e6 6 ♗e2 ♘c6 7 0-0 ♗e7 8 ♗e3 0-0 9 f4 ♗d7

By playing 9 ... ♗d7 Black creates basic support for the carrying out of his regrouping operation in the centre with 10 ... ♘xd4 11 ♗xd4 ♗c6 and only then will he play e6-e5. Then the bishop will defend the d5 square. The pawn will frequently remain at e5, limiting the activity of the White bishops, and the standard pawn operation on the queenside will take place with gain of time, since the Black pawn will advance to a5 in one move.

Now White cannot get anywhere with 10 ♘db5 ♕b8 11 a4 ♖d8 12 ♗f3 ♗e8 13 ♕e2 a6 or 10 ♗f3 e5! or 10 ♗d3 ♘xd4 11 ♗xd4 e5 12 ♗e3 ♘g4!

A 10 ♔h1
B 10 ♕e1

10 ♘b3 will be examined in the next chapter.

A

10 ♔h1 (79)

The "simply useful" prophylactic move is often encountered in practice but it is not, obviously, the most energetic move.

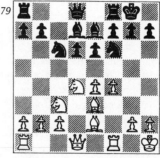

79

10 ...   ♘xd4

After 10 ... a6 the game transposes into the Classical Scheveningen. An original idea of Suetin — 10 ... ♕b8!? 11 ♗f3 ♖fc8 12 ♕e2 ♘xd4 13 ♗xd4 e5 14 ♗e3 ♗e6 15 ♕f2 b5 was employed successfully in the game Klovsky–Suetin, 1968: 16 f5?! (16 fe de 17 ♘d5=) 16 ... ♗c4 17 ♖fd1 b4 18 ♘e2 d5! 19 ♗g5 de! 20 ♗xf6 ef with advantage to Black.

11   ♗xd4

12 ♕xd4 is also quite playable. The queen occupies a strong and quite safe position in the centre. White can count on success in the centre and even on the queenside, especially if Black plays conventionally, for example 11 ... ♗c6 12 ♖ad1 ♕c7 13 f5 e5 14 ♕d3

🖺fd8   15 ♘d5 ♗xd5   16 ed 🖺dc8
17 c4 ♕d8   18 b4! ±, Dementiev-
Kopylov, 1972. Instead of 12 ...
♕c7 12 ... d5   13 e5 ♘e4 may
bring equality. 12 ... ♕a5 leads to
a tough fight, i.e. 13 f5 e5 (13 ...
♕e5!?   14 ♕d3 h6   15 ♗f2 🖺fd8)
or 13 b4 ♕c7   14 b5 ♗d7 (also
possible is 14 ... ♗e8 △ ♘f6-d7-c5)
15 e5 🖺fd8! and also 12 ... ♕b8
13 ♗f3 🖺d8   14 ♕c4 🖺c8   15 ♕e2
b5 16 ♗d4 b4, Vogt–Bonsch, 1981.

11   ...   ♗c6

12   ♗d3

The attempt to shift the play to
the queenside with 12 ♗f3 is not
promising. After the exchange
Black will have space to manoeuvre
and he will equalise without difficulty, i.e. 12 ♗f3 ♘d7   13 a4 e5!
14 ♗e3 ef   15 ♗xf4 ♘e5   16 ♗xe5
de 17 ♗e2 ♕d4! or 16 ♗e2 ♗g5 17
♗g3 🖺e8   18 ♘d5 🖺c8   19 c3 ♗h4,
Cirić–Krogius, 1965.

There is also a stereotyped
operation which works against 12
♕d3 ♘d7   13 ♕g3 e5! By playing
12 ♗d3, white would like to create
pressure in the centre and prepare
an attack on the kingside.

12   ...   ♘d7

It is also possible to play 12 ...
a6, but the retreat of the knight is
more logical. Black tries not only
to limit both of his opponent's
bishops, by placing a pawn at e5,
but also to exchange one of them
after ♘d7-c5. *(80)*

13   ♕e2

An interesting concept. White
prevents the exchanging operation
♗f6 and tries to bring his rook into
the game with 🖺f1-f3-h3. The more

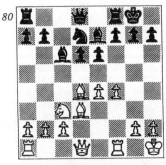

aggressive 13 ♕h5 achieves the same
goals, apparently, but this is not
really the case. The placement of
the queen turns out to be the fac-
tor which allows Black to create a
solid defence in a number of ways,
i.e. 13 ... g6   14 ♕h3 e5!   15 fe de
16 ♗e3 ♗g5 or even 13 ... ♗f6!
14 e5 g6!   15 ♕e2 de   16 fe ♗g7
17 🖺ae1 ♕h4.

13   ...   e5

This is by no means obligatory,
but it is consequential. It is not
easy to prove an advantage for
White after 13 ... ♘c5, for example 14 ♗xc5 dc   15 e5 ♕b6!
16 🖺ab1 🖺ad8   17 ♘e4 ♗xe4 18
♕xe4 g6   19 b3 🖺d4 =. There is a
sufficiently solid alternative in 13
... a6   14 🖺ad1 b5   15 🖺f3 e5   16
♗e3 ♗f6!   17 🖺h3 (17 ♘d5 ♗xd5
19 ed 🖺e8!   19 fe ♘xe5   20 🖺h3
g6 =) 17 ... ef   18 e5 g6! In the
game Liberzon–Boleslavsky, 1966,
White showed a profit from the
system with 13 ♕e2: 13 ... a6   14
🖺ad1 ♕c7   15 🖺f3 e5   16 ♗e3 ef
17 ♗xf4 ♗f6   18 🖺h3 g6?   19 ♗c4
♘e5   20 ♘d5 ♗xd5   21 ♗xd5 🖺ac8
22 c3±, but even here Black would
have obtained a comfortable game
if he had played 18 ... ♗e5!   19

♘d5 ♗xd5 20 ed ♗xf4! (also possible is 20 ... g6) 21 ♗xh7+ ♔h8 22 ♗d3+ ♗h6 23 ♕e4 f5! ∓.

After 13 ... e5 14 ♗e3 ef 15 ♗xf4 ♕c7 16 ♘d5 ♗xd5 17 ed ♗f6 the chances are approximately level.

B

    10   ♕e1

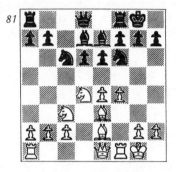

This is the most energetic plan, which is based on the goal of attacking the king. Black can of course return to a Classical formation by playing 10 ... a6, 10 ... ♕c7 11 ♕g3 a6 or even 10 ... ♖c8 11 ♖d1 a6 12 ♔h1 b5 13 e5 ♘e8 14 ♕g3 ♕c7 15 ♖d2 ♘xd4 16 ♗xd4 ♗c6 17 ♗d3 with a small initiative for White, Vogt–Beni, 1979.

    10   ...   ♘xd4
    11   ♗xd4   ♗c6

Black need not hurriedly disclose the future position of his queen. Here he undertakes the first part of his opening strategy, intending to carry out the advance e6-e5.

B1 12 ♕g3
B2 12 ♗d3

B1

    12   ♕g3   g6!? *(82)*

This is an interesting concept by Korchnoi. Black radically liquidates spontaneous threats on the g7 square and cuts off the diagonal for the White bishop, should it move to d3. Theory considers 12 ... ♕a5 equally worthwhile, the idea of which is revealed in the variations 13 ♗d3? ♕b4! 14 ♕f2 ♘g4 and 13 ♗f3 ♖fd8 14 ♖ae1 d5 15 ed ♗c5! There is a third variation which supports the solidity of the move 12 ... ♕a5: 13 a3! g6 14 ♗d3 ♘h5 15 ♕f2 ♘xf4 16 ♕xf4 e5 17 ♕f2 ed 18 ♕xd4 ♕c5 =. It seems to us that it is in this variation where White can improve his play. Thus instead of 14 ♗d3, 14 f5 is stronger with a powerful initiative because of the distance of the Black queen from the kingside. Even later, instead of 17 ♕f2, 17 b4 is a much stronger move.

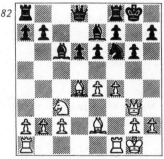

    13   f5!?

This is the continuation which is both most energetic and most fully in accordance with the logic of the position. Quiet play is not likely to disclose a defect in Black's last move: the weakening of the complex of dark squares in the region of the king's fortress. Here are some characteristic examples:

a) **13 ♕e3 ♕a5** 14 e5 de 15 fe ♘d5 16 ♘xd5 ♕xd5 17 ♗f3 ♕c4 = or 13 ... ♘d7 14 ♖ad1 ♕a5 15 ♕d2 ♗d8 16 ♗e3 ♘f6 =

b) **13 ♗f3 b5** 14 a3 a5 15 ♖ad1 b4 16 ab ab 17 e5 ♗xf3 18 ♕xf3 bc 19 ef ♗xf6 20 ♕xc3 ♗xd4+ =, Minić–Korchnoi, 1964.

c) **13 ♗d3 ♘h5** (13 ... b5?! 14 f5! e5 15 ♗e3 b4 16 ♗c4! ♔h8 17 ♘d5 ±) 14 ♕f2 ♘xf4 15 ♕xf4 e5 16 ♕f2 ed 17 ♕xd4 ♕a5 18 ♔h1 (18 ♘d5? ♗xd5 19 ♕xd5 ♕xd5 20 ed f5 ∓, Evans–Shamkovich, 1980) 18 ... ♕e5! with an equal game, Zhdanov–Kapengut, 1966.

> 13   ...   e5
> 14   ♗e3   ♘xe4

14 ... ♗xe4 15 fg ♗xg6 is quite dangerous: 16 ♗h6 ♕b6+ 17 ♔h1 ♖fc8 18 ♖ab1 △ h2-h4-h5, which is a most unpleasant threat. Now Black has no active counterplay, so the acceptance of the pawn sacrifice is fully justified. But suppose that there is counterplay, i.e. 14 ... b5!? 15 a3 a5 16 hg fg 17 ♗h6 ♖e8? ...

> 15   ♘xe4   ♗xe4

Despite his extra pawn, Black's position looks dangerous in view of the weakness of his king's fortress, and the threat of f5-f6 and lack of necessary coordination in the operations of his forces.

> 16   ♗h6

A useful move which also drives the rook from the defence of the kingside. 16 ♗d3 is weaker: 16 ... ♗xd3 17 cd ♔h8 18 fg fg 19 ♗h6 ♖f6 20 ♖f3 ♗f8 or 17 ... d5!? 18 fg hg 19 ♕xe5 ♗d6 20 ♕d4 ♖e8

with chances for both sides.

> 16   ...   ♖e8

Black falls under a strong attack after 16 ... ♕b6+ 17 ♔h1 ♕xb2 18 ♗xf8 ♖xf8 19 ♗d3 ♗xd3 (19 ... ♗d5!? 20 c4 ♗c6 21 fg hg 22 ♗xg6 fg 23 ♕xg6+ ♔h8 ±± Vogt, but unclear according to Nunn, who gives 24 ♖xf8+ ♗xf8 25 ♖f1 ♗g7 26 h4 ♕e2 27 ♖f5, where he advises Black to take the perpetual check.) 20 cd ♕d4 21 ♖ac1 b5, Vogt–Möhring, 1977, and 16 ... ♗xc2 17 ♗xf8 ♗xf8 18 fg hg 19 ♕f3 ♕b6+ 20 ♔h1 ♗f5 21 ♗c4!, Veröci–Savereide, 1978.

> 17   ♔h1

Although White's attacking formation seems most dangerous there are no concrete mating threats. Now White threatens to chase the bishop from e4 with 18 ♗b5 ♗c6! 19 ♗c4, thereby weakening the defences of the king even further. It is terrible to have to recommend that Black defend the position with 17 ... ♔h8 18 fg fg, but it takes a lot of nerve (and optimism) to adopt another defence, such as 17 ... ♗f8 18 ♗xf8 ♖xf8 19 f6 ♔h8. In that case Black's entire defence rests on the power of the ♗e4 and the defensive manouvre ♖g8 and g5, for example 20 c3 g5! or 20 ♕g5! ♕c8 (20 ... ♗xc2? 21 ♖f3! ±) 21 ♗f3 ♕f5 22 ♕h6 ♖g8 23 ♗xe4 ♕xe4. The position on the board which arose at move 15 is typical and useful for independent analysis of the methods of attack and defence in general. Although we placed the symbol "∞" on this position, our sympathies, it must be admitted, lie with the White side.

B2

12   ♗d3

This move doesn't have the advantages of 12 ♕g3. Moreover, the manoeuvre of the bishop gives Black more opportunities to choose a future plan, since he does not have to worry about the defence of the g7-square.

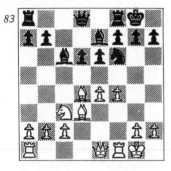

12   ...   ♞d7

Black tries to either effect the exchange of dark squared bishops, which will reduce the number of threats against his king, or to limit the activity of the White bishops by the routine e6-e5. Prophylaxis is obviously premature: 12 ... g6 only increases the power of the ♗d4. After 13 ♖d1 a6 14 ♔h1 b5 15 e5 de 16 ♗xe5! (16 fe is insufficient: 16 ... ♕xd4 17 ef ♗xf6 18 ♗xg6 ♕g4 19 ♞e4 fg! ∓) 16 ... ♞d7 17 ♗e4 and the White bishops develop strong pressure.

There is, however, an interesting manoeuvre which rarely occurs in the Sicilian Defence: 12 ... ♕d7!? which threatens ♞g4 and e6-e5. On 13 h3 Black is prepared for

active operations on the queenside with 13 ... b5 14 a3 a5, but even 13 a4 ♞g4 14 ♕g3 cannot prevent Black from obtaining an acceptable game with 14 ... f5! 15 ef ef 16 h3 ♗f6 17 ♞e2 ♞h6 18 ♕f2 a6 19 ♞c3 ♔h8 20 ♖ae1 ♞g8 21 ♗c4 ♖ae8 =, Matanović–Udovčić, 1965. Black's threat of ganging up on the e4-square ties down the white pieces.

White played more interestingly in the game Robatsch–Malich, 1971: 13 ♖d1 b5 14 ♗xf6!? ♗xf6 15 e5 ♗e7 16 f5, but Black's position turned out to be sufficiently solid after 16 ... ef 17 ♗xf5 ♕c7 18 ♞d5 ♗xd5 19 ♖xd5 de 20 ♕xe5 ♕b6+ 21 ♔h1 ♗f6 = Instead of 16 f5 Tal advises 16 ed ♗xd6 17 ♞e4 ♗xe4 18 ♗xe4, but even here White's advantage is minimal.

13   ♖ad1

Even on 13 ♕g3, 13 ... e5 is possible, e.g. 14 ♗e3 ef! 15 ♗xf4?! ♕b6+ 16 ♔h1 ♕xb2 ∓ or 14 fe de 15 ♗xe5 ♞xe5 16 ♕xe5 ♕b6+ 17 ♔h1 ♕xb2 18 ♖ad1 ♕a3! or 15 ♗e3 ♗c5! =

13   ...   e5

13 ... ♕c7 leads to a more conservative fight after 14 ♔h1 ♗f6 15 ♗xf6 ♞xf6 16 ♕h4 ♖fe8 17 ♖de1 e5. Boleslavsky's proposed 18 f5 does not, apparently, promise White much after 18 ... ♖ad8 19 ♖e3 ♕e7 20 ♖g3 ♔h8 21 ♕g5 ♕f8 22 ♖e1 d5.

14   fe   de

This is the simplest road to equality, although 14 ... ♞xe5 15 ♔h1 ♗f6! 16 ♕e2 ♞d7! is also solid. The excellent base on e5 guarantees Black a good game, for

example 17 ♗c4 ♗xd4 18 ♖xd4
♛b6 19 ♖xd6 ♛xb2 20 ♛d2 ♘e5,
Matanović-Korchnoi, 1965.

15	♗f2	♗c5
16	♗c4	♛b6
17	♗b3	

After 17 ♘d5 ♛xb2 18 ♗xc5
♘xc5 19 ♘e7+ ♚h8 20 ♘xc6 bc
White has no compensation for the
sacrificed pawn: 21 ♗xf7 ♛xc2!
22 ♖c1 ♛xe4.

| 17 | ... | ♘f6 |

The game is level. In order to
liquidate Black's battery along the
diagonal a7-g1, White must make
exchanges, and in this case the
weakness of the Pe4 takes away
any hope he might have for the
advantage.

13 10 ♘b3

1 e4 c5 2 ♘f3 ♘c6 3 d4 cd 4 ♘xd4
e6 5 ♘c3 d6 6 ♗e2 ♘f6 7 0-0 ♗e7
8 ♗e3 0-0 9 f4 ♗d7 10 ♘b3

The retreat of the knight is the
most unpleasant response to 9 ...
♗d7. Avoiding the exchange, White
liquidates Black's opening strategy
and in the majority of cases achieves
a position which is discussed in the
chapter on the Maroczy bind,
where the bishop often stands
badly on d7.

Since there are no threats out-
standing against Black, he can spend
a couple of moves coordinating the
operation of his pieces. The problem is, however, that the centre is
entirely under White's control, and
counterplay on the queenside is too
slow compared to White's pawn
storm on the kingside.

We examine the variations:

A 10 ... a5
B 10 ... ♛c7
C 10 ... a6

A

     10   ...   **a5** *(84)*

A seemingly active, but strategically faulty move. White obtains
the excellent outpost b5 for his
knight and interrupts the free
manoeuvring of Black's pieces.

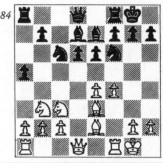

84

There is no great hope for the
central advance ... d6-d5, its effect
in any case being dubious.

     11   **a4!**

Not only does this transfix the
pawn at a5, but it also secures the
base on b5. The move 11 a3 is
illogical, as Black can equalise after
11 ... a4 12 ♘d4 (12 ♘d2?! d5! 13
ed ed ∓) 12 ... ♘xd4 13 ♛xd4 ♗c6
14 ♗f3 ♘d7 = Fichtl–Savon, 1974.

     11   ...   **e5**

The move 11 ... e5 has two
goals. Firstly, it takes away the d4
square from the ♘b3. Secondly,
Black hopes to advance ... d6-d5
without allowing White to push
past with e4-e5.

It is dangerous to delay this
move – 11 ... ♘b4 12 ♗f3 ♗c6?! 13
♘d4! g6 (13 ... ♛b8 14 ♛e2 ♖e8

15 ♖ad1 ♔h8 16 ♘db5 ♖a6 17
♖d2 ♖d8 18 ♖fd1 d5 19 e5
♘d7 20 ♕f2! ± Klovan–Vasyukov,
1968.) 14 ♖f2 e5 15 ♘xc6! bc
16 fe de 17 ♕f1 ± Karpov–Spassky,
1974.

12   ♔h1

There is another set-up for White
which promises Black a difficult
time: 12 ♖f2 ♘b4 13 ♗f3 ♕c7
(The manoeuvre 13 ... ♖c8 14
♔h1 ♖c4 also turns out to be ineffective after 15 fe de 16 ♖d2
♕c7 17 ♕g1! ♗d8 18 ♖ad1 ♗c6
19 ♗c5 with a clear advantage,
Geller–Reshevsky, 1970.) 14 ♖d2
b6 15 ♕e2. After 15 ... ♖fe8 16
fe de 17 ♖ad1 ♖ab8 (Christiansen–
Zichichi, 1980), Black holds the
balance with difficulty.

12   ...   ♘b4
13   ♗b5!

In the set-up with 12 ♖f2 White
left the bishop in a passive position.
Here, however, it wishes to play a
more active role, especially considering that Black would find an
exchange of light-squared bishops
unpalatable.

13   ...   ♗c6

After 13 ... ♗g4?! 14 ♕d2 ♖c8
15 ♖ac1 (15 ♕f2? ♖xc3!) 15 ...
♗e6 16 fe! White obtains a big
advantage with unexpected speed,
Suetin–Sax, 1976.

14   ♗xc6!   bc
15   fe   de
16   ♕e2!

Black has managed to liquidate
the weaknesses at d5 and b5, but
despite that, his problems have increased. The pawns at a5 and c6 are
very weak, and counterplay along

the c-file has been ruled out. On the
other hand, White has outposts on
c5 and especially at c4. It is not
clear how Black will be able to
create some chaos on the board,
in order that he might justify his
chosen plan and make some use of
his weak pawns. Certainly a simple
plan of campaign will not suffice,
for example 16 ... ♕c8 17 ♗c5
♗xc5 18 ♘xc5 ♘d7 19 ♘xd7
♕xd7 20 ♘d1 ♖ad8 21 ♘e3
(Moiseyev–Klein, 1978). Only after
16 ... ♘a6 17 ♕c4 ♕c7 is there any
hope for a successful defence.

B

10   ...   ♕c7

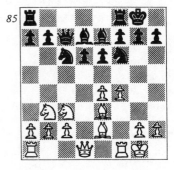

85

If Black wishes to adopt a waiting strategy then this move contains more prospects than 10 ... a6,
which needlessly weakens the pawn
structure. 10 ... ♕c7 is essential in
any event, if Black wants to go
hunting for the ♘b3. The immediate 10 ... ♘a5 is no good, since
after 11 e5 ♘e8 12 ♗d3 de 13 fe
♘xb3 14 ab ♗c6 15 ♗f4 White holds
a large spatial advantage.

The attention of tournament
players should also be turned towards the manoeuvre 10 ... ♕b8 △

b7-b5, for example 11 ♔h1 b5!
12 ♗xb5 ♘xe4. Black also stands
quite comfortably after 11 a4
♘b4! 12 ♗f3 ♖d8 13 ♖f2 ♗c6
14 ♘d4 ♗e8 15 ♖d2 d5 16 e5
♘d7. Petrushin–Godes, 1975.

After 10 ... ♕c7 White must
choose the appropriate moment for
the advance of his g-pawn:
B1 11 g4
B2 11 ♗f3

B1

   11 g4

There is a tempting idea to try
to outwit Black by luring him into
playing the useless (in the given
situation) move ... a6: 11 ♘b5 ♕b8
12 ♗f3 a6?! 13 ♘c3 ♕c7 14 g4 ±.
But instead of 12 ... a6, Black plays
12 ... ♘a5! and achieves equality,
exploiting the undefended white
knight: 13 ♘xa5 ♗xb5 14 c4 ♗d8!
15 cb ♗xa5 16 e5 de 17 fe ♖d8 =.

   11 ... d5!

11 ... ♖fd8 (or 11 ... ♖fc8) 12 g5
♘e8 probably gives Black fully adequate defensive capabilities, but he
does not, at first glance, seem to
have a very active position. Nevertheless, the old adage "an attack on
the flank should be parried by a
counterthrust in the centre" still
rings true.

   12 ed *(86)*

White can hang on to a small advantage after 12 e5, for example 12
... ♘e4 13 ♘xe4 de 14 c3 ♖fd8 15
♕b1 or 12 ... ♘e8 13 ♘b5 ♕c8 14
♗d3 g6.

   12 ... ♘b4!

An excellent discovery by Pritchett. Now after 13 de ♗xe6 Black's
pieces come alive and immediately

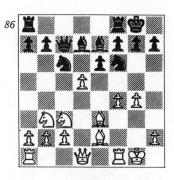

make their presence felt against
White's pawn storm. This unveils
the dark side of the immediate
advance g2-g4. The pawn structure
defending the White king is quite
hopeless, and this gives Black good
chances in the coming struggle.

Instead of 12 ... ♘b4, 13 ...
♘xd5 14 ♘xd5 ed is weaker. After
15 ♗f3! (dangerous is 15 ♕xd5
♘b4 16 ♕e4 ♖e8 or 15 ... ♖ad8!)
White holds on to his bishop and
with it the fortress surrounding his
king, in additional to his positional
advantage.

   13 ♗f3 ♘bxd5
   14 ♘xd5 ♘xd5
   15 ♗xd5 ed

The weakened pawn cover of the
White king and the bishop pair are
full compensation for the weakness
of the Pd5.

B2

   11 ♗f3! *(87)*

This is doubtless a wiser decision
than 11 ... g4. Black is not dis-
playing any activity, so White can
take time to increase his control
of the centre and keep his hand
hovering over that pawn on g2.

Besides 11 ♗f3, 11 ♔h1 ♖fd8

12 ♕e1 is also played, but after 12 ... ♖ac8, and later (against g2-g4) ♗e8, there arises a similar situation.

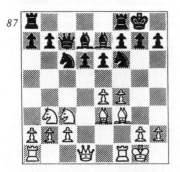

87

11   ...   ♖fd8

Here Black unprofitably changed direction in Klovan–Beliavsky, 1974, and came under a fierce attack after 11 ... ♘a5?! 12 e5 de 13 fe ♘xb3 (Taking the pawn leads to a loss of a piece: 13 ... ♕xe5 14 ♗d4 ♕c7 15 ♘xa5 ♕xa5 16 ♗xf6) 14 ef ♗c5 15 ab! ♗xe3+ 16 ♔h1 (Up to this point we are following analysis published by Boleslavsky in 1973.) 16 ... ♖fd8 17 ♗e4 ♗c6 18 ♕f3 ♗h6 19 ♗xc6 ♕xc6 20 ♔h3 ♖d2 21 ♖a4 ♖ad8 22 ♖g4! ♔f8 23 ♕h4! ±. This means that it is necessary to bring the rook into the game:

This is the most worthwhile move, and not only because it looks forward to the construction with ♗e8 and ♘d7. In the game Honfi–Hübner, 1974, Black obtained satisfactory play after 11 ... ♖ac8 12 ♕e2?! (Better is 12 ♘b5 ♕b8 13 c4 a6 14 ♘c3 ♖fd8 15 ♗b6 ♖f8 16 g4.) 12 ... ♘a5 13 ♘xa5 ♕xa5 14 g4 ♗c6 15 g5 ♘d7 16 ♖ad1

♖fd8 17 ♗g2 b5 18 a3 b4 19 ab ♕xb4 20 ♘c1 and now 20 ... ♗f8!

12   ♘b5!

If White plays an immediate 12 g4, then Black has either 12 ... ♗e8 or 12 ... ♘a5, as the ♗d7 is defended by the rook. After 13 g5 ♘e8 14 ♘xa5 ♕xa5 15 ♕e1 ♗f8! Black can finally hope for active counterplay based on the advance of his b-pawn.

The manoeuvre 12 ... ♘a5 is also available against other moves by White, say 12 ♖f2 or 12 ♕e2. This is another advantage of the move 11 ... ♖fd8.

Against 12 ♕e2 Black can construct a strong defence by 12 ... ♗e8 as well, i.e. 13 ♖ad1 ♘d7 14 g4 a6 15 g5 b5 16 a3 ♘c5 17 f5 ♘xb3 18 cb ♘e5 19 f6 ♗f8!

12   ...   ♕b8

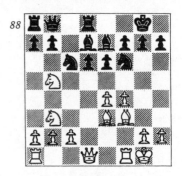

88

13   c4

13 a4 is less dangerous for Black: 13 ... e5 14 ♘c3 ♘b4 15 ♕d2 ♗g4! 16 ♕e2 ♗xf3 17 gf ♘h5 =, Balashov-Kuzmin 1974.

After 13 c4 there arises a critical position for the waiting strategy which was initiated by 10 ... ♕c7. Praxis has shown that after 13 ...

a6 14 ♘c3 b5 15 c5! b4 16 ♘a4
♝e8 17 ♛e1 dc 18 e5! ♘d5 19
♝xc5 ♛b5! 20 ♝xe7 ♘cxe7 21
♘ac5 a5 22 ♖c1 ♖ac8 Black has
sufficient counterplay: 23 ♝xd5
♘xd5 24 ♘e4 a4 25 ♘bc5 a3 26
ba ♘c3! ∓, Diesen-Rodriguez,
1976. But Black can also regroup
before pushing the b-pawn: 14 ...
♝e8 15 ♛e2 ♘d7 △ ... ♘c5, and
only then b7-b5.

The opening phase of the game
is completed. White has a spatial
advantage and some initiative, but
Black's position is viable and without weakness. The entire battle
lies ahead.

C

10   ...   a6

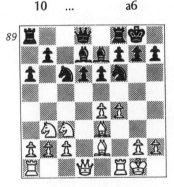

A waiting move which ensures
a peaceful life for the queen on c7
and provokes the opponent into
premature activity. By playing 10
... a6, Black must be prepared to
spend some time in "dull defence",
relying on the solidity of his
position.

White has a choice here. He can
either play 11 a4, cutting off any
possible activity on the part of his
opponent, or he can carry out his

own plan of attack, throwing Black
immediately on the defensive.

C1 11 ♝f3
C2 11 a4

C1

11   ♝f3

An immediate 11 g4 would be
a blunder. Black can play 11 ... b5
12 g5 ♘e8, after which White will
not be able to simultaneously main-
tain the pawn chain e4-f4-g5, and
also find a useful square for the
♘c3 to go to when attacked by the
b-pawn: For example, 13 ♝f3 b4
14 ♘e2 e5 ∓ or 13 ♛d2 b4 14
♘a4 ♖b8 15 ♝xa6? ♘a5! ∓

11   ...   ♖b8

11 ... b5 12 e5 de 13 fe ♘xe5
14 ♝xa8 ♛xa8 is a tempting exchange sacrifice which leads to
complications which favour White:
15 ♝d4! ♛b8 16 ♝xe5 ♛xe5 17
♖xf6 ♝d6 18 ♖f3 ♛xh2+ 19 ♔f2
♝c6 20 ♛h1 ±, Makarichev-
Moiseyev, 1968. Nor does 11 ...
♛c7 12 g4! b5 give Black equality,
because of 13 g5 ♘e8 14 a3. Black
cannot play 14 ... e5 due to 15 f5,
and if he adopts a waiting tactic he
will be buried: 14 ... ♖b8 15 ♛e2
♛c8 16 ♛g2 a5 17 ♖f2 a4 18 ♘c1,
and nothing will stop the attack on
the king, Suetin-Polugayevsky, 1966.
There is another interesting set-up
which Black can adopt: 11 ... ♛c7
12 g4 ♖fb8 13 g5 ♘e8 14 ♝g2
b5, which was encountered in the
game Hartston-Langeweg, 1967.
The drawback to this arrangement,
however, is the passivity of the
knight at e8.

12   g4   ♝e8

The difference between the

moves 11 ... ♕c7 and 11 ... ♖b8 are clearly illustrated by the variation 12 ... b5 13 g5 ♘e8 14 ♕d2 ♘c7 15 a4! (Tal considers 15 ♕g2 to be best, △ 16 f5 or 16 e5.) 15 ... b4 16 ♘e2 d5 17 e5. Here the choice of move at the 11th turn becomes important, as White's chances in this position are clearly better.

$$\begin{array}{lll} 13 & g5 & ♘d7 \\ 14 & ♗g4 & b5 \\ 15 & h4 & ♘b6 \end{array}$$

The plan of defence initiated by 12 ... ♗e8 is well known as far back as Ilyin-Zhenevsky-Sämisch, 1925, which was reached via 10 ♕d2 ♕b8 11 ♘b3 ♖fd8 12 ♖ad1 ♗e8 13 ♗f3 ♘d7 14 ♕f2 a6 15 ♖d2 ♕c7 16 ♖fd1 ♖ab8 etc.

Although Black's position seems a bit cramped, it appears that his defensive resources are sufficient to hold off White's attack: 16 f5 ♘c4 17 ♕e2 ♗d7!

C2

11   a4!

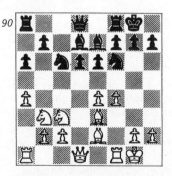

White not only refuses to allow the pawn to get to b5, but threatens in some circumstances to play a4-a5, stopping the b-pawn from reaching even the b6 square, as the a-pawn will then become rather difficult to defend, having to be supported by pieces. With his next moves Black must make a decision — to allow, or not to allow, the White pawn to reach a5, and more importantly, whether to advance the b-pawn.

The immediate blockade of the a-pawn with 11 ... ♘a5 has its drawbacks. The most important one is the weakened control over the e5 square. After 12 e5! ♘e8! (12 ... de 13 fe ♘xb3 14 ef ♗c5 15 ♗xc5 ♘xc5 16 fg is bad (±), as is 13 ... ♘e8 14 ♘xa5 ♕xa5 15 ♕xd7 ±) 13 ♘xa5 ♕xa5 14 ♘e4 ♕c7 15 ♗d4 ♗c6 16 ♗d3, Dvoiris-Kuzmichov, 1979 (△ 16 ... ♖d8? 17 ♘f6+! ±) or 14 ♕d2 ♕c7 15 ♗d4 f6 16 ♕e3! de 17 fe fe 18 ♗b6 ♕c8 19 ♖xf8+ ♗xf8 20 ♖d1! ♘d6 21 ♕xe5 ♘f5 22 a5! White solidly holds on to the initiative, Kapengut-Mikhailchishin, 1973.

Here the path divides:
C21 11 ... ♖ac8
C22 11 ... b6

C21

11   ...   ♖ac8

Praxis has eliminated other defensive formations, which do not come to terms with the threatened advance a4-a5. For example, 11 ... ♘b4 12 a5! ♗c6 13 ♗b6 ♕b8 14 ♕d2 (△ 15 ♘d1) 14 ... d5 15 e5 ♘d7 16 ♗d4 b5 17 ♗g4! g6 18 ♖fe1 ♖c8 19 f5! gf 20 ♗xf5! with devastation, Karpov-Cobo, 1972; or 12 ... d5 13 e5 ♘e4 14 ♗d3 (Karpov considers 14 ♗b6 ♕c8 15 ♘xe4 de 16 c4 △ ♕d2 ± to

be a stronger method.) 14 ... ♘xd3
15 cd ♘xc3 16 bc ♖c8 17 ♕d2
♕c7 18 ♖fc1 ♗b5 19 ♗d4 ♕d7
20 ♕e3 ♗a4 21 ♘c5 ±, Geller–
Bukić, 1967.

11 ... e5 is weak. Sax–Hulak,
1976, continued 12 ♘d5! ♘xe4?!
13 fe de 14 ♗d3 ♘f6 15 ♗b6 ♕c8
16 ♘xf6+ ♗xf6 17 ♖xf6 gf 18
♕h5 ±.

12 a5 *(91)*

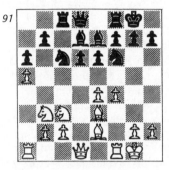

The prophylactic move 12 ♔h1
would allow Black to carry out his
blockading plan 12 ... ♘a5, which
was discussed above. In this case
after 13 e5 ♘e8 14 ♘xa5 ♕xa5 15
♕d2 ♗c6 16 b4 ♕c7 17 b5 ab 18
ab ♗xg2+(Tukmakov–Polugayevsky,
1972), the ♖c8 did its work. Other
continuations also lead to an equal
game: 15 ♗f3 ♗c6 16 ♗d4 de 17
fe ♖d8 18 ♗xc6 bc 19 ♘e2 ♘c7,
Geller–Polugayevsky, 1978, or 15
♘e4 ♕c7 16 a5 ♕xc2! 17 ed ♘xd6
18 ♘xd6 ♗xd6 19 ♖c1 ♕e4!. Another variation which fails to obtain
any advantage for White is 13 ♘d2
♕c7 14 ♕e1 ♘c6 15 ♕f2 ♘b4
16 ♖fc1 ♗c6 17 ♗b6 ♕b8.

12 ... ♕c7
The game Torre–Gheorghiu, 1981

led to a quick draw after 12 ... ♘b4
13 ♗f3 ♗c6 14 ♘d4 ♕c7 15 ♖f2
d5. But White could have played
more strongly on his last move: 15
f5, with which he would have retained the initiative since 15 ... e5?
would be answered by 16 ♘xc6 bc
17 ♘a4! ±.

13 ♗b6 ♕b8
14 ♕d2!

The conventional 14 ♗f3 just
loses time. After 14 ... ♘b4 15
♖f2 e5! 16 fe de 17 ♖d2 ♗e6
18 ♘d5 ♗xd5 19 ed e4! 20 d6
♗d8 21 ♖a4 ♗xb6 22 ab ♘d3!
Black even managed to gain the
advantage, Pritchett–Hartston,
1975, but this is due only to
White's error after an equal position had been reached in the
opening.

14 ... ♘b4
15 ♖fc1!

Here is the point of White's
manouevres. After 15 ♖ac1 complications unexpectedly arise – 15
... ♖xc3 16 bc ♘a2! Now, on the
other hand, White wishes to go
hunting for the knight, for example: 15 ... ♗c6 16 ♘d1! d5 17
e5 (17 c3?! ♘xe4 18 ♕e3 ♗d6!
is unnecessarily sharp) 17 ... ♘e4
18 ♕e3, arriving at a clear positional advantage after 18 ... ♗d7
19 c3 ♘c6 20 ♘f2. Black has no
choice.

15 ... e5
16 f5

The miserable position of the
knight – 16 ... ♗c6 17 ♘d1 d5
18 c3 ♘xe4 19 ♕e1 – forces Black
to enter into an inconclusive operation in the centre: 16 ... d5 17

♘xd5 ♘bxd5 18 ed ♗xf5. Black
has succeeded in emerging from
the opening without material loss,
but he has not achieved equality.
After 19 c4 it will be difficult for
him to erect a blockade against
White's threatening pawn chain on
the left side.

C22

11   ...   b6

By comparison with the favourable results in the classical Scheveningen, the set up with b6 is complicated by the position of the
bishop at d7. Located far away
from its home square on b7, it
leaves the defence of the a-pawn
to other pieces. Moreover, it eases
White's burden of defending the
e-pawn, and sits on a useful trans-
feral square in the Black camp. It
will take two moves to return the
bishop to b7, and White can make
use of this time to improve his
position. All of this promises difficulties for Black in the system
with 11 ... b6; continuing but not
hopeless, difficulties, which require
patience and precision in the
defence.

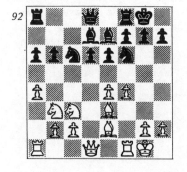

12   ♗f3

White has quite a wide range of
plans to choose from, from the
shelling of the a and b pawns to an
attack on the king itself. As far as
the majority of these plans are con-
cerned, the choice is purely a matter
of taste. To be perfectly honest,
the plan with 12 ♗f3 is only one of
several promising strategies.

Let us first consider some of the
other schemes and their fine points:
a) **12 ♖f2 ♕c7 13 ♕f1!** ♘b4 14
♗f3 ♖ac8 15 ♖d2 ♗c6 16 ♕f2
♘d7 17 ♘d4 ♗b7. White's manouevres were elegant but leisurely, and
Black, having regrouped, obtained a
fully satisfactory position.
b) **12 ♔h1 ♕c7 13 ♕e1.** White re-
groups and starts to play along the
lines of the classical Scheveningen,
preparing a piece attack on the king.
But in this case his queenside moves
(a4 and ♘b3) give Black a new
possibility for counterplay: 13 ...
♘b4!? 14 ♘d4 e5! 15 fe de 16
♕g3. White needs just one move to
catch his breath and defend the
pawn on c2. Black, therefore, must
find the best manner of defence
of the queen, in order to force the
white knight off d4 immediately ...
Black has the following possibilities
in this position: 16 ... ♕d6 17
♖ad1! ed 18 e5 ♘e4! 19 ed (Black
has an elegant manner of defence
after 19 ♘xe4 ♕g6 20 ♖xd4 ♗xa4
21 c3 ♘c2) 19 ... ♘xg3+ 20 hg
♗xd6 21 ♖xd4 ♗c5 22 ♖xd7
♗xe3 23 ♗c4! ♘xc2 24 ♖dxf7
♖xf7 25 ♖xf7 ♔h8 26 ♘d5 ♗c5
27 ♘c7 and White wins a pawn;
16 ... ♘e8 17 ♘f5 ♗xf5 18 ef ♔h8

(18 ... Nxc2 19 Nd5! is dangerous)
19 Rac1 Nf6 with complicated, but
approximately equal play; and
finally 16 ... Rfc8 17 Bh6 g6 18
Nf5 Bxf5 (18 ... Bd8 is also fully
playable) 19 Rxf5 Nxc2 20 Raf1
Qd6 and Black is successfully
defending.

c) 12 g4 Bc8 13 g5 Nd7 14 Qd2
Re8 15 Bf3 Bb7 16 Bg2 Bf8 17
Rf3! with an initiative for White
on the kingside.

By playing 12 Bf3, White at
first wishes to place his queen on e2
and assure the cooperation of his
rooks. Only then will he push forward the g-pawn.

    12   ...   Qc7 *(93)*

There is another set-up which
deserves analysis: 12 ... Rb8 13
Qe2 Qc8! 14 Rad1 Na5 15 e5 Ne8
16 Nxa5 ba 17 Bc1 Rb4! 18 Be4
de 19 fe Bc5+ with equal chances.
But the solidity of this arrangement may be called into question
by 14 Bf2 △ Bg3 or Bh4, where it
is by no means clear that Black can
equalise.

A solid, but passive, position was
reached in the game Ribli–Spassky,
1973: 12 ... Rc8 13 g4 Be8 14
Qe2 Nb4 15 g5 Nd7 16 Qg2 Kh8
17 Kh1 Nc5.

    13   Qe2!

A very powerful position for
the queen. Here it participates in
the battle on the entire board,
tying down the enemy rook to the
defence of the a-pawn and preparing to transfer to g2 in support
of the kingside pawn storm. The
immediate 13 g4 Rfd8 14 g5 Ne8
and 13 ... Bc8 14 g5 Nd7 15 Bg2

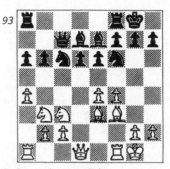

Re8 are also possible.

It pays to examine a rather similar situation, arising after 13 Kh1,
which is frequently reached via the
classical Scheveningen as well, by
the move order 6 Be2 a6 7 0-0 Be7
8 f4 0-0 9 Kh1 Nc6 10 Be3 Qc7
11 a4 Bd7 12 Nb3 b6 13 Bf3. The
move 13 Kh1 is less energetic and
less worthwhile than 13 Qe2, and
it is reasonable to assume that Black
will achieve equality here more
easily. Here are two recommend-
ations for Black:

a) 13 ... Rab8 14 g4 (On 14 Qe2
Black manages to reorganize with
14 ... Na5! 15 Nd2 (see also note a,
p. 17) 15 ... b5 16 ab ab 17 e5
Ne8 18 Qf2 Nc6 with equality,
Vogt–Tompa, 1979) 14 ... Bc8 15
g5 Nd7 16 Bg2 Re8 17 Nc1 Bf8
18 Nd3 b5, with equality, Geller–
Mukhin, 1973.

b) 13 ... Rfd8 14 Qe2 Be8 15
Bf2 Nd7 16 Bg3! Rdc8? (16 ...
Nc5 =) 17 Rad1 Nf6 18 e5! de 19
fe Be7 20 Nd4 Nxd4 21 Rxd4
Ra7 22 Rg4! with an attack for
White, Geller–Korchnoi, 1971. Or
16 Nd5!? ed 17 ed Nce5 18 fe
Nxe5 19 Bd4, Timoshchenko–
Platonov, 1975, with equal chances

after either 19 ... ♘xf3 20 ♖xf3
♗f8 or 19 ... ♗f8!? 20 ♗xe5 de
21 d6 ♗xd6 22 ♗xa8 ♖xa8.

13   ...   ♖fc8!

Black intends to regroup with
♗e8 and ♘d7, so he transfers his
rook to a more useful position, instead of allowing it to be shut in
by his kingside pieces.

Against 13 ... ♗c8 Boleslavsky's
14 ♕c4 (△ 15 ♘d5) forces the ugly
answer 14 ... ♗d8 (so that if 15
e5?!, 15 ... d5!).

An interesting, but very passive
defence is 13 ... ♗e8 14 g4 ♘d7 15
g5 ♘c5 16 ♗g2 f6!? 17 h4 ♗f7 18

f5 ♔h8 ±, Spassky–Petrosian, 1973.

14	g4	♗e8
15	g5	♘d7
16	♕g2	

This is the position which is
important for the evaluation of the
viability of Black's opening play
and chosen method of defence.
Above all White holds a large
amount of territory and consequently he carries out the plan
indicated in the note to 14 ♕e2,
but there is no real likelihood of
success. Black maintains a strong
defensive position, but there is no
great promise of active counterplay.

14 White fianchettos: 6 g3

The fianchetto of the king's bishop is one of the most solid methods of play available to White against the Scheveningen. The bishop on g2 paralyzes Black's play on the queenside, and hinders the advance d6-d5. Therefore the pawn storm on the kingside, which White will undertake only after he completes his development, will be all the more dangerous. Black's first task is to find the optimal deployment of his pieces, in order that he can initiate counterplay on the queenside. Many of the positions which will be examined in this chapter can be arrived at via a number of move orders, including not only the classical Scheveningen, but the Paulsen and Taimanov variations as well.

When White develops his bishop at g2, Black is faced with the same problems as in the Classical variation – whether or not to play ... a6, where should the ♘b8 go, and whether it is economical, in terms of time, to develop the kingside, etc.

(1 e4 c5 2 ♘f3 d6 4 d4 cd 4 ♘xd4 ♘f6 5 ♘c3 e6 6 g3)

A 6 ... ♘c6

B 6 ... a6 △ ♘bd7
C 6 ... a6 △ ♘c6

A

	6	...	♘c6
	7	♗g2	

The absence of pressure in the centre allows Black to put off castling for a while. First he can take prophylactic measures against the positional threat of ♘xc6 △ e4-e5. Now:

A1 7 ... ♘xd4
A2 7 ... ♗d7 (others)

A1

	7	...	♘xd4
	8	♕xd4	

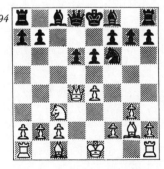

94

By exchanging knights Black avoids the positional threat of ♘xc6, but the strength of the ♗g2 is enhanced. Moreover, White has a very strong centre and threatens to play e5, opening the long diagonal. Therefore Black must not delay the transfer of his bishop to c6.

8   ...   ♗d7

The natural method of development – 8 ... ♗e7 9 0-0 0-0 lands Black in trouble after 10 e5! de 11 ♕xe5, after which it is very difficult for Black to develop his queenside, i.e. 11 ... ♕b6 12 a4 ♗d6 (12 ... ♗d7 13 a5 ♕a6 14 ♖d1! △ ♗f1) 13 ♕b5! ♕c7 14 a5 a6 15 ♕b6! with a clear advantage, Larsen–Kavalek, 1975.

9   e5

On the solid 9 0-0 Black will have time to reinforce his centre with 9 ... ♕c7.

9   ...   de
10   ♕xe5   ♗c6

This is the easiest way to parry the two threats, 11 ♗xb7 and 11 ♘b5. On the other hand, Black will be left with the problem of a weak pawn on c6, and White will retain a small but lasting positional advantage after 11 ♗xc6+ bc 12 0-0 ♗e7 13 b3 ♘d7 14 ♕e4 ♗f6 15 ♗b2 0-0. It seems, however, that Black's defensive resources will prove sufficient.

The other possible try for Black is 10 ... ♗b4 11 0-0 ♕b8 12 ♗f4 ♕xe5 13 ♗xe5 0-0-0 is connected with a pawn sacrifice: 11 ♗xb7 ♖b8 12 ♗g2 ♖b5 13 ♕e2 ♕c7. It demands thorough testing.

A2

7   ...   ♗d7

This move is played most frequently, in order to avoid the

breaking up of the pawns on the queenside. But is this really so terrible? Let's consider the position after 7 ... ♗e7 8 0-0 0-0 9 ♘xc6 bc 10 e5 de 11 ♕xd8 ♖xd8 12 ♗xc6 ♖b8

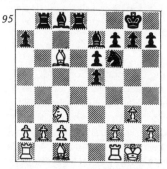

95

White's pawn majority on the queenside is balanced by the play of the rooks along the b- and c-files, and one mustn't forget that Black's pawns can advance along the e- and f-files. Here is an instructive example of Black's play from the game Larsen–Anderson, 1981: 13 ♖d1 ♗d7! (Black can afford to exchange bishops, but not rooks, as after 13 ... ♖xd1 14 ♘xd1 the ♗c1 would quickly enter the game.) 14 ♗xd7 ♘xd7 15 ♔f1 ♖b7! 16 ♘a4 ♖c8! 17 c3 f5 18 b3 ♔f7 19 c4 e4. White will have an advantage in the endgame, but for the moment there is a very double edged middlegame on the board.

8   0-0

White can retreat his knight, avoiding an exchange on d4, but as we shall see this exchange does not relieve Black's difficulties.

8   ...   ♗e7

8 ... a6 transposes into B.

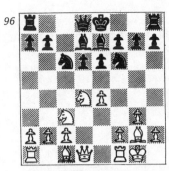

96

9 ♘ce2

In this position White has a wide choice of active and complicated plans, but in general all of them involve a strengthening of the centre followed by an attack on the flank. We examine a few of them:

a) 9 ♗e3 0-0 10 ♕e2 ♕a5 (also possible is 10 ... ♘xd4 11 ♗xd4 ♗c6 12 ♖fd1 ♕a5) 11 ♖ad1 ♘xd4 12 ♖xd4 e5 13 ♖d2 ♗e6 with an equal game.

b) 9 ♖e1 0-0 10 ♘xc6 ♗xc6 11 e5 de 12 ♗xc6 bc 13 ♕xd8 ♖fxd8 14 ♖xe5 ♗b4 or 11 a4 ♕d7 12 ♖e3 ♖fd8 13 ♖d3 ♘e8 14 b3, Browne–Petrosian, 1972 with approximately equal play.

c) 9 b3 0-0 10 ♗b2 ♖c8 11 ♘xc6 ♗xc6 12 a4 a6 13 ♖e1 ♕c7 14 ♕e2 ♖fe8 15 ♖ad1 ♕b8 16 ♖d2 d5! with a complicated struggle, Shamkovich–Sax, 1979.

d) 9 ♘db5 ♕b8 10 ♗g5 0-0 11 ♗xf6 ♗xf6 12 ♕xd6 ♖d8 13 a4 a6 14 ♕xb8 ♖axb8 15 ♘d6 ♘d4 16 ♘xb7 ♖xb7 17 e5 ♖xb2 18 ef gf with complex play, Wedberg–Sznapik, 1980.

e) 9 ♘de2 ♕b8!? 10 h3 b5 11 a3 a5 or 9 ... 0-0 10 b3 ♖c8 11 ♗b2 ♕a5 12 h3 ♖fd8 13 ♔h1 ♗e8 14

♕e1 b5 15 a3 ♕b6 16 ♖d1 b4 17 ab ♘xb4 18 ♖d2 a5 19 ♘d4 ♖c5! 20 ♘d1 d5! and Black has taken over the initiative.

f) 9 h3 0-0 10 ♘de2 ♕b8 11 a4 ♘b4 12 g4 ♖d8 13 g5 ♘e8 14 ♗e3 d5 15 ed ed 16 ♘xd5 ♘xd5, Iskov–Ligternink, Amsterdam, 1982.

By playing 9 ♘ce2, White hopes to place a pawn on c4, in which case the pawn-fangs c4 and e4 will control the centre of the board. The momentary weakening of the d5 square cannot be exploited: 9 ... d5 allows White to obtain the advantage by 10 ed ♘xd5 11 c4!

9 ...   0-0
10 c4

In the game Tseshkovsky–Kasparov, 1981, White tried to strengthen his left flank by the less obliging 10 a4 ♖c8 11 c3 (11 ♘b5 d5!) 11 ... a6 and then attack on the kingside. After 12 h3 ♕c7 13 g4?! Black quickly proved his counterplay in the centre – 13 ... d5! 14 ed ♘xd5 15 ♗xd5 ed 16 ♘f4 ♗c5 17 ♘b3 ♗a7 18 ♕xd5 ♗e6! 19 ♘xe6 fe 20 ♕e4 ♖xf2! and obtained a strong attack.

10 ...   ♖c8
11 b3   a6!

Now this move is most timely and is in no way a mere prophylactic. After 12 ♗b2 b5! 13 cb ♘xd4 14 ♘xd4 ab 15 ♕d2 ♕b6 16 ♖ac1 ♖fd8 the chances are equal, Gligorić–Boleslavsky, 1953.

B

6 ...   a6

Black delays the choice of destination of the ♘b8, and in the end puts it on d7.

7	♗g2	♛c7
8	0-0	♝e7

There is no great profundity involved in the delay of the development of the ♞b8, it is just that Black wants to avoid ♞xc6. Instead of 8 ... ♝e7, 8 ... ♝d7 is sometimes met. But it does not make sense to begin direct play on the queenside without the mobilisation of the kingside, given the placement of the White pieces. Usually after 8 ... ♝d7, White plays 9 ♖e1, and Black has nothing better than to return to known paths, i.e. 9 ... ♞c6 10 ♞xc6 bc 11 ♞a4 ♖b8 12 c4 c5 13 ♞c3 ♝e7 14 ♝f4 0-0 15 e5 ♞e8 16 ♛d2 with a positional advantage.

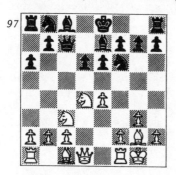

97

9   ♞de2

White must now decide how to develop the ♝c1 and also prepare a pawn storm on the kingside. Toward this goal he will transfer the knight to g3. As Black has not yet developed the ♞b8 White can also initiate the pawn storm immediately: 9 f4 0-0 10 g4! ♞c6 11 ♞xc6! bc 12 g5, i.e. 12 ... ♞d7 13 f5 ef 14 ef d5 15 ♔h1 ♝d6 16 ♛h5 ♖e8 17 f6 g6 18 ♛h4 ♞c5 or 12 ... ♞e8 13 f5 ef 14 ef d5 15

♔h1. In each case there arises a double-edged position with approximately equal chances.

9 ♞ce2 is weaker, and can be met by 9 ... ♞bd7 10 b3 ♞c5!

After 9 ♛e2 Black gets a good game with 9 ... ♞c6!

9	...	♞bd7
10	h3	0-0
11	g4	♖fd8

Not 11 ... ♞c5 12 g5 ♞fd7? in view of 13 b4!

12	♞g3	b5

Apparently best. The natural 12 ... ♖ab8 13 g5 ♞e8 14 f4 b5 15 a3 ♝b7 allows White to begin the attack with 16 f5.

13	e5	

In case of 13 g5 ♞e8 14 a3 ♝b7 15 f4 d5 Black saves a valuable tempo, striking at the centre after 15 ed ♞b6!

13	...	de
14	♝xa8	♞b6
15	♛e2	

White cannot save the bishop: 15 ♛f3 ♞xa8 16 ♛xa8 ♝b7 17 ♛a7? ♝c5 with a decisive advantage for Black.

15	...	♞xa8

Now White must take measures against threats along the a8-h1 diagonal, for example: 16 f4 ♝c5+ 17 ♔h2 (17 ♝e3 ef ∓) 17 ... ♝d4, or 16 ♖d1 ♖d4 17 ♝e3 ♖c4! or 16 ♖e1 ♝b7 17 ♛xe5 ♝d6 18 ♛e3 ♞b6. Black has sufficient compensation for the sacrificed exchange.

We conclude by examining variations with the knight on c6, which has a more considerable body of tournament praxis, especially in the past. As we noted earlier, this variation is relevant not only to the Scheveningen System, but to the Paulsen and Taimanov variations as well.

C

6 ... a6
7 ♗g2 ♛c7

Black can, if he so wishes, adopt a set up which does not include this move, for example 7 ... ♗d7 8 0-0 ♞c6 9 ♗e3 ♗e7 10 ♛e2 0-0

Nevertheless, praxis has shown that c7 is the only useful square for the Black queen against the fianchetto of the bishop by White. This is understandable; given the ideal placement of White's pieces, Black has no real chance to undertake active operations immediately. Therefore his best plan against the system with g3 is to regroup his force. So after 11 ♖ad1 ♛c7, we obtain a typical opening position, from which the middlegame can now develop. Before undertaking pawn operations on the kingside, White must retreat his knight, in order to avoid the standard type of counterattack with ♞xd4 and e6-e5. 12 ♞b3 b5 13 a3. Such a prophylactic moves gives Black

time to organize effective counterplay, for example 13 ... ♖ac8 14 f4 b4 15 ab ♞xb4 16 ♞d4 ♖fd8 17 g4 e5 18 ♞f5 ♗xf5 19 ef d5! (Klovan–Platonov, 1964) or 13 ... ♖ab8 14 f4 b4 15 ab ♞xb4 16 ♖c1 (Black was threatening 16 ... ♞xc2 17 ♛xc2 ♗a4!) 16 ... ♖fc8! 17 h3 ♗c6 18 ♞d4 ♗a8 19 ♗f2 ♛c4 20 ♛e3 ♗d8! (Dubinin–Estrin, 1962), promising Black excellent counterplay. Of course, instead of 10 ♛e2 White has a wide range of plans, but the positions which arise from these alternatives generally transpose into material considered below.

8 0-0 ♞c6

This move is the most exact, as after 8 ... ♗d7 9 ♖e1! ♞c6 White obtains a good position with 10 ♞xc6 bc (10 ... ♗xc6 11 ♞d5!?) 11 ♞a4 ♖b8 12 c4 c5 13 ♞c3 ♗e7, reaching a favourable variation for White, as the ♗d7 is misplaced. On 8 ... ♗e7 9 f4! 0-0 the lack of a threatened ♞xd4 allows White to begin flank operations immediately with 10 g4 ♞c6 11 ♞xc6 bc 12 g5.

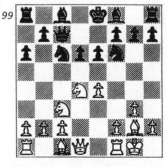

After 8 ... ♞c6 White can fortify

his position in the centre still further, leaving the pawn storm on the kingside to the second phase of the middlegame. Or he can limit his region of operations to the kingside. It pays to consider the middlegame strategy of the first type, as it best of all illustrates the prospects of the pawn storm:

9 ♘de2 ♗e7 10 h3 ♗d7 11 ♔h1 b5 12 a3 0-0 13 g4 ♔h8 (13 ... ♖fd8 14 g5 ♘e8 is another solid defence) 14 ♘g3 b4 15 ab ♘xb4 16 g5 ♘g8 17 f4 (It is obvious that without the aid of the f-pawn White will be unable to penetrate Black's fortress, but now Black opens up the centre) 17 ... d5! 18 ed ed. Black has a fully playable game, as it is dangerous to capture the pawn – 19 ♘xd5 ♘xd5 20 ♕xd5 ♗b5! 21 ♖e1 ♖ad8 – analysis by Bondarevsky.

Now we consider instances of a central strategy by White: 9 b3 ♗e7 10 ♗b2 0-0 11 ♘ce2 e5! 12 ♘xc6 bc 13 c4 ♗g4 14 f3 ♗h5 15 ♘c3 ♘d7 16 ♔h1 ♘c5 with equal play, Shianovsky–Spassky, 1962, or 9 ♖e1 ♗e7 10 ♘xc6 bc 11 e5 de 12 ♖xe5

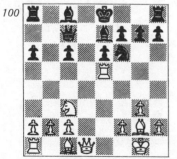

100

An original position! Instead of the usual pawn storms, there is lively piece play on the board. On 12 ... ♘d5 13 ♘xd5 cd 14 ♗f4 ♗d6 there follows 15 ♕xd5 ♗xe5 16 ♕xe5! If 12 ... ♗b7 13 ♗f4 ♗d6 White carries out a positional sacrifice of the exchange – 14 ♖xe6+! fe 15 ♗xd6 ♕d7 16 ♘c5! ♕xd1 17 ♖xd1 ♖d8 18 ♖e1 ♔f7 19 ♘e4! ♗xe4 20 ♗xe4 ♖he8, notwithstanding his material advantage, Black has an uphill fight for a draw, Browne–Langeweg, 1972. A still more amazing rook journey was proposed by Boleslavsky in answer to 12 ... ♗d6 – 13 ♕f3! ♗d7 14 ♖g5 ♔f8 15 ♖xg7 ♔xg7 16 ♗h6+ ♔g6 17 ♕e3! ♕a5 18 ♘d5! with unavoidable mate, or 14 ... ♖g8 15 ♕xf6! gf 16 ♖xg8+ ♗f8 17 ♗h6 ♔e7 18 ♗e3! with a strong attack. Only 12 ... 0-0 13 ♗f4 ♕b7 allows Black to obtain an equal game. It is considered that after 14 ♖e3 ♖d8 15 ♖d3 ♖xd3 16 ♕xd3 ♗d7 17 b3 ♗e8 18 ♕e2 ♖d8 19 ♘a4 ♘d5 20 ♗d2 White has the better chances, Barczay–Espig, 1976. This, it seems, is true, but Black can improve his play, for example, with 14 ... ♗c5 instead of 14 ... ♖d8. Then if 15 ♖d3 ♘d5 16 ♘xd5 ed! the way is clear for the white-squared bishop. Black, in our opinion, has solved all of his recurring problems, i.e. 17 ♖b3 ♕a7.

Returning to diagram 99, we consider two more options for White:

a) 9 ♗e3 ♗e7 10 ♕e2 ♗d7 11 ♖ad1 0-0. This position was examined above, in the case where the White knight journeys far from the kingside with 12 ♘b3. But White can also play without removing his knight from the centre: 12 f4 ♘xd4 13 ♗xd4 ♗c6 14 f5 e5 15 ♗e3 b5 (Sax–Cvetković, 1974) or 12 h3 b5 13 a3 ♘xd4 14 ♗xd4 ♗c6 15 g4 ♖fe8 16 f4 ♕b7, Lein-Jansa, 1965.

b) 9 a4 ♗e7 10 ♘b3 h6!? It is difficult to recommend such a method of defence. Instead of this move, one can play 10 ... b6 along the lines of the defence to the Maroczy bind in the classical Scheveningen. After 10 ... h6 White can reply 11 f4 0-0 12 g4 ♗d7 13 h4 b5 14 g5 ♘h7 15 ♗e3 b4 16 ♘e2. Black's opening play has not turned out well. The White king is surrounded by his own pieces, and he has the wall e4-f4-g5-h4, where the pawns act as if they are stones on a "go" board, forming a border on the kingside. The counterthrust 16 ... d5 leads only to the loss of a pawn after 17 ed ed 18 ♕xd5 ♖ac8 19 a5! ♘b8 20 ♘ed4! and White dominates the entire board, Nunn-Tal, 1982.

Summing up, the system with g3 is a very solid method of play for White, especially if he does not hasten to intensify the struggle. The basic merit of this system is its apparent harmlessness, especially when compared with the very sharp systems 6 g4 and 6 f4. If Black is aware of the subtleties of the position in the Sicilian Scheveningen, however, he can obtain a solid position against 6 g3 even if he does not know all of the complexities of the variations.

15 Keres Attack

1 e4 c5 2 ♘f3 e6 3 d4 cd 4 ♘xd4
♘f6 5 ♘c3 d6 6 g4

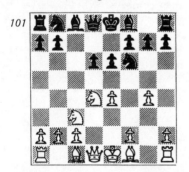

101

This early and aggressive advance of the pawn was inaugurated into tournament praxis by Panov in 1939. A bit later Keres began to adopt the variation regularly, and the system with 6 g4 received international recognition as the Keres Attack. Years passed, and the evaluation of individual lines changed, but the system with 6 g4 remains one of the most aggressive and dangerous formations for White. At first the Keres Attack was a tempting manner of saving time by comparison with the system involving 6 g3, and White arranged his forces with ♗g2, 0-0, h3 and ♘d4-e2-g3, later advancing the f and g pawns.

This was considered normal and has been applied up to the present time by a number of grandmasters. Now, however, the plan with queenside castling, involving ♗e3, ♕d2, and 0-0-0 is considered more dangerous for Black, as the kingside pawns advance quickly.

There are a number of move orders which sidestep the Keres Attack. If one leaves he knight on g8 and plays 4 ... ♘c6, for example. Then, however, White can play 5 c4 or 5 ♘b5 d6 6 ♗e2 ♗e7 and only after 7 0-0, then ... ♘f6. The move 4 ... ♘c6 is the Taimanov Sicilian, which is outside the scope of our book. A more original plan for White was played in Zaitsev–Fet, 1980, which continued 4 ... d6 5 ♘c3 ♗e7 6 g4! a6 7 ♗e3 b5 8 ♗g2 (8 ♖g1 ♗b7 9 a3 would have been more exact, as White could then answer 9 ... h5 with 10 g5!, stalemating Black's kingside.) 8 ... ♗b7 9 0-0 h5 10 gh ♘d7 11 a3 ♕c7 12 f4 ♘gf6 13 ♕e2 ♖xh5 14 f5! e5! 15 ♘e6 fe 16 fe ♕c4! 17 ed+ ♔xd7 with a draw, although Black's position holds the better prospects.

Naturally, the adoption of one

move order or another is a matter of taste, fashion, and sometimes even the constitution of the players. Even without examination, however, of all the fine points of the Keres Attack, one can conclude a priori that the thrust of the g-pawn cannot decide the battle, since Black's first five moves are a logical and natural system of development.

There is adventure, at first sight, anyway, in the move g4, which is supported by deep positional thought. Exploiting the fact that Black has for some time made moves which were not particularly active, even if they are useful, White rushes his pawn to g5, which not only secures a spatial advantage on the kingside, but also tries to set up full control over the central squares. The profit from his entire opening strategy hangs on the success White has in fulfilling this task. At the same time the advance of the g-pawn to g5, without having previously completed his development and before seeing to the safety of his king, can create severe weaknesses in the White camp. Nevertheless, Black must not try to casually refute this advance by immediately undertaking operations in the centre, where White pieces dominate the action.

Therefore 6 ... d5 almost forces the following position, which is quite bad for Black: 7 ed ♘xd5 8 ♗b5+ ♗d7 9 ♘xd5 ed 10 ♕e2+ ♗e7 11 ♘f5! The game Nikitin–Cherepkov, 1958, continued 11 ... ♔f8 12 ♗xd7 ♘xd7 13 ♗f4 ♕a5+

14 c3 ♖e8 15 ♘xe7 ♕c5 16 ♗e3 ♕xe7 17 0-0-0 ±.

Sometimes Black plays 6 ... ♗e7, which usually transposes into one of the variations below. It has no independent significance, although there are a few subtleties which must be observed.

Thus after 7 g5 ♘fd7 8 ♘db5 ♘b6 9 ♗f4 e5 10 ♗e3 ♗e6 11 f4 ef 12 ♗xf4

102

Black sacrifices a pawn to deliver his king from the centre and obtain good play: 12 ... 0-0! 13 ♕d2 (13 h4 f6 14 ♗xd6 fg) 13 ... ♘c6 14 ♘xd6 (14 0-0-0 ♗c4! ∓ Mednis–Amos, 1970) 14 ... f6!

The economy of 6 ... ♗e7 can be well illustrated in the following system: 7 g5 ♘fd7 8 h4 ♘b6! 9 ♗e3. After 9 ... d5 White has not even the single tempo he needs to continue his development with ♕e2 and 0-0-0, but 10 ♗b5+ ♗d7 is also fully acceptable for Black. If Black does not want to allow the bishop to b5, he can also play 9 ... 0-0 10 ♕e2 d5, since after 11 0-0-0? e5! he will be able to follow up with ... d4.

In the system without ... ♘c6,

where play continues 7 g5 ♘fd7 8 h4 a6 9 ♗e3 b5 10 a3 ♗b7 11 ♕d2 *(103)*

103

the "normal move" 11 ... ♘b6 (11 ... ♘c5 12 f3 ♘c6 is better, but still ±.) is a mistake because of the position of the bishop on e7, which allows White to obtain a strong attack by sacrificing a piece with 12 ♘xe6! fe 13 ♕d4! ♘c4 14 ♕xg7 ♔d7 15 ♗xc4 bc 16 0-0-0 ♕f8 17 ♖xd6+!, Karklins–Commons, 1972.

It is more difficult to evaluate the consequences of the move 6 ... e5. Black weakens the d5 square, but can count on counterplay on the dark squares of the kingside. White has a choice between two natural continuations: 7 ♗b5+ ♗d7 8 ♗xd7+ ♕xd7 9 ♘f5 h5 10 ♗g5 ♘h7 (If 10 ... ♘xg4?, then 11 h3!) 11 ♗d2 hg 12 ♕xg4 g6 13 ♘e3 ♗h6 12 0-0-0, Liberzon–Murei, 1978, and 7 ♘f5 h5 8 f3! (Black is given more possibilities after 8 g5 ♘xe4 9 ♘xg7+ ♗xg7 10 ♘xe4 d5; or 8 ♗g5 hg 9 ♘e3 ♗e6 10 ♕d2 ♘c6) 8 ... hg 9 fg g6 10 ♘e3 ♗e7 11 ♗g2 ♘c6 12 h3 ♘d4 13 ♕d3 ♗e6 14 ♗d2 ♘d7 15 0-0-0

♘c5 16 ♕f1, as in Brasket–Benjamin. As the reader will notice, in both cases White manages to retain his positional advantage, but it seems to us that this has only happened because of inaccurate play on Black's part. The continuation 6 ... e5, which stabilises the centre, is not without inner logic and deserves the careful attention of the reader.

We will now embark upon a journey through the three variations which are most commonly met in tournament practice. 6 ... h6 is the subject of the present chapter.

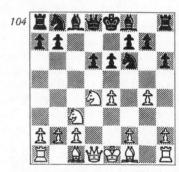

104

This way Black tries to keep the ♘f6 in place, where it can participate in the battle for the centre, and also hold up the kingside pawn storm. It is by no means easy to achieve these ends, however, in that the advance of the h-pawn practically rules out kingside castling, and it will take some time to get the king to the queenside. White can now play

A 7 ♖g1

B 7 ♗g2

C 7 ♗e3

D 7 g5
A

7   ⊞g1

White wants to chase the knight with the help of his pawns, and eliminates the opposition of the rooks on the h-file. The knight can be challenged with the direct 7 h4, of course, in which case it is not absolutely necessary that the rook move to g1. Usually after 7 h4 ♞c6 8 ⊞g1 play transposes below, but the other natural reply, 7 ... ♝e7, can give the game an original flavour, for example:

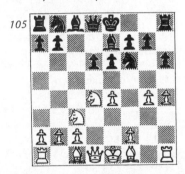

a) 8 ⊞g1 d5 9 ♝b5+ ♚f8 10 e5!? (10 ed ♞xd5 11 ♝d2 is not advisable, since after 11 ... ♝f6 12 ♞f3 ♞xc3 13 ♝xc3 ♝xc3 14 bc ♕xd1 15 ⊞xd1 ♚e7 Black's chances are preferable.) 10 ... ♞fd7 (10 ... ♞e4 11 ♞xe4 de looks dangerous, since after 12 g5 hg Black is faced with 13 ♝xg5, but after 13 ... a6 14 ♝a4 ♕a5+ 15 c3 ♕xe5 16 ♝xe7+ ♚xe7 17 ♕g4 g6 or even an immediate 17 ... ♞d7 there does not seem to be any real compensation for the sacrificed pawn.) 11 ♕e2 (Radulov has proposed a solid, if not particularly aggressive, for-

mation for White's pieces: 11 ♞f3 ♞c6 12 ♝f4 g6 13 ♕d2 ♚g7, where Black's defences are in good shape.) 11 ... ♝xh4 12 ♝e3!? ♞xe5 13 0-0-0 ♞bc6 14 ♞b3 a6 15 ♝xc6 ♞xc6 16 f4 ♝e7 17 g5! White has a strong initiative and a big lead in development in return for the two sacrificed pawns, Sokolov–Stoll, 1981/82. Sokolov's idea is quite interesting and holds good prospects for White.

b) 8 ⊞h3 d5! (After 8 ... ♞fd7 9 g5! hg 10 hg ⊞xh3 11 ♝xh3 the sacrifice on e6 is becoming a real threat.) 9 ♝b5+ ♚f8 10 e5 ♞fd7 (10 ... ♞e4 deserves consideration.) 11 ♝f4 (11 ♕e2!?) 11 ... ♕b6 12 ♞b3 (Hübner's advice is hardly better: 12 ♕d2 ♞c6 13 ♞xc6 bc 14 ♝f1.) 12 ... ♞c6 13 ♕e2 a6 14 ♝xc6 bc 15 0-0-0 a5 and Black clearly has the initiative, Torre–Hübner, 1979.

c) 8 ♕f3 h5 9 gh ♞xh5 10 ♝g5 ♞c6 11 0-0-0 ♝xg5+ 12 hg ♕xg5+ 13 ♚b1 ♞xd4 14 ⊞xd4 ♝d7 15 ⊞xd6 ♝c6 16 ♝e2 g6 with equal chances.

d) 8 ♝g2 g6 9 g5 hg 10 ♝xg5 (10 hg ⊞xh1+ 11 ♝xh1 ♞fd7 12 ♞db5 ♞b6 13 ♝f4 e5 14 ♝e3 a6 13 ♕xe7 ♚xe7 =) 10 ... ♞c6 11 ♞db5 ♞h5 12 ♝f3 a6 13 ♝xe7 ♚xe7 14 ♝xh5 ⊞xh5 and the initiative moves over to Black, Matulović–Sax, 1976.

7   ...   ♞c6

A useful and worthwhile move, but not the only answer. Black has other continuations, 7 ... a6 and 7 ... ♝e7, which secure favourable conditions for the advance of his d-pawn.

Now White has a choice.

A1   8 ♗e3
A2   8 h4

A1

8   ♗e3

Here we will consider the plan where White does not hasten to advance the h-pawn, but prefers to first complete his development. This is in accordance with one of the fundamental ideas of 6 g4: The Black king finds it difficult to escape from the centre.

Instead of 8 ♗e3, 8 ♗e2 is sometimes played, but after 8 ... d5!, or 8 ... ♕a5 9 ♘b3 ♕c7 10 h4 d5!, Black has an excellent game. The move 8 ♗e3 is more effective because it fortifies White's position in the centre.

8   ...   d5

Any delay with this pawn advance in the centre will allow White to carry out his kingside pawn storm, for example: 8 ... a6 9 h4! ♕a5 10 ♘b3 ♕c7 11 g5 hg 12 hg ♘d7 13 g6! The inclusion of 8 ... a6 9 h4 before playing d5 robs the thrust of its effect: 9 ... d5 10 ed ♘xd5 (10 ... ed? 11 g5! hg 12 gh ±) 11 ♘xd5 ed (11 ... ♕xd5? 12 ♗g2! ♕a5+ 13 c3 ±) 12 ♕e2 ♗e7 13 0-0-0, and it is difficult for Black to create counterplay and guarantee the security of his king.

9   ♗b5

White forces the ♗c8 to take up a passive position. Defending the knight with the queen is not on: 9 ... ♕d6? 10 f4 ♘xe4 11 ♘xe4 de 12 ♘xc6 bc 13 ♕xd6 winning, or 9 ... ♕c7 10 ed ed 11 ♕e2 ♗e7

12 g5 hg 13 ♗xg5 with strong threats.

9   ...   ♗d7
10   ed   ed
11   ♕e2   ♗b4!

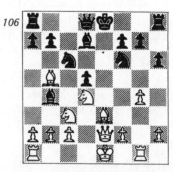

106

At first sight this seems extraordinarily risky, but, as analysis shows it is a justified decision. White cannot make a profit out of the discovered check because both of his most important pieces are on the e-file.

12 ♘xc6   ♗xc6!

12 ... bc is inferior: 13 ♗c5+ ♘e4 14 ♗xb4 cb 15 ♘xd5.

12 ... ♗xc3+ leads to an immediate catastrophe after 13 ♗d2+! Black's train of thought becomes clear after 13 ♗c5+ ♔d7!!. Unexpectedly, a very sharp position arises: 14 0-0-0 (but not 14 ♗xb4 ♖e8! ∓) 14 ... ♗xc3! (The white bishop turns out to be poisoned meat: 14 ... ♗xc5? 15 ♘xd5 ♔c8 16 ♗xc6 bc 17 ♕a6+ ♔b8 18 ♘xf6 ♕xf6 19 ♖d7 ♕f4+ 20 ♔b1 ♕b4 21 ♕xc6 ♖c8 22 ♕d5 f6 23 a3 ♕b6 24 ♖g3 winning.) 15 bc ♖e8 16 ♕d3 ♕a5 17 ♕f5+ ♖e6 18 ♖xd5+ ♔c8! 19 ♗xc6 bc 20 ♖e5 g6! and Black seizes the initiative.

13	0-0-0	♗xc3
14	♗d4+	♘e4
15	♗xc3	0-0

Black has fully solved his opening problems. After 16 ♗d4! ♛a5! 17 ♗xc6 bc 18 f3 ♘g5! 19 h4 ♖fe8 20 ♛d3 ♘e6 his counterplay may prove dangerous.

A2

8   h4

107

8   ...   d5!

Even here, this is the most active form of the battle for the centre, although the reality of the move g4-g5 makes Black's problems much more complicated. Attacking the centre with 8 ... e5 also deserves attention. We have already noted the special points of this form of pawn structure in our remarks concerning the move 6 ... e5. The results from the inclusion of the two White moves 7 ♖g1 and 8 h4 may turn out to be in Black's favour, for example: 9 ♘f5 h5 10 ♗g5 hg 11 ♘d5 (11 ♘e3 ♗e7 ∓) 11 ... ♗xf5 12 ♗xf6 ♛a5+! 13 c3 ♗xe4 14 ♗b5+. To those who enjoy defending the small centre we can recommend a less forcing variation of the type 8 ... ♘fd7 9 g5 hg 10 hg g6, or

even 8 ... g6 right away, which, however, guarantees White a prolonged initiative.

An advance of the kingside pawn chain with 8 ... h5 does not, in our opinion, solve Black's opening problems. White retains a spatial advantage and the initiative, i.e. 9 g5 ♘g4 10 ♗e2 ♛b6 11 ♗xg4 ♛xd4 12 ♗e3 ♛xd1+ 13 ♗xd1 ♗d7 14 ♘b5 ♔d8 15 ♗e2 a6 16 ♗b6+ ♔c8 17 ♘c3 △ f4 and 0-0-0, or 9 gh ♘xh5 10 ♗g5 ♘f6 (The character of the struggle is hardly affected by 10 ... ♛b6 11 ♘b3 a6 12 ♗e3 ♛c7 13 ♗e2.) 11 h5 ♛b6 12 ♘b3!? ♘xh5 13 ♖h1 g6 14 ♗e2 ♗d7 15 ♛d2! (15 ♗xh5 gh 16 ♖xh5 ♖g8 ∞) a6 16 0-0-0 ♛c7 17 ♔b1.

9   ♗b5

A typical manoeuvre, which forces the Black bishop to occupy a passive position. Two other attempts to enforce the initiative are available to White:

a) **9 ♘xc6** bc 10 g5!? hg 11 hg ♘d7 (The chances seem to be equal after 11 ... ♘e4 12 ♘xe4 de 13 ♛xd8+ ♔xd8 14 ♗g2 ♖h4! 15 ♖h1 ♖xh1 16 ♗xh1 f5 17 gf gf 18 ♗xe4 ♗d7 or 13 ♛g4 ♛a5+! 14 c3 ♛f5!) 12 g6 f6 13 ed cd 14 ♗b5 ♗b4 15 ♛e2 ♛c7! 16 ♗d2 ♛e5, Ivanović–Sznapik, 1981, with a complicated and double-edged fight.

b) **9 ed** ♘xd5 10 ♘xd5 ♛xd5 11 ♗g2 ♛a5+ 12 ♗d2 ♛e5+ 13 ♗e3 ♗d7 14 ♘xc6! ♗xc6 15 ♗xc6+ bc 16 ♛d4!, Belyavsky–Ghinda, 1980. Having a slight lead in development, White proposes to head into an endgame, where he will have the better chances thanks to his active bishop and the defects in Black's queenside pawn structure. Apparently, it is not worthwhile for Black to simplify and go into an endgame where he has a draw at best. The idea 13 ... ♘b4!? deserves consideration, in order to put the knight on d5. After 14 c4 ♗c5! 15 ♔f1 (15 ... ♗xd4 was threatened, and 15 ♘f3 would be parried by the simple 15 ... ♕c7) 15 ... 0-0! 16 a3? ♖d8! White's last move is obviously for illustrative purposes only, in order to point out the sort of dangers which White faces. Still, Black's chances are no worse.

9 ... ♗d7
10 ed ♘xd5

Because of the threat of 11 g5 Black cannot decline the exchange of knights.

11 ♘xd5 ed

108

12 ♗e3!

The attempt to attack directly gives Black good counterplay, as Liberzon has shown: 12 ♕e2+ ♗e7 13 ♘f5 ♗xf5 14 gf ♔f8! 15 c3 ♗f6 16 ♗e3 ♕a5! or 13 ♗e3 0-0 14 ♗xc6 bc 15 g5 c5. By sacrificing a pawn, White tries to bring the queenside pieces into the game in the quickest way possible.

12 ... ♕xh4

In the game Karpov–Spassky, 1980, Black accepted the pawn sacrifice in another guise: 12 ... ♗e7 13 ♕d2 ♗xh4 14 0-0-0 ♗f6 15 ♘f5 ♗xf5 16 gf a6 17 ♗xc6+ bc and fell under an attack after 18 ♗c5. The loss of two tempi on the journey of the black bishop is very risky. As later analysis showed, Black could have achieved a quite comfortable position by playing 13 ... ♘xd4 14 ♗xd7+ ♕xd7 15 ♗xd4 ♕e6+ 16 ♔f1 0-0 △ 17 ♖e1 ♕a6!.

13 ♕e2

If the queen occupies the f3 square, then Black can castle queenside immediately. With the queen on e2 it is not so easy for the Black king to flee the centre.

13 ... ♘xd4
14 ♗xd4+ ♕e7
15 ♗xd7+ ♔xd7
16 ♗e3

In the complicated endgame which arises after 16 ♕xe7+ ♗xe7 17 ♗xg7 ♖he8! 18 0-0-0 ♗g5+ 19 ♔b1 ♔c6, the activity of Black's pieces compensates for the defects in his pawn structure.

16 ... ♖d8
17 0-0-0 ♔c8

Black will not be able to hold on to his extra pawn because he will have to expend time on the development of his kingside pieces and in the defence of the pawn weaknesses on the queenside, but his position is still tenable, i.e. 18 ♕b5 a6 19 ♕b3 ♕b4! 20 ♖xd5 ♕xb3 21

Xd8+ ♔xd8 22 ab ♗d6 or 18 ♕f3!
♕e4! 19 ♕xf7 ♖d7 20 ♕f5 ♕xf5
21 gf b6 22 ♗d4 h5!

B

7 ♗g2

At first sight, a modest move,
but a very venomous and logical
conception, the basis of which is
the classical regrouping of White's
pieces before the initiation of the
kingside pawn storm. White does
not harass the f6 knight but plays
for development, in order to prove
that 6 ... h6 was a waste of time.

The other deployment of the
bishop: 7 ♗e2 ♘c6 8 ♗e3, allows
Black to equalize with the standard
counter-thrust 8 ... d5!, i.e. 9 ed ed
10 0-0 ♗b4!

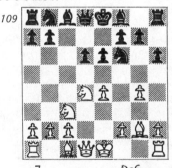

7 ... ♘c6

7 ... a6 and 7 ... ♗e7 are also
possible, and customarily transpose
or lead to situations of the type 7
... a6 8 h4 d5 or 7 ... ♗e7 8 h4 g6
9 g5 hg 10 hg ♖xh1+ 11 ♗xh1 ♘h5
12 ♗f3 ♘g7 13 ♗e3 ♘c6 14 ♕d2
♘xd4 15 ♗xd4 e5 with complicated play. It would be a mistake
for Black to undertake an immediate break in the centre with 7 ...
e5 8 ♘f5 h5 9 g5 since he doesn't
have the move 9 ... ♘xe4. 7 ... d5 is

also faulty on account of 8 ed
♘xd5 9 ♘xd5 ed 10 h3! (but not
10 ♕f3 ♘c6 11 ♗e3 ♘e5) 10 ...
♘c6 11 ♗e3 and Black has no
counterplay as compensation for
his chronically weak d-pawn.

8 h3! ♗d7

Another scheme of development
may also be recommended: 8 ...
♗e7 9 ♗e3 (9 ♘de2!?) 9 ... ♘e5
10 f4 ♘c4 11 ♗f2 ♗d7 12 b3 ♕a5
13 ♕d3 ♘a3 14 0-0 ♖c8 15 ♘ce2
0-0 16 c3 ♖fd8 17 ♖ac1, Hort–
Andersson, 1980) or 9 ... ♘xd4 10
♕xd4 e5 11 ♕d3 a6 12 0-0-0 ♗e6
13 f4 b5 14 f5. In each case Black
can fight for equality. A passive
formation such as 8 ... ♘xd4 9
♕xd4 ♗d7 10 f4 ♘c6 11 ♗e3 ♗e7
12 0-0-0 ♘d7 leaves Black with a
dreary defence.

9 ♗e3 ♗e7
10 ♕e2

The old method 10 ♘de2 0-0 11
0-0 is also interesting, although
after 11 ... ♘a5 12 b3 b5 13 a3
(13 e5 de!) ♕c7 14 ♕d2 ♖ac8
Black has counterplay. Contemporary defensive theory also holds
10 ... g5 in high regard, e.g. 11 ♕d2
♘e5 12 b3 ♕a5 13 f4 gf 14 ♗xf4
♗c6 15 ♕d2 h5 16 g5 ♘h7 16 h4
♘f8 △ ♘fg6. Here all of Black's
forces are strengthening the fortress
of the outpost at e5.

10 ♕e2 introduces a more logical
and more promising plan, first
applied by Grandmaster R. Byrne.

10 ... a6

Black cannot do without this
move. On 10 ... ♖c8 11 f4 ♘xd4
12 ♗xd4 ♕a5, 13 e5 de 14 ♕xe5!
is strong, giving the advantage to

White, Byrne–Estevez, 1973.

11 f4   ♛c7
12 ♕f2!

White makes it more difficult for Black to castle queenside, and practically forces Black to undertake some sort of action in the centre, which in the given situation only slightly improves his position: 12 ... ♘xd4 13 ♗xd4 e5 14 ♗e3 (14 ♗b6?! ♛c4! =) 14 ... ef 15 ♗xf4 ♗e6 16 0-0-0 ♘d7 17 ♖hf1 0-0-0 and Black has no counterplay which compensates for White's positional advantage.

C

7   ♗e3   a6

Most frequently 7 ♗e3 will transpose to previously analysed positions, i.e. after 7 ... ♘c6 8 ♖g1, or 8 h3 ♗d7 9 ♗g2. The position after 7 ... a6 is reached by another move order as well: 5 ... a6 6 ♗e3 e6 7 g4 h6 (i.e., from a Najdorf Sicilian). There are two alternatives to 7 ... a6 which deserve consideration:

a) 7 ... e5 8 ♗b5+ ♗d7 9 ♗xd7+ ♛xd7 10 ♘f5 g6 11 ♘xh6 ♗xh6 12 g5 ♘g4.

b) 7 ... ♗e7 8 ♕f3 ♘c6 9 ♘xc6 (9 ♖g1!?) 9 ... bc 10 0-0-0 e5! 11 ♖g1 ♘h7! (but not 11 ... ♗e6 12 h4 ♘h7 13 g5! hg 14 hg ♘xg5 15 ♛g3 f6 16 f4 ef 17 ♗xf4 ♛b6 18 ♗xd6 with a clear advantage for White, Belova–Minogina, 1981.)

Neither of these ideas has had a great deal of practical experience, which would allow us to reach definite conclusions on their merits. In our opinion 7 ... ♗e7 is no less promising than the text.

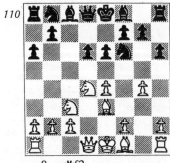

8   ♕f3

This move introduces an original transfer of the queen, and it has a tremendous amount of accumulated praxis, which distinguished it from these other continuations, which are of varying worth and interest:

a) **8 h4 b5?!** 9 a3 ♗b7 10 ♗g2 d5?! 11 g5 hg 12 hg ♖xh1+ 13 ♗xh1 ♘xe4 14 ♘xe6! ♘xc3 15 ♛h5! ±, Tseshkovsky–Mikhailchishin, 1981. Naturally, Black's play on the queenside, which he has not yet developed, is ineffective, but even 8 ... ♘c6 leads to White's advantage after 9 ♖g1, as has been discussed previously. Black can get counterplay, however, with 8 ... e5!? 9 ♘f5 g6, i.e. 10 ♘xh6 ♗xh6 11 ♗xh6 ♖xh6 12 g5 ♖h8 13 gf ♗e6 14 ♘d5 ♘d7!

b) 8 ♛e2 b5 (8 ... ♘c6 is possible.) 9 a3 ♗b7 10 f3 ♘bd7 11 h4 d5 12 ed ♘xd5 13 ♘xd5 ♗xd5 14 0-0-0 ♛c7 with a complex struggle, Sax–Ghinda, 1979 (15 ♘xb5?! ab 16 ♖xd5 b4!).

c) 8 ♖g1 ♗e7 9 ♕f3 ♛c7 10 h4 ♘fd7 11 g5 ♘e5 12 ♛g3 hg 13 ♗xg5 ♗xg5 14 hg (14 ♛xg5 ♛e7!) 14 ... ♘bc6 15 ♘b3 ♗d7 16 0-0-0 0-0-0 17 f4 ♘g6 with complications,

Velimirović–Hübner, 1979.
d) 8 f3 b5 9 ♕d2 ♗b7 10 0-0-0 ♘bd7 11 a3 ♖c8 with equal chances, according to Geller.

8 ...   ♘bd7

Now 8 ... e5 is insufficient because of 9 ♘f5 g6 10 ♘xh6 ♗xh6 11 g5 ♘g4 12 gh ♘xe3 13 ♕xe3 ♗e6 14 0-0-0, or 9 ... ♗e6 10 0-0-0 g6 11 g5 hg 12 ♘xd6+ ♗xd6 13 ♗xg5 ♗g4 14 ♕xf6 ♕xf6 15 ♗xf6 ♗xd1 16 ♗xh8 ♗f3 17 ♖g1, Novikov–Avshalumov, 1981, with a clear advantage for White in each case.

8 ... ♘c6 is quite possible, forcing White to defend the g-pawn. Now White must continue 9 ♖g1, as 9 ♕h3 ♘xd4 10 ♗xd4 e5! is not on. There was a beautiful attack in the game Horvath–Zinsel, 1980, which illustrates the punishment that awaits those who go pawngrabbing in the opening: 9 ... ♘e5 10 ♕h3 ♘exg4? 11 ♖xg4 e5 12 ♘f5 g6 13 ♖h4 gf 14 ef d5 15 0-0-0 d4 16 f4. Black could have obtained excellent counterplay, however, if he had played 10 ... ♘g6! 11 f4 e5!, i.e. 12 fe de 13 ♘f5 ♗b4 14 ♘xg7+ ♔f8 15 ♗xh6 ♔g8!

9 ♕h3 (111) ♘c5

Now on 9 ... ♘e5 there follows 10 g5!, but again the counterthrust 9 ... e5 looks promising, leading to a very sharp situation after 10 ♘f5 g6 11 g5 (11 ♘g3 ♘b6! 12 ♗e2 h5 13 ♕h4 ♗e7! ∓ Ermenkov–Polugayevsky, 1978) 11 ... gf 12 ef d5 13 0-0-0 d4 14 gf dc 15 ♗c4 ♕xf6 16 f4 ♘c5. These complications ended in Black's favour in Sax–Gheorghiu, 1981, so instead of 10 ♘f5 White should continue more peacefully. After 10 ♘b3 ♘b6 11 f3 ♗e6 the chances are equal.

10 f3   e5
11 ♘b3   ♗e6

The exchange 11 ♘xb3 is premature, as it allows White to take control of the centre with 12 ab ♗e6 13 ♗c4! ♗xc4 14 bc ♕c8 15 ♕f1!

12 ♘xc5

After 12 0-0-0 ♘xb3 13 ab ♕a5 14 ♔b1 ♖c8 Black obtains counterplay along the c-file and in the centre, in conjunction with the advance d6-d5. By exchanging on c5, White liquidates these counterchances and tries to take command of the d5-square.

12 ...   dc
13 ♕g3   ♗d6

The pawn sacrifice 13 ... ♗e7 14 h4 ♕a5 15 ♕xe5 0-0-0 is known from the game Sax–Tukmakov, 1978. It does not give Black sufficient counterplay after 16 ♗c4! ♗d6 17 ♗xe6+ ♔b8 18 ♕f5 fe 19 ♕xe6 ♖he8 20 ♕f7! Perhaps Black can improve somewhere along this chain of moves, but the position after 13 ♕g3 does not give Black any foundation for playing so sharply, when the sides are equally developed.

14 0-0-0 ♕e7

14 ... ♕c7 is a blunder on account of 15 ♝b5+.

Now Black has secured the right to castle queenside and has solved all of his opening problems.

D

7 g5 hg
8 ♝xg5

112

This is the most widely applied and logical reaction to 6 ... h6. Now after 8 ... a6 a position arises which is reminiscent of the Najdorf Sicilian, while after 8 ... ♞c6 the position resembles a Rauzer Attack. With the g and h pawns off the board, however, we have a situation which is clearly not in Black's favour, since his king cannot hide on its own flank, and this severely limits his choice of acceptable formations for his pieces. The fact that Black has a rook controlling the semi-open h-file does not change the evaluation of the position, since the play will take place in the centre of the board. The fundamental problem facing Black is therefore the evacuation of his king from the battle zone.

D1 8 ... a6
D2 8 ... ♞c6
D1

8 ... a6 *(112)*
9 ♝g2

It is difficult to give preference to any other plan. Both 9 f4 ♞bd7 10 ♕e2 (10 ♕f3!?) 10 ... ♝e7 11 0-0-0 ♞h5 12 ♝xe7 ♕xe7 13 ♕e3 ♞df6 14 ♝e2 e5, Kavalek–Szabo, 1967, and 9 ♕d2 b5 10 a3 ♞bd7

11 f4 ♝b7 12 ♝g2 ♕c7 13 0-0-0 ♞b6 14 ♕e2 ♞c4 15 h4, Kosten-Kurajica, 1980, lead to complicated struggles, and the choice of plan is largely a matter of taste. With the bishop on g2, Black should probably put his queen's knight on c6, since after 9 ♝g2 ♞bd7 10 ♕e2 ♕c7 11 0-0-0 White can more easily develop an attack.

9 ... ♝d7
10 ♕e2 ♝e7
11 0-0-0 ♕c7

White controls a great deal of space, but Black's defences are solid. Both 12 f4 ♞c6 13 ♞f3 ♞h5 14 ♝xe7 ♞xe7 15 ♕d2 ♞g6 16 ♞e2 0-0-0 and 12 h4 ♞c6 13 f4 0-0-0 14 f5 ♚b8 leave White with a small initiative, but Black has more chances to equalize.

D2

8 ... ♞c6 *(113)*
9 ♕d2

This is the most frequently played move, though it is quite possible that 9 ♞b3 is more promising, since then the queen can be placed on either d2 or e2, for example 9 ♞b3 a6 10 f4 ♕c7 11 ♕e2 b5 (or 11 ... ♝e7 12 ♝g2 ♝d7 13 0-0-0 ± or 11 ... ♝d7 12

0-0-0 🖀c8 13 ♗g2 b5 ±). The game Karasev–Krogius, 1971, continued 12 0-0-0 b4 with a complicated battle, but 12 a3! is stronger, limiting Black's counterplay while retaining his edge on the kingside.

There is another move order, which is even more subtle: 9 h4! ♛b6 10 ♘b3, with which White retains his choice of squares for the queen, but at the same time Black is forced to waste time on withdrawal, i.e. 10 ... a6 11 ♛e2 ♛c7 12 0-0-0 b5 13 ♗h3 ♗e7 (13 ... b4!? 14 ♘d5 ed 15 ed+ ♘e7) 14 f4 ♗b7 15 🖀he1 e5 16 fe ♘xe5 17 ♛g2 ±, Zhuravlev–Pyaeren, 1977.

9 ... ♛b6

It is useful to drive the knight from its active position in the centre, but Black must not delay. Both 9 ... ♗d7 10 0-0-0 ♛b6 11 ♘db5! 0-0-0 12 ♘a4, Zaitsev–Zhelyadinov, 1966, and 9 ... ♗d7 10 0-0-0 a6 11 f4 ♛b6 12 ♘f3! ♛c7 13 e5, Nikitin–Goldin, 1971, give White a clear advantage.

Now the knight must leave the centre, because both 10 0-0-0 ♘xd4 11 ♛xd4 ♛xd4 12 🖀xd4 a6 13 f4 (13 ♘a4 ♘d7!) 13 ... ♗d7

14 e5 ♗c6! and 10 ♗e3 ♘g4 11 ♘a4?! ♛d8 12 ♗g5 ♘xd4! favour Black, as does 10 ♘db5 a6! 11 ♗e3 ♛d8 12 ♘d4 ♘g4 13 ♗g5? ♘xd4.

10 ♘b3 a6

Interesting, although hardly strategically correct, is Magerramov's idea 10 ... ♘e5 11 ♛e2! (11 ♗e2 🖀h3!) 11 ... ♗d7. There are two ways in which White can obtain the advantage: 12 0-0-0 🖀c8 13 f4 ♘c4 14 🖀d4 ♘a5 15 ♛d2 ♘xb3 16 ab ♘g4 17 ♗e2 ± Chiburdanidze-Erenskam 1978, and 12 f4 ♘eg4 13 e5! ♗c6 14 ef gf 15 ♛xg4 ♗xh1 16 ♗xf6 🖀xh2 17 ♗d4, which is in textbook style.

It is still more dangerous to move the knight one move later: 10 ... ♗d7 11 0-0-0 ♘e5. Mariotti-Balashov, 1976 continued 12 ♗e3! ♛c7 13 f4 ♘c4 14 ♗xc4 ♛xc4 15 e5! de 16 fe ♘d5 17 ♘xd5 ed 18 ♘a5! ±, where Black has no compensation for his lagging development.

11 0-0-0 ♗d7

The plan with 11 ... ♛c7 (Δ b7-b5-b4), seems risky, since the king is still in the centre, thus making suspect early queenside operations. Nevertheless, praxis has not yet managed to find a reliable way to stamp "±" on it.

a) 12 ♗e3 b5 13 ♗g2 b4 14 ♘a4 🖀b8 15 f4 e5 16 h3 ♗e6 (16 ... ♗d7 17 ♛f2! ♘d4 18 ♘xd4 ed 19 ♗xd4 ♗xa4 20 e5! with an attack.) 17 ♛f2 ♘d7 with a complicated game, Shershnev–Pokrovsky, 1973/74.

b) 12 f4 b5 13 ♗g2 b4 (13 ... ♗b7 14 ♛e3! b4 15 ♘a4 ♘d7 16 e5 d5

17 f5! +, Razuvayev–Commons, 1978) 14 ♘a4 e5 15 fe de =, Ghinda–Nun, 1979.

After 11 ... ♗d7 the game takes on a more peaceful character.

Black has managed to avoid serious danger and has not had great difficulty in completing his development. All the same, however, he has not managed to reach equality, since White is setting the pace on all parts of the board. Black's king position on the queenside will not be sufficiently solid, and the coordination of his pieces in such a cramped space will prove difficult. The game can now develop in several directions, dictated by the next few moves, but in each case White will have an initiative.

a) **12 ♗e3 ♕c7** 13 f4 b5 14 ♗g2 ♖c8, Stein–Krogius, 1964/65.

b) **12 ♗f4 ♘e5** 13 ♗e3 ♕c7 14 f4 ♘c4 15 ♗xc4 ♕xc4 16 e5, Romanishin–Krogius, 1971.

c) **12 ♗g2 ♘e5?** (More solid is 12 ... ♕c7 or 12 ... ♗e7) 13 f4 ♘c4 14

♕d4 ♕c7 15 e5! ♘h7 16 ♗h4 ±, Chiburdanidze–Kushnir, 1970.

d) **12 f4 ♕c7** 13 ♗e2 b5 14 a3 b4 15 ab ♘xb4 16 ♗f3 ♖b8? (16 ... ♖c8! 17 ♔b1 e5 =) 17 e5 de 18 fe ♘h7 19 ♗e3 ±, Zaitsev–Padevsky, 1980.

12   h4

The most common plan. White liberates his rook, and plans to push the pawn to h5 with the help of his bishop, after which the support for the ♘f6 begins to shake.

12   ...   ♕c7

In principle, Black should be able to do without this move, for example 12 ... ♗e7 13 ♗e2 0-0-0 14 h5 ♔b8 15 f4 ♗c8 16 ♗f3 ♘g8. The queen move, which liberates the path for the Pb7, is more active.

13   ♗e2   ♗e7

13 ... b5 14 a3 b4 15 ab ♘xb4 16 h5 ♗e7 17 f4 ♖c8 18 ♔b1 e5 is also quite possible. By leaving the pawn on b7, Black prepares a hiding place for his king.

14   f4   0-0-0
15   h5   ♔b8
16   ♗f3   ♗c8
17   ♕e3

This position, which is characteristic of Black's defensive set-up, was reached in Spassky–Ribli, 1976. Black's position is solid, but passive. Therefore it should come as no surprise that most of the evaluations of 6 ... h6 conclude that it is comparatively passive and not quite sufficient for equality.

16 Keres Attack with 6 . . . a6

1 e4 c5 2 ♘f3 e6 3 d4 cd 4 ♘xd4
♘f6 5 ♘c3 d6 6 g4 a6

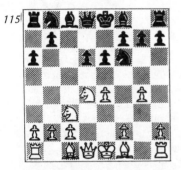

In this chapter we will consider
the variation where Black starts off
by developing the queenside, without moving the ♘b8 to c6. With
this approach he tries to cut down
on White's active operations and
create pressure on the a8-h1 diagonal as quickly as possible, target-
ing the Pe4. The big drawback to
this method is obvious – the ♘d4
is "unmarked" and this makes
Black's counterplay much more
difficult to obtain.

7   g5!

If White stops to think about
fortifying his centre or playing on
the queenside, his kingside attack
will quickly disappear, and then
the defects of his position, caused
by the early advance of the g-
pawn, will become important. On
7 ♗g2 Black can continue 7 ... ♘c6,
without worrying about 8 ♘xc6 bc
9 e5 because of 9 ... ♘d5 10 ed
♕xd6 11 ♘e4 ♕c7 12 c4 ♘f4! 13
♗xf4 ♕xf4 14 ♘f6+ ♔e7! Planinc-
Ribli, 1973. After 7 a4 Black has
a wide choice of continuations:
7 ... ♘c6, 7 ... d5, 7 ... e5. In each
case the advance of the flank pawn
by White proves ineffective.

It is worth paying some attention
to the move 7 ♗e3, because positions from the Najdorf Sicilian can
be reached. Therefore, besides 7 ...
h6, which was considered previously, we will look at three other
continuations.

a) 7 ... b5 8 g5 b4?! 9 gf bc 10
fg ♗xg7 11 b4! (11 b3 ♘d7 12
♖g1 ♗f6   13 ♕h5! is not bad,
either, as White has the initiative,
Tseshkovsky-Dvoiris, 1980.)

b) 7 ... d5 8 e5 ♘fd7 (8 ... ♘e4 9
♘xe4 de 10 ♗g2 ♕a5+ 11 ♕d2
♕xe5 is also possible.) 9 f4 ♗e7
10 ♕f3 ♘c6 11 0-0-0 g5! 12 ♕h3
♘xd4 13 ♗xd4 gf 14 ♔b1 ♗c5

with equal chances, Tseshkovsky-Palatnik, 1980.

c) **7 ... e5!** 8 ♘f5 g6. Since e3 is occupied, all that is left for White is the gambit 9 g5 gf 10 ef, which was introduced into tournament praxis by the Hungarian chessplayer Perenyi. The sacrifice of a piece sharply intensifies the situation, but in our opinion White does not have sufficient compensation after 10 ... d5 11 ♕f3 d4 12 0-0-0 ♕c7.

7   ...   ♘fd7

Here White must choose a plan:

A 8 ♗g2
B 8 ♗e3

A

8   ♗g2

White tries to carry out the kingside pawn storm immediately, without wasting time on prophylactics.

Sometimes 8 ♗c4 is played, which invites Black to fall into the trap 8 ... b5? 9 ♗xe6 fe 10 ♘xe6 ♕a5 11 ♗d2! ± But instead of 8 ... b5? the ♘d7 can take up an active position, which gives Black sufficient time to regroup:

a) **8 ... ♘e5** 9 ♗e2 (9 ♗b3 ♘bc6

10 ♘xc6 ♘xc6 11 ♗e3 ♗e7 12 f4 ♘a5 =) 9 ... b5 10 a3 ♘bc6 11 ♗e3 ♘xd4 12 ♕xd4 ♘c6 13 ♕d2 ♗e7 14 f4 0-0 15 0-0-0 ♕a5 =

b) **8 ... ♘b6!** 9 ♗e2 (9 ♗b3 d5! 10 ed ed =) 9 ... e5 (9 ... d5 is also possible.) 10 ♘b3 ♗e6 11 ♗e3 ♗e7 =

8   ...   b5

8 ... ♘c6 is more solid, of course, but as we are dealing with the analysis of lines with 6 ... a6 where Black does not play ... ♘c6, we shall not consider it here.

Black can also try to place his king on the queenside with 8 ... ♕c7 9 0-0 ♘c6 10 ♘de2 b5 11 a3 ♗b7 12 ♘g3 ♘b6 13 f4 0-0-0!? where the two sides have castled to the less common flank. Now White's pawn storm is weakened, but the position of Black's king on the queenside does not allow him to carry out active operations and his limited manouvering space makes it difficult to obtain counterplay in other regions of the board. Besides, White can play more strongly, i.e. 10 ♘xc6 bc 11 f4 d5 ±.

9   f4

White also maintains a marked initiative after 9 ♗e3 ♗b7 10 0-0, i.e.

a) **10 ... ♘b6** 11 ♕g4 ♘c4 12 ♗c1 g6 13 b3 ♗g7 14 ♖d1 ♘c6 15 ♘ce2!, Liberzon–Espig, 1972.

b) **10 ... ♘c5** 11 a3 ♘c6 12 f4 ♗e7 13 ♕g4 ♘xd4 14 ♗xd4 e5 15 fe ♘e6, Sax–Georgiev, 1980.

9   ...   ♗b7

10   f5!?

An interesting gambit attack, which picks up the pace of the game sharply. Once again, White can choose to develop an attack quickly without resorting to drastic measures:

a) **10 a3** ♘b6 **11 0-0** ♕c7 **12** ♔h1 g6 **13 f5**, Damjanović–Petrosian, 1978.

b) **10 0-0** b4 (10 ... ♘c6 is more solid.) **11** ♘ce2 ♘c5 **12** ♘g3 d5 **13 e5** ♘c6 **14** ♗e3 g6 **15 a3!** ♘xd4 **16** ♕xd4 ba **17 b4!**, Sveshnikov–Georgadze, 1978.

c) **10 h4** ♘c6 **11** ♗e3 ♖c8 (the only move.) **12 0-0** ♗e7 **13 f5** ♘xd4 **14** ♗xd4 e5 **15** ♗e3 ♘b6 **16 f6!**, Holmov–Donchenko 1980.

    10   ...   b4

Black cannot afford to open lines with 10 ... ef **11** ♕e2! or 10 ... e5 **11** ♘de2 ♗e7?! **12 f6!** gf **13** ♘g3! fg **14** ♘f5 ±, so he must sharpen the position.

    11   fe

The withdrawal of the knight by 11 ♘ce2 is not only unprofitable for White, but even eases Black's task.

    11   ...   bc
    12   ef+

After 12 ed+ ♘xd7 **13 0-0** or **13** ♘f5+ White also gets the initiative "for free", and these also seem dangerous.

    12   ...   ♔xf7
    13   0-0+   ♔e8!

This position has not yet appeared in tournament praxis, but a good deal depends on its evaluation. Can Black restrain the activity of the ♘d4? It seems to us that White has an attack which compensates him for the sacrificed material. Still, it is hardly worth pawn

grabbing here. After 14 ♕f3 ♘e5 **15** ♕xc3, Black's defence is still not easy, but after **14** ♘e6! ♕b6+ **15** ♔h1 White is putting some very difficult problems before his opponent.

B

    8   ♗e3

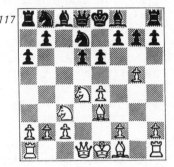

117

This is the most popular continuation. There has been so much tournament activity in these lines that there is a wide range of alternatives, which include some very interesting plans:

a) **8 a4** ♘c6 **9** ♗e3 ♘de5 **10** ♗e2 (10 ♘b3 ♘a5) 10 ... ♘xd4 **11** ♕xd4 ♘c6 **12** ♕d2 Δ f2-f4 guarantees a spatial advantage. The idea of exchanging the ♘d7 for the ♘d4 is often met in practice, but it is too slow and therefore has little effect.

b) **8** ♖g1 b5 **9 a3** ♘b6 **10** ♖g3!? ♗b7 **11** ♗g2 ♘bd7 **12 b3** g6 **13** ♗b2 e5! **14** ♘de2 h6 **15 h4** hg **16 hg** ♗e7 **17** ♕d2 ♘c5, Brueggemann–Espig, 1979. Although Black has seized the initiative, White's formation with 10 ♖g3 and 11 ♗g2 is original and deserves further polishing.

c) **8 f4** b5? (8 ... ♘c6 **9** ♗e3 ♗e7

reaches a position which will be analysed later.) 9 f5 ef (9 ... ♘e5!?) 10 ♘xf5 ♘e5 11 ♗f4 ♘8c6 12 ♘d5 ♗e6 13 ♕e2 ♖c8 14 0-0-0, Belyavsky-Vogt, 1980. White has a strong attack.

d) **8 h4** b5 9 h5 ♗b7 (9 ... b4 10 ♘ce2 ♗b7 11 ♘g3 ♘c5 12 ♗g2 d5 13 g6 hg 14 hg ♖xh1+ 15 ♗xh1 de 16 gf+ ♔xf7 ∞ requires detailed analysis.) 10 ♗g2 ♘c6 11 a3 ♖c8 with a complicated position which is favourable for White, Cardoso-Petrosian, 1975.

　　8　　... b5

Continuations such as 8 ... ♕c7 or 8 ... ♗e7 are too passive.

　　9　a3!

A modest, but quite useful move, which fixes the Black pawn duo for a considerable time. Now White can again occupy himself with the organization of a storm on the kingside.

The advance 9 a4 initiates play all over the board and can lead to success only if there is a difference in the abilities of the players. The game Smyslov-Vogt, 1977, continued 9 ... b4 (9 ... ba!?) 10 ♘a2 ♗b7 11 ♗g2 ♘c5 12 ♘xb4 ♘xe4? (12 ... ♗xe4 13 ♗xe4 ♘xe4 14 ♕g4 d5 =) 13 ♕g4 d5 14 ♘d3 ♗e7 15 h4 ♘d7 16 0-0 0-0 17 ♖fd1 ♖c8 18 c3 and although White achieved success, no one else has taken up this "wide" strategy for White.

White's attack may prove to be dangerous after 9 f4 ♗b7 (9 ... b4?! is weaker, as White has gained a tempo after 10 ♘ce2 ♗b7 11 ♗g2 ♘c5 12 ♘g3 ♘bd7 13 0-0.) 10 f5!?

b4. Tal considers that after 11 fe! bc 12 ef!+ (12 ed+ ♘xd7 ∓) 12 ... ♔xf7 13 ♗c4+ ♔e8 14 0-0 or 14 bc, White has great attacking possibilities, although there is no obvious direct method of continuing the attack.

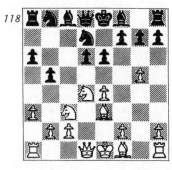

　　9　　...　　♘b6!

Praxis has already passed judgement on the transfer of the knight to c5, and it is a negative one since there is no real threat to the e-pawn, and the ♘c5 will hinder Black's traditional counterplay along the c-file: 9 ... ♗b7 10 ♕d2 ♗e7 11 h4 ♘c5 12 f3! ♕c7 13 0-0-0 ♘bd7 14 ♗xb5! ± , Fischer-Najdorf, 1960. Or 9 ... ♗b7 10 ♖g1 ♘c5 11 ♕g4 ♘bd7 12 0-0-0 ♗e7?! 13 f4! ♘xe4 14 ♘xe4 ♗xe4 15 ♗g2! ♗xg2 16 ♕xg2 0-0 17 f5 ef 18 ♘xf5! ± , Vasyukov-Dzhindzhihashvili, 1972.

Usually the moves 9 ... ♘b6 and 9 ... ♗b7 lead to one and the same positions.

　　10　　♖g1

10 ... h6 is a good reply to **10 f4**, as after 11 g6 ♕h4+ and the position of both kings is shaky. 10 ♕d2 finds the White queen in an insufficiently aggressive post. Korsun-

sky–Timoschenko, 1979, continued
10 ... ♗b7 11 0-0-0 ♘8d7 12 f4
♖c8 13 ♗d3 ♘c4 14 ♗xc4 ♖xc4
15 ♖he1 ♘c5! 16 ♗g1 ♗e7 17 b3
♖xc3! ∞.

10 ♗g2 ♘8d7 11 f4 looks sufficiently solid, White already threatens to break through with f4-f5-f6,
and on 11 ... e5 he can answer 12
♘c6! ♕c7 13 ♘b4 ±, but not 12
♘f5? g6! 13 ♘xd6+ ♗xd6 14
♕xd6 ♘c4 15 ♕d3 ♘xb2 16 ♕d5
♘c4! 17 ♗h3 0-0! 18 ♕xa8 ♕a5
19 ♗d2 ♘7b6 ∓, Estrin–Espig,
1971.

The direct plan of attack is also
an interesting thought: **10 h4 ♗b7
11 h5 ♘8d7 12 ♖h3!?** After 12 ...
♗e7 13 g6! ♗f6 14 ♕g4 ♕e7 15
gf+ ♔xf7 16 0-0-0 The Black king
is in serious danger, Pokojowczyk–
Sznapik, 1978. White stands better
after 12 ... ♘c5 13 ♕g4 ♕d7, as
well.

With the rook move White prepares a direct pawn storm, which
has the Pe6 as its target. The light
squared bishop finds work without
moving from its square.

10   ...   ♘8d7

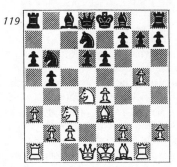

119

11 h4
Puzzling complications arise if the
f-pawn advances: 11 f4 ♗b7 12 f5
e5 (12 ... ef 13 ef ±) 13 ♘e6!
Shamkovich published exhaustive
analysis in the January 1979 issue
of *Chess Life and Review*. The basic
variation runs 13 ... fe 14 ♕h5+!
♔e7! 15 fe ♔xe6 16 0-0-0! ♔e7
17 g6 ♘f6 18 ♗g5! ♕e8 19 ♗h4!
♘d7 20 ♗h3 ♔d8 21 ♗xd7 ♔xd7
22 ♗xf6 gf 23 ♕f5+ ♕e6 24 g7
♕xf5 25 gh = ♕! ♗h6+ 26 ♔b1
♗xe4! 27 ♖g7+! ♗xg7 (27 ...
♔e6 28 ♘xe4!) 28 ♕xg7+ ♔e6
29 ♘xe4 ♕xe4 30 ♕c7! ±. This
is beautiful and complicated, re-
quiring practical tests.

11   ...   ♗b7
12 h5   g6
It would be dangerous for Black
to allow g5-g6.

13 ♖h1!
The culminating point of the
opening battle. Black has not
managed to create real counterplay, and White's initiative on the
kingside threatens to become dangerous. On 13 ... ♗g7, 14 hg hg 15
♖xh8+ ♗xh8 16 ♘dxb5! ab 17
♘xb5 might occur, and after 13 ...
♖g8 14 hg hg 15 ♖h7 ♗g7 16 ♕f3
♘f8 17 ♖h1 Black is faced with a
difficult defence. Apparently, then,
Black should deviate from the
above analysis by· meeting either 8
♗e3 or 8 ♗g2 with 8 ... ♘c6, but
this method of defence, as we re-
marked earlier, is reserved for the
next chapter.

17 Keres Attack with 6 . . . ♘c6

1 e4 c5 2 ♘f3 d6 3 d4 cd 4 ♘xd4 ♘f6 5 ♘c3 e6 6 g4 ♘c6!

The most logical answer to White's flank attack. By continuing to develop his pieces naturally, Black creates pressure in the centre of the board, which requires his opponent to solve the problem of the knight on d4.

Another logical developing move, 6 ... ♗e7, has already been discussed.

7 g5

White cannot manage without this move, since after 7 ♗g2 the g4-pawn falls to 7 ... ♘xd4, while on 7 ♗e3 or 7 h3, both 7 ... ♗e7 and 7 ... d5 are good.

In chasing the knight from f6, White guarantees that he will dominate the centre for some time.

7 ... ♘d7

It would be a mistake to exchange knights before the ♗f8 has emerged. After 7 ... ♘xd4 8 ♕xd4 ♘d7 the White queen seriously hinders the development of Black's kingside. One of the first games in which 6 g4 was played, Keres–Bogoljubow, 1943, continued 9 ♗e3 a6 10 ♗e2 ♕c7 11 f4 b6 12 f5 ♘e5 13 fe fe 14 a4 ♗e7 15 h4 ♕c5 16 ♕d2 ♕c7 17 ♖f1 ♗b7

18 ♗d4 ♖f8 19 0-0-0 ±.

After 7 ... ♘d7 White is at a crossroads. He can either begin active operations in the centre, or prepare an attack on the Black king with either pieces or pawns.

A 8 ♘db5
B 8 ♗e3

A

8 ♘db5

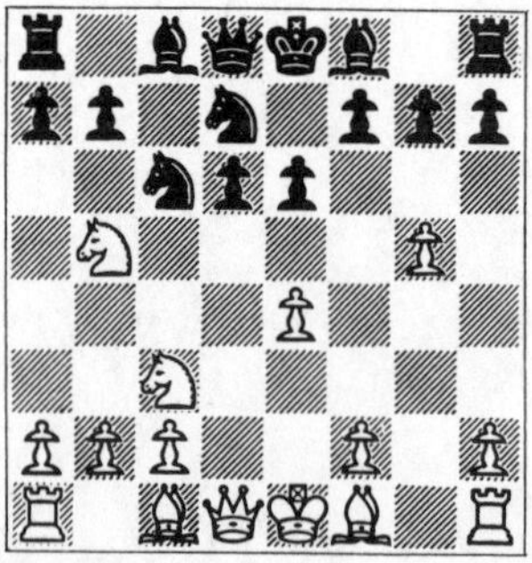

There are positional considerations which allow White to create concrete threats early in the game. These include the weakness of the Pd6, which is an important pawn for Black and the possibility to increase the pressure on this pawn; while on the other hand Black's pieces find it difficult to manoeuvre, limited for a time to a small portion of the board.

8 ...   ♘b6

This is the only acceptable square for the knight, since 8 ... ♘de5 provokes the advance of the f-pawn: 9 f4 ♘g6 10 h4 or 10 ♗e3 a6 11 ♘d4 ♘xd4 12 ♕xd4 ±. If 8 ... ♘c5 9 ♗f4 ♘e5 (9 ... e5 allows 10 ♘d5! ♘e6 12 ♗e3 ±), then 10 b4! ♘a6 11 a3 ♗e7 12 ♗g3! is strong, since the ♘b5 will cut off the Black pieces for a long time.

9 ♗f4   ♘e5

Less subtle, but quite possible is the method of defence with 9 ... e5 10 ♗e3 ♗e6, where Black fixes his central pawn structure for no essential reason.

10 ♕h5! *(121)*

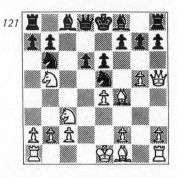

The entire attack is based on this move, which is not at all obvious. The queen not only liberates d1 for the rooks, but thereby enables the Pd6 and ♘e5 to be attacked. On the edge of the board it holds several hidden threats, such as 11 ♗xe5 de 12 g6!

It is tempting, at first glance, to force Black to forfeit his castling privilege with 10 ♗xe5 de 11 ♕xd8+ ♔xd8 12 0-0-0+ ♗d7 13 ♗e2 a6 14 ♘d6 ♗xd6 15 ♖xd6 but White is worse in the endgame in view of the weakness of his kingside pawns: 15 ... ♔c7 16 ♖d3 h6! 17 ♖f3 ♖af8 18 ♖g1 g6, Vitoliņš–Kapengut, 1976.

10 ...   ♘g6!

Black cannot kick the knight with 10 ... a6 because of 11 0-0-0! ab 12 ♗xe5 ±.

The natural reaction 10 ... g6 surprisingly only helps White: 10 ... g6 11 ♕h3! ♗d7 (11 ... a6 12

0-0-0 ♘bc4 13 ♗xc4 ♘xc4 14 ♘xd6+ ♗xd6 15 ♗xd6 ♕b6! 16 ♘a4 ♕c6 17 ♕c3! ±) 12 0-0-0 ♕b8 13 ♕g3! and catastrophe on the d6 square is inescapable.

Praxis also frowns upon 10 ... ♗d7?! 11 ♗xe5 de (11 ... g6? 12 ♗xd6 ±) 12 g6 a6 13 gf+ ♔e7 14 ♘a3 ♕c7 15 0-0-0 g6 16 ♕h4+ ♔xf7 17 ♘c4 ♘xc4 18 ♗xc4 ♗e7 19 ♕g3! and White has a clear advantage because of the hopeless position of the Black king and the real threat of an attack via h2-h4-h5, Szabo–Ivkov, 1973.

11 ♗g3

The bishop must retreat, since 11 ♗xd6 ♗xd6 12 ♖d1 is refuted by the unexpected resource 12 ... 0-0! 13 ♘xd6 ♕e7! Lagging in development, and with his king still in the centre, White must then turn his thoughts toward achieving an equal game despite his healthy extra pawn.

By retreating the bishop to g3, White holds the d6 pawn under observation, trying to create an attack on the king by playing in the centre.

Against the other retreat, 11

♗e3, we recommend 11 ... a6 12 ♘d4 d5! 13 0-0-0 ♗b4 14 ♘de2 0-0 13 h4 ♘c4 16 ed ♕a5! with extra-ordinarily complex play.

11 ...   a6
12 ♘bd4   ♗e7

12 ... h6 would be a mistake on account of 13 gh ♖xh6 14 ♕a5!, and it will be difficult for the Black king to escape. 12 ... d5!, however, deserves attention along the lines that have just been discussed.

13 0-0-0   ♗xg5+
14 ♔b1   0-0
15 ♖g1

By sacrificing a pawn, White has managed to create pressure in the centre and on the kingside. After 15 ... ♗f6 16 f4 ♕c7? 17 ♖d3! White quickly obtained an attack in the game Chiburdanidze–Kozlovskaya, 1979, but this would not have happened if instead of 16 ... ♕c7, Black had played 16 ... e5! 17 fe ♘xe5 with a strong defensive position and an extra pawn for Black.

B

8 ♗e3

The most precise move order. White does not commit his king's bishop to one diagonal, and at the same time liberates his queen from the necessity of guarding the ♘d4. Castling queenside enters into his plans.

Still, it is not so easy for Black to solve his opening problems after 8 ♗g2, either. The advance d6-d5 will be more difficult, and Black will have to spend some time before he can hope to find counter-play. After 8 ... a6 we reach a position that can arise by trans-position after 6 ... a6, and we now give the analysis which was promised back in Chapter 15.

122

a) 9 ♗e3 ♘de5 10 0-0 h6 11 gh ♕h4 12 ♘f3 ♘xf3 13 ♕xf3 g6 14 ♖ad1 ♗xh6 with a complicated game, Ubilava–Anikayev, 1976.

b) 9 f4 ♕b6 10 ♘b3 h6 11 ♕e2 hg 12 ♗e3 ♕c7 13 fg ♘ce5 14 0-0-0 b5, and again Black has a satisfactory position, Byrne–Peters, 1975.

c) 9 h4 (This is the most dangerous plan. The f-pawn, as will be seen in the examples below, is best left on its home square for the time being.) 9 ... ♘xd4 (On 9 ... ♕c7, 10 h5 is a strong reply.) 10 ♕xd4 b5 11 a4! (Against the conventional 11 ♗e3 ♗b7 12 f4, Black succeeds in creating counterplay by 12 ... ♖c8 △ ... ♖c4.) 11 ... e5 12 ♕d1 ba 13 f4 ♗b7 14 f5 ♖c8 15 0-0. White's chances are preferable, Razuvayev–Ree, 1975.

Let us return to the plan with 8 ♗e3. Now Black must reveal his opening strategy, and the decision which he now takes will largely dictate the moves of the coming battle.

With his next move Black can either take his king away from the centre and then prepare counterplay in the middle of the board, or he can force the advance of the d-pawn, or he can leave his king in the centre and force counterplay on the queenside.

B1 8 ... ♗e7
B2 8 ... ♘b6
B3 8 ... a6

B1

8 ... ♗e7

The beginning of a most natural and worthwhile plan. White must now unveil his plans, since the Pg5 is threatened.

Sometimes the knights are exchanged immediately, but this does not allow Black to escape difficulties: 8 ... ♘xd4 9 ♕xd4 ♘e5 (9 ... a6 see Keres-Bogoljubow, 1943, p. 120.) 10 ♗e2 ♘c6 11 ♕d3 ♗e7 12 ♗f4 0-0 13 0-0-0 e5 14 ♗e3 ♗e6 15 ♘d5 ♕a5 16 a3, Nunn-Jansa, 1979. This example gives a pretty good picture of the battle which takes place when the knights are exchanged early in the game. White need not attack the position of the Black king with pawns. He holds a long lasting initiative which guarantees him complete domination of the centre, and Black's pieces will be tied to the defence of the Pd6. Against 8 ... ♘de5 (△ 9 f4 ♘xd4 10 ♗xd4 ♘c6), we can recommend 9 ♘b3 after which Black has a choice between coming to terms with the retreat of the knight after f2-f4, or securing its position in the centre with the aid of an original, but strategically

risky, operation: 9 ... h6 10 hg g5!? 11 ♗e2 ♕f6.

After 8 ... ♗e7 White must either transfer his big guns to the kingside or prepare the pawn storm.

B11 9 h4
B12 9 ♖g1!

B11

9 h4

In principle it is not very important which pawn moves forward. If 9 f4 one must consider the possibility of 9 ... h6, although the double-edged play after 10 hg ♖xh6 11 f5 ♗h4+ 12 ♔e2 ♗g5?! 13 ♘db5, or 10 g6 ♗h4+ 11 ♔d2 is profitable for White.

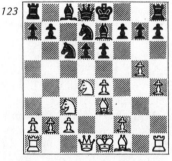

123

9 ... 0-0

This looks risky, but as praxis shows, it is an acceptable method of defence. Its positive points are clear. Black can take up arms for the operations in the centre and on the queenside. In order to succeed in the attack, White must create flaws in the pawn protection of the Black king, and this is a complicated matter.

Besides, instead of 9 ... 0-0 Black can play 9 ... ♘b6, since on 10 f4 he will have a choice between 10 ...

d5 and 10 ... h6, which is not un-profitable for him in the situation: 11 ♗g2 hg 12 hg ♖xh1+ 13 ♗xh1 ♘c4! 14 ♗c1 ♕b6 or 11 gh ♗xh4+.

9 ... a6 usually leads to a trans-position of moves, especially if White plays 10 ♕d2, for example 10 ... ♘xd4 11 ♕xd4 0-0 12 0-0-0 b5 13 ♖g1 ♖b8! 14 h5 b4 15 ♘d5?! (15 ♘e2 e5! 16 ♕c4 ♘c5 ∞) 15 ... ed 16 h6 ♘e5 17 f4 ♕c7 ∞, Pokojowczyk-Timoshchenko, 1979. Sometimes we find the plan of attack with 10 ♕e2, in which case White can use both central files for his operations in the middle of the board. What can happen to Black if he plays imprecisely can be seen in the game Karpov-Dorfman, 1976: 10 ♕e2 ♕c7?! 11 0-0-0 b5 12 ♘xc6! ♕xc6 13 ♗d4! b4 14 ♘d5! ed 15 ♗xg7 ♖g8 16 ed ♕c7 17 ♗f6 ♘e5 18 ♗xe5 de 19 f4 ±. If Black had played the standard 10 ... ♘xd4 (instead of 10 ... ♕c7), then the game might have taken on a more double-edged character after 11 ♗xd4 0-0 12 0-0-0 b5, for example 13 a3 ♗b7 14 f4 ♕a5 or 14 ... ♖c8, △ 15 h5? e5 16 ♗e3 ♖xc3 etc.

10   ♕d2

It is still too soon to determine the position of the ♗f1.

a) 10 ♗c4 ♘b6 11 ♗b3 (or 11 ♗e2) 11 ... d5 12 ed ed 13 ♕e2 ♗b4 = Ivkov-Gligorić, 1966.

b) 10 ♗g2 a6 11 f4 ♘xd4 (11 ... ♖e8 12 0-0 ♗f8 13 f5?! ♘de5! is possible, if somewhat passive.) 12 ♕xd4 b5. The ♗g2 can hardly be said to assist the pawn storm. After

13 ♕d2 ♘b6 14 b3 ♕c7 15 f5 d5!; 13 f5 d5!; or 13 h4 b4! 14 ♕xb4 (14 ♘a4 e5 15 ♕xb4? d5! ∓) 14 ... ♖b8 15 ♕d4 e5 16 ♕d2 ef 17 ♗xf4 ♖xb2 (Savon-Espig, 1972), complications arise which are fa-vourable for Black, while if 13 0-0-0-0-0 ♕a5 14 a3 ♖b8 or 14 f5 b4 the chances in the coming battle are roughly equal.

c) In answer to **10 f4** Black should not hasten to play e6-e5, since after 10 f4 ♘xd4 11 ♕xd4 e5 White saves an important tempo, and this can lead to a position which holds few prospects for Black in view of the chronic weakness of the Pd6. Black can quietly develop his pieces on the queenside, with-out worrying about the advance of the f-pawn, and anticipate the move-ment of the queen to d2, for ex-ample: 10 ... a6 11 ♕d2 ♘xd4 12 ♕xd4 b5 13 0-0-0 ♗b7 14 ♗e2 e5 or ♕a5 with an acceptable game. The fight in the game Dobosz-Danailov, 1979, is worth analysing: 11 ♕f3 ♖e8 12 0-0-0 ♗f8 13 g6 fg 14 ♗c4 ♘b6 15 ♗b3 ♘a5 16 h5 g5 17 fg ♘bc4.

Besides 10 ... a6, Magerramov's 10 ... d5!? awaits practical tests. Play may continue 11 ed ed 12 ♗g2 ♖e8 13 ♘xd5 ♗c5.

Besides 10 ♕d2, White can place his queen on e2, but this does not set any new problems before Black, if he plays either 10 ... ♘b6 or 10 ... a6.

10   ...   a6 *(124)*
11   0-0-0

It is possible that 11 f4 ♘xd4 12 ♕xd4 b5 13 0-0-0 ♗b7 14 ♖g1

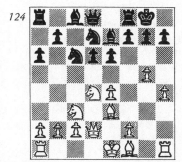

124

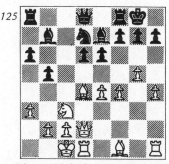

125

is slightly more accurate. In this case the standard break 14 ... e5 15 fe ♘xe5 leads to a simple positional advantage for White: 16 ♗e2 ♖c8 17 ♘d5 ♗xd5 18 ed ♖e8 19 ♔b1 ♗f8 20 ♕d2 ♕e7 21 ♗d4 ♕b7 22 ♗c3, Katz-Timoshchenko, 1981. Instead of 14 ... e5, 14 ... ♕a5 should be played, forcing 15 a3.

| 11 | ... | ♘xd4 |
| 12 | ♗xd4 | |

As we have already noted in our remarks to 9 ... 0-0, the capture with the queen leads to double-edged play with possibilities for both sides.

| 12 | ... | b5 |
| 13 | a3! | |

A necessary prophylaxis, since the direct 13 f4 gives Black rich counterplay: 13 ... b4 14 ♘e2 ♗b7 15 ♗g2 a5 16 ♘g3 b3! or 14 ♘a4 e5 15 ♗e3 ef 16 ♗xf4 ♕a5 17 ♗xd6 ♗xd6 18 ♕xd6 ♕xa4 19 ♗c4 ♕a5 20 g6 ♕e5!, Schöneberg-Tukmakov, 1967.

13	...	♗b7
14	f4 *(125)*	
14	...	♕a5

The conventional 14 ... e5 15 ♗e3 ef 16 ♗xf4 ♘e5 leads to a

position which favours White after 17 ♘d5 ♖c8, since the ♗e7 has few prospects.

After 14 ... ♕a5 the attack with 15 g6 fg 16 ♗h3 is parried by the simple 16 ... e5. On 15 ♔b1, 15 ... ♗d8! 16 ♗e3 ♘c5! merits study, for example 17 ♗g2 ♗c7 18 h5 b4 19 ab ♕xb4 20 g6 ♖ab8 or 17 b4 ♕xa3 18 bc ♗a5!

B12

| 9 | ♖g1! *(126)* |

With this move White prepares to launch a piece attack on the kingside, should Black castle short. The rook intends to travel along the path g1-g3-h3. Moreover, standing on g1, the rook increases the effectiveness of the pawn storm and defends the Pg5.

9 ♕h5, with the same goal, gives Black good counterplay because of the weakness of the g-pawn: 9 ... g6! 10 ♕d1 (10 ♕h6 ♗f8!) 10 ... ♗xg5 11 ♗xg5 ♕xg5 12 ♘xc6 bc 13 ♕xd8 ♖b8! 14 h4 ♕c5 ∓, Pirc-Cirić, 1965.

| 9 | ... | ♘b6! |

This manoeuvre with the following advance of the pawns in the centre has special value as a universal method of fighting against

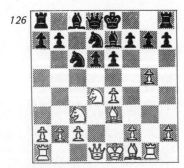

126

the attack with 6 g4.

Black can count on equality, by playing along the lines of the customary "sicilian" methods, for example 9 ... a6 and then:

a) **10 ♕h5 0-0 11 ♖g3 ♖e8 12 0-0-0 (12 ♖h3 ♘f8) 12 ... g6 13 ♕e2 ♗f8 14 ♔b1 ♕c7 15 h4.** In the game van Riemsdyck–Najdorf, 1978, Black played 15 ... ♘xd4? 16 ♗xd4 b5 17 h5, and White's attack, in which the ♗d4 plays an active role, proved dangerous. After 15 ... b5 the chances would have been about equal.

b) **10 ♕d2 0-0 11 0-0-0 ♘xd4 12 ♗xd4 b5 13 f4 (13 a3 ♖b8 14 ♖g3 ♖e8) 13 ... b4 14 ♘a4 ♕a5 15 b3 ♗b7 16 ♗g2 e5!** or 12 ♕xd4 b5 13 f4 ♕a5 14 f5 b4 15 g6 (15 f6 ♗d8! 16 fg ♖e8) 15 ... hg 16 fe bc 17 ed ♗f6 18 ♕d5 ♕b4.

c) **10 h4 0-0 11 h5 ♘xd4** (11 ... ♘de5 12 f4 ♘xd4 13 ♗xd4 ♘c6 14 ♗e3 =) **12 ♕xd4 ♘e5 13 ♗e2** (13 ♖g3!? ♗xg5 14 0-0-0 ∞) 13 ... ♘c6 14 ♕d2 b5 15 0-0-0 (15 a3 ♕a5 16 f4 b4 or 15 g6 ♗f6) 15 ... ♕a5 16 g6 b4.

d) **10 ♗e2 0-0 11 f4 ♖e8 12 ♕d2 ♘xd4 13 ♗xd4 b5 14 a3 ♗b7 15 f5 ♘e5! 16 0-0-0 ♕c7!** Balashov–

Spassky, 1976.

The examples given above give some indication as to how the attack and defence should run in similar positions. Success will go to the one who creates his attack more quickly.

10   ♕h5

The consistent realisation of his conception.

On 10 ♖g3, 10 ... d5 is good, after which 11 0-0-0 may follow. 10 ... d5 is also a good reply to 10 f4: 11 ed ed 12 ♕f3 ♗b4 13 ♘xc6 bc 14 ♗d4 0-0 15 0-0-0 ♗f5 ∓, Damjanović–Ree, 1970. 10 ... e5 is also good: 11 ♘f5 ♗xf5 12 ef d5! 13 ♗xb6 ♕xb6. White gets no result from 10 ♗b5 ♗d7 11 ♕h5 g6 12 ♕e2 either. After 12 ... ♖c8! 13 0-0-0 0-0 14 ♘xc6 (14 f4?! is weaker: 14 ... ♘a5 15 f5 ef 16 ef d5! ∓. Gheorghiu–Najdorf, 1966.) 14 ... ♗xc6 15 ♗xc6 ♖xc6 16 f4 ♘c4 17 f5 ♕a5 and Black has an excellent game.

10   ...   g6

10 ... 0-0 is dangerous here: 11 ♖g3 ♘xd4 (11 ... g6? 12 ♕h6 ♘xd4 13 ♖h3 ±) 12 ♗xd4 (12 ♖h3 ♘xc2+ 13 ♔d2 h6!) 12 ... e5 13 ♗xb6, and White retains the advantage because of his domination of the d5-point. But 10 ... ♘e5 deserves study, since the tempting 11 ♗b5+ ♗d7 12 ♘xe6 is parried simply by 12 ... g6 13 ♘g7+? ♔f8 14 ♕h6 ♔g8! ∓.

11   ♕e2   e5
12   ♘b3   ♗e6 (127)

This complicated position has not yet appeared in tournament praxis. It is difficult to evaluate.

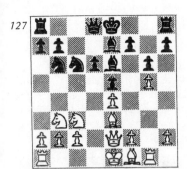

127

The direct play for domination of the d5-square does not bring the desired result: 13 ♗xb6 ab! 14 ♘d5 ♗xd5 15 ed ♘d4! 16 ♘xd4 ed 17 ♕b5+! ♔f8!; 13 0-0-0 ♘c4 14 ♘c5 ♘xe3 15 ♘xe6 is somewhat better, but then Black has a choice between the queen sacrifice 15 ... ♘xd1 16 ♘xd8 ♘xc3 17 bc ♖xd8, and the quieter continuation 15 ... fe, which leads to a roughly level game.

B2

    8   ...   ♘b6

An interesting move which conforms to the logic of the position.

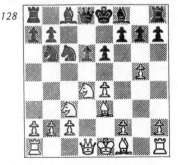

128

The first time this move was seen was in the game Krogius–Petrosian, 1958. The future world champion connected the idea with the occupation of c4 by his knights. This took a lot of time, and after 9 ♕d2 ♘e5 10 0-0-0 a6 11 f4 ♘ec4 12 ♗xc4 ♘xc4 13 ♕e2 b5?! 14 f5 g6 15 ♖hf1 ♗g7 16 h4 White's position was clearly superior.

In our opinion the manoeuvre ♘d7–b6 deserves to live. It can be compared with one of the fundamental rules of chess strategy: "A pawn attack on the flank should be met by a counterthrust in the centre." By transferring the knight to b6, Black does not usually encounter difficulties in the realization of the liberating advance d6-d5, and sometimes e6-e5. His bishops are well employed, and the ♗f8 can move directly to b4.

    9   ♕d2   ...

In our opinion, this is the arrangement of pieces which is most likely to give Black trouble. Against other continuations methods have already been worked out which give Black sufficient means to create counterplay.

a) 9 f4 d5 10 e5 ♗b4 11 a3 ♗xc3+ 12 bc ♘a5! 13 ♘b5 ♘bc4

b) 9 h4 d5 10 ♗b5 ♗d7 11 ed ed 12 ♕e2 ♗e7 13 0-0-0 0-0

c) 9 a4 ♘a5 10 f4 d5! 11 ed ♘xd5 (11 ... ed 12 ♗g2 ♗b4 13 0-0 0-0! = is also possible) 12 ♗b5+ ♗d7 13 ♘xd5 ed

d) 9 ♗b5 ♗d7 10 ♘b3!? a6 11 ♗e2 ♗e7 12 h4 0-0

e) 9 ♕e2 ♗e7 (9 ... ♘xd4 10 ♗xd4 ♕xg5 11 ♕b5+! ♕xb5 12 ♘xb5 ♔d7 13 ♘xa7 ♖xa7 14 ♗xb6 ♖a8 15 ♗b5+ ♔e7 16 0-0-0 ♗d7 =) 10 h4 d5 11 0-0-0 0-0 12 ♗g2 ♘e5 13 ♘b3 ♗b4.

9	...	d5
10	ed	ed
11	0-0-0	♗e7
12	♗b5!	

The passive placement of Black's pieces is more important than the Pd5! In the game van Riemsdyck–Tal, 1979, a double edged endgame arose after 12 ♘b3 0-0! 13 ♘xd5 ♘xd5 14 ♕xd5 ♕xd5 15 ♖xd5 ♘b4 16 ♖e5 ♗d6 17 ♖a5 b6 18 ♗g2 ba.

12	...	♗d7
13	♘b3!	

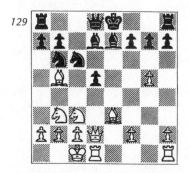

129

This is a position which is critical for the evaluation of 8 ... ♘b6, but by no means for the evaluation of the entire plan involving the transfer of the knight to b6 with the aim of securing the advance d6-d5.

In the diagrammed position White obtained the advantage in the game Kremenetsky–Andrianov, 1980 after 13 ... ♘c4?! 14 ♕xd5 ♘xe3 15 fe a6 16 ♗xc4 ♗e6 17 ♕e4, but much stronger, in our opinion, is 13 ... ♗e6 which maintains the defensibility of Black's position. Even if this evaluation doesn't hold up, the idea ♘d7-b6 still has its viability on the 9th and 10th moves.

B3

8	...	a6

Here we will examine Black's attempts to force play on the queenside. The analysis of this position is interesting since this situation may arise under different move orders, such as 6 ... a6 7 g5 ♘d7 8 ♗e3 ♘c6.

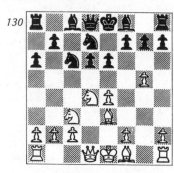

130

9	♕d2

There are other continuations here, of course, and possibly some of them are equally worthy. We consider 3 interesting ideas.

a) 9 h4 ♕c7 10 ♕e2 b5 11 ♘xc6 ♕xc6 12 ♗d4 ♗b7 13 0-0-0 0-0-0 14 a3 ♘b6 15 ♖h3 and White's chances are better, Korsunsky–Eingorn, 1979.

b) 9 ♖g1 ♕c7 10 f4 b5 11 a3 ♖b8 12 ♕d2 ♘c5 with a double-edged game, Sax–Tringov, 1978.

c) 9 a4 ♘de5 10 ♘b3 d5!? 11 ed ed 12 ♕xd5 ♗g4! 13 ♗g2 ♕xd5 14 ♗xd5 ♘b4 15 ♗e4 f5 with chances for both sides, Bronstein–Tal, 1976.

9	...	♕c7
10	0-0-0	♘xd4
11	♕xd4	b5
12	h4	♖b8

White has an advantage in space and holds the initiative, but as Hort–Andersson, 1973, shows, the battle lies ahead: 13 ♔b1 b4 14 ♘a4 ♗b7 15 b3.

So, the Keres Attack (6 g4) is a dangerous weapon against the Scheveningen system of the Sicilian Defence. It requires boldness, enterprising play and exactitude from both sides — attack and defence.

18 Alternative 6th Moves for White

1 e4 c5 2 ♘f3 e6 3 d4 cd 4 ♘xd4 ♘f6 5 ♘c3 d6

In this chapter we will consider three systems where opposite side castling is employed, in which White plays f2-f4 later than move 6. Fashion has passed these systems by, but they are still fully viable.

A 6 ♗g5
B 6 ♗e3
C 6 ♗b5+!?

A

6 ♗g5

131

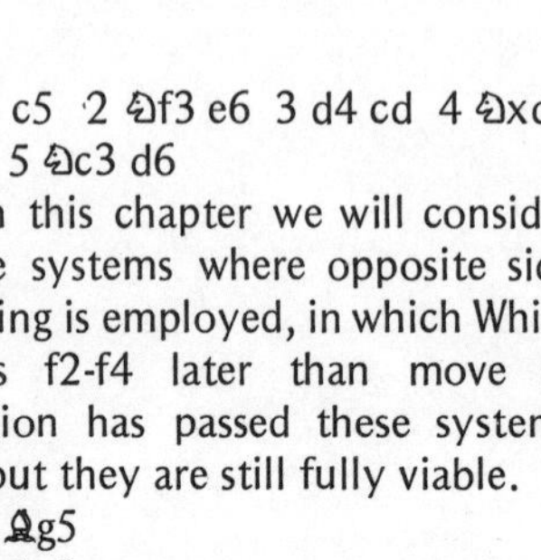

Quite logical and very useful, but all the same this move is taken up only infrequently. Its major drawback is the wide range of opening systems available to Black on his 6th move. Thus after 6 ... ♘c6 we have the Rauzer Attack,

while 6 ... a6 leads to the Najdorf.

Besides that, if both sides castle short the ♗g5 reduces White's attacking possibilities partly because White must now be more careful in playing f2-f4.

Here we will consider only those variations which are independent of the Rauzer and Najdorf variations.

6 ... ♗e7

After 6 ... h6 7 ♗xf6 ♕xf6 8 ♕d2 a6 9 f4 Black is too far behind in development. The formation with 6 ... ♘bd7 7 ♘db5 h6 8 ♗f4 ♘e5 9 ♕d4! is also dangerous, as Black loses a pawn after 9 ... a6 10 ♘xd6+ and 11 ♗xe5.

7 ♕d2

On 7 f4 h6 8 ♗h4 there follows the combinational liquidation 8 ... ♘xe4 9 ♗xe7 ♘xc3 10 ♗xd8 (If 10 ♕g4, then 10 ... ♔xe7 11 bc g6 gives Black a pawn and a strong position.) 10 ... ♘xd1 11 ♖xd1 ♔xd8 12 ♘b5 ♘c6 13 ♘xd6 ♔e7 15 c3, Steiner–Najdorf, 1935. Black's chances in the endgame are no worse. It can be shown that the same exchanging combination can be played in answer to 7 ♕e2 as well: 7 ... h6 8 ♗h4 ♘xe4

9 ♕xe4 ♗xh4 10 ♘f3 ♗e7 with advantage to Black, Gutman–Ghinda, 1981. But it is not quite that simple. Instead of the mistaken move 9 ♕xe4?, White had an interesting choice between 9 ♕b5+ and 9 ♗xe7 ♘xc3 10 ♕c4! ♔xe7 11 ♕xc3, giving him a good attack for the pawn. This combination does not work against 7 ♕d2: 7 ... h6 8 ♗h4 ♘xe4 9 ♗xe7 ♘xd2 10 ♗xd8 ♘xf1 11 ♗c7 ♘a6 12 ♗xd6.

7 ... a6
8 0-0-0 b5

Even here Black can play ♘c6 and transpose into the Rauzer attack.

9 ♗d3

Moves such as 9 a3 ♘bd7 10 f3 do not fit in with the concept of queenside castling.

9 ... ♗b7
10 f4

More solid is 10 ♖he1 ♘bd7 11 f4.

10 ... b4?!

10 ... ♘bd7 is apparently solid and correct. By grabbing a pawn, Black is left seriously behind in development.

11 ♘ce2 ♘xe4

132

12 ♗xe4 ♗xe4
13 ♗xe7 ♕xe7
14 ♘g3 d5
15 ♖he1

White has brought all of his pieces into the game and with his next move recovers the pawn, since 15 ... f5 is not on because of 16 ♘gxf5 ef 17 ♘xf5. His advantage is beyond doubt.

B

6 ♗e3

Here the game returns to the Scheveningen fold after 6 ... ♗e7, although it is quite possible to give examples of reckless play such as 7 h4!? 0-0 8 ♘b3 ♘c6 9 ♗d3 a6 10 ♕e2 b5 11 0-0-0 ♘b4 12 g4 with double-edged play, Bellon–Andersson, 1980.

6 ... a6
7 ♕f3 ♘bd7

The development of the knight at c6 is also possible, for example 7 ... ♘c6 8 0-0-0 ♗d7 9 ♕g3 ♕b8 10 f4 b5 11 e5 de 12 ♘xc6 ♗xc6 13 fe b4 14 ♘e2 ♘e4 15 ♕f4 g5!? 16 ♕f3 ♗g7 17 h4 ♕b7 (Fedorowicz–Kaplan, 1980, or 7 ... ♕c7 8 0-0-0 ♘c6 9 ♗e2 ♗e7 10 ♕g3 0-0 11 f4 ♗d7 12 e5 ♘e8 13 ♔b1 ♖c8 14 ♗d3 de 15 fe ♘xe5 16 ♗f4 ♗d6, Ljubojević–Andersson, 1975. Both examples demonstrate well the peculiarities of the play in the dynamically equal positions which arise from this manner of development.

8 0-0-0 ♗e7
9 ♗e2

White's plan of attack becomes clear. At first the g-pawn will advance, chasing the ♘f6 and guaranteeing White domination in the centre. Only then will the Pf2 advance. These situations which arise closely resemble the Keres Attack in goal and method. Here are two characteristic fragments, which show how the struggle may develop:

a) 9 ... ♕c7 10 g4 ♘e5 11 ♕h3 b5 12 g5 ♘fd7 13 f4 b4 14 ♘b1 ♘c4 15 ♗xc4 ♕xc4 16 b3 ♕c7 17 g6 ♘f6, Ljubojevic–Sax, 1975.

b) 9 ... 0-0 10 g4 ♕c7 11 g5 ♘e8 12 ♖hg1 b5 13 a3 ♖b8, Sax–Vogt, 1975.

The positions which arise are characterised by great dynamism and approximately equal chances. To the extent that the possibilities of complicating the struggle are great, success will come to the more enterprising player.

C

6   ♗b5+!? *(133)*

This is a very interesting idea of the Latvian master Vitolins. White plays to develop his pieces quickly. The evacuation of his king to the queenside is in accordance with his fundamental strategy, as the ♖a1 will thereby enter the game. The fight will take place along the central diagonals.

6   ...   ♘bd7

The other defence to the check — 6 ... ♗d7 — leads to approximately equal play after 7 ♕e2! and now either:

a) 7 ... a6 8 ♗xd7+ ♘bxd7 9 ♗g5 ♗e7 10 0-0-0 0-0 11 f4 ♖c8 12 ♔b1, Vitolinš–Timoshchenko, 1981.

b) 7 ... ♘c6 8 ♗e3 a6 9 ♗xc6! bc 10 0-0-0 c5 11 ♘b3 ♕c7 12 g4

♗c6 13 f3 ♗b7 14 g5 ♘d7 15 h4 0-0-0 16 ♖d2 ♗e7 17 ♖hd1 c4, Boitkevič–Sokolov, 1980.

7   ♗g5   ♕b6

For the sake of rapid development White does not put too high a price on his bishop pair. Thus on 7 ... a6 there follows 8 ♗xd7+ ♗xd7 9 f4. Perhaps instead of 7 ... ♕b6 or 7 ... a6 Black should also try to develop quickly with 7 ... ♗e7.

8   ♗xf6   gf
9   ♕d3   a6
10   ♗xd7+   ♗xd7
11   0-0-0

In the end a position has arisen in which Black has the two bishops, but this is not yet meaningful. Black's strong pawn centre will be weakened if any of the pawns should advance, and therefore the bishops will not be able to taste freedom for a long time. Chances stand approximately equal, as Bagirov's analysis shows: 11 ... ♕a5 (11 ... 0-0-0 △ ♔b8, ♗c8 is more passive.) 12 ♔b1 b5 13 f4 b4 14 ♘ce2 ♗e7 15 f5 e5 16 ♘b3 ♕b5.

6 ♗b5+ certainly deserves further analysis and practical testing.

19 6 f4!

(1 e4 c5 2 ♘f3 e6 3 d4 cd 4 ♘xd4 ♘f6 5 ♘c3 d6 6 f4)

Here we discuss systems where White tries to seize the initiative by potent means. In such situations castling queenside usually enters into his plans, storming the king-side with his pawns aided by the especially active position of his queen. The rook on d1 will exert appreciable pressure on the centre, and only the white-squared bishop may, at first play the role of a spectator. In this respect the system we consider here is similar in character and tempo to the Veli-mirović attack, which will be examined in the later chapters.

      6 ...   ♘c6

Doubtless the most logical answer, although praxis of recent years has demonstrated the via-bility of two other continuations:

a) 6 ... ♕b6!? *(134)*

As the pawn stands at f4 this thrust by the queen makes it more difficult for White to castle short and also hinders the development of the ♗c1. But these difficulties are quickly overcome, and there are several good methods by which White can obtain an advantage.

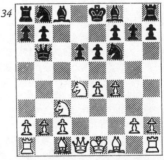

134

a1) 7 ♘b3 ♘c6 8 ♗e2 (on 8 ♗d3, 8 ... d5 9 e5 ♘d7 10 ♕e2 ♘c5 is to be considered) 8 ... ♗e7 9 ♗f3 0-0 10 ♕e2 a5 11 ♗e3 ♕c7 12 a4 b6 13 0-0 ±, Timoshchenko–Mikhail-chishin, 1973.

a2) 7 ♘f3 ♘c6 8 ♗d3 ♗e7 9 ♕e2 0-0 10 g4 (The sacrifice of the b-pawn – 10 ♗d2 ♕xb2 11 ♖b1 ♕a3 12 0-0 – also has good pros-pects, but throwing the g-pawn forward is sharper.) 10 ... ♘xg4 11 ♖g1 ♘f6 (The position after 11 ... f5!? 12 ef ef 13 ♗d2! ♗h4+! 14 ♔f1 ♘d4 15 ♘xd4 ♕xd4 16 ♘b5 ♕c5 17 h3, Gulko–Tukmakov, 1970, resembles a puzzle.) 12 ♗d2 ♘b4 13 0-0-0 ♘xd3+ 14 cd g6. White has good perspectives on the g-file, now that his g-pawn is gone, but Black's position shows no weakness and it will not be easy for White to smash through.

a3) 7 a3 ♘c6 8 ♗e3 ♗d7 (The pawn at b2 is poisoned: 8 ... ♕xb2 9 ♘a4! and the queen is trapped.) 9 ♗e2. Later White will play ♕d2 and decide where to put his king. It is possible that this unassuming pawn move might prove best of all, underlining the harmlessness of the thrust of the Black Queen.

b) 6 ... ♗e7 7 ♗e3 (Black has no big problems after 7 ♗d3 0-0 8 0-0 ♘c6 9 ♘f3. 9 ... ♘b4 10 ♕e1 b6 and 9 ... e5 10 ♕e1 ef 11 ♗xf4 ♘g4 12 ♘d5 ♘ge5 and even 9 ... b5!? 10 ♘xb5 ♕b6+ 10 ♔h1 ♘xe4 12 ♗xe4 ♕xb5 13 b3 ♗f6 are all relatively acceptable, but we advise that Gutman's recommendation be tried: 9 ... b6 10 ♕e1 ♘d7 11 ♕g3 ♘c5. Black destroys the ♗d3, reducing White's attacking potential, and seizes control over the key squares d4 and e5.) 7 ... 0-0 8 ♕f3 e5! (In this manner Black avoids the unpleasant and complex plan of attack after ♘xc6 and f4-f5.) 9 ♘f5 (Other retreats by the knight will be examined in the analysis of 6 ... ♘c6.) 9 ... ♗xf5 10 ef.

10 ... ♕a5 (The pawn sacrifice 10 ... e4 11 ♘xe4 ♘xe4 12 ♕xe4 doesn't achieve anything tangible after either 12 ... ♗h4+ 13 g3 ♖e8 14 ♕xb7 ♖xe3+ 15 ♔f2 or 12 ... d5 13 ♕d3 ♘c6 14 a3! ♗f6 15 0-0-0 ♖e8 16 ♔b1 ♘a5 17 g4 ♘c4 ♗c1 ♕b6 19 ♕b3!, Yudasin-Lukin, 1981) 11 0-0-0 (Also fully possible is 11 ♕xb7, although after 11 ... ♘bd7 12 ♕a6 ♕c7 13 0-0-0 ♖fc8 14 ♕a4 Black has something resembling counterplay.) 11 ... e4 12 ♕h3 ♖c8 13 ♗d4 ♘c6 14 ♗c4 ♕b4. Here is an inteesting fragment from the game Kupreichik-Sigurjonsson, 1980: 15 ♗xf6 ♗xf6 16 ♗b3 ♘d4 17 ♘d5! ♖xc2+ 18 ♔b1 ♘xb3 19 ♘xf6+ gf 20 ♔xc2 ♖c8+ 21 ♔b1 ♘d2+ 22 ♔a1 ♖c2 23 ♕a3! ♕xa3 24 ba. In this sharp endgame White's chances are more real as his king enters into the game quickly. (But in Halifman-A. Sokolov, 1982 Black managed to improve with 24 ... d5 25 ♖c1 ♖c6! with equal chances – tr.)

7   ♗e3

Other continuations are connected with the retreat of the knight from the centre, 7 ♘f3 being the most interesting of them, having been analyzed in the variation 6 ... ♕b6 7 ♘f3. Of course, Black is not obliged to play ... ♕b8. Van Mil-Ligterink, Amsterdam 1982, preferred 7 ... ♗e7 8 ♗d3 0-0 9 0-0 ♘d7 10 ♕e1 b6 11 ♗e3 ♗b7 12 ♕g3 ♖c8. But why retreat from the centre so soon?

7   ...   ♗e7

Again a move of the type "most logical and natural". But Black's position is not so poor that there is only one equalizing method available. The space which White holds in the centre is still insufficiently fortified, and Black can try to exploit this immediately by moving forward one of his central pawns. But 7 ... d5 leads only to a strengthening of White's position in the centre after 8 e5! ♘xd4 9 ♗xd4 ♘e4 10 ♗d3.

Of more significant interest is 7 ... e5!, after which an attack in the centre is inescapable. Now if 8 ♘xc6 bc 9 f5, Black does not waste time on ♗f8-e7 but quickly advances his pawn to d5: 9 ... ♕a5 10 ♕f3 ♖b8 11 0-0-0 d5 12 ed ♗a3!. In the event that the knight retreats to f3, 8 ... ♘g4 9 ♗g1 ef or 9 ♗d2 ♕b6 must be considered. There remains only 8 ♘de2, bringing the knight to the defence of the pawn on 8 ... ♘g4 9 ♗g1! But the clumsy configuration ♘e2, ♗f1 will unavoidably cost White time, as he must redeploy them more usefully on the right flank. Black should exploit this circumstance. A good example is Shibarevich–Andersson, 1978: 8 ♘de2 ♗e7 9 ♕d2 a6 10 h3 b5 11 ♘g3 ♕a5 12 ♗e2 ef 13 ♗xf4 ♗e6 14 0-0 0-0 and Black has the initiative.

Another method of counterplay for Black turned out to be unexpectedly promising because of the economising on kingside development: 7 ... ♗d7 8 ♕f3 a6 9 0-0-0 ♕c7 10 g4 ♘xd4 11 ♗xd4 (11 ♖xd4 d5!? 12 ed ♘xd5 13 ♘xd5 ed 14 f5 ♗c6 15 ♗f4 ♕a5 16 ♕e3+ ♔d7, Chudinovsky–Pokrov-

sky, 1980) 11 ... e5 12 fe de 13 ♕g3 ♗d6! 14 ♗e3 ♗e6. Black has no problems, but what about White . . .

There is very little practical experience with the moves 7 ... e5 and 7 ... ♗d7, but they are both worthy of analysis.

8 ♕f3

The queen takes up a good position. Without interfering with the development of his pieces, White not only prepares kingside operations but also restrains Black's queenside play.

Gaprindashvili has sometimes played 7 ♘f3 and ♕e2, feeling that the f3-square is best left to the knight. Sometimes 8 ♕e2 is played in the present position, with similar ideas:

136

The fundamental advantage of the move 8 ♕e2 is that it is little explored, and this puts Black on his own. The disadvantages are also obvious: the road for the ♗f1 is blocked and the king can only castle onto the queenside. Black has a rich choice of developmental schemes:
a) 8 ... e5 9 ♘f3 a6 10 0-0-0 ♕a5 11 ♔b1 =, Gaprindashvili–Kushnir, 1972.

b) **8 ... ♘xd4 9 ♗xd4 0-0 10 0-0-0
♛a5 11 ♗f2?!** (11 ♛e1 b6! =) **11
... d5! 12 ♗e1 de 13 ♘d5 ♛xd5!
14 ♖xd5 ed 15 ♗c3 ♗e6 =**

c) **8 ... 0-0 9 0-0-0 d5! 10 e5 ♘d7
11 ♛h5 ♖e8 12 ♗d3 ♘f8 =**

          8   ...   ♛c7

The last developing move, with
which Black takes control of the e5
square, liquidating the possibility
of the unpleasant opposition of the
♖d1 and ♛d8 and defending the
♘c6, with the option of the standard pawn march by the rook and
knight pawns. Black also retains
the option of evacuating his king
to the queenside.

          9   0-0-0

It goes without saying that this
is the continuation which is most
principled and unpleasant for Black.
The solid plan with 9 ♗d3 and
eventual kingside castling will be
considered below.

We now examine:

A 9 ... a6
B 9 ... 0-0

A

          9   ...   a6

Black prepares queenside castling, and in the hope of carrying
that out awaits a quiet development of White's pieces, for example
10 ♗d3 ♗d7 11 ♖hg1 0-0-0. It
ought to be mentioned that drastic
operations in the centre may prove
fatal: 9 ... ♘xd4 10 ♗xd4 e5 11
fe! ♗g4 (11 ... de 12 ♛g3 ♗d6 13
♛xg7 ±) 12 ♛g3 ♗xd1 13 ♛xg7
♖f8 14 ef ±.

          10   g4!

In this way White forces Black
to castle short, after which the
game will take on a very sharp
character. Another continuation,
10 ♖g1, finally puts to rest the
idea of e6-e5, but allows Black,
besides castling kingside, to play
10 ... ♗d7 11 g4 0-0-0 12 g5
♘e8, although his position is then
a bit crowded.

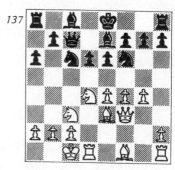

137

          10   ...   0-0

Since the centre has not yet been
opened up, it is possible to delay
the evacuation of the king, although this strategy is not without danger. Two continuations
deserve analysis:

a) **10 ... ♘d7 11 g5 b5 12 ♗d3**,
and now not 12 ... ♗b7 13 ♛h3
♘c5?! (13 ... 0-0-0!?) **16 g6! b4
15 gf+ ♔xf7 16 ♘xe6 ♘xe6 17
♘d5+**, Gutman–Petkevich 1976,
but immediately 12 ... ♘c5 intending ♗d7 and later, perhaps, queenside castling.

b) **10 ... ♘xd4 11 ♗xd4** (11 ♖xd4
b5 12 g5 ♘d7 13 h4 ♗b7 14 f5
♘e5 15 ♛h3 ef ∞) **11 ... e5 12 fe
de** (12 ... ♗xg4 13 ♛g3 ±) **13 ♛g3
♗d6 14 ♗e3 0-0!** (14 ... ♗xg4 is
dangerous because of 15 ♖d3! or
even 15 h3 ♗xd1 16 ♛xg7 ♖f8
17 ♛xf6 ♗h5 18 ♗b5+ ab 19

⊘xb5 ±) 15 g5 ⊘e8! 16 ⊘d5 ♕c6! (Just so! 16 ... ♕a5 loses to 17 ⊘f6+! gf 18 gf+ ♔h8 19 ♖g1 and further ♗h6 with a mating attack. On 16 ... ♕c6 17 ⊘f6+ Black has the retreat 17 ... ♔h8, and the ♗d6 is defended after 18 ⊘xe8 ♖xe8.) 17 h4 ♗e6, Sikorallyin, 1976. Thanks to the outpost at d5 White's position is preferable, but Black has possibilities of counterplay on the queenside and can count on eventual equality.

    11   g5   ⊘d7
    12   ♖g1   b5

The attempt to build a fortress with 12 ... ⊘xd4 13 ♗xd4 ♖e8 (△ ... ♗f8) is unjustifiably passive. After 14 f5 g6 15 ♗f6! ♗f8 16 fg fg 17 e5! ⊘xe5 18 ♗xe5 de 19 ⊘e4 ♗g7 20 ⊘f6+ ♗xf6 21 gf ♖f8 22 ♗d3! White obtained a strong attack in Kupreichik-Pjaaren, 1975.

It seems that 12 ... ⊘xd4 13 ♗xd4 places the white bishop in a strong position, and is therefore uncomfortable for Black unless he can improve somewhere in the concrete variation. Here 13 ... b5 gives White a clear advantage after 14 f5! ⊘e5 (14 ... b4 loses to 15 ♗xg7! bc 16 ♖g3! ♗b7 17 ♗xc3 ♖fc8 18 fe! ⊘e5 19 ef+ ⊘xf7 10 g6 ±, Petrzhelka-Mikhailov, 1975) 15 ♗xe5 de 16 f6 ♗c5 17 fg ♖d8 18 ♖g3 ♖xd1+ 19 ⊘xd1, Andersson-Espig, 1969.

    13   ♕h5 *(138)*

On the basis of the beautiful game Haritver-Popov, 1976, this position is considered to be favourable for White: 13 ... ⊘xd4

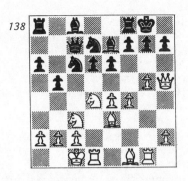

138

14 ♗xd4 b4 15 ♖d3! ♖e8 16 ♖h3 ⊘f8 17 g6! fg 18 ♖xg6! e5 19 ⊘d5 ♕d8 20 ♗c4! ±. But Black's defensive resources are sufficiently great, if he does not help White transfer his ♖d1 to h3. After the logical 13 ... b4! the tempting sacrifice 14 ⊘d5 ed 15 ⊘xc6 ♕xc6 16 ed ♕c7 17 ♗d4 doesn't work: 17 ... ⊘c5! (17 ... ⊘e5?! 18 fe de 19 g6! ±) 18 ♗xg7! ♗f5! ∓, or 17 ♗d3 g6 18 ♕h6 ♖e8! 19 ♗d4 ♗f8 20 ♕h4 ⊘c5 ∓. This means that in answer to 13 ... b4 White must retreat with 14 ⊘ce2, but then 14 ... g6! 15 ♕h6 ♖e8! 16 ♖g3 ♗f8 17 ♕h4 ⊘c5 or 15 ♕h4 ⊘c5 16 ⊘g3 ♗d7 leads the game into a complicated, double-edged situation.

The break 13 f5 instead of 13 ♕h5, does not have any great force: 13 ... ⊘de5 14 ♕h3 b4! 15 ⊘a4 ef! (Better than 15 ... ⊘xd4 16 ♗xd4 ef 17 ⊘b6!) 16 ⊘xf5 (16 ef ⊘xd4 17 ♗xd4 g6!) 16 ... ♖b8 = and steers play into a fully acceptable position for Black.

B

    9   ...   0-0

The most natural and at the same

time boldest move for Black. This method of development immediately puts the king in the face of a pawn storm, but on the other hand, why should he fear an attack if he has not made any antipositional moves?

10 ♘db5

This sets more complicated problems before Black. The other, more obvious White moves do not require great accuracy in the carrying out of the defence:

a) **10 ♗e2 a6** (It is also worth trying 10 ... e5 11 ♘f5 ♗xf5 12 ef 罝ac8 △ ... 罝fd8) 11 g4 ♘xd4 12 ♗xd4 b5 (The ♗e2 defends the queen, so the break 12 ... e5 13 fe ♗xg4 (13 ... de 14 ♕g3) doesn't work on account of 14 ef ♗xf3 15 fe ♕xe7 16 ♗xf3) 13 g5 ♘d7 14 ♕h5 ♗b7 15 f5 e5 16 ♗e3 罝fc8 17 f6 b4! 18 fe bc 19 ♗d3 罝e8 gives Black an obvious advantage, Chekhov-Hort, 1976.

b) **10 罝d2 a6** 11 g4 ♘xd4 12 ♗xd4 e5 16 ♗e3 ♗e6 =

c) **10 g4!** is a thoroughly venomous continuation:

This requires exact and energetic action from Black. 10 ... ♘xd4

11 ♗xd4 e5 12 fe de 13 ♕g3!

The critical position of the variation. The most natural, and even conventional reply is **13 ... ♗d6**, which at first glance eliminates the basis for White's threats. Actually, after either 14 ♘b5 ed! 15 ♕xd6 ♕d6 16 ♘xd6 ♘xg4 or 14 ♗f2 ♗b4! 15 g5 (15 ♘d5 ♘xd5 16 ed renders absurd White's entire opening strategy based on 10 g4.) 15 ... ♘h5 16 ♘d5 ♘xg3 17 ♘xc7 ♘xh1 18 ♘xa8 ♘xf2 the Black knight consumes more than its White counterpart. The move 14 ♗e3!, however, makes Black's life extraordinarily difficult. Now White can obtain a completely winning endgame after 14 ... ♗b4 15 g5 ♘h5 16 ♘d5! ♘xg3 17 ♘xc7 ♘xf1 18 罝hxf1 ♗h3 19 ♘xa8 ♗xf1 20 罝xf1 罝xa8 22 罝d1 △ 罝d7, Grünfeld-Dur, 1981. The effect of the pawn sacrifice **13 ... ♕a5** 14 ♗xe5 ♗e6 is entirely unclear, so it seems that the evaluation of 10 g4, and indeed of the entire plan with 8 ... ♕c7, hinges on the results of analysis and praxis of the position which arises after **13 ... ♘g4** 14 ♘d5 ♕d6, or even 14 ... ♕d8, preparing ... ♗h4 and ... ♕g5+. It seems to us that Black's house is in order. But what do you think?

After studying the fine points of the attack and defence of 10 g4, it is not difficult to evaluate the consequences of the play in other variations: 10 罝g1 ♘xd4 11 ♗xd4 e5 12 fe de 13 ♕g3 ♗d6 (Now the retreat of the ♗d4 is less harmful to Black, especially since the g2 pawn is still on its home square, and White's only serious threat is ②b5, for example 14 ♗e3 ♗b4! 15 ♗g5 ♗xc3 16 ♗xf6 ♗xb2+! 17 ♔b1 g6 ∓) 14 ②b5 ♕a5! 15 ②xd6 ed 16 ♗c4 ♗e6 also gives Black excellent counter-chances.

10	...	♕b8
11	g4	a6
12	②d4	②xd4
13	♗xd4	

White's 10 ②db5 manoeuvre is cunning, forcing Black to react to the advance of the g-pawn in a manner which is not as energetic as one would wish. But this is closer to a fine point than an achievement, and Black's defensive resources are sufficient. We examine two possibilities:

B1 13 ... e5!
B2 13 ... b5

B1

| 13 | ... | e5! |

Simplest, most solid, and correct: countering a flank attack with a counterthrust in the centre. Black will be able to achieve fully equal play, since White is forced to enter into a long simplifying variation.

| 14 | g5 | ♗g4! |

A necessary subtlety. After 14

... ed 15 gf ♗xf6 16 ②d5 Black does not have the move ... ♕d8, while 15 ... dc 16 fe cb+ 17 ♔b1 ♖e8 18 f5! gives White a decisive attack.

| 15 | ♕g3! | ed |
| 16 | gf | |

A strong attack seems to arise after 16 ♖xd4 ♗e6 17 f5, but the counter-combination 17 ... ②xe4! 18 ♖xe4 d5! turns the tables.

16	...	dc
17	fe	cb+
18	♔b1	

The Black pawn on b2 only serves to protect the White monarch.

| 18 | ... | ♗xd1 |
| 19 | ef = ♕+ | ♕xf8 |

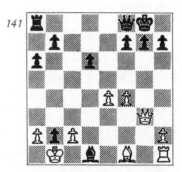

Black has a material advantage and a strong position. All he has to do is avoid trying to defend his surplus on the queenside — remember the remark on 18 ♔b1 — and then the most that White can count on is a restoration of material equality at the cost of placing the initiative in Black's hands, e.g.

a) **20 ♗c4 ♗h5 21 ♕h3 g6 22 ♕d7 b5 23 ♗d5 ♖e8.**

b) **20 ♖g1! g6! (20 ... ♖c8 21 ♗d3! ±; 20 ... d5 21 ♕d3 ♕c5 22 ♖g5!**

±) 21 ♕d3 ♗h5 22 ♕d5! ♕h6! The "highlight" of Black's plan. Now the rook will defend the f7 point, while the queen prepares to compete in the "pawn eating contest": 23 ♕xb7 ♖f8 24 ♖g5 ♗f3! 25 h3 ♕h4! or 23 ♖g5 ♖f8 24 ♗c4 b5 25 ♗b3 ♗e2! or 23 ♗c4 ♖f8 24 ♕xd6 ♗f3 25 f5 ♗xe4 26 f6 ♖e8 27 ♕e7 ♕f8.

B2

| | 13 | ... | b5 |
| | 14 | g5 | ♘d7 |

This route also brings Black equality in the end, but the path is lined with dangers which are difficult to escape unless one is completely familiar with the fine points of the situation.

15 ♗d3

The most logical and natural continuation, when employed in conjunction with the following knight sacrifice. There is not to be seen a more effective way of developing the attack. The plan with 15 h4 is just too slow: 15 ... b4 16 ♘e2 e5 17 ♗e3 ef 18 ♘xf4 ♘e5 19 ♕g3 ♗b7 20 ♘d5 ♗xd5 21 ♖xd5 ♕c7 22 ♗d4 ♖fc8. The cautious 15 a3, on the other hand, allows Black to find the soft spot in the defence of the opposing monarch: 15 ... b4 16 ab ♕xb4 17 ♕h5 ♘c5! 18 ♖g1 ♖b8 19 b3 ♗b7! (Analysis by Shamkovich).

	15	...	b4
	16	♘d5!?	ed
	17	ed	*(142)*

The two strong bishops bear down on the target area and if White is allowed to bring his heavy guns in, the attack will soon bring

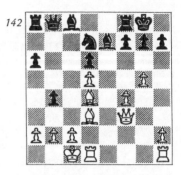

142

the game to an end with a favourable result for him. How should one escape the standard type of sacrifice which arises after, say, 17 ... ♘c5? 18 ♗xh7+ ♔xh7 19 ♕h5+ ♔g8 20 ♗xg7, etc? Black must immediately cut off the working diagonal of the ♗d3, advancing one of the kingside pawns which are protecting his monarch: 17 ... f5 or 17 ... g6. But will his defences be able to withstand the coming onslaught in any event?

17 ... g6!

Just so! 17 ... f5 leads to the loss of the game, as in Tal–Larsen, 1965, which continued 18 ♖de1 ♖f7 19 h4 ♗b7 20 ♗xf5 and White achieved victory. The latest analysis shows that Black cannot fend off the attack even after the improvement 18 ... ♗d8!, when the decisive combination is 19 ♗xg7 ♔xg7 20 ♕h5!, and there is no defence against the threat of 21 ♕h6+ ♔g8 22 g6.

18 ♖de1

The advance of the White h-pawn seems more dangerous here. 18 h4 ♘c5 19 h5 ♘xd3+ 20 ♖xd3 ♗f5 21 hg!, but according to analysis by Shamkovich, Black has a defence: 21 ... fg! 22 ♖xh7 ♔xh7 23 ♖e3 ♕c7 24 ♕e2 ♖a7!! 25 ♗xa7 ♗d8! 26 ♗d4 ♔g8 27 ♕h2 ♕h7. The direct 18 ♕h3 does not achieve its goal after 18 ... ♘f6 19 ♕h6 ♘h5 20 ♗e2 ♖e8 21 ♗xh5 ♗f8! ∓. With the text move White tries to stop the bishop from reaching f8.

18 ... ♗d8
19 ♕h3 ♘e5

19 ... ♗b6 loses to 20 ♗xg6! fg 21 ♖e7.

20 ♕h6 ♗b6!

Black repulses the attack: 21 ♗xb6 ♘xd3+ 22 cd ♕xb6 23 h4 ♗g4 ∓, although there is still some pressure in the position, especially in the variation 21 fe ♗xd4 22 ♖e4! ♗f2!! 23 ♖f1 ♕a7 or 23 e6 fe 24 de ♗b7!.

This analysis requires practical testing, of course, but all the same one can conclude that in the tremendous complications after 13 ... b5 14 g5 ♘d7 Black's chances are no worse.

20 Alternative 8th Moves for Black

1 e4 c5 2 ♘f3 e6 3 d4 cd 4 ♘xd4 ♘f6 5 ♘c3 d6 6 f4 ♘c6 7 ♗e3 ♗e7 8 ♕f3

In this chapter we consider:

A 8 ... ♗d7
B 8 ... e5

A

8 ... ♗d7

Black does not yet determine the position for his queen. His immediate plans call for the exchange of knights on d4 and the transfer of the bishop to c6, after which the advance e4-e5 will be rendered temporarily difficult. On the other hand, his own break d6-d5 is facilitated. Obviously, other schemes of development are also possible: 8 ... ♘xd4 9 ♗xd4 0-0 10 0-0-0 ♕a5, where the battle will rage for a short while around the e5-square, the contrasting objectives being e4-e5 and e6-e5. Who is braver? The direct 11 e5 de 12 fe ♘d7 gives Black an object of attack at e5. The prophylactic move 11 ♕g3 runs into the blatant 11 ... ♘h5 12 ♕g4 (12 ♕e3 ♘xf4!) 12 ... ♘f6 13 ♕g3 ♘h5, drawing. It is possible that the solution to the position is hidden in the variation 11 ♗xf6 ♗xf6 12 ♖xd6

♗xc3 13 ♕xc3 ♕xa2 14 ♔d2! ♕a4 15 ♗d3 b6 16 b3 ♕a3 17 e5 ♗b7 18 ♖a1, putting Black in a difficult defensive position.

9 0-0-0

With the king still in the centre the thrust 9 g4 is risky — 9 ... ♘xd4 10 ♗xd4 e5! 11 fe de 12 ♗xe5 ♕a5!

9 ... 0-0

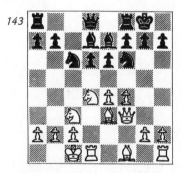

143

If Black delays for even one move, the advance of the g-pawn will become dangerous, i.e. 9 ... a6 10 g4 ♘xd4 11 ♖xd4!, as White has a clear advantage after either 11 ... d5 12 ed ♘xd5 13 ♘xd5 ed 14 ♕xd5 ♗c6 15 ♕e5! or 11 ... e5 12 fe ♘xg4 13 ed ♗f6 14 ♘d5!

10 ♖g1

The most natural continuation. White intends to advance the g-pawn, in which case it is entirely possible that the g-file will be opened, when the ♖g1 will play an important role. In this position White has a number of alternatives, but none of them achieves much:

a) 10 ♘db5 ♕b8 11 g4 a6 12 ♘d4 ♘xd4 13 ♖xd4 ♗c6 14 g5 ♘d7 15 ♖g1 ♖e8 =

b) 10 ♘b3 a5! 11 ♘d2 (11 ♘a4 e5 12 f5 ♘b4 13 ♘b6 a4! 14 ♘d2 a3! ∓) 11 ... e5! 12 f5 ♘d4 13 ♗xd4 ed 14 ♘e2 ♕b6! 15 ♘c4 ♕c5 16 ♖xd4 ♗b5. Black has a strong initiative for the pawn.

c) 10 ♗e2 ♘xd4 11 ♗xd4 ♗c6 12 g4 ♕a5 (12 ... d5!?) 13 g5 ♘d7 14 ♖hg1 b5

144

The diagrammed position is very useful for anyone who wishes to increase his combinational skill. Besides 15 ♕h5 △ ♕h6 e.g. 15 ... g6 16 ♘d5! ed 17 ♕h6 or 15 ... ♘e5! 16 fe de 17 ♗e3 b4, the position hides within itself the interesting variations 15 ♖d3! and 15 f5, but in each case Black will beat back the attack.

10 ... ♘xd4
11 ♗xd4 ♗c6

Once again one must not forget about the possibility of the move 11 ... ♕a5, although in this case 8 ... ♗d7 does seem rather superfluous. On 12 g4 Black can sacrifice a pawn with 12 ... d5, and on 12 e5 ♘e8! (12 ... ♗c6? 13 ef ♗xf3 14 fe △ gf ±) and the consequences of the following operation are unclear: 13 ♕xb7 ♘c7 14 ed ♗xd6 15 ♗e5 ♗xe5 16 fe ♖fb8 17 ♕f3 ♗e8 with the threat of ... ♕b6.

12 g4 d5

Once again a question arises for those who are fond of attacking. How serious is White's attack after 12 ... ♕a5 13 g5 ♘d7 14 ♕h5? It seems to us that it is very serious indeed, but what is your opinion?

The answer: 14 ... b5 15 f5 b4 16 ♗xg7! with a rout; 14 ... e5 15 fe de 16 ♗e3 g6 17 ♕h6 ♖fd8 18 ♗c4 ♘f8 19 ♘d5! and finally, 14 ... ♖fd8 15 f5 ef 16 ♗c4! with strong threats. This is not surprising. By comparison with the analogous idea on the 11th move, here the White pawn succeeds in getting to g5, chasing away the ♘f6. As a result the defence of the Black king is already compromised, and his chances for success in the centre of the board are reduced.

13 e5

It is quite dangerous and illogical to open the centre: 13 ♗xf6? ♗xf6 14 ed ed, and even more so to go after the pawn: 15 ♘xd5 ♗xd5 16 ♕xd5. After 16 ... ♕b6! the two invalids at b2 and g1 cannot be cured immediately.

13   ...   ♘e4!
14   ♔b1   ♗c5!

It is very difficult to transform White's small spatial advantage into something tangible, as Black has no weaknesses or "bad" pieces in the position.

B

8   ...   e5

By this move Black tries to avoid the position with castling on opposite sides. By creating an obstacle in the way of White's castling long, he agrees to accept the difficulties which will arise as a result of pawn weaknesses on the queenside.

The counterthrust ... e5 is also playable on the previous move, that is, in place of 7 ... ♗e7. It seems even stronger, as on 8 ♘xc6 bc 9 fe Black can reply 9 ... ♘g4! 10 ♗f4 ♕b6. 8 ♘f3!, however, guarantees White an opening advantage due to his lead in development after 8 ... ♘g4 9 ♕d2 ♘xe3 10 ♕xe3 ef 11 ♕xf4.

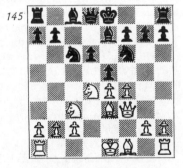

145

9   ♘xc6

The retreat of the knight does not place any serious questions before Black:

a) 9 ♘f5 ♗xf5 10 ef ♘d4 11 ♗xd4 ed 12 ♘b5 ♕a5+ 13 c3 dc =

b) 9 ♘de2 – a cunning idea. In view of the positional threat 10 f5, which would severely limit the operational scope of the ♗c8, Black must either exchange immediately on f4, which would only help the White knight find its best square, or be prepared to exchange his bishop for the knight. There are two acceptable plans here: 9 ... ef 10 ♘xf4 0-0 11 h3 ♘e5 12 ♕f2 b6 13 ♗d4 ♗b7 14 0-0-0 ♕c7 15 ♖e1 ♗c6 16 g4 ♕b7 17 ♕g2 ♘fd7 with complicated play, as in Bronstein-Furman, 1965, or 9 ... ♗g4 10 ♕f2 ♕a5 11 ♘g3 0-0 12 h3 ef 13 ♗xf4 ♗e6 and Black's chances are no worse. We prefer the second option but this is largely a matter of taste. We like it because of the difficulties faced by the White knight.

c) 9 fe (Δ 9 ... de 10 ♘f5 ♗xf5 11 ef ♘d4 12 ♗xd4 ed 13 0-0-0) fails to generate an advantage for White, since Black can replace 9 ... de with the more interesting plan 9 ... ♘xe5!? 10 ♗b5+ ♔f8 (One can also play simply with 10 ... ♘fd7 11 ♕e2 0-0) 11 ♕e2 ♘fg4. At the cost of the right to castle Black obtains the strong point e5 and the possibility of developing his light pieces conveniently. The game Ruderfer-Lepeshkin, 1966 continued instructively: 12 ♗f4 a6 13 ♗a4 ♘g6 14 ♗g3 h5 15 0-0-0 h4 16 ♗e1 ♘f4 17 ♕f3 ♘e5! 18 ♕f1 h3 19 g3 ♗g2 20 ♗d2 ♗g4 =.

9   ...   bc

Here our analysis divides:

B1 10 fe

B2 10 f5
B1

10 fe de

Grandmaster Zaitsev has proposed a paradoxical idea in this position: 10 ... ♘g4!? 11 ed ♕xd6 12 ♗f4 ♘e5 13 ♕g3 ♗f6. Actually, with such weaknesses in his pawn chain Black is prohibited from carrying on the struggle by positional methods, and the pawn sacrifice, which gives him good piece play, is the logical solution. White does not have a wide choice of continuations which can provide him with an advantage. Thus on 14 ♗c4, 14 ... ♕e7! is very strong, threatening ... ♘xc4 and ... ♗h4. The soundest continuation, 14 ♗d3 ♖b8 15 ♘d1 (15 0-0-0 ♖xb2!) leads to a position where the extra pawn plays no part.

11 ♗c4 0-0

The pawn islands at a7 and c6 and the pressure along the f-file are the price which Black has had to pay in order to interrupt the aggressive plans of his opponent. On the other hand, he obtains the option of creating play on the b-file.

146

12 h3!

White is forced to play this prophylactic move, since on the natural 12 0-0 Black has the strong exchanging manoeuvre 12 ... ♘g4! 13 ♖ad1 ♘xe3! in his arsenal. The acceptance of the queen sacrifice — 14 ♖xd8 ♗xd8! — is dangerous, while 14 ♗xf7+ ♔h8 15 ♕xe3 ♕b6! 16 ♕xb6 ab leads to a position where the activity of Black's pieces compensates for the loss of the pawn.

By taking away the square g4 from the Black pieces, White leaves his opponent to find other ways of creating active counterplay. White's chances lie either in the organization of an attack on the king with the help of the open f-file, or in the exchange of heavy pieces and exploitation of the weaknesses of the pawns at a7 and c6 in the endgame.

Praxis has shown that Black stands no worse in this position, but equality cannot be achieved in any old way. The following examples illustrate the dangers which lie before Black: 12 h3 ♕a5 13 0-0 ♗c5 14 ♔h1 ♗d4? 15 ♗g5! ♗e6 16 ♗xf6 ♗xc4 17 ♕g4 g6 18 ♕g5 ± or 12 ... ♗b4 13 0-0 ♗xc3 14 bc ♗e6 15 ♗b3 ♕a5 16 ♗g5! ♕c5+ 17 ♔h2 ♘d7 18 ♕g3 ♔h8 19 ♖ad1 ♘b6 20 ♖f6 ±, Kuzmin–Furman, 1966. The dark-squared bishop is necessary for the defence of the king.

12 ... ♗e6!?

The beginning of a strategically risky plan. Black completely abandons his pawn structure in an attempt to obtain counterplay thanks to White's occupation with castling. But in spite of the fact that the move 12 ... ♗e6 has a considerable amount of practical experience about it, one must not forget about the direct defence via the manoeuvre 12 ... ♘e8 13 0-0 ♘d6, after which the bishop must retreat from its key post on c4 and yield one of the diagonals to its Black counterpart. In our opinion Black obtains fully satisfactory play in these variations: 14 ♗d3 ♗e6 15 b3 ♕a5 16 ♘e2 (16 ♘a4 ♘c4! =) 16 ... c5; 14 ♗b3 ♕a5 15 ♖ad1 ♗a6 16 ♖f2 ♘c4 or 15 ♖fd1 ♘b5! 16 ♘a4 ♘c7 △ ... ♗e6.

13   ♗xe6

Without detailed analysis it is difficult to understand when the black c-pawn stands better on c6 and when it is better off on c5, where it only seems to get in the way of his dark-squared bishop. Praxis has confirmed, however, that if Black does not leave this pawn on c5, but pushes it to c4, he can obtain good counterplay thanks to the opening of the line, for example 13 ♗b3 c5 14 ♕e2 ♖b8 (One can also play an immediate 14 ... c4 15 ♗xc4 ♘h5! 16 ♕xh5 ♗xc4 17 ♔f2 f5! with strong counterplay) 15 ♗xe6 (Somewhat better is 15 ♖b1 ♗xb3 16 ab, but even here after 16 ... ♖b4! 17 ♗g5 c4 Black has everything under control; and on 15 0-0, 15 ... ♕c8! is quite strong.) 15 ... fe 16 0-0 (after 16 b3? White must fight for equality: 16 ... c4! 17 ♕xc4 ♕c8! 18 0-0 ♕xc4 19 bc ♖b4!, Tal–Balashov, 1973. Tal could not

manage to salvage a draw.) 16 ... ♖xb2 17 ♕c4 ♕c8! Thanks to his extra doubled pawn Black dominates more squares in the centre and therefore has the better chances. After 13 ♗b3 c5 14 ♗xe6 fe 15 ♕e2 Black carries out his basic plan of counterplay, which is connected with the position of the White king in the centre: 15 ... c4! 16 ♕xc4 ♘h5! 17 ♕xe6+ ♔h8 18 ♘d5 ♗h4+ 19 ♔d2 ♘g3 20 ♖hd1 ♕a5! 21 ♔c1 ♘e2+ 22 ♔b1 ♖ab8 with a mating attack.

Therefore White must keep an eye on the Pc6 until the completion of his development.

13   ...   fe

14   ♕e2

If White manages to get his king out of the centre in the near future then the rest of the game will be a mere matter of technique, given the weakness of the Black pawn chain. For example: 14 ... ♖b8 15 0-0! ♖xb2 16 ♖ab1! ♖b4 17 ♕a6 ♕c7 18 a3 ♖xb1 19 ♖xb1 ♖a8 20 a4! ± Hübner–Petrosian, 1970.

14   ...   ♕b8

The knight sacrifice looks quite tempting, after which Black will have a beautiful pawn chain. There are two ways of bringing this about, but in each case White holds on to the advantage: 14 ... ♕a5 15 ♕c4 ♘d5 16 ed cd 17 ♕a4 ♕c7 18 0-0-0 d4 19 ♘e4 ♕b7 20 ♗g5! and 14 ... ♘d5 15 ed ♗h4+ 16 ♔d1 cd 17 ♗c5!.

With the move 14 ... ♕b8 Black activates his queen, in order to limit the actions of her White counterpart.

15   ♖ab1!

On 15 0-0 ♕xb2 16 ♕c4 there follows 16 ... ♕b4 17 ♕xe6+ ♔h8. Black obtains sufficient counterplay against 15 0-0-0 ♕b4 16 a3 ♕a5 17 ♕c4 by 17 ... ♔h8, for example 18 ♖d3 ♖fe8 19 ♘a4 ♘h5 20 ♖c3 ♘f4, Kuindzhi–Balashov, 1974.

15 ...   ♘e8

Since the movement of the ♖a1 has eliminated the possibility of queenside castling, the sacrifice of the knight deserves consideration: 15 ... ♘d5!? 16 ed ♗h4+ 17 ♔d1 cd 18 ♗c5 ♖c8! when it will be difficult for White to coordinate his pieces.

16 ♗f2   ♘d6
17 0-0   ♕b4

White has managed to bring his king to safety, but Black has activated his queen, bringing the square c4, which is of the utmost importance to him, under control. The only remaining task is to find a good working position for his bishop. After 18 a3 ♕c4! 19 ♖fe1 ♗d8! 20 ♖ad1 ♕xe2 21 ♖xe2 ♘c4 Black transfers his bishop to b6 and equalises: 22 ♘a4 ♗b6 23 ♘xb6 ab 24 b3 ♘xa3 25 ♗xb6 ♘b5.

B2

10 f5! (147)

An interesting conception of the Belgian Master Boey. White would like to fix the pawn structure in the centre, and disregarding the open b-line, place his king on c1, in order to enable the g-pawn to advance with greater effect. To this end the white pawn on f5 serves to cut off the Black pieces from the defence

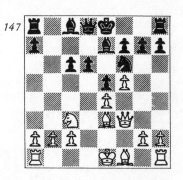

147

of their king, should he move to g8. The ♗f1 will move over to b3, where it will dominate the a2-g8 diagonal, holding the critical d5 and f7 squares under his thumb.

The beautiful pawn chain c6-d6-e5, which permits Black to control the entire centre, is in reality a defensive liability, as it limits the manouvering space of the Black pieces. The Pc6 even blocks the "Sicilian line" (c-file), obtaining in a less than equal exchange the b-file. If play develops quietly Black will be able to exchange his passive bishop and consolidate his position, but he can have little hope of the quiet life, as White is ready to begin his kingside pawn storm at the earliest opportunity. Therefore Black must find active and rapid countermeasures, and this almost automatically requires him to destroy his central fortress when his d-pawn thrusts forward. Dangers lie ahead, and although at first glance there appear to be several tempting plans for development, this only confuses matters, as not all of them can be added to the list of acceptable continuations once they have undergone the test of analysis.

10   ...   ♕a5

The immediate break d6-d5 leads to serious difficulties as the pawns at d5 and e5 will only become objects of attack, and making the position of the Black king in the centre insecure. The negative evaluation of the move 10 ... d5 is based on the variations 11 ed ♘xd5 12 ♗b5! ♘xe3 13 ♗xc6+ ♔f8 14 ♕xe3 ♖b8 15 ♖d1 ♕c7 16 ♘xd5 ♕xc6 17 ♘xe7 ± or 11 ... cd 12 0-0-0 e4 13 ♕h3! ♕a5 14 ♗b5+ ♔f8 15 g4 ± .

Black cannot create good conditions for the break by interpolating 10 ... 0-0 11 0-0-0! After 11 ... d5 (Here the transfer of the knight is insufficient: 11 ... ♘d7 12 h4! ♘b6 13 g4 ±) 12 ed cd the opposition ♖d1-♕d8 and the impossibility of the advance ... d4 (because of the opposition ♕f3-♖a8) conspire to ruin Black's game. After 13 ♗c4! e4 14 ♕e2 ♕c7 15 ♘xd5 White's advantage is obvious, Ree–Reshevsky, 1974.

10 ... g6 is not sufficient for equality. Black attempts to achieve several pawn exchanges on the kingside and thus liquidate White's threats of a pawn storm, but after 11 g4 h5 12 g5 ♘g4 13 f6! ♘xe3 14 ♕xe3 ♗f8 Black will not be able to unravel his pieces on the kingside without material loss.

Another kingside prophylactic also proves inadequate: 10 ... h5, intending to prevent g2-g4. Black does hold up the advance of the white pawns temporarily, but at a tremendous cost, as his king will

find difficulty in locating a solid position. As long as the game is not opened up this will not be felt, for example 11 ♗c4 ♘d7 12 0-0-0 ♘b6 13 ♗b3 ♗a6 14 ♔b1 ♘c4 15 ♗c1, but how will the ♖h8 get into the play?

Black can regroup more successfully if he undertakes the manoeuvre immediately: 10 ... ♘d7 11 ♗c4 ♘b6 12 ♗b3 ♗a6 13 0-0-0 ♘c4. There is an amusing knight tour in the variation 14 ♕e2 ♘xe3 15 ♕xa6! ♕c8! (15 ... ♘xd1 16 ♕xc6+ ♔f8 17 ♖xd1 ±) 16 ♕xc8+ ♖xc8 17 ♖de1 ♘g4 18 h3 ♘f6 19 g4 ♘d7! The negative aspect of this leisurely manner of regrouping is the absence of active counterplay for Black, although after 14 ♔b1 ♕c7 15 ♗c1 0-0-0 he does have a solid position.

10 ... ♖b8 is also possible, usually leading to a transposition of moves after 11 0-0-0 ♕a5 12 ♗c4 0-0 13 ♗b3. Deviations from this transposition involving the advance of the g-pawn are hazardous: 12 g4 d5 13 ed ♖xb2! 14 ♔xb2 ♗a3+ ∓ or 13 g4 d5 14 ed ♖xb2 15 d6 ♕xc3 16 ♗b3 ♖xb3 17 de ♕b2+ 18 ♔d2 ♖d3+! 19 ♔xd3 e4+ etc.

Playing the queen to a5 is a flexible continuation which not only breaks the opposition ♖d1-♕d8, but also frees the d8 square for the rook.

11   ♗c4!

White must reckon with the appearance of the bishop on b4, for example 11 g4 d5 12 ♗d2 ♗b4, and if 11 0-0-0, Black can

either apply a similar plan, 11 ... d5
12 ed ♗b4, this time as a gambit
after 13 ♗d2 0-0 14 dc ♖b8, or he
can exchange the light-squared
bishops by 11 ... ♗a6 12 ♗xa6
♕xa6 and then castle queenside.

By transferring his bishop to b3
via c4, White not only avoids this
exchange, but also solidly defends
the Pb2.

148

11 ... ♗b7

Not particularly subtle, but a
solid enough continuation. When
Black advances the Pd6, both of his
bishops will find employment.
Black must find the most profitable, and at the same time fastest,
method of opening the centre,
otherwise the move 10 ... ♕a5 will
turn out to be a mere waste of time.
In that case White will get his play
on the kingside moving first. Thus
the transfer of the knight to b6,
which we also considered on the
last move, is still too slow, this time
because the queen has abandoned
d8: **11 ... ♘d7** 12 0-0-0 ♘b6 13
♗b3 ♗a6 14 f6! gf 15 ♖xd6!
♗xd6 16 ♕xf6 ♔d7 (16 ... ♖f8
17 ♕xd6 ♖d8 18 ♕xc6+ ♖d7 19
♘c5 ♖g8 20 ♗xf7 ±) 17 ♖d1 ♖ad8

18 ♕xd6+ ♔c8 19 ♕xc6+ ♔b8
20 ♘d5 ±.

The immediate break with **11 ...
d5** leads to gambit play: 12 ed
♗b4 13 ♗d2 e4 (13 ... 0-0 14
0-0-0 cd 15 ♘xd5 ±) 14 ♘xe4
♗xd2+ 15 ♘xd2 0-0 16 0-0-0 cd
17 ♗b3, when Black does not have
sufficient counterchances.

The manoeuvre **11 ... ♗a6** is
sufficiently solid and promising, as
Black tries to first eliminate the unpleasant White bishop and only
then begin operations in the centre.
After 12 ♗b3 (Weaker is 12 ♕e2
♗xc4 13 ♕xc4 0-0! 14 ♕xc6 ♖fc8
∓) 12 ... 0-0 13 0-0-0 ♘d7 14 g4
♘c5 there arises a critical position,
where White must part with one of
his bishops. The exchange 15 ♗xc5
ends up in Black's favour after 15
... dc! 16 h4 (16 ♖d7 ♗g5+) 16 ...
c4! 17 ♗a4 ♖ac8 △ ... ♗b4. 15 g5
♘xb3+ 16 cb d5 leads to a sharp
position where it is difficult to
definitively evaluate the chances,
for example, 17 f6 ♗b4! 18 fg
♖fd8 or 17 ed ♗b4 18 ♗d2 cd!
(Weaker is 18 ... ♗xc3 19 ♗xc3
♕xa2 20 dc ♕xb3 21 ♕e4 ♖fe8
22 g6 ±) 19 ♕xd5 ♕c7 20 ♖he1
♖fe9 △ ... ♖ad8.

One can also recommend the
plan with **11 ... ♖b8**, when the
d6-d5 break is carried out in conjunction with an attack on the
weakest point in the White position
− the Pb2. In this case 12 ♗b3 does
not promise White much: 12 ... d5!
13 ♗d2 ♗b4 (13 ... d4? 14 ♘d5
♕d8 15 ♘xf6+! ♗xf6 16 0-0-0 0-0
17 h4 △ g4 with a decisive attack.)
14 0-0-0 d4 15 ♘b1 0-0 16 a3

♗xd2+ 17 ♘xd2 ♘d7 18 g4 ♘c5 =, Sigurjonsson–Olafsson, 1976. After the bold 12 0-0-0, however, there arises an exceptionally interesting situation, in which Black is temporarily given the possibility of exploiting the weakness of the b2 square which is now needed for the defence of the White king.

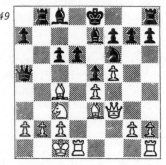

149

For this he has only one route — the ♗e7 must immediately enter the game by **12 ... d5!?** The variations after 13 ed resemble a puzzle, and although today White is weathering the storm, who can say what will happen tomorrow? You can check these variations for yourself: 13 ... ♖xb2! (Inferior is 13 ... ♗a3?! 14 ba ♕xc3 because of 15 ♗xa7! ♕b2+ 16 ♔d2 ±) 14 d6! (It is dangerous to take the rook: 14 ♔xb2 ♕a3+! 15 ♔b1 ♕xc3 16 ♗b3 cd 17 ♗xd5 [White obtained the advantage by another route in Balashov–Andersson, 1978: 17 ♗g5 ♕c7 18 ♗xf6 ♗xf6 19 ♗a4+ ♔f8 10 ♕xd5] 17 ... e4! 18 ♕e2 0-0 19 ♗b3 ♘d5! 20 ♗d4 ♕xd4 =) 14 ... e4! 15 ♘xe4 ♖xc2+! 16 ♔xc2 ♗xf5 17 ♖d4 ♗xd6 18 ♖f1 ♗g6 19 ♖xd6 ♗e4+ 20 ♕xe4+ and White

enters into a decisive counterattack.

Praxis has shown that a more fundamental preparation for the advance of the d-pawn is **12 ... 0-0** 13 ♗b3, and this plan is more promising. Now instead of the sacrifice of a rook at b2, Black can give it up for the bishop on b3, immediately freeing the king from worries along the a2-g8 diagonal, for example 13 ... ♖xb3 14 cb d5 15 ed cd. In the game Gaprindashvili–Hartoch, 1976, White won after 16 ♖xd5! ♘xd5 17 ♘xd5 ♗d6 18 ♘f6+ gf? 19 ♗h6, but 18 ... ♔h8 would have left the outcome uncertain, as both kings would have found themselves in danger. The validity of the plan with 11 ... ♖b8 can also be shown by more quiet means: 13 ... ♘d7 (Instead of 13 ... ♖xb3) 14 g4 ♘c5 15 ♗xc5 dc 16 h4 ♖b4! 17 a3 ♖d4! where the chances are equal.

12   0-0-0   0-0
13   g4

White must hurry, since 13 ♗b3 only wastes time, the Black king having already left the centre. After 13 ... d5! we have:

a) 14 ed cd 15 ♘xd5 (15 ♗xd5 e4! 16 ♗xe4 ♘xe4 17 ♘xe4 ♕xa2) 15 ... ♗xd5 16 ♗xd5 e4! 17 ♗xe4 ♖ab8 18 ♗d5 ♖xb2 19 ♔xb2 ♗a3+ 20 ♔b1 ♘xd5 21 ♕xd5 ♕xd5 22 ♖xd4 ♖b8+ with a draw.

b) 14 ♗d2 ♗b4! (worse is 14 ... d4? 15 ♘d5 ♕d8 16 ♘xf6+! ♗xf6 17 h4 with an attack) 15 a3 ♗xc3 16 ♗xc3 ♕c7 17 ed cd 18 ♕g3 ♘e4 19 ♕xe5 ♕xe5 20 ♗xe5 ♘f2 with an unclear game.

13   ...   d5

14   g5!

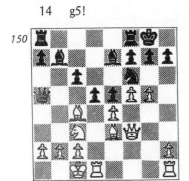

150

The culmination of the struggle. Since the White pawn storm is in full flight and the opening of the g-file is inescapable, Black must hang on to the one piece which is so critical for the defence of his king – the dark-squared bishop. Therefore the natural 14 ... dc 15 gf ♗xf6 would be a mistake, since the unexpected 16 ♖d6! creates an unstoppable attack: 16 ... ♖fd8 17 ♖xf6! gf 18 ♕g3+ ♔f8 (There is no salvation in 18 ... ♔h8 19 ♕h4! ♖d6 19 ♖g1 ♖g8 21 ♖xg8+ ♔xg8

22 ♗h6 mating.) 19 ♘a4!! ♕xa4 20 ♗c5+ ♔e8 21 ♕g8+ ♔d7 22 ♖d1+ etc. 14 ... ♘xe4 15 ♘xe4 de 16 ♕e2 is also clearly insufficient, as there is no defence to the threat of destruction by either g6 or f6.

There is only one defence for Black in this perilous situation, but it is sufficient: 14 ... d4 15 gf ♗xf6 16 ♗d2 dc 17 ♗xc3 ♕c5. Black has managed to escape the direct attack. He is still a bit worse because of his defective pawn structure on the queenside, but even after 18 b3! ♖ad8 19 ♖xd8 (19 ♔b2 ♖d4!) 19 ... ♖xd8 20 ♔b2 White's advantage is not very large. Of course, to play such a sharp variation with Black only to wind up in a quiet endgame is not to everyone's taste, but as the attentive reader will already have noticed, there are other branches of the analysis given above which are also promising. Black's position in the variation with 10 f5 can be considered fully playable and solid.

21   9 ♗d3 a6

1 e4 c5 2 ♘f3 e6 3 d4 cd 4 ♘xd4
♘f6 5 ♘c3 d6 6 f4 ♘c6 7 ♗e3
♗e7 8 ♕f3 ♕c7 9 ♗d3 a6
A 10 0-0
B 10 ♘b3
A

10   0-0   0-0

151

This position is often reached by another move order: 1 e4 c5 2 ♘f3 ♘c6 3 d4 cd 4 ♘xd4 e6 5 ♘c3 a6 6 ♗e3 ♕c7 7 ♗d3 ♘f6 8 0-0 ♗e7 9 f4 d6 10 ♕f3 0-0. By comparison with the classical Scheveningen White has managed to get his bishop to d3 in just one move, and even the queen has managed to take up her fighting position immediately instead of adopting the two-step manoeuvre ♕d1-e1-g3. White does not fear the exchange of bishop for

knight after ♘c6-b4xd3, since in this case he will be able to occupy the open c-file quickly and strengthen his position in the centre. Now neither 11 g4 nor 11 ♕h3 will bear fruit because of 11 ... ♘xd4 12 ♗xd4 e5, and therefore he must find another method of strengthening his position.

11   ♔h1

An intelligent prophylactic. By taking his king away from the g1-a7 diagonal, White avoids the standard liberating manoeuvre 11 ... ♘xd4 12 ♗xd4 e5 13 fe de 14 ♕g3 ♗c5!

Nevertheless, praxis has shown that the direct 11 ♖ae1 does not by any means ease Black's problems in the opening. Thus after 11 ... ♘xd4 12 ♗xd4 e5 13 fe de 14 ♕g3

152

14 ... &c5 15 &xc5 ₩xc5+ 16 &h1
Black cannot count on the defensive plan 16 ... &h8 17 &xf6 gf 18
₩h4 &g8, because White can play
17 &d5! &xd5 18 ₩xe5 &e6 19
c4! which requires serious repair
work. Only here does the strength
of 11 &ae1 make itself felt, as on
19 ... ₩c7 there follows 20 ed, and
the ₩e5 is protected by the rook.
Black has hopes for counterplay in
the centre after 19 ... f6!? 20
₩xe6 &b4 21 &b1 &ae8, but it is
necessary to test this idea thoroughly. Besides 16 ... &h8, Black
can play 16 ... &e8 or 16 ... ₩d6,
but in each case White puts his
knight on d5 and dictates the play.
But Black can exploit the position
of the king on g1 in another way.
Returning to the diagram we have
14 ... &e6! after which it is clear
that the Pe5 is immune: 15 ₩xe5
&d6 16 ₩g5 &xh2+ 17 &h1 h6!
or 15 &xe5 ₩c5+ 16 &h1 &h5!
The advance of the knight to d5
does not work: 15 &d5? &xd5 16
ed &c5! 17 &xc5 ₩xc5+ 18 &h1
e4!. There remains only 15 &h1,
which allows Black to regroup with
15 ... &d7 16 &e3 &fe8 17 &d5
&xd5 18 ed g6, which equalises
in the end.

A more complicated situation
for both sides arises if Black declines the simplification and answers
11 &ae1 with 11 ... &d7, completing his development. After 12
₩g3 (Clearly inferior are 12 g4
&xd4 14 &xd4 e5 or 12 &de2 b5
13 g4 b4 14 &d1 &c8 or 12 &b3
b5 13 a3 b4 or 12 a3 &ab8 13
₩g3 b5 14 &f3 b4) there arises

another interesting Sicilian position,

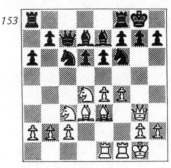

in which it is necessary to compare
the positive and negative aspects
of the &d3 with the classical
Scheveningen where it stands on
e2. After 12 ... b5 13 e5 de 14 fe
&e8 15 &f3! White stands clearly
better, while he also has a strong
attack in the event of 12 ... &h5
13 ₩h3. For example: 13 ... &xf4
14 &xf4 &xd4 15 e5 &f5 16 g4
de 17 gf ef 18 f6 &c5+ 19 &f2!
&xf2+ 20 &f1! h6 21 ₩g4 g5 22
₩h5. Or 13 ... &xd4 14 ₩xh5 g6!
(14 ... &c6? 15 &f3! ±; 14 ...
&f6? 15 f5 &e5 16 f6! gf 17
&xf6! ±) 15 ₩h3 &c6 16 f5 ₩d8
17 &h6 &e5 (17 ... &e8! 18 e5!
&xe5 19 &xe5 de 20 fg hg 21
&xg6!) 18 &xf8 &xf8 19 f6. Only
12 ... &h8 maintains Black's defences and avoids immediate catastrophe, although after 13 &f3 he
has no real chances of equalising.

11 ...   &d7
The immediate 11 ... b5 gives
White a strong attack after 12 e5!
&xd4 13 &xd4 de (13 ... &b7?
14 ₩h3 ±) 14 &xe5 ₩b7 15 ₩h3.
There is however another strategy
which deserves consideration: 11 ...

&fd8!?   12 a3 &xd4 13 &xd4 b5
14 &ae1 &e8 15 &g3 &b7 16 e5
de. Instead of 14 &ae1 White can
try to attack right away with 14 e5,
but this leads the game into the
twilight zone after 14 ... de 15 fe
&xd4! 16 &xa8 &g4 17 &e2 &xe5
or 14 ... de 15 &xe5 &a7 16 &e4
&b7! 17 &xf6 &xf6 18 &xf6+ gf
19 &h5 &d4! 20 &xh7+ &f8.

    12   &Eae1

    12 &g3 b5 13 e5 de 14 &xc6
&xc6 15 fe is another method of
attack based on an attempt to exploit the weakness of the g7 square
in the variation 15 ... &d7 16 &f4
&c5 17 &h6. After 17 ... g6 18
&xf8 &xf8, however, White is left
with the exchange and problems
involving the defence of the Pe5.
The play enters a new arena, where
White's advantage is not very large.

    12   ...   b5

    13   a3

    13 g4 is a less original manner of
carrying out the attack, and it is
important to show the immediate
refutation 13 ... &xd4 14 &xd4 e5
15 fe (15 &d5 &xd5 16 ed &h4!)
15 ... de 16 &d5! &d6!, but one
should also take note of the puzzling
game Mikhailchishin-Taborov,1978,
where instead of 14 ... e5, Black
played 14 ... &c6 15 g5 &d7 16
&d5! &d8 17 &h5 (The correct
continuation was 17 &e3!, but then
we would have been deprived of the
following turn of events!) 17 ...
ed 18 &f3 &e5! 19 fe g6
(*154*) 20 &xh7+! &xh7 21
&h3+ &g8 22 ed6 f6 23 e5!!
White is a whole queen down,
but he peacefully strengthens the

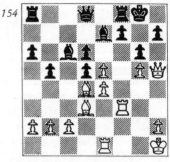

position of his pieces. 23 ... &xd6
24 ef!! Who needs the Black bishop!
24 ... &f7 25 &h6 &e8. Only after
detailed analysis was the correct
defence discovered: 25 ... &f8! 26
&xg6+ &h8 27 &e7! &e8! 28 &f5!
&c8!! 29 &xc8 &xc8 30 h4! &h7.
In the game there was 26 &xg6+
&h8 27 &h6+ with a draw by perpetual check. This fantastic game
illustrates the huge tactical potential of the Sicilian, despite the fact
that both players have castled on
the same side.

    13   ...   &Eab8!

    Black threatens to open the
b-file.

    14   &xc6   &xc6

    15   &h3!   &Ebd8!

    The only way of cutting off the
threat which lies hidden in the advance of the e-pawn.

    16   &d4

    The break 16 e5 de 17 fe is not
dangerous. On the contrary, after
17 ... &xe5 18 &b6 &xd3! 19 cd
&d6 20 &g1 &d8 it is the Black
side that dictates the play. Now
White again threatens to advance
the e-pawn, and if 16 ... g6, he has
17 f5, which is quite dangerous.
Black has no choice.

16   ...   e5!
17   fe   de

Black can be satisfied with the result of the opening. All of his pieces are participating in the game, and his king position is solid. 18 Ae3 is obviously not dangerous for Black, and neither is the forcing variation 18 ᐰd5 Axd5 19 Axe5! ₩xe5 20 ed ₩xb2 21 ᙏxf6 g6 =, Novopashin-Korchnoi, 1962.

B

10   ᐰb3

White adopts radical means of preventing the exchanging operation in the centre, temporarily consigning his knight to a passive position.

10   ...   b5
11   0-0   Ab7 *(155)*

This position also arises in the Paulsen variation after 1 e4 c5 2 ᐰf3 e6 3 d4 cd 4 ᐰxd4 a6 5 ᐰc3 ₩c7 6 Ad3 ᐰc6 7 Ae3 ᐰf6 8 0-0 b5 9 ᐰb3 Ae7 10 f4 d6 11 0-0. Less exact is 11 ... 0-0, though it is risky for White to play 12 e5 because of 12 ... de 13 fe ᐰxe5 14 ₩xa8 ᐰeg4!, but there is an alternative method of attack 12 g4!. This attack is not dangerous if the correct defence is applied: 12 ... b4 13 ᐰe2 e5 14 f5 (14 g5 ᐰg4 15 f5 ᐰxe3 16 ₩xe3 ₩a7!) 14 ... d5! 15 ᐰg3 Ab7 16 g5 de 17 ᐰxe4 ᐰxe4 18 Axe4 ᐰd4, Ghizdavu-Fernandez, 1972. Both 12 e5 and 12 e4 would be utterly pointless after 11 ... Ab7. Other continuations after 11 ... 0-0, for example 12 ᙏae1, 12 a3 or 12 a4, lead to a complicated struggle.

White has a pretty wide selection here in his plan of attack.

a) He can play all over the board with 12 a4 b4 13 ᐰe2 ᐰa5 14 ᐰxa5 (After 14 ᐰbd4 ᐰc4 15 Ac1 d5 16 e5 ᐰe4 Black has everything under control, Spassky-Bukhtin, 1960) 14 ... ₩xa5 15 g4 ₩c7 16 g5 ᐰd7 17 ᐰd4 g6 with a complicated game.

b) He can apply preliminary prophylaxis on the queenside: 12 a3 ᙏc8! (On 12 ... 0-0, there is the interesting line 13 ₩h3! b4 14 ᐰa4 ba 15 ᙏxa3 d5 16 e5 ᐰe4 17 ᐰbc5!) 13 ᙏae1 0-0 14 ₩h3 b4. Another puzzle. On 15 ab ᐰxb4 16 e5 de 17 fe there follows 17 ... ₩xe5! 18 ᙏxf6 ᐰxd3! and Black goes over to the attack. Kupreichik sacrificed a knight against Tal in 1970: 15 ᐰd5! ed 16 ed ᐰb8 17 Ad4 g6 18 ᙏf3 and won, but later the incorrectness of the sacrifice was demonstrated: 18 ... Axd5 19 ᙏfe3 Ad8! 20 ₩h4 ᐰbd7 21 ₩h6 ₩b7 22 ᙏg3 Ab6!

c) He can prepare an attack on the king with 12 ₩h3. As praxis has shown, it is not necessary for Black to castle here. He can also play both 12 ... ᙏc8 and 12 ... ᐰb4 13 a3 ᐰxd3 14 cd e5. He can even try

12 ... h5! 13 ♔h1 ♘g4 14 ♗g1 g6
15 ♖ae1 ♗f6 16 e5 de 17 ♘c5
♗c8 18 ♕f3 ♖b8. In the opinion
of Gutman, who has worked out
similar methods of defence with the
king in the centre, the chances are
equal here.

Well, what happens if Black does
castle? If White doesn't mate, then
what is his queen doing on h3?
12 ... 0-0 13 ♖ae1 (The pawn sacrifice is incorrect: 13 e5? de 14 fe
♘xe5 15 ♗f4 ♕b6+!) 13 ... ♖ad8
(One can also play 13 ... ♖ac8 14
a3 b4, transposing into the above-
mentioned game Kupreichik–Tal.)
14 g4 ♘b4 15 g5 ♘d7 16 f5 ♘xd3
17 cd ef! 18 ef ♖fe8. It becomes
clear that the head-on attack does
not work: 19 f6 ♗f8 20 fg ♗xg7
21 ♖xf7 ♔xf7 22 ♕xh7 ♖xe3! 23
♖xe3 ♘e5 and the position of the
White king will soon become an
object of Black's counterattack,
keeping in mind that the ♗b7 has
no counterpart on the White team.

The most natural preparation for
the attack is to develop the ♖a1.

12   ♖ae1   ♘b4!

We have already considered what
can happen to the Black king if he
castles kingside. It is impossible to
recommend 12 ... 0-0-0 as White's
pieces in the centre are well placed
for a queenside attack. After 13 h3
♘d7 14 ♕f2 ♖dg8 15 a4 b4 16
♘b5! the White attack is well
under way, Ciocaltea–Andersson,
1974. 12 ... ♖c8 is possible although
it leads to well known positions after
13 ♕h3 ♘b4 14 a3 ♘xd3 15 cd 0-0
16 ♕g3 e5 =, Gheorghiu–Stein,

1971.

The move 12 ... ♘b4 is logical
because it removes the opposing
light-squared bishop from the game,
and reduces White's attacking potential.

13   a3   ♘xd3
14   cd   d5

Castling short is another solid
continuation, but the text move
undermines the Pe4 and again
creates pressure in the centre, so it
is more promising and timely. If
Black delays for even one move,
14 ... ♖c8 15 ♕h3, the advance of
the d-pawn will prove to be a mistake after 16 e5.

15   ♗d4

The weakness of the e-pawn
does not allow White time to pile
up on the c5 square: 15 ♖c1 de
16 ♘xe4 ♗xe4! 17 de ♕b7 18 ♘c5
♗xc5 19 ♗xc5 ♘xe4.

15   ...   de
16   ♘xe4

The activity of the White pieces
is of a fleeting nature, but the defects of his position are permanent.
Black has two promising methods
of fighting for the initiative: 16 ...
0-0 17 ♗xf6 ♗xf6 18 ♘xf6+ gf 19
♕g3+ ♔h8 20 ♕h4? ♖g8 or even ...
♕e7; and 16 ... ♗d5! 17 ♖c1 ♕d8,
when Black holds the strong bishop
and a pawn chain without any
defects.

Thus the deployment of the
White pieces with kingside castling
is interesting and dynamic, but it
gives Black chances ... if he knows
the subtleties of the variations well.

22 6 f4 a6

1 e4 c5 2 ♘f3 d6 3 d4 cd 4 ♘xd4 ♘f6 5 ♘c3 e6 6 f4 a6

In this chapter the Scheveningen systems with f4 will be considered, where White develops his ♗f1 not on e2, but on d3, and the ♘b8 enters the game via d7, either immediately or after a few moves.

      7   ♗e3

Sometimes this position is reached via a move order which is characteristic of the Najdorf: 5 ... a6 6 ♗e3 e6 7 f4 etc.

There is another fully acceptable system in which 7 ♗d3 is played before developing the ♗c1.

156

In this case the queen will often go to e2 to support the advance of the e-pawn, and the ♗c1 will find itself on d2, in order that it not get in the way of the queen and where it can defend the ♘c3. This allows White to play on the queen-side, a rather unusual strategy in the Scheveningen. A sharp situation arises which is extremely dynamic, rather like that after 7 ♗e3.

Here are some characteristic examples of the struggle after 7 ♗d3:

a) 7 ... ♘bd7 8 ♕f3 (The position after 8 0-0 ♕b6 9 ♗e3 ♕xb2 10 ♘cb5 ab 11 ♘xb5 ♖a5 is interesting for analysis.) 8 ... ♕c7 9 a4 (after 9 g4 or 9 ♗e3 the play develops along lines discussed elsewhere in the text) 9 ... ♘c5 10 0-0 b6 11 ♗d2 ♗b7 12 b4 ♘cd7 13 ♖ae1 ♗e7 14 ♕h3 0-0-0 15 ♕e3 ♖he8 16 ♕e2 with a threatening initiative for White on the queen-side, Ghizdavu–Ayansky, 1971.

b) 7 ... ♕c7 8 0-0 b5 9 a3 ♗b7 10 ♕e2 ♘bd7 11 ♔h1 ♗e7 12 ♗d2 ♖c8 13 b4! ♘b6 14 a4 ba with a complex game, in which the White pieces play the more active role, Gufeld–Espig, 1980.

c) 7 ... b5 8 e5 (More solid is 8 0-0 ♗b7 9 ♕e2 e5 10 ♘b3 ♘bd7 11 ♗d2 ♗e7 12 ♘d1!?) 8 ... de

9 fe ♘d5 (9 ... ♘fd7 10 ♘xe6!
leads to a massacre) 10 ♕g4 ♘b4!
11 0-0 ♘xd3 12 cd ♗c5 13 ♗e3
0-0 14 ♔h1 ♗xd4 15 ♗xd4 ♗d7
with a complicated struggle, where
Black's chances are no worse,
Kupreichik–Anikaev, 1979.

d) 7 ... ♘c6 8 ♘f3 (8 ♗e3 has
already been discussed) 8 ... ♗e7
9 0-0 ♕c7 10 ♔h1 b5 11 e5 de
12 fe ♘d7 13 ♗f4 ♘c5 =

It is difficult to give preference
to one bishop move over the
other, so we will limit ourselves
to the observation that the system with 7 ♗d3 is less well-known.

White can generally keep to himself the intended positions of the
bishops, playing 7 ♕f3 ♕b6 (White's
initiative will develop even more
quickly if the knight is allowed to
remain at d4: 7 ... ♕c7 8 g4 b5
9 g5 ♘fd7 10 a3 ♗b7 11 ♗d3
♘c5 12 f5 e5?! 13 ♘de2 ♘bd7
14 ♗e3 ♗e7 15 ♘g3 g6 16 0-0-0
♘xd3 17 ♖xd3 with a vice-like
grip on Black's position, Balashov–
Najdorf, 1980.) 8 ♘b3 ♕c7 9 g4 b5
10 ♗d3. Here Black can choose
between 10 ... h6?! 11 h4 b4
12 ♘e2 h5 13 g5 ♘g4 14 ♗d2
♕b6 15 g6 fg 16 e5; 10 ... b4 11
♘e2 ♗b7 12 g5 ♘fd7 13 ♗e3;
and, finally, 10 ... ♗b7 11 g5
♘fd7 12 ♗e3, but in each case
White retains the initiative.

After 7 ♗e3 Black must choose
the moment for tossing his b-pawn
into the game, as that is, after all,
the point of ... a6.

A 7 ... ♕c7
B 7 ... b5

A

7 ...   ♕c7

At the moment no one can say
whether it is necessary for Black to
force the advance of his Pb7, and
it is difficult to predict whether
normal developing moves might
damage the Black position so early
in the opening stages of the game.
By playing 7 ... ♕c7, Black retains
the option of transposing into the
classical Scheveningen with the
knight on c6.

Besides 7 ... ♕c7, one can even
play 7 ... ♘bd7, for example 8 ♕f3
e5! 9 ♘f5 g6 10 ♘g3 ef 11 ♗xf4
♘e5 12 ♕f2 ♗e7 13 0-0-0 ♕a5 or
8 ♗d3 b5 9 e5 de 10 ♘c6 ♕c7 11
fe ♗b7 12 ef ♗xc6 with complicated play. Perhaps the best reply
to 7 ... ♘bd7 is 8 a4, intending a
binding strategy.

The path divides:
A1 8 ♕f3
A2 8 g4

A1

8   ♕f3

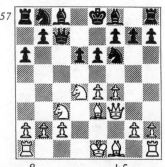

157

8 ...   b5

Further delaying the advance of
the b-pawn frees White's hands for
play in the centre.

a) 8 ... ♗e7 9 0-0-0 (On 9 g4 Black

can undertake operations in the centre with 9 ... d5!? 10 ed ♗b4!) 9 ... ♘bd7 10 g4 ♘c5 11 g5 ♘fd7 12 ♕h3 b5 13 g6 b4 14 gf+ ♔xf7 15 ♘ce2 and White has good prospects thanks to the unstable defence of the Black king, as Tal has demonstrated.

b) **8 ... ♘bd7** 9 g4 (on 9 0-0-0 the best continuation is 9 ... b5 10 ♗b3 b4 11 ♘b1 ♗b7 12 ♘d2 with complicated play — Tal) 9 ... b5 10 g5 b4 11 gf bc 12 fg ♗xg7 13 b3 ♗d3 14 ♖g1 ♗f6 15 ♕h5 ♘c5 16 b4 ♘xe4 17 ♘xe6 with a strong attack, Ligterink–Tan, 1967.

    9   ♗d3

9 g4 ♘fd7 10 ♗d3 ♗b7 leads to a transposition of moves. Since the merits of b5-b4 are not clear, White should not waste time on the prophylactic 9 a3.

    9   ...   ♗b7
    10   g4   ♘fd7

Fully possible is 10 ... ♘c6 11 g5 ♘d7, but it is better for Black to retain the choice of square for the ♘b8.

    11   0-0-0   b4

Less commital, and also quite playable is 11 ... ♘c5 △ ... ♘bd7.

After 11 ... b4 the game Kupreichik–Zilberstein, 1976, continued 12 ♘ce2 ♘c5 13 ♔b1 ♘bd7 14 ♖hf1 g6 15 f5, where Black obtained counterplay which proved sufficient to equalize, by playing 15 ... ♘e5.

A2

    8   g4 *(158)*

A logical continuation in the spirit of the Keres attack, which forces Black to react energetically

in order to avoid a bind.

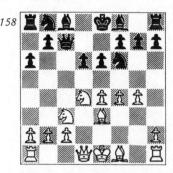

158

    8   ...   d5!

After **8 ... b5?!** 9 g5 ♘fd7 10 ♗g2! ♘b6 11 0-0 ♗b7 12 ♕e2 Black will not succeed in creating sufficient counterplay. On 12 ... ♘c4, 13 ♗f2 is good as 13 ... ♘xb2? is not on because of 14 ♘cxb5, and if 12 ... ♘8d7 13 a4 b4 14 ♘d1 e5 15 fe de 16 ♘b3 ♗e7 17 ♘a5 0-0 18 ♘xb7 ♕xb7 19 b3 Black is relegated to passive defence, Romanishin–Balashov, 1975. With the queen on c7, however, it is possible that 8 ... h6 might also turn out well i.e. 9 g5 hg 10 fg ♘fd7 11 g6 ♘e5 12 gf+ ♔xf7!?

    9   e5   ♘fd7
    10   a3

Keres, defending this ordinary modification of the attack g2-g4, considered this prophylactic move worthwhile, since on 10 ♕f3 the ♗f8 will manage to get into the game: 10 ... ♗b4! 11 ♘e2 ♘c6 12 0-0-0 ♘b6 and Black has been allowed to achieve an acceptable formation for his pieces.

    10   ...   g5!?

It is possible to play more

traditionally with 10 ... ♘c6 11 ♕f3 ♘c5 △ ... ♗d7 and ... 0-0-0. With the unexpected thrust on the king's wing Black begins a risky, but as yet unrefuted play against the white pawn centre. The game Keres–Bilek, 1960, continued 11 f5 ♘xe5 12 ♕e2 ♘bc6 13 0-0-0 ♗e7 14 ♗g2 ♗d7 15 ♗xd5! and White quickly developed a strong attack. According to the latest analysis the capture 11 ... ♕xe5 is not playable because of 12 ♕d2 ♗c5 13 0-0-0 ♘c6 14 h4 ♗xd4 15 ♗xd4 ♘xd4 16 ♕xd4 ♕xd4 17 ♖xd4 with a consequent attack on the kingside pawns. In our opinion, however, this position can hardly be considered profitable for White. After 17 ... gh 18 ♖xh4 ♘f8 △ ... ♗d7, ... ♖g8, and ... 0-0-0 Black has no problems. The idea 10 ... g5 deserves further testing.

B

7   ...   b5

159

8   ♕f3

White begins a standard deployment of his forces, optimally concentrating their influence in the centre of the board.

Instead of 8 ♕f3, Keres proposed an interesting pawn sacrifice: 8 e5 de 9 fe ♘d5 10 ♘xd5 ♕xd5 11 ♗e2!? ♕xe5 12 ♕d2, considering it profitable for White. After 12 ... ♗b7 13 ♗f4 ♕c5 14 0-0-0 ♗e7, however, White's advantage in development is not so great, and the squares along the d-file are well defended. In the game Gipslis–Sigurjonsson, 1976, Black managed to hold off the attack: 15 ♘b3 ♕c8 16 ♗d6 ♕d8! 17 ♕b4 ♗xd6 18 ♖xd6 ♕g5+ 19 ♖d2 ♕e7 20 ♘c5 0-0, retaining his extra pawn.

8   ...   ♗b7!

A necessary move, hindering the advance e4-e5.

Now White must make a critical decision: to slow down or not to slow down the later advance of the Pb5.

B1 9 a3
B2 9 ♗d3

B1

9   a3

This prophylactic will hold up the b-pawn for a while, and, at first glance, strengthens White's position in the centre. Black, however, gains time to further his development.

9   ...   ♘bd7
10   ♗d3   ♗e7

It seems that this is the most suitable continuation. Hardly promising is the combination 10 ... ♖c8 11 0-0 ♖xc3 12 bc ♘c5 because Black's lack of development makes it difficult for him to create any real counterplay. After 13 ♕e2 (13 a4 ba! 14 ♖fb1 ♗a8 ∓) 13 ... ♘fxe4 14 c4 bc 15 ♗xc4 ♗e7 16 f5 e5 17 ♘b3 White's advantage is obvious. But there is an interesting idea involving the fianchetto of the dark-squared bishop: 10 ... g6 11 0-0 &g7 12 &ae1 0-0 13 &h3 &c8. The weakness of the Pd6 is not important, while the Pg6 cuts off the activity of the &d3. There is no question that work will be found for the &g7 along the a1-h8 diagonal. Thus on 14 &f3 an exchange sacrifice is playable: 14 ... &xc3 15 bc &xe4. The best move for White is 14 f5!, however in our opinion after 14 ... ef! 15 ef &e5 Black has a good game.

11   0-0   0-0

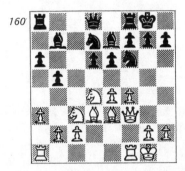

160

11 ... &c8 also deserves consideration. Black can engage in active operations even with his king uncastled because the opposition &b7-&f3 makes it difficult for White to operate in the centre or on the kingside. In the game Smyslov-Tan, 1963, White could not manage to gain the upper hand: 11 ... &c8 12 &ae1 &c5 13 g4 g6 14 g5 &fd7 15 &g3 e5! 16 &f3 0-0 17 f5 &e8 18 &h4 d5 =

Also possible is 11 ... &c7 12 &ae1 &c5, giving Black a strong position. Apparently, White's best

is 13 &f2. The direct 13 g4, according to analysis by Keres, gives Black a good game on either 13 ... d5 or 13 ... h5 14 g5 &g4 15 f5 d4 16 &f4 &b6.

12   &ae1

White completes his mobilization and prepares to free the queen from the defence of the e-pawn. He can't do without this move, since on 12 &h3 &c8! 13 g4 the standard exchange sacrifice 13 ... &xc3 14 bc &xe4 is strong.

12   ...   &ac8

A knight on c5 would interrupt the c-file and thereby reduce Black's possibilities. After 12 ... &c5 13 &h3 &xd3 14 cd &d7 15 &f3 &f6 16 &f2 White's position deserves preference.

13   &h3

On 13 g4 there is a good possibility for Black in 13 ... &xc3 14 bc &c5 15 &f2 &a5 16 g5 &fd7, where the weakness of the White pawns on the queenside is full compensation for the sacrificed exchange. Incidentally, Black can also carry the play into the centre with 13 ... g6 14 &de2 e5 15 f5 d5!

With the move 13 &h3 White eliminates the threat of 13 ... &xc3 14 bc &xe4, since now there would follow 15 &xe4 &xe4 16 &xe6! ±

13   ...   &c5!

14   &f2

On 14 e5 de 15 fe Black can capture on d3: 15 ... &xd3 16 cd (16 ef &xf6 ∓) 16 ... &d5! ∓.

Now White has defended the Pe4 and prepares the advance g2-g4-g5. Black must not hasten to capture on d3 now, because the White centre will be strengthened and the c-file opened. Nor should Black hurry to break in the centre with d6-d5, for example, 14 ... d5? 15 e5 (15 ed ⟨⟩xd3 16 cd ⟨⟩xd5 17 ⟨⟩xe6 fe 18 ♕xe6+ ♖f7 ∓) 15 ... ⟨⟩fe4 16 ♗xe4 ⟨⟩xe4 17 ⟨⟩xe4 de 18 f5 ef 19 ⟨⟩xf5 ♖xc2 20 ♖d1 ♕e8 21 ♖d7! ±.

14   ...   g6
The pawn pair e4-f4 gives White some advantage in the centre, but Black, apparently, can quickly carry out a break in the centre with e6-e5 or d6-d5 and level the chances.
B2
9   ♗d3   ⟨⟩bd7
It is possible to advance the b-pawn immediately: 9 ... b4 10 ⟨⟩ce2 ⟨⟩bd7 11 g4, but this only transposes into positions considered below. Anyway, it is better to play a useful developing move.

There is another plan of defence which deserves analysis: 9 ... ♗e7 10 g4 g6!? 11 g5 ⟨⟩h5 12 0-0-0 ⟨⟩d7 13 f5 ⟨⟩e5 14 ♕h3 b4 15 ⟨⟩ce2 ⟨⟩xd3+ 16 cd ♗xg5 17 fe ♗xe3+ 18 ♕xe3 0-0 = Platonov-Dzhindzhihashvili. The move 9 ... ♗e7 is evidently solid, since on 10 g4 there is also the natural regrouping manoeuvre 10 ... ⟨⟩fd7 11 g5 ⟨⟩c5.

10   g4 *(161)*
It goes without saying that this is the most aggressive continuation, but 10 0-0 is the most natural move, and it brought White rapid success in the game Christiansen-Reshevsky, 1977: 10 ... b4 (10 ... ⟨⟩c5?! −11

a3! ± as the placement of the rook on c8 is ineffective here.) 11 ⟨⟩ce2 ⟨⟩c5 12 ⟨⟩g3 h5? 13 a3 h4 14 ⟨⟩ge2 ⟨⟩fxe4 15 ⟨⟩xe6! fe 16 ab ⟨⟩g3 17 ♗g6+ ♔d7 18 ♕g4 ⟨⟩xe2+ 19 ♕xe2 ⟨⟩e4 20 ♗d4 ⟨⟩f6 21 ♖fe1 ± Instead of 12 ... h5, Black should play simply 12 ... ♗e7, with a promising and solid position, for example 13 a3 d5! or 13 f5 e5 14 ⟨⟩de2 d5.

161

The plan with g4! in which White intensifies the aggression of his opening by threatening to advance the g-pawn, is very dangerous for Black.
10   ...   b4
Other than this advance, which is connected with bold play in the centre, there are two other plans which deserve analysis, and possibly recommendation.
a) 10 ... h6 11 0-0-0 ♖c8 12 ⟨⟩ce2 ⟨⟩c5 13 ⟨⟩g3 ⟨⟩xd3 14 ♖xd3 g6 15 ♖f1 h5 16 gh (16 g5 h4!) 16 ... ⟨⟩xh5 17 f5 ef 18 ⟨⟩dxf5 gf 19 ⟨⟩xf5 ♖h7 20 ♔b1 ♕c7 with a double-edged game, Kupreichik-Tukmakov, 1978.
b) 10 ... ⟨⟩c5 11 g5 b4 (On 11 ... ⟨⟩fd7 12 a3 is also good) 12 gf bc

13 fg ♗xg7   14 b4!? (Also interesting is 14 ♖g1 cb 15 ♖b1 ♕a5+ 16 ♔e2; 14 bc ♕c7 15 ♖b1 0-0-0 16 ♔e2 leads to a double-edged game after either 16 ... f5!? or 16 ... ♖he8 17 ♖hg1 ♗h8 18 f5 e5, Hübner-Portisch, 1980)   14 ... ♘xd3+ 15 cd ♖c8 16 ♕h5! or 15 ... ♕e7 16 ♖g1 ♗f6 17 ♖ac1 ♖c8 18 ♕h5 ♔d7 19 e5! with an attack, Sigurjonsson-Helmers, 1982.

11   ♘ce2   e5!?

Without this counterthrust the move 10 ... b4 would only have led to an improvement in the position of White's forces, for example 11 ... ♘c5?! 12 ♘g3 and then 12 ... ♕c7 13 0-0 g6 14 f5! (Balashov advises opening up the play on the queenside with 14 a3 ba 15 ♖xa3) 14 ... gf 15 gf e5 16 ♗g5 ♗e7 17 ♗xf6 ♗xf6 18 ♘h5 ♕e7 19 ♘b3 or 12 ... g6 13 0-0-0 ♘xd3+ 14 cd ♗g7 15 f5 ef 16 ♘dxf5 gf 17 ♘xf5 ♗f8 18 ♖hf1 ♕d7 19 ♗d4 ♕e6 20 ♔b1, Balashov-Gheorghiu, 1977, or 12 ... d5 13 e5 ♘fe4 14 0-0-0 ♕a5 15 ♔b1, with White retaining the initiative in each case.

The possibility of operations in the centre by Black when his king has not yet castled depend on tactical considerations and therefore demand detailed analysis.

12   ♘b3

The most active evacuation, 12 ♘f5, does not get in the way of Black's operations. After 12 ... d5 13 ♘fg3 ♗c5! 14 g5 de 15 ♘xe4 ♘xe4   16 ♗xe4 ♗xe4   17 ♕xe4 ♗xe3 18 ♕xe3 0-0 19 0-0-0 ♕c7 20 ♔b1 ♖ac8, Balashov-Spassky, 1978, the chances turn out to be equal. By retreating the knight to b3 White hinders the intended transfer of the bishop to c5.

12   ...   d5

A bold decision, unexpectedly giving Black a serious initiative in the centre, based on the unfortunate position of the White queen on f3. As a result it will be Black, not White, who will dictate the pawn structure in the centre.

13   ♘g3

Black players come to this position unwillingly, basing their fear of this move on two games: 13 ... ef 14 ♗xf4 de 15 ♘xe4 ♘xe4 16 ♗xe4 ♗xe4   17 ♕xe4+ ♕e7 18 ♕xe7+ ♗xe7   19 0-0-0 0-0-0 20 ♖he1 ♖he8 21 ♘d4 with a decisive advantage for White, Kupreichik-Magerramov, 1978; and 13 ... ♗e7 14 0-0-0 ♕c7   15 g5 de 16 ♘xe4 ♘xe4 17 ♗xe4 ♗xe4 18 ♕xe4 0-0 19 f5 ♖fd8 20 f6! also with a clear edge for White, Ligterink-Panno, 1980. The situation is less clear after 13 ... de 14 ♘xe4 ♘d5 15 0-0-0 ♕c7 16 f5 ♗e7 17 g5 ♘xe3 18 ♕xe3 h6

In our opinion, however, the position after 13 ... ♕c7 14 g5

♘xe4   15 ♘xe4 ♖c8!? is problematic. Such a sharp intensification of the struggle logically arises from the decision to advance the b-pawn on move 10. After 16 ♘g3 d4 17 ♗e4 ♗xe4 18 ♕xe4 de 19 0-0-0 both sides have equal and good winning chances. Additional analysis is required before a final assessment can be made.

23 Systems with f4 and ♛d2

In this chapter we will examine systems in which White plays f2-f4 and develops his queen at d2.

1 e4 c5 2 ♘f3 ♘c6 3 d4 cd 4 ♘xd4 e6 5 ♘c3 d6 6 f4 ♘f6 7 ♗e3 ♗e7 8 ♗e2 0-0 9 ♛d2

163

Here is another position in which opposite side castling is possible. The construction with 9 ♛d2 has its own peculiarities. The ♗e2 will help the g-pawn advance to g4, and it can later be employed on the a8-h1 diagonal. The ♛d2 creates threats in the centre and can transfer to g2 to add to the attack on the Black king and support a bishop on f3.

The drawback of this plan lies in its slowness, which allows Black to create counterplay on the queen-side. Instead of 9 ♛d2 White can transform his position by playing 9 ♘f3 a6 10 ♛e2 ♛c7 11 0-0-0, but this does not change our evaluation of White's chances. After 11 ... ♘xd4 12 ♗xd4, for example, Black has sufficient counterplay: 12 ... e5 13 ♗e3 ♗e6 14 f5 ♗c4 15 ♛d2 b5 16 g4 b4 17 ♘a4 d5 18 ♘b6 ♖ab8.

Now Black can adopt one of the following defences:
A 9 ... a6
B 9 ... e5

On 9 ... ♗d7, 10 ♘db5 is unpleasant, for example 10 ... ♘e8 11 0-0-0 a6 12 ♘d4 ♘xd4 13 ♗xd4 ♗c6 14 ♗f3 ♘f6 15 g4 ♛a5 16 g5 ♘d7 17 ♔b1, and the threat of 18 ♘d5 puts Black on the defensive.

A

9 ... a6

This move is required if Black wishes to adopt the standard plan of counterplay and in order to liquidate threats against the Pd6.

10 0-0-0 ♛c7

Even here the manoeuvre 10 ... ♗d7 11 g4 ♘xd4 fails to earn equality because of 12 ♛xd4 (Also possible is 12 ♗xd4, but by capturing with the queen White does not lose a tempo playing ♗f3.) 12 ... ♗c6 13 g5 ♘d7 14 h4 ♖c8 15 h5! e5 16 ♕d2 ef 17 ♗xf4. If Black tries to transfer the bishop (♗c8-d7-c6), then the move a7-a6 will prove to have been a waste of time. On 10 ... ♕c7 it is logically connected with Black's developmental plans.

Fully possible is 10 ... ♘xd4, which offers chances for both sides after 11 ♗xd4 e5 12 ♗e3 b5 13 ♘d5 ♘xd5 14 ed ef 15 ♗d4 ♗f5!, Timoshchenko–Vilela, 1981.

10 ... d5! is worthy of serious consideration. If White closes the centre with 11 e5, then he risks coming under an immediate attack: 11 ... ♘d7 12 ♘b3?! b5 13 ♗f3 ♘a5.

11   g4   b5
It is dangerous for Black to play 11 ... ♘xd4 12 ♗xd4 e5, intending to win the g-pawn. After 13 ♗e3! b5 14 a3! ♗xg4 15 ♗xg4 ♘xg4 the pawn is no compensation for White's tremendous positional advantage: 16 ♘d5 ♕b7 17 ♖hg1 ♘xe3 18 ♕xe3 f6 19 f5! The advance of the d-pawn deserves analysis: 11 ... d5 12 ed ed!? 13 g5 ♘e4 14 ♘xd5 ♕d8.

12   g5
Regardless of the menacing pawn trio (e4, f4, g5), it seems that White has a long way to go before he can create any concrete threats. Before striking at the heart of Black's centre, the Pe6, and the transfer of the heavy pieces to the h-file, many moves are required. This is a long, and therefore un-

realistic, campaign. Or so it seems.
12   ...   ♘d7
The exchange 12 ... ♘xd4 13 ♗xd4 ♘d7 transposes below.
13   f5!
A rather direct, but quite logical continuation of the attack, in which there is an unexpected role for the ♕d2.

164

An extraordinarily confused position, in which the central question is: Whose pawns are more dangerous?
13   ...   b4
After 13 ... ♘xd4 14 ♗xd4 b4! 15 f6! the bishop occupies a very important position and guarantees White a prolonged initiative without any great hardship: 15 ... bc 16 ♗xc3 ♘c5 17 fe ♕xe7 18 e5 de 19 ♕e3 ♘d7 20 ♗f3.
The text is more complicated — and more dangerous!
14   f6   gf
15   ♖hg1!
This is Tseitlin's move, which boldly and effectively livens up the position. The struggle will require boldness in attack on White's part, and Black will have to play very exact defence.

15 ... f5

15 ... bc loses immediately to 16 ♕xc3 ♘xd4 17 gf+ ♔h8 18 fe ♕xc3 19 ♗xd4+. No better is 15 ... ♔h8 16 ♘d5! ed 17 ♘xc6 ♕xc6 18 ♗d4.

16 g6!

Instead, Itkis–Popov, 1977, saw 16 ef bc 17 ♕xc3 ♘de5 18 f6 ♗d8 19 ♗f4 ♘g6 20 ♕h3 ♔h8 and White ran out of steam. The evaluation of the variation hinges on the position which arises after 16 g6. There is a lot of work to be done here by the analysts.

B

9 ... e5!

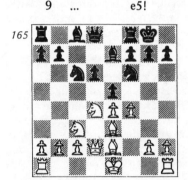

165

A new, and as yet untried continuation. Black has put his king away and now opens up the centre, in order to give his bishops something to do. He knowingly weakens the Pd6, considering the corresponding weakness of the Pe4 to be sufficient compensation.

10 ♘f3

10 ♘f5 is not good: 10 ... ♘xe4! 11 ♘xe7+ ♕xe7 12 ♘xe4 ef. 10 ♘xc6 bc 11 fe de leads to an equal position, since the weaknesses of the Pc6 and Pe4 are identical. The move 10 ♘b3 deserves attention, though, as it cuts off the effect of the occupation of g4 by Black's pieces. Thus 10 ... ♘g4 is not good because of 11 ♗xg4 ♗xg4 12 f5, while the exchanges after 10 ... ef 11 ♗xf4 ♖e8 12 0-0-0 ♗f8 13 ♗xd6 ♗xd6 14 ♕xd6 ♕xd6 15 ♖xd6 ♘xe4 16 ♘xe4 ♖xe4 are in White's favour after 17 ♗f3. Apparently Black should answer 10 ... ef 11 ♗xf4 ♗e6, and now after 12 0-0-0 he can play 12 ... ♘e5, 12 ... ♗xb3 13 ab ♘e5, or even 13 ... ♕a5.

10 ... ef
11 ♗xf4 ♗g4!

With this bishop manoeuvre (△ ♗h5-g6) Black increases his pressure on the e-pawn and has the possibility of achieving equality, for example: 12 0-0-0 ♖e8 13 ♗c4 ♗h5 14 ♘g5 ♘e5! or 13 h3 ♗h5 14 ♖he1 ♕a5 15 ♗b5 ♖ac8 16 ♔b1 ♗f8 = Ghinda–Jansa, Bucharest 1982.

The system of defence with 9 ... e5 is no less promising than that with the double-edged 9 ... a6, but it requires practical testing.

24 Sozin Attack 6 ♗c4

1 e4 c5 2 ♘f3 ♘c6 3 d4 cd 4 ♘xd4 ♘f6 5 ♘c3 d6

This move order has been adopted frequently, even though White can then transpose to the Rauzer Attack with 6 ♗g5. Nowadays the Sozin Attack is usually reached by a different move order: 1 e4 c5 2 ♘f3 ♘c6 3 de cd 4 ♘xd4 e6 5 ♘c3 ♘f6 6 ♗e3 d6 7 ♗c4 or 1 e4 c5 2 ♘f3 d6 3 d4 cd 4 ♘xd4 ♘f6 5 ♘c3 e6 6 ♗e3 ♗e7 7 ♗c4.

6 ♗c4

This natural move was well known even before the Scheveningen System entered into praxis. Then, however, the development of the ♗ on c4 was an attempt to discourage the construction with g6 and ♗g7. Thus, for example, the opening of the game Schlechter–Em. Lasker, 1910, continued 6 ... g6 7 ♘xc6 bc 8 e5! ♘g4 9 e6 f5 10 0-0 ♗g7 11 ♗f4 ♕b6 12 ♗b3 ♗a6 with complicated play. But the move 6 ... g6 is insufficient for equality, since after 7 ♘xc6 bc 8 e5 ♘g4 9 ♗f4! Black has difficulty in developing, while 9 ... d5 10 ♘xd5 ♗g7 11 ♘c3 leads to a clear advantage for White. Black can,

however, fianchetto his king's bishop if he plays the preliminary move 6 ... ♗d7. In this case after 7 ♗b3 g6 there arises a position from the Dragon variation, with its peculiarities and difficulties. White can castle short in this case, for example 8 0-0 ♗g7 9 ♗e3 0-0 10 h3 ♖c8 11 ♕d3?! ♘e5 12 ♕e2 ♖xc3 13 bc ♘xe4 14 ♕e1 ♕c7 ∓, Hennings–Taimanov, 1967. Of course his prospects will be better if he castles long. While we cannot analyse this sort of position exhaustively, as it is the theme of other books, we will give a few characteristic examples: 6 ... ♗d7 7 ♗b3 g6 8 f3 ♘xd4 9 ♕xd4 ♗g7

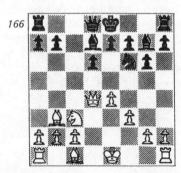

166

a) 10 ♗g5 ♕a5 11 ♕e3 0-0 12 ♗h6

🛇fc8 13 0-0-0 ♕c5 14 ♕d2 ♗h8 =
b) **10 ♗g5** 0-0 11 0-0-0 h6 12 ♗h4
♗c6 13 ♕e3 ♘d7?! (13 ... ♕a5 is
more solid) 14 🛇xd6 g5 15 🛇g6!
e6 16 🛇xg7+ ♔xg7 17 ♗f2 ±,!
Tal–Stein, 1969.
c) **10 ♗g5** 0-0 11 ♕e3! b5 12 h4
a5 13 a4 ba 14 🛇xa4 🛇b8 15 h5
🛇xh5 16 g4 🛇f6 17 ♗h6 ±
Ciocaltea–Stein, 1970.

After 8 f3, Black does not have
to exchange on d4, but can transpose to the Yugoslav Attack of the
Dragon with 8 ... ♗g7 9 ♗e3 0-0
10 ♕d2 or adopt Fischer's recommendation 8 ... 🛇a5!? 9 ♗g5 ♗g7
10 ♕d2 h6 11 ♗e3 🛇c8 12 0-0-0
🛇c4 13 ♕e2 🛇xe3 14 ♕xe3 ♕a5
15 f4 0-0 16 h3 e6 =, which he
gave in 1969.

In answer to 7 ♗b3 Black would
seem to be presented with a choice
between the "dragon" 7 ... g6 and
the Scheveningen 7 ... e6, since
nothing good comes out of other
continuations.
a) 7 ... a6 8 ♗e3 🛇g4?! 9 🛇xc6 bc
10 ♕f3 🛇f6 11 e5 ±
b) 7 ... 🛇c8 8 f3 a6 9 ♗e3 ♕a5
(or 9 ... 🛇a5 10 ♕d3 b5 11 g4 ±)
10 ♕d2 e6 11 0-0-0 ♗e7 12 g4 ±

In answer to 7 0-0 Black can
play 7 ... e6 and be satisfied that he
has avoided the dangerous positions
with opposite wing castling and
arrived at the Sozin Attack. Should
he instead try to head for the
regions of the Dragon with 7 ... g6,
he may have to contend with
Boleslavsky's interesting idea 8
🛇xc6!?, i.e. 8 ... ♗xc6 9 ♗g5 ♗g7
10 🛇d5! ♗xd5 11 ed 0-0 12 🛇e1
or 8 ... bc 9 f4 ♕c7 10 e5! de 11

fe ♕xe5 12 ♗xf7+ ♔xf7 13 ♕xd7,
with a clear positional advantage
for White in either case.

6 ... e5 is not worthy of recommendation, since after 7 🛇de2 or
even 7 🛇f5 counterplay for Black,
which might compensate for the
weakness of the d5 square, is no-
where to be seen.

The interesting manoeuvre 6 ...
♕b6, intending to drive the white
knight from the centre, is considered in Chapter 27.

At this point we should pause
to consider some further peculiarities of the move order. On 1 e4 c5
2 🛇f3 🛇c6 3 d4 cd 4 🛇xd4 e6 5
🛇c3 d6 6 ♗c4, Black has nothing
better than 6 ... 🛇f6, since in
answer to the thrust 6 ... ♕b6
White has the strong move 7 ♗e3!
In this case it is dangerous to
accept the pawn with 7 ... ♕xb2
8 🛇db5 ♕b4 because of the weakness at d6 and the lag in development. After 9 ♗e2 there is no
satisfactory continuation for Black,
for example 9 ... a6? 10 🛇b1 ♕a5
11 ♗b6! ± or 9 ... ♕a5 10 ♗d2!
♕d8 11 ♗f4 🛇c5 (11 ... e5 12
🛇d5!) 12 ♕d4! ±.

There is yet another move order
which gives Black the privilege of
an unusual knight tour: 1 e4 c5
2 🛇f3 e6 3 d4 cd 4 🛇xd4 🛇f6
5 🛇c3 d6 6 ♗c4 ♗e7 7 ♗e3 0-0
8 ♗b3 🛇a6!?, a rarely applied but
interesting system, which somewhat resembles the Sozin, where
Black tries to get rid of the ♗b3
right away. On c5, however, the
knight stands better than on a5,
as it now threatens the Pe4. White

must make maximum use of his centralised knight, otherwise the initiative will move to his opponent. It is worth analysing two plans of development for White's pieces:

a) **9 f3 ♘c5 10 ♕e2** (The queen stands a bit better here than on d2, as after 10 ♕d2 a6 11 g4 ♕c7 12 g5 ♘fd7 13 h4 b5 14 g6 ♘e5 15 gf+ ♖xf7 the Pf3 is attacked, although perhaps White can keep the position sharp by playing 16 ♕g2.). 10 ... a6 11 g4 ♕c7 12 g5 ♘fd7. Here, together with 13 0-0-0 (and why not 13 0-0?!), there is the logical, but risky, storm on the Pe6: 13 f4 b5 14 f5.

b) **9 f4 ♘c5 10 ♕f3.**

167

10 ... a6 (On 10 ... d5, Novo-pashin–Tal, 1962, 11 ed ed 12 0-0 ♖e8 13 f5! ± is good.) Here White cannot continue with a queenside castling plan, since the e-pawn is weak and under pressure from the ♘c5: 11 0-0-0 ♕c7 12 g4 b5 13 f5 ♘fxe4! ∓ or 13 e5 de 14 fe ♘fe4! ∓, Hübner–Ree, 1971. 11 g4 is not good either because of 11 ... d5 12 e5 ♘fe4.

That leaves 11 0-0 ♕c7 12 f5, in order to keep the ♗c8 from

reaching b7 by tying it to the defence of the e-pawn. The reply 12 ... e5 allows White to take the initiative with 13 ♘de2 ♘xb3 14 cb h6 15 ♘g3 b5 16 ♘h5! ♗b7? 17 ♗xh6. If Black keeps the pressure in the centre, however, there does not seem to be any way for White to cleanly gain the advantage, for example 12 ... b5 13 fe fe 14 ♕h3 ♘xb3 15 ab b4 16 ♘a4 e5 17 ♘f5 ♖b8 or 12 ... ♘xb3 13 cb ♗d7 14 ♖ac1 ♕d8 15 fe fe 16 ♕h3 ♕e8!, and in both cases Black has sufficient counterplay. The system with 8 ... ♘a6 deserves further tests, and analytical work.

6   ...   e6

The conceptual support of the move 6 ♗c4 changed sharply after praxis had demonstrated the viability of the small centre with e6 and d6. Almost 50 years ago the Soviet master Sozin proposed, in answer to 6 ... e6, a strategically rich and well-constructed system for White, which now bears his name.

The Sozin Attack is one of the sharpest methods of struggle against the Scheveningen set up. Both the development of the bishop at c4 and the advance of the f-pawn to f5 (and sometimes even the g-pawn to g5) are intended to weaken the d5 square. If Black tries to get rid of the bishop by exchanging a knight for it, his possibilities for queenside play will be sharply reduced.

7   ♗b3

For 7 a3 see Chapter 25.

If 7 0-0 ♗e7 8 ♗e3 0-0 9 f4,

Black can immediately carry out a counterthrust in the centre with 9 ... d5 10 ed ed. After 11 ♗e2 ♖e8! 12 ♔h1 ♗a3 13 ba ♖xe3 his advantage is obvious, Grünfeld-Taimanov, 1950.

After 7 ♗b3, Black has two plans. He can first complete the evacuation of his king from the centre or he can immediately undertake queenside operations. The first plan will be considered here while the second is in Chapter 25.

7 ... ♗e7
8 ♗e3

It is not worth tarrying with the development of the dark-squared bishop, since without the support of the ♗c1 and ♖a1 it is difficult to achieve anything in the centre. Thus on 8 f4 Black has 8 ... ♘xd4 in addition to the obvious 8 ... 0-0. After 9 ♕xd4 Black can adopt one of two routes:

a) the very sharp **9 ... e5!?** 10 fe de 11 ♕xe5 (11 ♗a4+ ♗d7) 11 ... 0-0 12 ♗g5 h6 13 ♗h4 ♘xe4 14 ♘xe4 ♗xh4+ 15 g3 ♗h3!, Batskan-Lotsov, 1970.

b) the simply sharp **9 ... 0-0** *(168)*

The queen, which seems so

168

threatening from its post at d4, only interferes with the quick completion of White's development. On 10 0-0 a good plan is 10 ... b6!, threatening 11 ... d5. After 11 ♔h1 ♗a6! we have:

b1) **12 ♖e1** d5! 13 ed ♘g4 14 ♘e4 ♗c5 15 ♕d2 ♕h4 16 g3 ♕h5 17 ♘xc5 bc ∓, Klavin-Boleslavsky, 1957.

b2) **12 ♖f3** d5! 13 ed ♗c5 14 ♕a4 ♗b7 15 ♗e3 ed 16 ♗d4 and now instead of 16 ... ♖e8 17 ♖d1 ♘g4, Fischer–Geller, 1962, 16 ... a6! 17 ♗xf6 gf would have won, as b6-b5 is unstoppable.

Instead of 11 ♔h1, 11 ♕d3 is stronger but even then after 11 ... ♘d7 12 ♗e3 ♗b7 13 ♖ad1 ♕c8! 14 ♘b5 ♘c5 Black has full-fledged counterplay. Black has no difficulties if White replaces 10 0-0 with the development of the ♗c1, for example 10 ♗e3 ♘g4! 11 0-0 (11 0-0-0 e5!) 11 ... b6 12 ♔h1 d5 13 ♗g1 ♗a6 or 10 ♗d2 a6 11 0-0-0 ♕c7 12 ♖hg1 ♘d7 13 g4 ♘c5 15 g5 b5.

Economising on the move 8 ♗e3 does not bring White results in the variation 8 0-0 0-0 9 ♔h1.

Black has two methods of equalising:

a) **9 ... ♘xd4** 10 ♕xd4 b6 11 ♗g5 (11 f4 ♗a6 etc) 11 ... ♗b7 12 ♖ad1 (12 f4 ♖c8 13 f5 ♖c5!) 12 ... ♕c8 13 f3 ♖d8

b) **9 ... ♘a5** 10 f4 b6 11 e5 ♘e8 12 f5 de! 13 fe ed 14 ef+ ♔h8 15 fe = ♕ ♕xe8 16 ♖xf8+ ♗xf8 17 ♕e2? ♗a6! ∓. In the game Neikirkh-Botvinnik, 1960, White refrained from 12 f5, but was destroyed because of the weakness of his first rank: 12 罝f3 ♘xb3 13 ♘c6 ♕d7 14 ♘xe7+ ♕xe7 15 ab f6! 16 ed ♘xd6 17 罝d3 ♘f5 18 罝a4 ♕e8 19 ♘e4 b5! 20 罝a5 &b7 21 ♘d6 ♘xd6 22 罝xd6 罝d8!

8 ... 0-0

The continuation 8 ... a6 will be examined in the next chapter. Now White has a choice:

A 9 f4
B 9 0-0

A

9 f4

With this move White retains the option to castle queenside.

169

9 ... ♘xd4

Other moves are inferior, i.e.

a) 9 ... &d7 10 ♕f3 ♘xd4 11 &xd4 &c6 12 f5 e5 13 &f2 b5 14 0-0-0 ±.

b) 9 ... ♘a5 10 ♕f3 b6 11 e5 de 12 fe &b7 13 ef &xf3 14 fe ♕xe7 15 ♘xf3 ♘xb3 16 ab ±.

c) 9 ... e5 10 fe ♘g4 11 &g1 ♘xd4 12 ♕xd4 ♘xe5 13 0-0-0 &f6 14 ♘d5 or 12 ... de 13 ♕xd8 罝xd8 14 ♘d5 &d6 15 0-0-0.

10 &xd4 b5!

The position after 11 a3 &b7 12 ♕e2 a5 arose in the game

Shaposhnikov–Gurevich, 1964, which continued 13 ♕xb5 ♕c7 14 ♕d3 a4! 15 &xa4 e5! 16 &e3 ef 17 &d4 d5 18 e5 ♘e4 19 &b5 &h4+ and Black had the advantage. In 1972 the idea with the sacrifice of the pawns was repeated in the fourth game of the Fischer–Spassky match.

11 e5 de
12 fe ♘d7

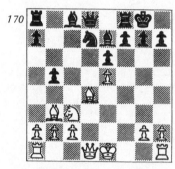

170

13 0-0

The defencelessness of the Black pawn is illusory, after 13 ♘xb5 ♕a5+ 14 ♘c3 ♘xe5 it is regained with plenty of interest. At the same time Black manages to retain both important diagonals with his bishops at b7 and c5, after which he can occupy himself with the plans for the siege of the Pe5.

The sharp continuation 13 ♕g4 &c5 14 0-0-0 can bring White success if Black plays inattentively, for example 14 ... ♕b6 15 ♘e4 &xd4 16 罝xd4 ♘xe5? (more solid is 16 ... ♔h8! 17 罝hd1 ♘xe5 18 ♕h5 f6! ∓) 17 ♘f6+ ♔h8 18 ♕h3 gf 19 罝h4 ±, Barle–Beliavsky, 1971. After 13 ♕g4 Black's chances are no worse: 13 ... b4 14 ♘e4

♗b7   15 ♘d6 ♗xd6   16 ed ♘f6
17 ♕g3 ♘h5   18 ♕g4 ♘f6 (analysis
by Gheorghiu), or 13 ... ♗c5   14
0-0-0 ♗xd4   15 ♕xd4 ♕g5+   16
♔b1 ♕xe5 ∓ (analysis by Krogius).

O'Kelly's recommendation 13
♕f3 ♖b8   14 ♘e4 ♗b7   15 0-0-0
does not bring with it the sharp
edge which can cause danger to
Black: 15 ... ♕c7   16 ♖he1 ♘c5
17 ♗xc5 ♗xc5 =

The text creates more problems
for Black.

          13   ...   a6
13 ... b4? 14 ♘e4 ♗b7   15 ♘d6!
♗xd6   16 ed ♕g5   17 ♕e2 ♗d5   18
♖ad1 ± was Fischer-Olafsson, 1961.
After 13 ... ♗c5 a sharp endgame
arises by force: 14 ♗xc5 ♘xc5   15
♕xd8 ♖xd8   16 ♘xb5 ♗a6   17 ♗c4
♖ab8, Fischer-Geller, 1962, in
which Black, despite being down a
pawn, managed to hold the balance
and eventually drew.

The reputation of the move 13
0-0, and consequently of the entire
plan with 9 ... ♘xd4, depends on
an evaluation of the position arising
from the text move.

          14   ♘e4
The game Fischer-Spassky, 1972,
continued more solidly but less
energetically with 14 a3 ♗b7   15
♕d3, and after 15 ... a5! 16 ♘xb5
♘c5!   17 ♗xc5 ♗xc5+   18 ♔h1 ♕g5
19 ♕e2 ♖ad8 White held the
balance only with great difficulty.

Direct attack is also not dangerous for Black: 14 ♕f3 ♘c5!   15
♗xc5 ♗xc5+   16 ♔h1 ♕c7!   17 ♘e4
♗b7   18 ♕g4 ♖ad8 ∓, Ciocaltea-
Gheorghiu, 1973. No better is 14
♕h5 ♗b7   15 ♖ad1 ♘c5!   16 ♗xc5

♗xc5+   17 ♔h1 ♕c7   18 ♖d3 ♖fd8
19 ♖h3 h6   20 ♖g3 ♖d2!   21 ♘e2
♖ad8!   22 ♘f4 ♖f2! ∓, Kuzmin-
Ermenkov, 1976. Also unimpressive
is 14 ♕g4 ♗b7   15 ♖ad1 ♘c5!   16
♔h1 ♘xb3   17 ab ♕c7   18 ♖d3
♖fd8 ∓ or 15 ♖xf7 ♔xf7   16
♗xe6+ ♔e8   17 ♕h5+ g6   18 ♕xh7
♕c7   19 ♖ad1 ♘xe5!, given by
Gheorghiu.

          14   ...   ♗b7
          15   ♘d6   ♗xd6
          16   ed   ♕g5

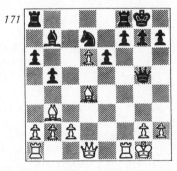

171

          17   ♖f2
The fundamental danger for
White lies not in the direct threat of
mate at g2, but in the advance of
the e and f pawns, which will significantly fortify Black's attacking
potential, for example 17 ♕e2 e5
18 ♗e3 ♕g6   19 ♖ad1 ♔h8   20 c3
♗e2   21 ♕f2?! f5!   22 ♕g3 ♕e8   23
♗g5 f4!   24 ♕f2 ♕g6   25 ♗e7 ♖f5!
26 ♖fe1 ♗c6 ∓, Klaman-Gligorić,
1972, or 20 h4 f5   21 h5 ♕f6   22
a4 f4! ∓, Browne-Donner, 1974.

If White can manage to retard
this pawn pair in the region of the
fifth rank, and then get his queenside pawn majority moving, both
his bishop pair and the passed pawn

on d6 will prove to be quite strong. The move 17 ♖f2 gives White more chances to solve these problems: the queen is freed from its defensive functions and the ♖f2 is hardly in a passive position. Two games by the master Bangiev illustrate well the possibilities of the White position:

a) **17 ... e5 18 ♗c3 e4?! 19 ♕f1! ♕g6 20 ♖e1! ♖ae8 21 ♖e3 ♘e5 22 d7! ♖e7 23 ♗xe5 ♖xe5 24 ♖xf7** with a rout, Bangiev–Shmarin, 1971.

b) **17 ... ♗d5 18 ♖d2! ♗xb3 (18 ... ♗c4 ±) 19 ab e5 20 ♗f2! ♖fc8 21 ♕e2 ♖c6 22 c4 ♖ac8 23 c5 ♕f5 24 ♖c1 ♕e6 25 ♖c3 f6 26 b4 ±**, Bangiev–Chernikov, 1975.

These games show that it doesn't pay for Black to hurry in the advance of the e-pawn. When it goes to e5 the power of the ♗b3 is sharply increased, while on e4 it cuts off Black's own bishop at b7. Black must force the play around the Pd6, and to that end the best move is ...

| 17 | ... | a5! |
| 18 | c4 | |

Now on 18 a4, 18 ... ♖a6! is very strong, i.e. 19 ♕d2 ♕xd2 20 ♖xd2 b4 21 ♗e3 ♖fc8 △ 22 ... ♗e4 and later ... ♖ac6. But after the text move the Pd6 also finds itself in danger.

| 18 | ... | a4! |

Not 18 ... ♖a6 19 c5! e5 20 ♗c3 ♕e3! 21 ♕e1! ♕xc5 22 ♗xa5 when it is not clear who stands better.

| 19 | ♗c2 | bc |
| 20 | ♗xa4 | ♖fd8 |

| 21 | ♗xd7 | ♖xd7 |
| 22 | ♗b6 | ♖c8! |

Black threatens ... ♖c6 or ... ♕e5.

B

| 9 | 0-0 |

The solid continuation, which we consider the main line. White takes his king out of the centre and prepares to complete his mobilisation with the moves f4, ♕f3, and ♖ad1. The character of future events is determined by Black's next moves. We consider:

B1 9 ... a6
B2 9 ... ♘xd4
B3 9 ... ♗d7
B4 9 ... ♘a5

B1

| 9 | ... | a6 |
| 10 | f4 | ♕c7 |

Black's plan is clear — preparation for b7-b5, but its realization demands exact play.

Apparently Black should not waste time on the manoeuvre ♘c6-a5, since then the White knight on d4 puts strong pressure on the centre. Thus after 10 ... ♘a5 11 ♕f3 ♕c7 White obtained a strong attack in Boleslavsky–Aronin, 1949 with 12 g4! b5 (12 ... ♘xb3 13 ab and 12 ... ♘c4 13 g5 ♘d7 14 ♘f5! are not adequate for Black) 13 g5 ♘d7 14 ♘xe6 fe 15 ♗xe6+ ♔h8 16 ♘d5 ♕d8 17 ♕h5.

On **10 ... ♗d7, 11 f5!** is very strong, as in Fischer–Larsen, 1971: 11 ... ♕c8? 12 fe ♗xe6 13 ♘xe6 fe 14 ♘a4 ±. Even if Black chooses the best reply — 11 ... ♘xd4 12 ♗xd4 ef 13 ef ♗c6 — White still stands better thanks to the activity of his bishops and strong pawn at f5. Actually, Fischer's idea works against this type of defence on the previous move as well: 9 ... ♗d7 10 f4 ♕c8 11 f5! (Also simple and strong is 11 ♕f3!) 11 ... ♘xd4 12 ♗xd4 ef 13 ♕d3! fe 14 ♘xe4 ♘xe4 15 ♕xe4 ♗e6 16 ♖f3 ♕c6 17 ♖e1 and notwithstanding his extra pawn, Black is fighting for a draw, Fischer–Larsen, 1971.

11   ♕f3   ♗d7!

Black improves the coordination of his pieces and prepares to advance his b-pawn. The move 11 ... b5 would have been premature in view of 12 e5! ♘xd4 13 ♗xd4 ♗b7 14 ef ♗xf3 15 fe ♕xe7 16 ♖xf3. The inadequacy of 11 ... ♘a5 has been shown above.

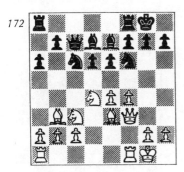

172

12   f5!

The most principled continuation. White begins an immediate attack against the Pe6, trying to provoke its advance, which will weaken the d5 square. Khenkin has demonstrated that other continuations allow Black to equalise without difficulty:

a) 12 g4 ♘xd4 13 ♗xd4 e5 14 fe de 15 ♕g3 ♗c6! 16 ♖ae1 ♗d6 17 ♗f2 b5 =

b) 12 h3 b5 13 g4 ♘xd4 14 ♗xd4

♗c6 15 g5 ♘d7 16 ♘e2 ♘c5 17 ♘g3 ♘xb3 18 ab e5 19 ♗e3 ef 20 ♗xf4 g6 =

c) 12 ♖ad1 b5 13 f5 ♘xd4 14 ♗xd4 b4 15 ♘e2 e5 16 ♗f2 ♗c6 17 ♘g3 a5; or 13 g4 ♘xd4 14 ♖xd4 e5 15 ♘d5 ♘xd5 16 ♖xd5 ef 17 ♗xf4 ♗e6 =

12   ...   ♘xd4
13   ♗xd4   b5

If 13 ... e5, White will take control of the d5 square with 14 ♗f2! (But not 14 ♗e3 ♗c6 15 g4 b5 16 g5 ♘xe4! 17 ♘xe4 ♕b7 ∓) 14 ... ♗c6 15 g4.

14   a3   a5
15   g4

White's position deserves preference, thanks to his active bishops. Khenkin gives the following variation: 15 ... b4 16 ab ab 17 ♖xa8 ♖xa8 18 g5 bc 19 gf ♗xf6 20 ♗xf6 gf 21 fe ♗xe6 22 bc, although the conversion of White's advantage in this position may turn out to be quite difficult in view of the paucity of material which remains on the board. All the same it is better for Black to play 15 ... h6, holding up the advance of the g-pawn, for example 16 h4 ♘h7 17 ♕g3 ♕d8.

B2

9   ...   ♘xd4
10   ♗xd4   b5 *(173)*

Black immediately initiates counterplay on the queenside.

Also possible are 10 ... ♕a5 and 10 ... b6.

The manoeuvre 10 ... ♕a5 is worthy of attention only in connection with 11 f4 e5!, but this has not yet been tested in the practical arena.

173

There are fewer prospects for Black after 10 ... b6 11 f4 ♗a6. The manoeuvre ♗c8-a6-c4, intending to exchange bishops, takes too much time and White will therefore succeed in bringing all of his pieces into the game: 12 ♖f3! (better than 12 ♖e1 ♛c7 13 f5 ♗c4 14 e5 de 15 ♗xe5 ♛c6!) 12 ... ♗b7! (Black can not achieve the d6-d5 break at a propitious moment: 12 ... ♛c7 13 ♖h3 ♖fd8 14 ♔h1 e5 15 ♗e3 ♗c4 16 f5 ♗xb3 17 ab ♛c6 18 ♗g5 d5 19 ♗xf6 de 20 ♛g4 ♗xf6 21 ♘xe4 ±) 13 ♛e2! (13 ♖h3 e5! 14 fe de 15 ♗xe5 ♗c5+ 16 ♔h1 ♘xe4 =) 13 ... d5 14 e5 ♘e4 15 ♖h3 g6 16 ♖d1. White stands better. Black has yet to resolve the problem of his ♗b7.

The continuation 10 ... a6 11 f4 b5 transposes to positions considered previously after either 12 a3 ♗b7 13 ♛d3 a5 or 12 e5 de 13 fe ♘d7.

     11   ♘xb5!

The quiet 11 a3 ♗b7 12 ♛d3 does not place any difficult questions before Black, who can play 12 ... a5!, as in Fischer–Spassky, 1972.

     11   ...   ♗a6

12	c4	♗xb5
13	cb	♘xe4
14	♛g4	♘f6
15	♛e2	

Thanks to his strong bishops and pawn majority on the queenside, White must stand better, especially if Black hastens with his pawn advances, i.e. 15 ... e5 16 ♗c3 ±. Fischer could not prove the advantage of the White side when he played against Korchnoi in 1970: 15 ... ♘d7! 16 ♛e3 ♗f6 17 ♗xa7 ♛a5 18 b6 ♗d8! 19 ♖ad1 ♘xb6 20 ♗xb6 ♗xb6 =. If White had chosen to play 16 ♖fd1 ♗f6 17 ♗e3, however, he could have counted on an advantage by advancing the a-pawn.

B3

9	...	♗d7
10	f4	♘xd4
11	♗xd4	♗c6

174

This variation does not significantly differ from the variation B2 which we have just examined. In any case White can play 12 ♛f3 b5 13 a3 a5 14 ♖ae1. At the same time there is no advantage for White in the manoeuvre 12 ♛d3 b5 13 e5 de 14 fe ♘d7! 15 ♘e4 (15

♘xb5? ♘c5 ∓) 15 ... ♗xe4 16
♕xe4 ♘c5 17 ♕e3 ♕c7 18 c3
♘xb3 19 ab a5 20 ♖f3 ♖ac8 =,
Minić–Sofrevsky, 1965, or in 12
♕e1 b5 13 ♖d1 b4 14 e5 bc 15
ef ♗xf6 16 ♕xc3 ♗xd4+ 17 ♕xd4
d5 18 f5 ♕b6 =, Neikirkh–Hartoch
1967. In most cases, however,
White plays 12 ♕e2 in the diagrammed position, preparing to
bring the ♖a1 into the game.

12 ♕e2   b5

Black cannot succeed in breaking up the White pawn pair by
playing e6-e5, since after 12 ... ♕a5
White plays 13 f5 and forces the
decisive weakening of the d5-
square: 13 ... e5 14 ♗f2 ♖ac8
15 g4 ♘d7 16 h4 h6 17 ♔g2 ♕d8
18 ♖h1 ♘c5 19 ♗xc5 dc 20 ♖ad1
±, Zuckerman–Spassov, 1967.

13 ♘xb5

Khenkin recommends 13 ♖ae1
b4 14 ♕c4! bc 15 ♕xc6 cb 16 f5
e5 17 ♗xb2, but after 13 ... a5!
14 a3 ♖b8 White hasn't achieved
anything. Simagin proposed another
idea: 13 ♖ad1 b4 14 e5 bc 15 ef
♗xf6 16 ♗xf6 ♕xf6 17 ♖xd6
♖ac8 18 f5! but this has not yet
made an appearance in tournament
play. 13 ♘xb5 is undoubtedly the
move that is most in accordance
with the demands of the position.

13 ...   ♗xb5

After 13 ... e5 14 fe! (but not
14 ♘xa7 ♗d7! 15 ♗f2 ♕b8 16
♕a6 ♘xe4 17 ♗d5 ♘xf2 18 ♗xa8
♘h3+ ∓) 14 ... de 15 ♗e3 a6 16
♘c3 ♘xe4 17 ♖xf7! Black is a
pawn down, Fischer–Nievergelt,
1959.

14 ♕xb5   ♘xe4

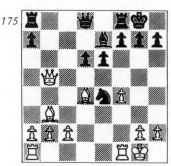

175

The evaluation of the entire plan
with 12 ♕e2 hangs on the assessment of this position. White has the
two bishops, but Black has the
knight in the centre. In order for
Black to make progress in this
position it is essential for him to
play d6-d5, but then While will
begin to attack the centre with f4-
f5 and c2-c4. White cannot achieve
victory with the help of the c-pawn
alone: 15 ♕d3 d5 16 c4 dc! 17
♗xc4 ♘d6 =, Bannik–Boleslavsky,
1955, or 15 ♕e2 d5 16 ♖ad1 ♗f6
17 ♗xf6 ♘xf6 18 c4 a5! 19 cd
a4! 20 ♗c4 ed 21 ♔h1 ♕a5 ∓,
Neikirkh–Simagin, 1965. First it is
necessary to activate the ♗b3, and
to this end the f-pawn is advanced.

15 f5!   ♗f6!

It is worthwhile to get rid of
one of the dangerous White bishops
immediately. Advancing the pawns
now only creates weakness: 15 ...
e5?! 16 ♗e3 ♘f6 (Somewhat
better is 16 ... ♗g5 17 ♕e2 ♗xe3+
18 ♕xe3 ♘f6 ±) 17 ♖ad1 ♘g4 18
♕e2 ♗g5 19 ♕xg4! or 15 ... d5?!
16 fe fe 17 ♕c6! ♕d6 18 ♖xf8+!
♖xf8 19 ♕xd6 ♗xd6 20 ♗xa7 ±,
Penrose–Petersen, 1961.

16 ♕d3!

It makes no sense for White to enter into the variation 16 ♗xf6 ♛xf6 17 fe ♛d4+ 18 ♔h1 fe! 19 ♗xe6+ ♔h8, but even 16 ♖ad1 ♗xd4+ ♖xd4 is insufficient for an advantage, as the ♖d4 is a bit awkward: 17 ... d5 18 ♖4d1 a5! 19 fe fe 20 c4 ♛c7! =, Neukirkh-Möhring, 1966.

16   ...   d5
17   ♗xf6

White does not strengthen his position by playing 17 ♖ad1, since the reply 17 ... ♛e7 creates the threat of exchanging the bishop with ... ♘c5, which would create level chances.

17   ...   ♘xf6
18   c4!

This must be played immediately, since after the preparatory 18 fe fe, 19 c4? is met by 19 ... ♛b6+ 20 ♔h1 ♘e4! ∓

18   ...   ♛b6+!

In the game Fischer-Lombardy, 1959, Black permitted the exchange of queens with 18 ... dc 19 ♛xd8 ♖fxd8 and obtained a bad endgame: 20 ♗xc4 e5 21 ♖fe1 e4 22 ♖ad1 ±

19   ♔h1   dc
20   ♛xc4   ef
21   ♖xf5   ♖ad8

White has a small positional advantage, which is guaranteed by his active bishop and pawn pair a2, b2, which faces a single counterpart on a7. Still, Black should be able to achieve a draw with exact defensive play.

B4

9   ...   ♘a5
10   f4   b6

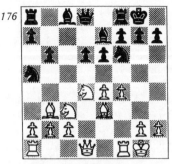

176

Now Black will have the possibility of exchanging the ♗b3 at an appropriate moment, but on the other hand he weakens his control over the e5 square and unleashes the ♘d4. The strength of the move can be seen in the variation 11 f5? e5 12 ♘de2 ♘xb3 13 ab ♗b7 14 ♘g3 d5! Nor does White gain any profit from another method of attack: 11 ♛f3 ♗b7 12 g4 ♖c8! 13 g5, since Black seizes the initiative by sacrificing the exchange with 13 ... ♖xc3! 14 gf! (Inferior is 14 bc ♘xe4 15 ♛g4 ♛c8! 16 ♖f3 ♘xb3 17 ab f5 18 ♛h4 e5 19 ♖h3 h6, Padevsky-Botvinnik, 1956) 14 ... ♖xe3 15 ♛xe3 ♗xf6 17 ♖ad1 ♘xb3 18 ab a6 19 e5 de! 20 ♘xe6? ♛c8 21 ♘xf8 ♛c6! with a strong attack, Rubezov-Borisenko, 1960. White's aspirations must be based on an immediate advance of the e-pawn.

11   e5   ♘e8

The exchange 11 ... de 12 fe ♘e8 gives White the opportunity to bring his queen into the attack on the Black king: 13 ♛f3 ♗b7 14 ♛g3 ♘xb3 15 ab ♛c7 and to create pressure along the f-file: 16 ♖f2. It is considered that 15 ...

♗c5 (instead of 15 ... ♕c7) 16 ♖ad1 ♕e7 equalises, but 17 ♘a4 guarantees a small advantage for White.

| 12 | f5 | de |

On 12 ... ef, 13 e6! ♘c7 14 ef+ ♔h8 15 ♘xf5 is strong.

| 13 | fe | ♘xb3 |

There was a curious game Geller-Batnikov, 1949, in which Black resigned after 13 ... f6 14 ♘f5 ♘xb3 14 ♘d5! ♘d4 16 ♘dxe7+ ♔h8 17 ♘g6+. With the bishop on e3, 13 ... ed is not good: 14 ef+ ♔h8 15 fe = ♕ ♕xe8 16 ♗xd4.

| 14 | ♘c6! | ♕d6! |
| 15 | ♕xd6! | |

Another curiosity — the game Bilek-Petrosian, 1961: 15 ♘d5? ♗h4! 16 ef+ ♖xf7 17 ♖xf7 ♘xa1! 18 ♕f1 ♗f6 18 ♘xf6+ ♘xf6 and this time it was White who had to resign.

| 15 | ... | ♗xd6 |
| 16 | ab | ♗xe6 |

Black needs good counsel here. He may well be destroyed by a combination of factors: the pawns at a7 and b6, the out of play rook at f8, and the restricted scope of his bishops.

| 17 | ♘xa7 | |

Gligorić gives another strong plan: 17 ♘b5 ♗d7 18 ♘cxa7 ♗c5 19 ♗xc5 bc 20 ♖a4 ♖b8 21 ♖a5.

| 17 | ... | ♖b8 |

No better is 17 ... ♘f6 18 ♗xb6 ♖fb8 19 ♘c6! ♖xa1 20 ♖xa1 ♖c8 21 ♘a7 ♖b8 22 ♘ab5! ♗f8 23 ♗c7! ± Kostro-Doda, 1957.

18	♖a6	♘f6
19	♖xb6	♖xb6
20	♗xb6	♖b8
21	♗f2	♘g4
22	♘ab5	

Black has no compensation for the sacrificed pawn and should lose, Fischer-Korchnoi, 1962.

25 Sozin 7 . . . a6

In this chapter we will consider plans where Black plays 7 ... a6, reaching positions which often arise from the Najdorf variation. First, however, we will look at the move 7 a3.

1 e4 c5 2 ᗌf3 ᗌc6 2 d4 cd 4 ᗌxd4 ᗌf6 5 ᗌc3 d6 6 ♗c4 e6 7 a3

White creates a haven for the bishop, so that it will not be exposed to an attack by Black's knight. Nevertheless, he loses an important tempo, and Black can take advantage of this to equalise in several ways. One can recommend the plans given below.

| | 7 | ... | | ♗e7 |

The game Minić–Timman, 1974, saw 7 ... a6 8 ♗e3 ♛c7 9 ♗a2 ᗌa5, but after 10 ♛e2 or 10 f4 b5 11 ♛f3 White stands well.

| | 8 | 0-0 |

In Vasyukov–Djurasević, 1961, White played 8 ♗a2 0-0 9 ♗e3 ♛c7 10 f4 a6 11 ♛f3 ᗌxd4 12 ♗xd4 e5! 13 ♗e3 ef 14 ♛xf4 ♗e6 15 0-0 ᗌfe8 16 ♗b3 ♗f8 and Black had an equal game.

	8	...		0-0
	9	♗a2		ᗌxd4
	10	♛xd4		b6! *(177)*

11 f4 does not work because of

177

11 ... d5! An original, but insufficient try is 11 b4!? ♗a6! 12 ᗌe1 ♛c7 13 ♗b2 ᗌac8 14 ♗b3 ᗌfd8 15 f4 ♗c4 Smirnov–Nikitin, 1965. There remains only the plan of pressuring the Pd6.

	11	♗g5		h6
	12	♗h4		♗b7
	13	ᗌad1		ᗌac8
	14	ᗌfe1

Against 14 ᗌd2 Black has the standard exchange sacrifice 14 ... ᗌxc3 15 bc ᗌxe4 16 ♗xe7 ♛xe7 17 ᗌd3 d5 18 ♛b4 ♛c7 19 ᗌh3 ᗌc8, Zhuravlev–Suetin, 1962.

| | 15 | ... | | ᗌc5! |

The game is level. White cannot play 15 b4 because of 15 ... ᗌxc3 16 ♛xc3 ᗌxe4 17 ♗xe7 ᗌxc3 18 ♗xd8 ᗌxd8! 19 ᗌa1 d5 ∓. Therefore Black will be able to regroup with ♕d8-c7 and ♖fd8, neutralising the pressure on the d-file.

We now turn to an analysis of 7 ... a6:
1 e4 c5 2 ♘f3 ♘c6 3 d4 cd 4 ♘xd4 ♘f6 5 ♘c3 d6 6 ♗c4 e6 7 ♗b3 a6

There are two major continuations for White:
A 8 ♗e3
B 8 0-0

Perhaps more exact, however, is the immediate advance of the f-pawn: 8 f4 ♘a5 9 f5! After 9 ... ♘xb3 10 ab Black has given up the opportunity of playing 10 ... b5, but a transposition into normal lines with 10 ... ♗e7 11 ♗e3 0-0, because Black has wasted time with ♘c6-a5xb3, allows White to place his forces in their best positions after 12 ♕f3, i.e. 12 ... ♗d7 13 g4! e5 14 ♘de2 ±, or 12 ... e5 13 ♘de2 d5?! 14 0-0-0! (14 ed? e4! 15 ♕h3 ♘xd5! 16 0-0-0 ♗xf5! ∓, Romanishin–Dorfman, 1976) 14 ... d4? 15 ♘xd4 ed 16 ♗xd4 ♕a5 17 e5! ± – Dorfman.

A

8 ♗e3

178

8 ... ♗e7

Black can try to get things moving on the queenside right away, for example 8 ... ♕c7 9 f4 ♘a5. But White's better development guarantees him an advantage after either 10 f5 or 10 g4!? d5 (10 ... e5 11 ♘f5 g6 12 fe de 13 ♗g5) 11 e5 ♘d7 12 0-0 ♘c4 13 ♗xc4 ♕xc4 14 ♕f3 ♕c7 15 ♖ae1 ♗b4 16 f5! ±, Vaisman–Mititelu, 1973.

There is another, more logical, continuation: 8 ... ♘a5 9 f4 b5!?, saving time by omitting the move ... ♕c7. On 10 e5 (10 0-0 is B) de 11 fe Black has a defence in 11 ... ♘xb3 12 ab ♘d5, and further 13 ♘c6 ♕c7 14 ♘xd5 ♕xc6, or 13 ♕f3 ♗b7 14 0-0 ♕d7. If White plays 10 f5!?, then after 10 ... e5 11 ♘de2 ♘xb3 12 ab Black, despite the fact that he is behind in development, will have a choice between 12 ... ♗e7 and the rather risky 12 ... b4, which took place in the game Parma–Tukmakov, 1971: 13 ♘d5 ♘xd5 14 ♕xd5 ♖b8 15 0-0 ♗e7 16 ♘g3?! (16 ♕c6+?! ♗d7 17 ♕xa6 would be another mistake because of 17 ... ♗b5! ∓, but there remain some chances for an advantage after 16 c4.) 16 ... ♖b5! 17 ♕c4 (17 ♕c6+ ♕d7 18 ♕xd7 ♗xd7 ∓) 17 ... 0-0 18 ♖ad1 ♗b7 19 ♕e2 f6! 20 c3 bc 21 bc ♕a8! with a complicated struggle.

By playing 8 ... ♗e7 Black guarantees that he will be able to castle whenever he feels the moment is right.

9 f4

It is possible to transpose to the Velimirović attack here with 9

♕e2 0-0 10 0-0-0.

9   ...   ♕c7

9 ... 0-0 would lead to variations considered above. With the move 9 ... ♕c7 Black saves time for the creation of active counterplay. White must now play energetically and the strategy adopted by Black leads to sharp, double-edged play.

Black can, of course, castle after a preliminary exchange on d4; 9 ... ♘xd4 10 ♗xd4 0-0. In this case the continuation of the game Hermlin-Shamkovich, 1972, is interesting: 11 ♕f3!? b5! 12 e5 (12 ♗xf6! would have been stronger.) 12 ... de 13 fe (13 ♗xe5 ♕b6!) 13 ... ♕xd4 14 ef ♗c5! 15 fg ♖d8 16 ♖ad1 ♕e5+ 17 ♕e4 ♖xd1+ ∓.

It is premature to play 9 ... d5 because White can close the centre with 10 e5 ♘d7 and stands much better after 11 ♕h5.

10   ♕f3   ♘a5

The continuation which most adequately fulfills the requirements of the position. This move proves useful whether White castles short or long. If Black sets up with **10 ... ♗d7**, then after 11 0-0-0 ♖c8 White does not have to contend with any serious problems. After 12 g4 g6 13 g5 ♘h5 14 f5 it is quite difficult for Black to co-ordinate his pieces. In the game Vasyukov–Titenko, 1961, White quickly obtained a crushing positional advantage after 14 ... ♘e5 15 ♕e2 ♘c4 16 f6 ♗d8 17 ♗xc4 ♕xc4 18 ♘b3.

On the natural **10 ... 0-0** 11 0-0-0 b5 White can play for complications with 12 e5! ♘xd4 13

♗xd4 (After 13 ♕xa8 ♘c6! 14 ef ♗xf6 15 ♘e4 ♗e7 White does not have sufficient compensation for the queen.) 13 ... ♘d7 14 f5, and it is difficult for Black to find a defence against the threats on three diagonals, for example:

a) **14 ... ♗b7** 15 ♕g3 de 16 fe fe 17 ♗xe6+ ±

b) **14 ... ♘xe5** 15 ♗xe5 de 16 ♕xa8 ♗b7 17 ♕a7 ♗c5 18 ♖d7! ♕xd7 19 ♕xc5 ±

c) **14 ... ef** 15 e6 fe 16 ♗xe6+ ♔h8 17 ♕xa8 ♗b7 18 ♕a7 ♖a8 19 ♘d5! ±

d) **14 ... de** 15 fe ed 16 ♘d5 ♗g5+ 17 ♔b1 ♕d8 18 e7! ±

11   0-0

A solid continuation which does not allow Black a great deal of choice, since after 11 ... 0-0 Black has an unsatisfactory position, as discussed previously. But White can play more sharply, and, it seems, more strongly with 11 g4! 0-0 12 g5 ♘d7 13 0-0-0 (13 ♗xe6?! allows Black to obtain counterplay with 13 ... ♘e5! 14 fe fe 15 ♕g3 ♘c4). Now the threat of ♗xe6 is very real: 13 ... b5 14 ♗xe6 ♘e5 15 ♘d5! ♕d8 16 fe fe 17 ♘xe7+ ♕xe7 18 ed ±. If Black captures on b3, 13 ... ♘xb3+ 14 ab, then after 14 ... b5 there follows 15 f5 ♘e5 16 ♕g3. This idea requires practical tests.

11   ...   b5

12   g4

12 a3 deserves attention, as it limits Black's activity on the queen-side, i.e. 12 ... ♘c4 13 ♗xc4 bc 14 g4. But in this position the only move which has been seen in practice is 12 e5 ♗b7 13 ♕g3 de 14 fe

♘h5 15 ♕h3 (Lovers of quick draws will enjoy the variation 16 ♗xe6 ♘xg3 16 ♗xf7+ ♔d7 17 ♗e6+ ♔e8 18 ♗f7+ etc.) 15 ... ♘xb3 (on 15 ... ♕xe5, 16 ♗xe6! is decisive: 16 ... ♘f6 17 ♖ae1 etc.) 17 ♘xb3 ♕xe5 18 ♘a5 b4! 19 ♘c4 ♕c7 20 ♕xh5 g6 21 ♕e2 bc with full-blooded play for Black, Bannik-Taimanov, 1954.

12	...	h5
13	g5	♘g4
14	g6!	♘xb3
15	gf+	♔xf7
16	ab	b4
17	♘d1	

17 f5 ♘e5 leads to unclear complications after 18 fe+ ♔g8 19 ♕g2 or even 19 ♘d5!?. The inventor of 14 g6, Khenkin, evaluated the position after 17 ♘d1 as favouring White. The threat of f4-f5 really is unpleasant for Black, and even after the best move − 17 ... ♗f6 − White has greater chances to achieve success, although the position remains sharp.

B

8 0-0

By playing 8 ♗e3 (A), White retained the option of castling long. In this variation, he castles short to bring the ♖h1 into the game, which has considerable significance in conjunction with the advance e4-e5.

| 8 | ... | ♘a5 |

Black cannot hold up 9 f4 by playing 8 ... ♕a5 9 f4 ♘xd4 10 ♕xd4 d5, since 11 ♗e3! ♘xe4 12 ♘xe4 de 13 f5! leads to a big advantage for White, given his development and the open centre.

| 9 | f4 | b5 |

Black hopes to tie his opponent's pieces to the defence of the e-pawn by playing ♗b7 and exchanging the ♘a5 for the ♗b3. Only then will he attend to the development of his kingside. The problem with this plan is Black's lagging development. In addition, White dominates the centre.

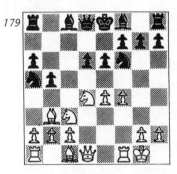

179

| 10 | ♗e3 | |

An immediate **10 e5** leads to great complications: 10 ... de 11 fe ♗c5! 12 ♗e3 ♘xb3 (12 ... ♘c6? 13 ♕f3! ±) 13 ab ♘d5 14 ♕f3 0-0 15 ♘xd5 ♕xd5 16 ♕xd5 ed 17 b4! ♗b6 18 c3 and White has little basis for playing for a win.

Unclear play arises after **10 f5** ♘xb3 11 ab e5!, i.e. 12 ♘dxb5 ♗b7! 13 ♘a3 ♘xe4 14 ♘xe4 (14 ♘c4 d5! ∓) 14 ... ♗xe4 15 ♘c4 ♕c7! 16 ♘e3! ± or 12 ♘de2 ♗b7 13 ♗g5!? (No advantage is gained by either 13 ♘d5 ♘xe4 14 ♗e3 ♖c8, or 13 ♕d3 ♕b6+ 14 ♔h1 ♕c6! 15 ♘g3 h5! or 13 ♘g3 h5 14 ♗g5 h4! 15 ♗xf6 ♕b6+ 16 ♔h1 hg! ∓) 13 ... ♕b6+ 14 ♔h1 ♘xe4 15 ♘xe4 ♗xe4 16 ♘c3 ♗b7! 17 ♘d5 ♕c5! 18 c4 bc 19 bc ♕xc4

20 ♘e3 with a complicated fight
ahead.

With the move 10 ♗e3 White
defends the ♘d4 and threatens the
break e4-e5, which would be most
unpleasant for Black. For example:
10 ... b4 11 e5! de 12 fe ♘xb3 13
ab bc 14 ef cb 15 ♖b1! gf 16 ♕f3
♗d7 17 ♘c6! with a rout. 10 ... e5
is also bad: 11 ♘f5 g6 12 fe ♘xb3
13 ab de 14 ♕xd8+ ♔xd8 15
♗g5 ±

        10   ...   ♘xb3
It might be possible to defend
against the e4-e5 break by the
simple 10 ... ♕c7, but then it would
be necessary to contend with 11
♕f3 ♗b7 12 ♗xe6 fe 13 ♘xe6 ♕d7
14 f5 or even 11 f5 e5 12 ♘de2
♗b7 13 ♘d5.

By playing 10 ... ♘xb3 Black
carries the struggle onto the a8-h1
diagonal.

        11   ab
Now the ♖a1 comes into the
game along the a-file. The attempt
to use an open c-file also comes
into consideration: 11 cb!? ♗b7 12
e5 ♘d5 13 ♘xd5 ♗xd5 14 f5 ♕d7
15 fe fe 16 ♖c1 g6 17 ♘f3 ♗e7
18 ♘g5 de 19 ♕g4 ±, Furster–
Osnos, 1970.

        11   ...   ♗b7
Even here activity with 11 ... b4
turns out to be premature: 12 ♘c6
♕c7 13 ♘xb4 d5 14 ♕d4! ♘xe4
15 ♘xe4 de 16 f5 ±.

        12   e5   de
Once again the advance of the
b-pawn only leads to unpleasantries:
12 ... b4 13 ef bc 14 f5! e5 15 fg
♗xg7 16 ♕g4 ♗f6 17 ♘e6 with a
strong attack, Matokhin–Karabanov,

1962.

        13   fe   ♘d7
If the knight goes to d5 White
obtains a clear positional advantage:
13 ... ♘d5 14 ♕f3 ♕d7 15 ♘xd5
♗xd5 16 ♕g3 g6 17 ♖ad1 ♕b7 (17
... ♗g7 is not on because of 18 c4!
bc 19 bc ♗xc4 20 ♘f5!) 18 ♗g5
♗g7 19 ♗f6.

With the move 13 ... ♘d7 Black
tries to create pressure on the Pe5.

        14   ♕h5   g6
        15   ♕h3   ♕e7

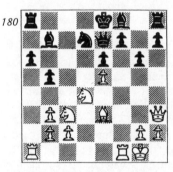

180

The critical position of the variation 10 ♗e3. All Black has to do is
play two moves, ... ♗g7 and ... 0-0,
and the weakness of the Pe5 will
prove decisive. Therefore White has
no time for manoeuvring: 16 ♘f3
♗g7 17 ♘g5 ♘xe5! 18 ♘ge4 (18
♗f4 h6 19 ♗xe5 hg!) 18 ... 0-0 19
♗g5 f6 20 ♗f4 b4! ∓. The consequences of the combination 16
♖ad1 ♗g7 17 ♗g5!? ♕xg5 are unclear. White can take a draw with
18 ♘xe6 fe 19 ♖xd7 ♔xd7 20
♖f7+ ♔d8 21 ♕d3+ ♗d5 22
♘xd5 ♔e8 23 ♘f6+, but the
attempt to achieve more than
that led to a catastrophe in
Damjanović–Krogius, 1967: 18

Ħxf7 ♔xf7 19 ♕xe6+ ♔f8 20 ♘d5 ♗xd5 21 ♕xd5 Ħe8 22 ♕d6+ ♕e7 23 Ħf1+ ♘f6 24 ♘e6+ ♔g8. But one must not pass judgement on the idea 17 ♗g5 on the basis of a single game. Krogius considers the plan 16 ♘dxb5 ab 17 ♘xb5 ♘xe5 18 Ħad1 ♗g7 19 ♘d6+ ♔f8 20 ♗c5 to be dangerous.

But if White is reluctant to sacrifice, then he has yet another interesting possibility at his dis-

posal: **16 Ħae1 ♗g7 17 ♗h6!**, which retains good chances for an advantage, as if 17 ... 0-0 18 ♗xg7 (17 ♘e4?! ♗xe5 18 ♘f3 ♗xb2! ∓) 18 ... ♔xg7 19 ♘e4 ♗xe4 20 Ħxe4 Ħac8 21 c3, with a good game. On 17 ... ♗xe5 18 Ħxe5 ♘xe5 White also stands better after 19 ♗g7 ♕c5 20 ♕e3! (20 ♗xh8 ♕xd4+ 21 ♔h1 ♕g4!) 20 ... ♘g4 21 ♕f4!

26 Sozin 6 . . . ♛b6

1 e4 c5 2 ♘f3 ♘c6 3 d4 cd 4 ♘xd4 ♘f6 5 ♘c3 d6 6 ♗c4 ♛b6

Those who do not wish to spend many moves on the razor's edge of the Velimirović attack might try this queen manoeuvre, which chases the White knight away from the centre.

181

The pawn sacrifice 7 ♗e3 ♛xb2 8 ♘db5 is incorrect: 8 ... ♛b4! 9 ♗d3 ♛a5 10 ♗d2 ♛d8 11 ♘d5 ♘xd5 12 ed ♘e5 13 ♗e2 a6 14 ♘d4 ♛c7 15 0-0 g6. Therefore the knight must move. We examine:

A 7 ♘xc6
B 7 ♘db5
C 7 ♘de2
D 7 ♘b3

A

7 ♘xc6 bc

8 0-0

At first sight innocuous, but actually a sufficiently venomous operation by White. At the cost of somewhat strengthening his opponent's pawn mass in the centre, he escapes problems along the c-file and prepares to sink his own pawn "fangs" into the centre of the board with c4 and e4, for example 8 ... e6 9 b3! ♗e7 10 ♗b2 0-0 11 ♛e2 e5?! 12 ♔h1 ♛c7 13 ♖ae1 ♘d7 14 ♘a4 ♗b7 15 ♗d3 ♖fe8 16 c4 ♗g5 17 ♛c2 h6 18 b4, and White has the initiative on the queenside, Karpov-Stein, 1971.

One can recommend two plans for Black:
a) 8 ... g6 9 b3 (9 ♛e2 ♘g4! 10 ♗b3 ♗g7 11 h3 ♘e5 12 ♗e3 ♛a5 13 f4 ♗a6 = Vasyukov-Mititelu, 1967) 9 ... ♗g7 10 ♗b2 0-0 11 ♛d3 a5 12 ♖ae1 ♗a6 13 e5 de 14 ♘a4 ♗xc4, Honfi–Cobo, 1972.
b) 8 ... e6 9 b3 (9 ♗g5 ♛c5 10 ♗xf6 ♛xc4) 9 ... ♗e7 10 ♗b2 0-0 11 ♛e2 ♘d7! 12 ♘a4 ♛c7 13 f4 ♗b7! 14 ♖f3 ♖ae8 15 ♖af1 (15 ♖g3 e5 15 ♛g4 ♗f6 =) 15 ... g6 16 ♗d3 (16 f5?! ef! 17 ♛e3 ♗f6 18 ♛h6 ♗xb2 19 ♘xb2 d5! ∓,

Hass–Radulov, 1975) and after an eventual c2-c4 a complicated position arises with chances for both sides.

B

	7	♘db5	a6
	8	♗e3	

It is quite dangerous for Black to take the pawn: 8 ... ♛a5 9 ♘d4 ♘xe4 10 ♛f3 f5 11 ♘xc6 bc 12 0-0-0! d5 13 ♘xd5 cd 14 ♗xd5 ♖b8 15 ♗c6+ ♚f7 16 ♗xe4 e6 17 ♖d5! ed 18 ♗xd5+ ♚e8 19 ♗d2 ♗b4 20 ♛h5+ with a decisive attack, Bednarski–Minev, 1975.

At the moment theory recommends that Black adopt a sufficiently solid, but not particularly promising set up: 8 ... ♛a5 9 ♘d4 e6 10 0-0 ♗e7, i.e. 11 ♗b3 0-0 12 f4 ♗d7 13 f5! ♘xd4 14 ♗xd4 ♖ac8 15 fe ♗xe6 16 ♘d5 ♗xd5 17 ed ♖ce8 18 c3 ♗d8! with approximate equality, Bilek–Hort, 1971.

After 8 ... ♛d8 a Velimirović attack can take place: 9 ♘d4 e6 (9 ... ♘g4! 10 ♘xc6 bc 11 ♗g5! ♛b6 12 ♛d2 h6 13 ♗h4 g5! 14 ♗g3!) 10 ♛e2 △ 0-0-0.

C

	7	♘de2	e6
	8	0-0	♗e7

The knight manoeuvre (♘d4-e2-g3), with the goal of strengthening the attacking potential on the kingside, was adopted by Fischer, and Ljubojević likes to play this way as well. *(182)*

	9	♗b3	0-0

9 ... a6 10 ♛d3 0-0 11 ♛g3! ♚h8 12 ♗g5 ♛c7 13 ♖ad1 ± was Ljubojević–Radulov, 1975. In the

182

position after 9 ... 0-0 we have a dynamic, typically Sicilian, situation, which is rich in tactical nuances, for example:

a) 10 ♚h1 ♘a5 11 ♗g5 ♛c5 12 f4 b5 13 ♘g3 ♗b7! (13 ... b4 is inferior because of 14 e5! de 15 ♗xf6 gf 16 ♘ce4 ♛d4 17 ♛h5 ♘xb3 18 ♛h6! ef 19 ♘h5 f5 20 ♖ad1! ± Fischer–Benko, 1958) 14 ♘h5 b4! 15 ♘a4 ♛c7 16 ♘xf6 ♗xf6 17 ♗xf6 gf 18 ♛g4+ ♚h8 19 ♛h4 ♖g8 ∓

b) 10 ♘g3 ♘a5 11 ♗g5 ♛c7 12 ♛d2 a6 13 ♖ad1 ♖d8 14 ♖fe1 b5! 15 ♘f5!? ef 16 ♗xf6 ♘xb3! 17 ab ♗xf6 18 ♘d5 ♛d7! 19 ♘xf6+ gf 20 ♛h6 ♗b7 with a sharp game, Ljubojević–Ribli, 1972.

D

	7	♘b3	e6
	8	♗e3	♛c7

It seems that this is the most dangerous reaction to Black's 6 ... ♛b6. Having lost time on the retreat ♘b3, White immediately regains it, chasing the queen with 8 ♗e3. Now White has a variation of the Scheveningen which is favourable for him.

| | 9 | f4 | |

The withdrawal of the bishop

to e2 would lead the game into the region of the Maroczy system: 9 ♗e2 a6 10 a4 b6 11 f4 ♗e7 12 ♘f3 ♖b8 13 ♕e2 ♘a5! 14 ♘d2 0-0, where Black has no problems.

In principle, White hopes to introduce sharp complications by 9 f4, for example 9 ... a6 10 ♕e2 b5 11 ♗d3 ♗e7 12 g4! h6 13 0-0-0 etc, although the fight which results cannot be described as anything more than complex.

White can play a bit less aggressively with 10 ♗d3 b5 11 a3 ♗b7 12 0-0 ♗e7 13 ♕f3 ♖c8 14 ♖ae1 0-0, which reaches a position examined earlier in which the chances are equal.

9   ...   ♗e7
10   0-0   a6
11   ♗d3

White can limit the movement of the b-pawn to the 6th rank, but then he must consider the exchange of bishops, for example 11 a4 b6 12 ♗d3 ♗b7 13 ♕f3 ♘b4 or 12 ... ♖b8 13 ♕e2 ♘b4 14 ♗f2 0-0 15 e5 ♘fd5 16 ♘xd5 ♘xd5 17 ♗d4 ♘b4!

11   ...   b5

Black need not hasten to castle, as then White would advance with g2-g4-g5 and the queen could be placed in a more aggressive position, for example 11 ... 0-0 12 g4! b5 13 g5 ♘e8 14 ♕h5! g6 15 ♕h6 ± Fischer–Saidy, 1967.

12   ♕f3   ♗b7
13   ♖ae1

The most natural continuation. On 13 ♕h3 the best response is to play 13 ... ♘b4 14 a3 ♘xd3 15 cd e5! 16 ♖ac1 ♕d8! = (17 g4? h5! ∓, Tukmakov–Csom, 1971). The advance 13 a4 would be parried by 13 ... b4 14 ♘e2 ♘a5, i.e. 15 ♗d4 e5 16 ♘xa5 ♕xa5 17 fe de 18 ♕f5 0-0! =

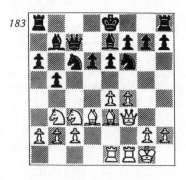

This is a typical position of the variation 6 ... ♕b6 7 ♘b3. White has completed his development and waits for Black to castle.

13   ...   ♘b4

Black delays castling and thereby hinders White's short-term planning, since it is too soon to start advancing the g-pawn. After 14 ♕h3 e5! 15 a3 ♘xd3 16 cd 0-0 17 ♖c1 ♕d8 or 14 ♕g3 g6 15 a3 ♘xd3 16 cd h5 17 ♖c1 ♕d8 (Vogt–Hort, 1971), Black has a solid position.

If Black can find a more dynamic answer to 7 ♘db5, then the move 6 ... ♕b6 will be a good answer to the invitation of the Velimirović attack using the move order 1 e4 c5 2 ♘f3 ♘c6 3 d4 cd 4 ♘xd4 ♘f6 5 ♘c3 d6 6 ♗c4.

27 Velimirović Attack

1 e4 c5 2 ♘f3 ♘c6 3 d4 cd 4
♘xd4 ♘f6 5 ♘c3 d6 6 ♗c4 e6 7
♗e3 ♗e7 8 ♕e2

With these moves one of the
sharpest variations of the Sicilian
Defence begins, in which White
plans to castle queenside and then
advance his g-pawn. He will place it
on g5, where it will drive away the
♘f6 and therefore not only strengthen his control over the centre,
but also allow White to bring his
pieces into an attack on the Black
king. Castling on opposite wings
speeds up the battle and increases
the importance of playing exactly
on every move. Both sides often
find it to their advantage to seize
or retain the initiative by sacrificing
material.

The Yugoslav Grandmaster Velimirović first worked out, and more
importantly, first successfully employed the system with 8 ♕e2 and
9 0-0-0 in practice. *(184)*

Black can now follow one of
two paths. He can first complete
his kingside development and then
begin his counterattack on the
queenside, or he can leave the king
in the centre, keeping the ♖h8 in
reserve, and immediately undertake

184

queenside operations and try to
place the initiative in his own hands.

In this Chapter we will consider
the play after the natural 8 ... 0-0
9 0-0-0 ♕c7, placing other 9th
moves in Chapter 28, and other
8th moves in Chapter 29.

    8   ...   0-0
    9   0-0-0

Now the battle lines are clearly
drawn. The ♖d1 will hinder central
operations by Black, so Black will
have to find counterplay on the
queenside. White has abundant
possibilities, including the advance
of the pawn to g5 creating attacking possibilities and the advance
f2-f4-f5, which threatens not only
to weaken Black's king position
with f5-f6, but also helps the light-
squared bishop to attack the

defender of Black's foothold in the centre – the Pe6, which controls the critical d5 square.

9 ...   ♛c7
10 ♗b3

One can try to attack immediately, without spending time on ♗c4-b3. Actually, this is not thought to be a good idea because Black can later use his active pieces to take advantage of the position of the bishop on c4. White achieves a reasonable endgame after 10 ♖hg1 a6 11 g4 ♘xe4 12 ♘xe4 d5 13 ♗d3 de 14 ♗xe4 e5 15 ♘f5 ♗e6 16 ♛f3 ♖fd8 17 ♗xc6 ♗xf5 18 gf ♛xc6 19 ♛xc6 bc 20 c4.

If Black tries 11 ... ♘a5, he can still transpose to a position considered later on after 12 ♗b3 ♘xb3 13 ab ♘d7. 12 ♗d3 would grant Black equality after 12 ... d5! 13 ed ♘xd5 14 ♘xd5 ed 15 ♛f3 ♗e6 (12 ... ♖d8!? 16 ♗xh7+ ∞) 16 g5 g6! 17 h4 ♘c4! 18 h5 ♘xe3, according to analysis by Savon.

Black might also try to save a tempo himself, omitting ... a6, i.e. 10 ... ♗d7 11 g4 ♘a5 12 ♗d3 (12 ♗b3 ♗c6 13 f3 d5 =) 12 ... ♖fc8 13 g5 ♘e8 △ ... ♘xc4, or even 10 ... ♘a5 11 ♗d3 e5 12 ♘f5 (12 ♘b3 ♗e6) 12 ... ♗xf5 13 ef d5.

10 ...   a6

Until the rook has gone to g1, the manoeuvre ... ♘a5 (△ ♘xb3) is a mistake. The fact of the matter is, that the ♗b3 and the ♘d4 are White's most dangerous pieces because they put pressure on the Pe6. Here the principle of personal marking (man-to-man coverage) from football (or basketball), is appropriate: The ♘c6 must continue to oppose the ♘d4, while the ♗b3 is the responsibility of the ♘f6, which will travel via d7 to c5, where he can then exchange himself for the bishop. After 10 ... ♘a5 the ♘d4 has no opposition, and White's kingside initiative rolls along: 11 g4! ♘xb3+ 12 ab a6 13 g5 ♘d7 14 f4 ♖e8 15 h4 b5 16 g6! hg 17 h5! ±.

Now White has a choice.

A 11 f4
B 11 ♖hg1
C 11 g4
D 11 ♔b1

A

11   f4

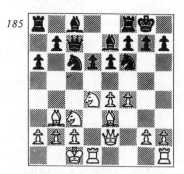

185

Here White tries to create pressure on the Pe6 and force a weakness at d5. This is a time consuming plan, however, and in sharp positions where the kings have fled to opposite sides of the board it is his safety which matters, and not pawns.

11 ...   ♘xd4
12 ♖xd4

The rook's place is not, of course, in the middle of a piece-filled board, but recapturing with the bishop is not on because of 12 ... e5 13 fe de! (13 ... ♗g4 14 ef ♗xe2 15 fe ±) 14 ♗e3 ♗g4, winning the exchange.

12	...	b5
13	♖f1	♖ab8!
14	a3	

The flaw in White's opening strategy is revealed. He is forced to compromise the defences of his own king, but he cannot inflict the same upon his opponent: 14 f5 is dangerous because of 14 ... b4 15 ♘a4 e5 16 ♖c4 ♕a5 17 ♖c6 ♗b7 18 ♗b6 ♕b5!

| 14 | ... | ♗d7 |
| 15 | f5 | a5 |

The initiative is in Black's hands and it looks very dangerous indeed.

B

| 11 | ♖hg1 |

186

Not wasting any time, White will push forward the g-pawn and prepare the way for the manoeuvre ♖g1-g3-h3.

| 11 | ... | b5 |

Now Black can also defend by transferring his knight to c5, but after 11 ... ♘d7 12 g4 b5 we reach a position which is examined in C.

| 12 | g4 | b4 |

With these moves, first seen in Matulović–Nikitin, 1966, the main line commences.

The plan with 12 ... ♘xd4 13 ♗xd4 ♘d7 will be examined in C.

12 ... ♘a5 also deserves consideration. The fact is, after 12 ... ♘a5 13 g5 ♘xb3+ 14 ab ♘d7 the ♖g1 would stand better on its original square, especially after the h-file has opened. In this context the move 11 ♖hg1 can be considered a loss of one (or sometimes two) costly tempi, and Black succeeds in creating counterplay with one move after another, leading to some rather puzzling situations, for example:

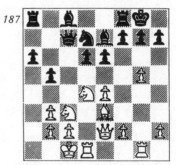

187

a) 15 h4 b4 16 ♘a4 ♗b7 17 g6 hg 18 h5 e5! ∓, Zuckerman–Paoli, 1970.

b) 15 ♖g3 ♖e8 16 ♕h5 g6 17 ♕h4 b4 18 ♘ce2 ♗b7 19 ♖h3 ♘f8.

c) 15 ♕h5 g6 16 ♕h6 ♖e8 17 ♖g3 ♗f8 18 ♕h4 b4 (18 ... ♗g7 19 ♖h3 ♘f8 20 e5 d5 ∞) 19 ♘ce2 ♗b7 20 ♖h3 h5 21 ♘g3 ♗g7.

d) 15 f4 b4 (15 ... ♖e8!?) 16 ♘f5!? ♘c5! (It is too dangerous for Black to play 16 ... ef: 17 ♘d5 ♕d8 18 ef ♖e8 19 g6! fg 20 fg ♗f6 21 ♕h5 hg 22 ♖xg6 ♗b7 23 ♗b6! ±) 17 ♘xe7+ ♕xe7 18 e5! bc! 19 ed cb+ 20 ♔xb2 (20 ♔b1 ♕a7 21 b4 ♘a4!) 20 ... ♕a7 21 ♕f2 ♘a4+ 22 ba ♕b7+ 23 ♔a3 ♗d7.

e) **15 ♘f5** ef 16 ♘d5 ♕d8 17 ef ♖e8 18 ♕f3 (18 g6!) 18 ... ♖b8 19 f6 ♗f8 20 g6 hg 21 ♖xg6 ♘e5 22 fg ♗e7! ∓ Cordova-Ermenkov, 1977.

13 ♘xc6

White's attack is less dangerous after **13 g5** bc 14 gf cb+ 15 ♔b1 ♗xf6. The pawn at e6 is still alive, and it hinders the operations of the ♘d4 and, more importantly, the ♗b3. In the game Matulović-Nikitin, 1966, there followed 16 ♕f3! ♗e5! 17 ♗h6 g6! 18 ♕c3! ♗d7 (Even stronger is 18 ... ♗b7 19 f4 ♗f6 20 ♗xf8 ♖xf8 21 ♗a4 ♕a5! or 20 e5 de 21 ♘xe6 fe 22 ♗xe6+ ♖f7 23 ♖d7 ♕xd7 ∓) 19 f4 ♗f6 20 ♗xf8 ♖xf8 21 ♗a4 ♖c8 and the game entered an endgame which is favourable to Black.

If White wishes to avoid the ensuing complications, he must be precise in his move order. After **13 ♘d5**, Stean-Velimirović, 1974 headed for a quiet position with equal chances after 13 ... ♘xd5! 14 ♘xc6 ♘xe3 15 ♘xe7+ ♕xe7 16 ♕xe3 a5 17 ♗a4 ♗b7 18 g5 ♖fc8.

13 ... ♕xc6

Of course it is less risky to play 13 ... bc 14 ♘xe7+ ♕xe7 15 ♗d4! cb+ 16 ♗xb2 ♗b7, but then Black will have a long uphill struggle for equality.

14 ♘d5!?   ed

No one has tried 14 ... ♘xd5 15

ed ♕b7 16 de fe, where Black can create counterplay by advancing his a-pawn: 17 f4 a5 18 f5?! a4 19 ♗xe6+ ♗xe6 20 fe b3 21 ♔b1 ♕e4! ∓

15 g5!

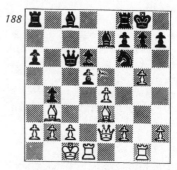

The key to White's attack. His threat to regain the sacrificed material with interest after ♗b3xd5 is quite real. Black must look to the weakened position of the White king, a result of the brief absence of the bishop, which embarks on a hunting journey (♗b3xd5xa8).

15 ...   ♘xe4

This is not greed, but above all an attempt not to allow the g-file to be opened and to keep the White rooks from entering the game. Practice has refuted 15 ... de 16 gf ♗xf6, which was once considered acceptable: 17 ♗d5 (17 ♗d4 leads only to equality after 17 ... ♗xd4 18 ♖xd4 ♗e6!) 17 ... ♕a4 and now Black is under heavy attack, as was demonstrated in the game Ostapenko-Yartsev, 1969: 18 ♕h5 ♗e6 (There is no salvation in 18 ... b3 19 ♗xb3 ♕d7 as White continues 20 ♖xg7+ ♗xg7 21 ♖g1 ♕h3 22 ♗d4 ±) 19 ♖xg7+! ♗xg7

20 ♖g1 ♖fc8 21 ♖xg7+! ♔xg7 22
♕h6+ ♔g8 23 ♗xe4 b3 24 ♗xh7+
♔h8 25 ♗f5+ ♔g8 26 ♕h7+ ♔f8
27 ♗h6+ ♔e8 28 ♕g8+ ♔e7 29
♗g5+ ♔d7 30 ♕xf7+ ♔c6 31 ♗xe6.

Boleslavsky tried to defend this
position in analysis with 31 ... ♕e4!
32 ♕d7+ ♔b6 33 ♗e3+ ♔a5, but
this only led to an evaluation of ±
on the 41st move: 34 ♗xb3 ♖c6
35 a4! (△ 36 ♗d2+, 37 a5+) 35 ...
♕h1+ 36 ♔d2 ♖ac8 37 ♕f5+ ♖c5
38 ♗xc5 ♖xc5 39 ♕f4 ♕c6 40 c3
♔b6 41 h4! ±. There is no way
for Black to resolve both of his
problems, the defence of the king
and the threatened promotion of
White's h-pawn.

16   ♗xd5   ♕a4!

Here there is no room for a
transposition of moves: 16 ... ♘c3
17 bc ♕a4 18 ♗b3! ♕a3+ 19 ♔b1
bc 20 ♗c1 ±.

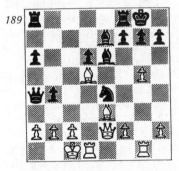

189

White must now choose between
taking the rook with the attendant
risk of falling under an attack, or he
can limit his recovery of material,
maintaining the active positions of
his pieces.

17   ♗xa8

The other capture (17 ♗xe4)
restores material equality and at
first glance seems to threaten combinational attacks on the Black
king. But after exact defence the
attack is repelled; 17 ... ♗e6! and
now:

a) 18 ♗xa8 ♖xa8 19 b3 ♕xa2 20
♗d4 ♖c8 ∓.

b) 18 g6 hg 19 ♗d4 ♕xa2 20 ♕h5
♖ac8 21 ♗xg6 hg 22 ♖xg6 ♖xc2+
23 ♔xc2 ♕c4+ 24 ♔b1 ♗f5+ 25
♔a1 ♗xg6 ∓, Pinkas–Kunstowicz,
1976.

c) 18 ♗xh7+ ♔xh7 19 ♕h5+ ♔g8
20 g6 fg 21 ♕xg6 ♗f6 22 ♗d4 b3!
23 ♗xf6 ♕f4+ ∓.

d) 18 ♗d4 g6! 19 ♗f6 ♗xf6 20 gf
♕xa2 21 ♕h5 ♕a1+ 22 ♔d2 ♕xb2
23 ♗xg6 fg 24 ♖xg6+ ♔h8 25 ♕h6
♕c3+ 26 ♔c1 ♖g8 27 ♖dg1 ♕a1+
∓ Rodig–Dueball, 1974.

17   ...   ♘c3
18   bc   ♗e6!

The success of Black's counterattack depends on the rapid mobilisation of his forces and the ability
to get them into the area of the
board where the action is taking
place. 18 ... bc would be a mistake
because of 19 ♖d4 ♕xa2 20 ♔d1! ±.

After 18 ... ♗e6 White cannot
hang on to his extra rook: 19 ♗e4
♕a3+ 20 ♔d2 ♕xc3+ with a draw
or 19 ♗d5 ♗xd5! (but not 19 ...
♕a3+ 20 ♔b1 ♗xd5 21 c4! ±) 20
♖xd5 ♕xa2 21 ♗d4 ♖e8! with
approximately equal chances. 19
♗d4 looks more promising, but
even here Black has sufficient
counterplay: 19 ... bc 20 ♗xc3
♖xa8 21 g6 hg 22 ♖xg6 ♕f4+
23 ♗d2 ♕f5 (Also possible is 23
... ♕e5!? 24 ♕xe5 de 25 ♖xe6

♗a3+ with a draw) 24 ♖g3 ♖b8.

C

11   g4

This direct continuation is the most logical and is dangerous for Black. First White chases the ♘f6 and only then chooses his plan of attack.

Black has a small selection of acceptable continuations here. Practical experience of the last 10 years has supported the conclusion that the only defensive plan is that connected with the knight tour ♘f6-d7-c5. This confirms opinions in the first edition of this book, published in 1969 (Russian edition by Nikitin alone – tr.). The knight manoeuvre achieved great popularity after Larsen's brilliant win over Fischer in 1970, and to that victory owes its reputation as an acceptable defence against both 11 g4 and 11 ♖hg1.

Now Black must decide whether he will capture the ♘d4 before manoeuvring the knight f6 to c5. In either case sharp and difficult to assess positions will arise, which require concrete and precise calculation.

C1 11 ... ♘d7

C2 11 ... ♘xd4

C1

11   ...   ♘d7

The goal of the knight manoeuvre is clear. Black wants to liquidate the ♗b3 at an appropriate time. But then the dark-squared bishop will be the only piece defending his king. To carry out the defence in such an economical manner requires Black to play with extreme accuracy and with an understanding of all of the subtleties of the position.

Again the path divides:

C11 12 ♘f5!?

C12 12 g5

Other moves are less promising:

a) **12 ♘xe6.** This combinational method of exploiting the weakness at d5 is not as effective as that considered in C11. 12 ... fe 13 ♗xe6+ ♔h8 14 ♘d5 ♕d8. The knight at d5 looks beautiful, but the beauty is only skin deep and the piece is really quite useless. After 15 ♗xd7 ♗xd7 16 ♗b6 ♕e8 17 ♘c7 ♕f7 18 ♘xa8 ♖xa8 White may be able to restore approximate material equality, but the initiative will belong to his opponent.

b) **12 f4.** Sometimes White tries to march the f-pawn up the board quickly, but without the light-squared bishop it is not possible for White to seriously expect success in the centre, for example 12 ... ♘c5 13 f5 ♘xb3+ 14 ab b5 15 ♖hf1 ♗d7 16 g5 b4 17 f6 bc 18 bc ♗d8 19 ♕h5 ♘xd4 20 ♗xd4 e5 ∞ Brueggeman–Semkov, 1978. Black can also follow Boleslavsky's analysis: 13 ... b5

14 ♖hg1 b4 15 ♘a4 ♗d7 16 ♘xc6 ♘xb3+ 17 ab ♗xc6 18 g5 ef 19 ef ♖e8! 20 ♘b6 ♕xb6! 21 ♗xb6 ♗xg5+ 22 ♖xg5 ♖xe2 =.

c) **12 ♗xe6 ♘xd4** obviously favours Black.

d) **12 ♖hg1** △ ♘f5 is worth analysing: 12 ... ♘c5 13 ♘f5 b5 (White will mount a menacing attack on the g-file if 13 ... ♘xb3+ 14 ab ef 15 gf!) 14 ♘xe7+ ♕xe7 15 g5 ♗b7 16 ♗d4 ♘xb3+ 17 ab e5 gave Black a worthwhile game in Lukhin-Zaichik, 1980, since the move 12 ♖hg1 turned out to be a waste of a valuable tempo.

C11

	12	♘f5	ef
	13	♘d5	♕d8
	14	gf	

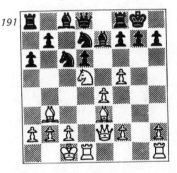

191

White has solid compensation for the piece: the light squared bishop has come to life, the excellent outpost square d5, and the cramping influence of the Pf5, which keeps the ♗c8 out of the game. He can also use the Pf2 to defend e4, or push it forward to destroy Black's potential base of operations at e5. At the same time, the threats along the opened g-file

are unpleasant for Black.

	14	...	♘a5

On 14 ... ♘f6 White crashes through with 15 ♖hg1 ♔h8 16 ♗b6 ♕d7 17 ♘c7 ♖b8 18 f4 ♘xe4 19 ♗e6! fe 20 fe ±.

	15	♖hg1	

After 15 ♘xe7+ ♕xe7 16 ♗d5 ♘f6 17 ♖hg1 ♔h8 18 ♕f3 ♘xd5 19 ♖xd5, Velimirović-Bukal, 1971, Black could have maintained his defences and held on to a small material advantage if he had played 19 ... ♘c6.

	15	...	♘xb3+
	16	ab	

Velimirović's analysis continues 16 ... ♔h8 17 ♗d4 f6 18 ♕g4 ♖g8 19 ♘f4 ♘e5 20 ♗xe5 fe 21 ♘g6+! hg 22 ♕h3+ ♗h4 23 ♖xd6 ♕e7 24 ♖dxg6 ±.

Still, Black is not forced to accept this "gift", but can play 12 ... ♘c5! instead, continuing to follow his plan of redeployment. We think that this gives him more opportunities to obtain active counterplay, for example:

a) **13 ♖hg1 b5** 14 ♗f4 ♘e5 15 ♕d2 ef! 16 ♘d5 ♘ed3+! 17 ♔b1 ♕d8 18 cd ♘xb3 19 ab fg ∓.

b) **13 ♘xe7+ ♕xe7** 14 g5 (14 ♕d2!? ♖d8) 14 ... b5 15 ♖hg1 ♗b7 16 ♕h5 b4 17 ♘a4 ♘xe4 18 ♖g4 g6 19 ♕h6 ♘a5 20 ♖h4 ♘xb3+ 21 ab f5! ∓

c) There is a very interesting quiet sacrifice: **13 ♘xg7 ♔xg7 15 g5,** but it has not yet been tried out in practice.

C12

	12	g5	♘c5 (192)
	13	♖hg1	

192

An immediate pawn storm would be much too slow and would provide Black with time for the creation of counterplay on the queenside: 13 h4 b5 and now:

a) **14 f3 &d7 15 ♕g2 b4 16 ♘ce2 ♘xb3+ 17 ab a5 18 g6 fg 19 h5 ♘xd4 20 ♘xd4 g5! 21 &xg5 &xg5+ 22 ♕xg5 h6 23 ♕g4 ♖f7 24 ♖hg1 a4! ∓** Fischer-Larsen, 1970.

b) **14 ♔b1 ♘xb3** (14 ... b4? 15 ♘d5! ed 16 ♘xc6 ♘xb3 17 ♘xb4! ♘c5 18 ♘xd5 ♕b7 19 &d4 &e6 20 ♘f6+! ±) **15 ab &d7 16 h5 ♘xd4?! 17 ♖xd4 &c6 18 g6 fg 19 hg h6 20 ♘d5! ed 21 ed &e8! 22 &xh6 &xg6!** with a sharp game, Roos-Codrua, 1970.

c) **14 ♘xc6 ♕xc6 15 g6?! ♘xb3+ 16 ab fg 17 h5 g5 18 h6 g6 ∓**

d) **14 g6 fg 15 h5 ♘xd4 16 ♖xd4 g5 17 h6 g6 18 ♖hd1 &d7** Zhelnin-Moscalev, 1978.

e) **14 h5 b4! 15 ♘a4 ♘xd4 16 ♖xd4 &d7! △ 17 ♖xb4 &b5 ∓**

The attack of the f-pawn is less dangerous: 13 f4 b5 14 ♖hf1 ♖b8 15 f5 b4!

With the text move White retains the possibility of bringing both rook and queen onto the h-file. This position still demands

study, because it often arises after a different move order: 11 ♖hg1 ♘d7 12 g4 ♘c5 13 g5 etc.

13 ...   &d7

A logical move which increases the coordination of the black pieces to the maximum. There is no need for the &c8 to watch over the b7 square. It is needed on d7, where it observes the squares along the important c8-h3 diagonal and defends the e6 pawn. But if one considers that the ♖a8 has its sphere of action on the queenside, and that the ♖f8 must stay and defend the king, then the coordination of these rooks is perhaps not essential, so one might save time by omitting ... &d7 and play **13 ... b5** *(193)*. The obvious game of "getting there first", does not leave White any choice. Since he doesn't have time to get the pawn roller moving he must attack the enemy king with his pieces:

193

a) **14 ♖g3 ♘xb3+ 15 ab b4 16 ♕h5 bc 17 ♖h3 h6! ∓**

b) **14 ♘xc6 ♘xb3+ 15 ab ♕xc6 16 &d4 b4** (16 ... ♖e8 17 &f6 &f8 is worth a try) **17 &f6!** (17 ♕h5 bc 18 ♕h6 cb+ 19 ♔xb2 e5 20 &xe5

♕xc2 21 ♔xc2 de 22 ♕b6 ♗e6 ±)
17 ... ♖e8! 18 ♘a4 (18 ♖d3 bc
19 ♖h3 ♗f8! 20 ♖xh7 ♔xh7 21
♕h5+ ♔g8 22 ♖g4 ♕b5! 23 bc
♕e2! ∓ Bonin-Shamkovich, 1976)
18 ... e5 19 ♗xe7 ♖xe7 20 ♕c4
(Perhaps 20 ♕e3!?) 20 ... ♖c7 21
♕xc6 ♖xc6 22 c4 bc = Didishko-
Mochalov, 1975
c) 14 ♕h5 g6 15 ♕h6 ♖fe8 16
♖g3 (16 ♘xc6?! ♘xb3+ 17 ab
♕xc6 18 ♗d4 ♗f8 19 ♕h4 b4
20 ♖d3 h5 ∓) 16 ... ♗f8 17 ♕h4
b4 (17 ... ♗e7) 18 ♘c6! (18 ♖h3
h5 — who wants to try 18 ...
♗g7 19 ♕xh7+ ♔f8? — 19 gh bc 20
♕f6 (20 ♘xc6 ♘xb3+ 21 ab e5! ∞)
20 ... ♔h7 21 ♘f3 ♘xe4 ∞ Mager-
ramov-Tal, 1974) 18 ... ♘xb3+ 19
ab ♕xc6 20 ♗d4! h5 21 gh ±
Pereira-Varabiescu, 1981. The
strength of the attack is more
seriously tested after 13 ... ♗d7
instead of 13 ... b5, by the move 15
... ♖fc8!, when White's play is inter-
rupted by the threat of mate on c2.

Mochalov has analysed the no
less complicated variation after 14
... b4!?: 15 ♘xc6 ♘xb3+ 16 ab
♕xc6 17 ♗d4 ♗b7! (17 ... ♖d8 18
♖d3! bc 19 ♖f3! ± Grigorov-
Spassov, 1975) 18 ♖g4! (18 ♘d5?
ed 19 ♕h6 ♕xc2+! 20 ♔xc2 ♖fc8+
△ 21 ... gh ∓ or 18 ♗f6 ♖fc8! ∓) 18
... bc! 19 ♖h4 cb+ 20 ♗xb2 ♕xe4!
21 ♖xe4 ♗xe4 ∓.

15 ♖g3 is even worse: 15 ... bc!
16 ♖h3 h6 17 ♖g1 ♘xb3+ 18 cb
♘xd4 (18 ... ♕a5!?) 19 ♗xd4 cb+
20 ♔xb2 e5 21 gh g6 22 ♖c3
♔h7! or 22 ♖xg6+ ♔h8! ∓.

d) The manoeuvre 14 ♗d5 might be
a serious argument against the move

13 ... b5. If 14 ♗d5!? ♗d7 15
♘xc6 ♗xc6 16 ♗xc5 dc 17 ♗xc6
♕xc6 18 e5 △ ♘e4. Accepting the
bishop sacrifice is dangerous: 14 ...
♘xd4 15 ♗xd4 ed? 16 ♘xd5
♕b7 17 ♘f6+! ♔h8 18 ♕h5 h6
19 gh g6 20 ♖xg6! ±±.
14 ♖g3
Again, the most energetic continuation. It is too late to march
the f-pawn: 14 f4 b5! 15 f5 b4!
16 g6 ♘xb3 17 ab fg 18 fg bc 19
♕h5 hg 20 ♖xg6 ♖f7 21 ♖h6 gh
22 ♖g1+ ♗g5 23 ♗xg5 ♖g7! ∓
Benjamin-Liberzon, 1980.
14 ... ♖fc8!
The idea behind this move is
to tie the ♘c3 to its place in view
of the threat of mate on c2. Simultaneously, a square is made available for manouvering the ♗e7. For
a short time the Black king will be
left to cope with potential incur-
sions of the White pieces by himself.
Eight years of experience, however,
has shown the viability of Black's
position.
15 ♕h5 g6
16 ♕h6 ♗f8
17 ♕h4 ♗e7 *(194)*
17 ... b5 18 ♖h3 ♘xb3+ 19 ab
♗g7!? is extraordinarily risky. 20
♕xh7+ ♔f8 21 f4 ♘e7 was played
in Vitomsky-Vitolinš, 1972, but it
has since been refuted: 22 ♘f3! e5!
(22 ... b4 23 ♗d4! e5 24 fe de 25
♗xe5 ± Donchev-Semkov, 1978)
23 f5 gf 24 ♘h4 (24 g6 f4!) 24 ...
f4 25 ♘f5! and there is no way
to stop White's attack.
This is the critical position, in
which it is up to White to decide
whether or not to accept the im-

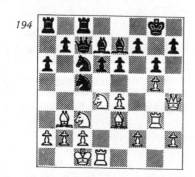

194

plicit offer of the draw: 18 ♕h6 ♗f8 etc. The alternative is to seek new avenues or objects of attack. Praxis and 12–15 ply analysis shows that Black's position can be defended, for example:

a) **18 ♖h3?!** h5 19 f4 ♘xd4 20 ♗xd4 ♘xb3+ 21 ab e5! ∓

b) **18 ♘f5** ♘xb3+ 19 ab ef 20 ♘d5 ♕a5 21 ♘xe7+ ♕xe7 22 ♗d4 ♕a1+ 23 ♔d2 ♕a5+ 24 ♔e2? (24 ♔c1 ♕a1+ draws) 24 ... fe 25 ♕h6! ♗g4+! 26 ♖xg4 ♘f5 0-1, Panchenko-Kochiev, 1973

c) **18 f4** b5 19 ♘xc6 ♕xc6 20 ♗d4 h5 21 ♖d2 b4 22 ♗d5 bc! 23 ♗xc6 cd+ ∓ Lysenko-Ioseliani, 1976

d) **18 ♘de2!** h5 19 f4 b5 20 f5 ♘xb3+ 21 ab b4 22 ♘f4 bc 23 bc ♕a5! 24 fg fg 25 ♘xg6 ♔g7 26 ♘xe7 ♘xe7 27 ♗d4+ e5 28 g6 ♘g8! 29 ♕xh5 ♘f6! ∓.

C2

    11   ...   **♘xd4**

The exchange of knights is advantageous, in principle. The rook does not occupy a significant position in the centre, the pressure on the e6 pawn is relieved and it will now be easier to play ... b7-b5.

There is one aspect to the position of the rook which is favourable, however, and that is that White will now have an extremely dangerous threat in e4-e5, as the rook will then be able to move over to h4. Only the most precise defence can neutralise this threat.

If one is going to exchange the knights, then this is the time to do so. Delay only results in a position which allows White favourably to carry out his attack: 11 ... b5 12 g5 (12 ♘xc6 ♕xc6 13 g5! ♘xe4 14 ♘d5 ♕b7 15 ♕f3 is also strong, ±) 12 ... ♘xd4 13 ♗xd4! ♘d7 14 ♕h5 ♘c5 15 ♖hg1. Now the ♗d4 plays an active, and possibly even decisive, role. The position which we have reached must be examined because it can also arise after 11 ♖hg1 b5 12 g4 ♘xd4 13 ♗xd4 ♘d7 14 g5 ♘c5 15 ♕h5.

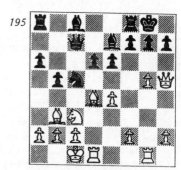

195

Here are two examples from praxis, which illustrate the method and strength of White's attack:

a) **15 ... ♘xb3+** 16 ab ♕d8 (16 ... b4? is inferior: 17 ♗f6 bc 18 ♕h6! ± or 16 ... f6?! 17 gf ♗xf6 18 ♗xf6 ♖xf6 19 ♘d5! ±) 17 ♖d3 e5 18 ♗xe5 b4 19 ♗f6! (△ 20 ♕h6)

19 ... ♗xf6 20 gf ♕xf6 21 ♘d5! ±.
b) 15 ... ♗b7 16 ♗f6 ♖fc8 17 ♖g4
b4 18 ♖h4 ♗xe4! 19 ♖xe4 bc 20
♖h4 ♘xb3+ 21 ♔b1 ± Bardonada–
Pavlov, 1974.

    12   ♖xd4   ♘d7

The counterthrust in the centre
with 12 ... e5 is not recommendable.
In his pursuit of a pawn Black
willingly weakens the d5-square and
sharply increases the power of the
♗b3. In response White has two
plans of attack, which make use of
these factors:
a) 13 ♖c4! ♕d8 14 g5 ♘d7 15
♖xc8! ♕xc8 16 ♘d5 ♗d8 17 h4,
and the ♗b3 is stronger than the
♖a8.
b) 13 ♘d5! ♘xd5 (13 ... ♕d7 14
♘b6 ♕xg4 15 f3 ♕h3 16 ♘xa8 ed
17 ♗xd4 ♗e6 18 ♘c7 ±) 14 ♖xd5
♗e6 15 ♖d3 ♖ac8 16 ♗d5 and
Black has no counterplay.

    13   g5   b5

This move is more elastic than
13 ... ♘c5, which removes the
knight from the kingside rather
early. Against 13 ... ♘c5 Grandmaster Bronstein has proposed an
interesting pawn sacrifice: 14 e5!
de 15 ♖h4 g6 16 ♖h6!? with the
idea of doubling rooks on the h-file
after playing h2-h4-h5. After 16 ...
f5 17 h4 ♘xb3+ ab White quickly
creates concrete threats, for example: 18 ... f4 19 ♗d2 b5 20
♖xh7! ♔xh7 21 h5 ♗xg5 22 ♘e4
♖f5 23 hg+ ♔g8 24 ♖h7 f3 25
♕e1 ♗xd2+ 26 ♕xd2 ♕xh7 27
♕d8+ ♔g7 28 gh ♔xh7 29 ♘d6
e4 30 ♕h4+ 1-0, Fillipov–Cask,
1975. Instead of 16 ... f5, 16 ... b5!
is evidently stronger: 17 ♗xc5! (17

h4 ♗b7 18 f3 e4! 19 f4 ♘d3+!) 17
... ♕xc5 18 ♘e4 ♕c6!, i.e. 19 h4
♗b7 20 f3 ♕d7 21 ♕e3 ♕d4! ∓

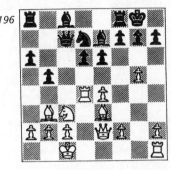

196

    14   ♕h5

The attack along the h-file with
the heavy pieces can be organized
quite quickly, and correspondingly
it seems more promising than the
pawn storm.
a) 14 h4 ♘c5 15 h5 ♗d7 (15 ... f5
16 ef ♖xf5 is another acceptable
defence.) 16 g6 a5! ∓
b) 14 f4 ♘c5 15 f5 (There is no
time for preparatory moves such as
15 ♖f1 or 15 ♕f2, since Black takes
the initiative after either 15 ... b4
16 ♖xb4 a5 or 15 ... f5 16 ef
♖xf5) 15 ... ef 16 ♘d5 (There does
not seem to be full compensation
for the pawn after 16 ef ♗xf5 17
♖f1 ♕d7! or 16 ♗d5 ♖b8 17 ef
♗xf5 18 ♖f1 ♕d7.) 16 ... ♕d8 17
ef (on 17 e5 Black can stave off the
attack with 17 ... ♘xb3+ 18 ab de
19 ♘f6+ ♗xf6 20 ♖xd8 ♗xd8 21
♗c5 ♖e8 ∓, but there is the interesting idea of attacking on the g-
file to be considered: 17 ♖g1 ♖e8
18 ♕f2 △ ♘f6+) 17 ... ♗xf5 18 ♖f1
♗e6 ∓
c) The pawn sacrifice 14 e5 leads to

puzzling complications, but if Black defends accurately he can repulse the attack:

c1) **14 ... de 15 Rh4 Rd8 16 Qh5** (16 Rg1 Bb7 17 Rxh7! g6! 18 Rh6 Bf8, but not 17 ... Kxh7? 18 g6+! 19 gf Rxg6!, according to analysis by Wagner in 1980) **16 ... Nf8 17 Ne4! Bb7 18 Nf6+! Bxf6!** (18 ...gf? 19 Rg1 f5 20 g6 fg 21 Bxe6+ Nxe6 22 Qxh7+ Kf8 23 Qh8+ Kf7 24 Rh7+ winning.) **19 gf Bxh1 20 fg Kxg7 21 Bh6+ Kg8 22 Qg5+ Ng6 23 Qf6 Rd1+!! 24 Kd1 Qd8+** – analysis by Velimirović.

c2) **14 ... Nxe5 15 Qh5** (on 15 Rh4 both 15 ... g6 and 15 ... Qc6! 16 Ne4 Ng6 are good) **15 ... Ng6 16 Rh1 Bb7 17 Rg3 Rfc8 18 Rh3 Nf8 19 Rdh4 Bg2! 20 Rg3 Qc6 ∓**

d) Besides 14 Qh5, White can begin his attack using his heavy pieces by playing **14 Rg1** (Δ Rg1-g3-h3). But since the rook has left the h-file, the manoeuvre Rd4-h4-h6, combined with h2-h4-h5, has lost some of its effect, and the pawn sacrifice after 14 ... Nc5 15 e5 now carries great risk, for example 15 ... Nxb3+ 16 ab de (But not 16 ... d5 17 Rh4 Qxe5? 18 Qd3 g6 19 Bd4! Qxg5+ 20 Rxg5 Bxg5+ 21 Be3 Bxh4 22 Qd4 Be7 23 Bh6! ±, Musil–Haag, 1974) 17 Rh4 g6, or 15 Rg3 g6! 16 e5 (16 h4 Rb8 17 h5 a5!) 16 ... de 17 Rh4 f5! After 14 Rg1 Nc5 15 Qh5 g6, 16 Qh6 doesn't work either: 16 ... f5! 17 gf Bxf6 18 h4!? Bxd4 19 Bxd4 Nxb3+ 20 ab e5 21 Bb6 Qf7! 22 Nd5 Be6 23 h5 Bxd5 24 hg Qf4+ wins.

By playing **14 Qh5**, White ex-cludes the possibility of 14 ... Nc5, since then 15 e5 will be significantly stronger.

14   ...   Rfd8!

This might seem risky, but it is a well calculated defence, in which the f8-square is made available for Black's minor pieces. Besides 14 ... Rfd8, Black has another continuation, which is based on the same defensive strategy: 14 ... g6 15 Qh6 Re8 16 Rg1 (16 e5 Bf8 17 ed Qb7!) 16 ... Bf8 17 Qh4 Rb8 18 Rg3 Bg7 19 Rd1 b4 20 Ne2 Nf8 21 f4 a5, Vetemaa–Panchenko, 1979. A similar idea is 14 ... Bb7 15 Rg1 g6 16 Qh6 Rfe8 17 f4 Bf8 18 Qh3 Rac8 19 Rg4 Nc5 20 Rh4 h5 21 gh Kh7 22 Rg4 a5 23 f5 a4 24 Qg3 ef 25 ef Rxe3 26 Qxe3 ab 27 Qg5! Kg8! Kyss–Foisor, 1979.

After 14 ... Rfd8 we reach the culminating point of the struggle.

15   Rhg1

The attack 15 e5 de 16 Rh4 Nf8 17 Ne4 Bb7 18 Nf6+ is refuted by 18 ... Bxf6!, which was already demonstrated in our remarks to 14 Qh5. At first glance, however, the attack against f7 looks dangerous after 15 e5 de 16 Nd5! ed 17 Bxd5, but after 17 ... ed 18 Qxf7+ Kh8 19 Bxd4 Bxg5+ 20 Kb1 Qe5! 21 Bxe5 Nxe5 Black has the advantage. Equally effective is the defence against 15 Nd5: 15 ... ed 16 Bxd5 Ne5! 17 f4! Bg4 18 Qh4 Rac8 19 c3 Be6 20 Bxe6 Ng6 21 Qg4 fe ∓, Kuzmin–Udovin, 1976.

15   ...   g6

Also possible is 15 ... Nc5, with

a similar idea, since on 16 e5 Black constructs his defence as follows: 15 ... g6 16 ♕h3 d5! 17 ♖h4 ♕xe5 18 ♗d4 ♘xb3+ 19 ab ♕f5 20 ♖xh7 ♕xh3 21 ♖xh3 e5 ∓

16 ♕h6

It is necessary to prevent the defence with h7-h5. The move 16 ♕h4 can only be played with the intention of advancing the f-pawn, but the the sense of White's previous moves is lost and complications arise: 16 ... ♘c5 17 f4 ♖b8 18 f5 a5 19 ♔b1 a4 20 ♘d5 ed 21 ♗xd5 ♗e6!. The resulting position favours Black, as seen in the game Radulov–Ribli, 1972.

16 ... ♗f8
17 ♕h4 ♘c5

Black can force a draw if he prefers, by playing 17 ... ♗e7.

18 ♖g3

This position is extremely sharp and quite difficult to evaluate. Keeping the status quo in the centre, each side plays on "its own" flank. After 18 ... ♖b8 19 ♖h3 Black has a choice between two risky, but apparently acceptable, continuations: 19 ... ♗g7!? 20 ♕xh7+ ♔f8 and 19 ... h5 20 gh ♔h7 21 ♕f6 b4!

D

11 ♔b1 *(197)*

A paradoxical move. White loses time playing a prophylactic move, which is little researched. The idea belongs to Velimirović.

11 ... ♘d7

One of the merits of White's 11th move is amply demonstrated in the game Velimirović–Csom, which inaugurated the variation:

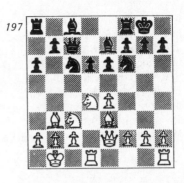

197

11 ... b5?! 12 ♘xc6 ♕xc6 13 ♗d4! ♗b7 14 ♖he1 ♕c7 15 a3 ♖ac8 16 f4! e5 17 fe de 18 ♘d5! ♗xd5 19 ed ed 20 ♕xe7 ♕xh2 21 d6 ♖ce8 22 ♗xf7+! etc.

12 ♕h5 ♘c5
13 g4 ♘xb3
14 cb!

A second subtlety of the prophylactic movement of the king is that White widens the scope of his operations to include the c-file. To achieve success against such a wide front requires great accuracy.

14 ... ♗d7
15 ♖hg1 ♘xd4
16 ♖xd4 f6!

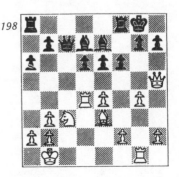

198

This position is rather unusual in the Velimirović attack. Black has not managed to advance his b-pawn, but he has fortified his defences and improved the coordination of his pieces. Velimirović considers that White holds the initiative after 17 ♖c1!, but Black has a solid position after the simple 17 ... ♗c6 18 ♘d5 ♕d8 19 ♘xe7+ ♕xe7. On 17 f4, Black can obtain roughly equal chances after 17 ... ♕d8 (The game Ligterink–Rodriguez, 1978, saw the less accurate 17 ... b5 18 f5 ♖ac8 19 g5! ef 20 g6! hg 21 ♖xg6 ♖f7 22 a3 ♗d8 23 ♖d1 ♕b7 24 ♖h6! ±±) 18 f5 ♕e8! 19 ♕h4 ♕f7.

The move 11 ♔b1 doubtless deserves further study.

28 9th Move Alternatives

Here we will examine those lines in which Black does not choose to enter into the lines considered in Chapter 27, but prefers to exit at move 9.

1 e4 c5 2 ♘f3 ♘c6 3 d4 cd 4 ♘xd4 ♘f6 5 ♘c3 d6 6 ♗c4 e6 7 ♗e3 ♗e7 8 ♕e2 0-0 9 0-0-0

At this point we ought to mention that if White castles short he will be invalidating his previous play and Black will not face any serious problems, for example: 9 0-0 ♘xd4 11 ♗xd4 ♕a5 12 ♖ad1 ♗d7 13 ♗b3 ♗c6 14 f4 e5 15 fe de 16 ♖f5 ♗c5! 16 ♗xc5 ♕xc5+ 17 ♔h1 ♖ad8 18 ♘d5 ♗xd5 19 ed e4! ∓, Hasin–Bradvarević, 1964, or 9 ... a6 10 ♖ad1 ♕c7 11 ♗b3 b5 12 a3 ♘xd4 13 ♗xd4 ♘d7 14 ♕g4 ♗f6 15 ♗xf6 ♘xf6 16 ♕g3 ♗b7 =.

White can also play 9 ♗b3, which just transposes into the normal lines after 9 ... a6 10 0-0-0. If he plays 9 ... d5 10 ed ed 11 0-0, he will enter a position where the play revolves around the isolated queen pawn.

A 9 ... d5
B 9 ... a6
C 9 ... ♘xd4
D 9 ... ♗d7
E 9 ... ♕a5

A

9 ... d5

This is a risky plan. Black hopes to pre-empt the coming pawn storm by activity in the centre, but he has not yet completed his development. With the king standing at c1 the isolation of the d-pawn after 10 ed ed does not play a major role, i.e. 11 ♗b3 ♖e8, 11 ♘f3 ♗e6, or 11 ♗g5 ♖e8 12 ♖he1 ♗g4 13 f3 ♗d7. The most solid reply to 9 ... d5 is Boleslavsky's recommendation 10 ♘f3!, in order to achieve active piece play in the centre, for example 10 ... ♘xe4 11 ♘xe4 ♕a5 12 ♗d2 ♕a4 13 ♗d3 de 14 ♕xe4 ♕xe4 15 ♗xe4 f6 (15 ...

♗d7 16 ♗g5! ±) 16 ♗e3 e5 17
♗d5+, although even here after 17
... ♔h8 △ ♗d7, ♖fd8, Black should
equalise.

Nor is 10 ♗b3 dangerous, be-
cause Black can play 10 ... ♘a5.
The advance 11 e5 will be in
Black's favour.

The opposition ♖d1-♕d8 allows
White to carry out an interesting
combination.

10 ♘xe6!?   fe
11 ed   ♘a5
12 de

White has enough pawns for the
piece, and if he manages to complete his pawn chain with f5 and
g4, then he will be very close to
victory.

12 ...   ♕c7

Another good method of defence is 12 ... ♕e8 13 ♗b5 ♘c6 14
♖he1 a6 15 ♗c4 b5 16 ♗b3 ♘a5
17 ♗d5 ♖b8, Zaitsev–Bitman, 1968.

13 ♗d5   ♘c6!

13 ... ♕e5? is bad: 14 f4 ♕f5 15
h3 ♗xe6 16 g4 ±, Zaitsev–Gik,
1967. By playing 13 ... ♘c6, Black
threatens to capture the bishop on
d5. On 14 ♗b3 he can even repeat
the position with 14 ... ♘a5. Perhaps 14 ♕c4 or 14 ♖he1 is stronger,
which leads to a complicated
struggle with somewhat better
chances for White.

B

9 ...   a6

This usually transposes back to
the main lines after 10 ♗b3, but
Black can adopt the original idea of
Grandmaster Belyavsky and play 10
... ♕e8!?. This way the queen participates in the defence of the king-

side, including the g6 square, should
White march his pawn all the way
from g2 to that square. The primary benefit of 10 ... ♕e8, however, is that it prevents 11 g4, since
that would lose a pawn to 11 ...
♘xd4 12 ♖xd4 e5. White can play
11 ♖hg1 ♘d7 12 g4 ♘c5 13 g5,
and apply the attacking methods
which we have considered elsewhere in these chapters. Velimirović recommends that White
play 11 f4 ♘d7 12 g4 ♘c5 13
♔b1 b5 14 f5 ♘xb3 (14 ... ♗f6
15 fe fe 16 ♘f5! ±, Velimirov-
Spassov, 1974) 15 ab, but after
15 ... ♗b7, Black, in our opinion,
has a solid position and well-
known counterplay on the queenside.

C

9 ...   ♘xd4
10 ♗xd4   ♕a5

This incarnation of the ♕a5
manoeuvre is less favourable for
Black than in E, since the White
bishop occupies a useful post at
d4. There is no need for White to
waste time retreating the Bishop
to b3.

11 e5

White also has a strong initiative after 11 ♖hg1.

11 ...   de
12 ♗xe5   b6
13 ♘b5

The correct piece. 13 ♗b5 fails
to 13 ... a6! 14 ♗c6 ♖a7 15 ♗b8
♗b7! 16 ♗xa7 ♗xc6 ∓.

13 ...   ♗a6
14 ♘c3   ♕a4
15 ♖d4

White has the initiative.

Bogdanović–Shamkovich, 1963 continued 15 ... ♗xb5 16 ♗xb5 ♕xa2 17 ♖hd1.

D

9 ... ♗d7

This move is intended to free a square for a rook.

10 f4!

10 ♗b3 is also possible, for example 10 ... ♕b8 11 f4 ♘xd4 12 ♖xd4 b5 13 f5! b4 14 fe fe 15 ♘b1 ±, or 13 ... ef 14 ef ♗xf5 15 g4 ♗e6 16 g5! ♘d7 17 ♗xe6 fe 18 ♕g4 ♘c5 19 b4 ±. Black can also try 10 ... ♖c8, after which he can obtain satisfactory play, according to Boleslavsky: 11 f4 ♘a5! 12 e5! de 13 fe ♘xb3+ 14 ab ♘d5 15 ♘xd5 ed 16 ♖hf1 ♗c5.

10 ... ♕b8
11 f5! ♘xd4
12 ♗xd4

Black must play 12 ... e5, in order to eliminate the threat of e4-e5, but after 13 ♗f2 White's advantage is indisputable.

E

9 ... ♕a5

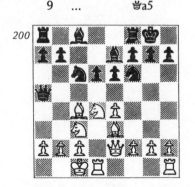

Black controls the e5-square and will carry out the manoeuvre ♗c8-d7-c6, followed by ♖ac8 and ♖fd8.

10 ♗b3

On 10 f4 Black's simplest reply is 10 ... ♘xd4 11 ♖xd4 ♗d7! 12 ♖f1 ♗c6 13 f5 d5!

10 ... ♘xd4

10 ... a6 is inferior in view of 11 ♖hg1 ♘xd4 12 ♗xd4 b5 13 g4 b4 14 g5 ♘d7 15 ♘d5! ed 16 ♗xd5 ♖b8 17 g6 with a very strong attack. Also bad is 10 ... ♗d7 11 ♘db5 ♘e8 12 f4 a6 13 ♘d4 ♘xd4 14 ♗xd4 ♗c6 15 f5!

11 ♗xd4 ♗d7
12 ♔b1

12 g4 is premature because of 12 ... e5!, but 12 f4 e5 13 ♘d5 ♘xd5 14 ed f6 15 ♗c3 ♕b6 16 g4 deserves consideration. The loss of a tempo entailed in defending the e-pawn with 12 f3 allows Black to obtain a good game by a number of means, for example 12 ... ♗c6 13 g4 d5 14 g5 ♘h5.

The move 12 ♔b1 forces Black to reveal his plan. It is a useful move in any event, since by defending the a-pawn with the king the bishop is freed from that responsibility. Moreover, the king is no longer on the c1-h6 diagonal.

12 ... ♗c6

On 12 ... b5 White has a choice between 13 ♗xf6 ♗xf6 14 ♖xd6 and 13 f4 e5 14 ♘d5 ♘xd5 15 ed ♗f6 (15 ... f6 16 fe fe 17 ♗xe5! ±) 16 ♗c3 ♕b6 17 g4 ±. If Black plays 12 ... ♖ad8, then 13 ♕e3! is good: 13 ... b6 14 ♗xf6! gf 15 ♘d5!! ♖fe8 (15 ... ed 16 ♖xd5 ♕a6 17 ♖h5 ♗g4 18 ♕g3 ±) 16 ♕h6! winning, according to analysis by Fischer.

13 f4 ♖ad8

Both sides have completed the redeployment of their pieces. White clearly has more chances to create active play. Play may continue 14 g4 d5 15 ed! ♘xd5 16 ♘xd5 ♗xd5 17 ♗c3 ♛c5 18 ♗xd5 ♖xd5 19 ♖xd5 ♛xd5 20 ♖d1 ♛c5 21 f5!, following analysis by Holmov. White can also try 14 f5! e5 (14 ... ef 15 ef ♖fe8 16 ♛d3 ±) 15 ♗f2 d5 16 ed ♘xd5 17 ♘xd5 ♗xd5 18 ♛xe5 ±, while the game Geller–Fischer, 1967, continued 14 ♖hf1

b5 15 f5! b4 16 fe bc 17 ef+ (Murey suggested 17 ♖xf6! gf 18 ef+ with a very strong attack.) 17 ... ♚h8 18 ♖f5! ♛b4 19 ♛f1! and White still obtained a strong attack.

We can sum up the lessons of these two chapters (27–28) as follows: The plan 8 ... ♗e7 9 0-0-0 0-0 leads to complicated and double-edged positions. Black's game is sufficiently solid, but he must play attentively and precisely in the defence.

29 Velimirović Attack: 7 . . . a6

1 e4 c5 2 ♘f3 ♘dc 3 d4 cd 4
♘xd4 ♘f6 5 ♘c3 d6 6 ♗c4 e6 7
♗e3 a6

At first glance this move seems
to violate Black's own opening
principle of rapid development, but
if he succeeds in gaining rapid
counterplay on the queenside his
play will be justified.

      8   ♕e2

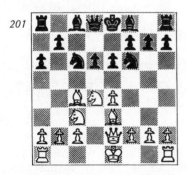

201

White can, of course, return to
the Classical Sozin with 0-0. Castling
queenside is riskier, but it is more
logical and more in the spirit of the
position, since White will soon be
able to concentrate the maximum
amount of firepower in the centre.

      8   ...   ♕c7

The direct action 8 ... ♘a5 9
♗d3 b5 meets with the strong reply

10 b4! After 10 ... ♘b7?! 11 0-0!
it is White who is attacking on
the queenside: 11 ... e5 12 ♘b3
♕c7 13 ♗d2 ♗d7 14 a4! ba 15
♘xa4 ♗e7 16 ♗e3 ±, Mestrović–
Polugayevsky, 1972. Of course, the
knight stands badly on b7, where it
only paralyzes Black's counterplay.
There are more chances in the
pawn sacrifice 10 ... ♘c4 11 ♗xc4
bc 12 ♕xc4. In the game de
Firmian–Zaltsman, 1979, White
obtained an advantage after 12 ...
♗b7 13 0-0 ♖c8 14 ♕d3 d5 15 e5
♘d7 16 ♗f4 ♗xb4 17 ♘ce2 ♗e7
18 ♕g3 g6 19 ♗h6, but 13 ... d5
14 ed ♘xd5 deserves analysis, as
both Black bishops will be employed.

    There is not much point to 8
... ♗d7 9 0-0-0 b5 10 ♗b3 ♕b8
(It is too late to play 10 ... ♗e7:
11 ♘xc6 ♗xc6 12 e5! ±) 11 g4
♘xd4 12 ♗xd4 e5. Exploiting his
lead in development, White profit-
ably opens up the game: 13 g5! ed
14 gf dc 15 e5! cb+ 16 ♔b1 ±.

      9   0-0-0

Practical players may well wish
to examine the immediate active
plan 9 ♗b3 ♘a5 10 g4, which
saves a tempo. It is too soon to

pass judgement on the counter-thrust 10 ... h5, as our only example is Brueggemann–Atanasov, 1978, which continued 11 g5 ♘g4 12 g6 ♘xb3 12 ab fg 14 h3 ♘xe3 15 ♕xe3 ♗e7 16 ♖g1 g5 17 ♘f3 g4 ∞. 11 gh must be tested, as it creates new objects of attack on the kingside. A more solid continuation than the game would have been reached had Black played 10 ... b5 11 g5 ♘d7.

202

Arriving at such a position, it is above all essential to precisely evaluate the consequences of sacrifices at e6, and this had better be done at home. Analysis shows that the variations of the sacrifice are not dangerous for Black. 12 ♗xe6 fe 13 ♘xe6 ♕c4! 14 ♕xc4 ♘xc4 15 ♘c7+ ♔d8 16 ♘xa8 ♘xe3 17 fe ♗b7 ∓, or 12 ♘xe6 fe 13 ♗xe6 ♘e5 14 ♘d5 ♕c4! 15 ♘f6+ gf 16 ♗xc4 (16 ♕h5+? ♔e7 17 ♗xc4 ♗g4 18 gf+ ♔d7! ∓) 16 ... ♗g4! 17 ♗xb5+ ♔f7 18 ♗xa6 ♗xe2 19 ♗xe2 ♘ac4 ∞

It is more natural to storm the e6 point with a pawn. 12 f4!? is met by 12 ... b4, and wild complications ensue: 13 ♘a4 ♗b7

(13 ... ♘xb3 14 cb! ♗b7 15 ♖c1!± or 13 ... ♘c5 14 ♘xc5 dc 15 ♗a4+ ♗d7 16 ♗xd7+ ♕xd7 17 ♘b3 ♕b5) 14 f5 e5 15 ♘e6 (The retreat 15 ♘f3?! is less bold and much less powerful: 15 ... ♘xb3 16 cb ♗xe4 17 0-0 ♕b7 18 ♘d2 ♗c6 19 ♖f2 ♕b5! ∓, Roth–Kasparov, 1980) 15 ... fe 16 fe ♘c5! 17 ♘xc5 dc 18 ♗d5 0-0-0 19 0-0-0 ∞ or 13 ♘d5!? ed 14 ed ♘c5 15 ♘c6! ♘xc6 16 ♗xc5+ ♗e7 17 ♗a4 ♗d7 18 dc ♗xc6 19 ♕f3 ♗xa4!? 20 ♕xa8+ ♔d7! 21 ♕xa6 (21 ♕xh8 ♕xc5 ∓) 21 ... ♗c6 22 ♗b6 ♖a8 23 ♕xa8 ♕xb6! ∓∓

After 9 0-0-0 Black can choose between:
A 9 ... ♘a5
B 9 ... ♗e7

Black cannot, however, play 9 ... b5 since after 10 ♘xc6 he is in trouble. White obtains the advantage after either 10 ... ♕xc6 11 ♘xb5 ♘xe4 12 ♘a7 ♕b7 13 ♘xc8 ♕xc8 14 ♗b3 △ ♗a4+, or 10 ... bc 11 ♕xc4 ♗b7 12 ♘e5 ♕xc4 13 ♘xc4 ♘xe4 14 ♘xe4 ♗xe4 15 f3 ♗d5 16 ♘b6.

A
9 ... ♘a5
Only now, when White's king has already fled to the queenside, must Black hurry with his counter-play.

10 ♗d3
On 10 ♗b3 Black should play 10 ... b5 11 g4 (11 f3 ♗e7 12 g4 0-0 13 g5 ♘h5! 14 f4 g6 15 f5 b4! 16 ♘b1 ♘xb3+ 17 ab e5! 18 f6 ed 19 fe ♕xe7 20 ♗xd4 a5 21 ♖hd1 ♖e8 ∓ Tal–Gipslis, 1981) 11 ... ♘xb3+ 12 ab. Now he can choose

between 12 ... ♗e7, transposing
into the main lines (B), or he can
explore uncharted territory with
either 12 ... ♗b7 or 12 ... g6 13 g5
♘h5.

10 ... b5!

Sticking to his plan. It makes no
sense to mix systems by playing 10
... ♗e7 11 g4 b5 12 g5 ♘d7 13
♘f5! ef 14 ♘d5 ♛d8 15 ef ♗b7.

203

Can the black pawn be allowed
to advance to b4, after which the
White knight will be temporarily
offside?

By placing his bishop on d3
White has sharply reduced the activity of the ♖d1, and for some
time to come his control of the
centre will be weakened. Therefore
it seems logical to play a prophylactic move which will give White
time to fortify his position later.

11 a3

Other continuations lead to
sharp and double-edged play:

a) 11 f4 b4 12 ♘b1 e5 (12 ...
♗b7!?) 13 ♘f5 g6 14 fe de 15
♗g5 ♘d7 with sharp play Ljubo-
jević-Musil, 1975.

b) 11 g4 b4 12 ♘b1 ♗b7 (the
risky 12 ... d5 is not so easy to

refute: 13 ed ♘xd5 14 ♗e4 ♘xe3!
15 ♛xe3 ♖b8 16 ♘d2 ♗d6 =
Kengis-Petrushin, 1980) 13 ♘d2
♗e7 (Here the rook on d1 is even
more passive and the opening of
the centre would be fully justified,
so why not 13 ... d5!?. The direct
attack will run out of steam quickly:
14 e5 ♛xe5 15 f4 ♛d6 16 f5 e5
17 ♗f4 ♘d7 ∓, Shlekis-Ivanov,
1977) 14 g5 ♘d7 15 f4 ♘c5 16
♔b1 d5 17 e5 0-0-0 or 17 ... ♘c4
with a complex game, as in Male-
vinsky-Shevelyev, 1979.

11 ... ♗b7

The fact that White had to take
time out for 11 a3 is a small victory
for Black, who can now use the
tempo to carry out his own preferred scheme of development. He
can therefore play the text, or the
equally straightforward 11 ... ♗e7.
Malevinsky-Petrushin, 1980
varied with 11 ... ♖b8 12 ♗d2
♘c4 13 ♗e1 ♗e7 14 f4 0-0 15 g4
d5! 16 ed ♘xd5 17 ♘xd5 ed 18
♘c6 ♗f6! 19 ♗xc4 bc 20 ♘xb8
♛xf4+ 21 ♗d2 ♛xb8 ∞

12 f4

12 g4!? is possible, as is 12
♗g5!? ♗e7 13 f4 0-0 14 ♘dxb5 ∞

12 ... ♗e7
13 ♖hf1 0-0
14 g4 d5!
15 ed

If 15 e5, then 15 ... ♘e4 is good.

15 ... ♘xd5
16 ♘xd5 ♗xd5
17 ♔b1 ♘c4

Black has a good game, Tisdall-
Dorfman, 1977.

B

9 ... ♗e7

White's target in the variations where Black castled at move 8 was the Black king, but the pressure on the centre played a less significant role. Now we will consider systems in which Black has not yet castled, but is prepared to do so at any moment. White must find a plan which is flexible enough to be appropriate whether Black's king remains in the centre, or flees to the flank.

Black does not spend a tempo castling, but tries to use the time saved to press home his queenside action, sometimes even playing in the centre. If he can force White to play just one inactive "extra" move, such as f2-f3, then his opening strategy is justified.

10 &b3

White can meet cunning with cunning, economising on the retreat of the bishop. To this end his best reply is 10 ♖hg1 with the obvious aim of advancing his g-pawn to g5, which will weaken Black's position in the centre.

Black has a number of obvious continuations, but none of them are quite sufficient to achieve equality:

a) 10 ... b5 11 ♘xc6 (After 11 &b3 0-0 12 g4 b4 13 ♘d5 we reach a well-known position) 11 ... ♕xc6 12 ♘xb5 ♘xe4 13 ♘a7 ♕b7 14 ♘xc8 ♕xc8. White still has a small edge, but Black can try to achieve counterplay on the b- and c-files.

b) 10 ... 0-0 transposes into the note to 10 &b3 after 10 ♖hg1 a6 on p. 190.

c) 10 ... ♘a5. Here White should probably return to the main lines with 11 &b3 since after 11 &d3!? b5 12 a3 (If White tries the direct 12 g4 then 12 ... b4 13 ♘a4 ♘d7 14 ♘b3 ♕c6! ∓ is good for Black.) and now Black has a choice between three comfortable plans:

c1) 12 ... &b7 △ d5.
c2) 12 ... ♘c4 13 &xc4 ♕xc4.
c3) 12 ... e5!? 13 ♘f5 &xf5 14 ef d5.

In each case Black has counterplay.

10 ... ♘a5

Black should not try for equality by bringing his king to the queenside: 10 ... &d7 11 g4 ♘xd4 12 ♖xd4 &c6 13 g5 ♘d7 14 f4 ♘c5 15 ♖hd1 ♘xb3+ 16 ab 0-0-0. After 17 ♕f2 b5 18 f5 Black has forfeited his right of play on the queenside and will be suffocated to death.

10 ... b5 is also unpromising because of 11 ♘xc6 ♕xc6 12 &d4 &b7 (On 12 ... 0-0, 13 ♘d5! is strong.) 13 ♖he1! 0-0 14 f4 ♖ac8 (Even after 14 ... ♕c7 15 e5!, White stands better) 15 ♘d5! ♕e8 (15 ... ed 16 ed ♘xd5 17 &xg7 ♘xf4 18 ♕xe7 ♔xg7 19 ♖xd6 ±) 16 ♘xf6+ gf 17 f5 e5 18 ♕h5! ♔h8 19 ♖d3 ♖g8 20 &xf7 and White has an excellent position, Hübner–Hort, 1972.

11 g4!

Just so! The attack with the f-pawn is not effective: 11 f4 b5 12 f5 ♘xb3+ 13 ab b4! 14 ♘a4 e5 15 ♘f3 &b7 ∓

By moving the g-pawn White tries to reduce the pressure on the e-pawn without holding up the attack.

    11   ...   b5

Belyavsky's interesting idea involves the blockade of the pawn storm: 11 ... ♘xb3+ 12 ab g6 13 g5 ♘h5. The consequences of the sacrifice 14 ♘f5 are not clear: 14 ... ef 15 ♘d5 ♕c6! 16 ♗d4 ♗xg5+ 17 ♔b1 ♖g8!, but not 17 ... 0-0? 18 ♕xh5! gh 19 ♘e7+ ♗xe7 20 ♖g1+, mating. A double-edged position arises after 14 f4 b5 15 f5 b4 16 ♘a4 0-0.

    12   g5   ♘xb3+
    13   ab   ♘d7

Both sides are poised for the battle. Black tries to pin White's pieces to the defence of the e-pawn, after which he will castle. White has completed his development and has a strong knight on d4, but it is not easy to find an active plan for him. There are two ways to fortify his position. First, he can advance his pawns on the kingside in order to break Black's wall of pawns by playing g5-g6. The second, combinational, method is employed when the Black king remains in the centre. In that case he will be subject to shelling from White's heavy artillery, which is concentrated on the open files in the centre.

14 b4?! is an ineffective and risky plan. White adopts radical measures which prevent the advance of Black's b-pawn, but the advanced pawn makes it easier for Black to open up lines. After 14 ... 0-0! 15 f4 a5 16 ♘cxb5 ♕b7 17 f5 ab! 18 f6 gf 19 ♖hg1 ♔h8 20 gf ♘xf6 21 ♗h6 ♖g8 Black has beaten back the attack and achieved

a clear advantage, Christiansen–Tukmakov, 1972.

Here our analysis separates into:
A 14 h4
B 14 ♘f5!?

If White advances the f-pawn (f2-f4), then the e-pawn comes under fire after 14 ... ♘c5. The plan with 14 h4 is more dangerous, since its aim (after f4-f5 and g5-g6) is not only to disrupt the Black pawn structure or deny his opponent the privilege of castling, but also, in some cases, to undertake operations along the h-file.

A

    14   h4

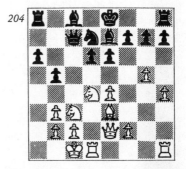

204

Castling can prove fatal for Black: 14 ... 0-0 15 g6! hg 16 h5 and besides that it would be in violation of his opening strategy: Castle when one's opponent makes an insignificant move.

14 ... ♘c5 seems natural enough, as it threatens to win the e-pawn after ... b4. It has a rather negative reputation based on the game Radulov–Hamman, 1968: 15 b4 ♘a4 16 ♖d3 ♕c4? 17 ♘b1! ♕xb4 18 c3 ♕a5 19 ♘c6 ±. It is doubtful that White can obtain an advantage

with 15 b4 and 16 ⬜d3, but the
move 16 ... ♛c4 is hardly the way
to play for Black. Instead, any
move of the ♝c8 or even 16 ...
♘xc3 17 ⬜xc3 ♛b7 would have
given Black a satisfactory game.
White should probably answer 14 ...
♘c5 with 15 h5, after which 15 ...
b4 16 ♘a4 leads to positions considered below.

14 ... ♝b7 is often played, creating the same threats on the e-pawn.
After 15 f3 b4 16 ♘a4 ♘c5 17 h5!
♘xa4 18 ba ♛a5! Larsen considers
that Black stands quite well. 15 h5!
places more difficult problems before Black. It is dangerous to take
the pawn, as Black will lose a lot of
time and fall under a powerful
attack, i.e. 15 ... b4 16 ♘a4 ♝xe4
17 f3 ♝b7?! 18 g6 hg 19 hg ⬜xh1
20 ⬜xh1 ♘c5 22 gf+ ♚xf7 23 ♘xe6
±, Podgayets–Butnoris, 1975.

There are other replies to 15 h5,
such as 15 ... b4 16 ♘a4 0-0-0; 15
... ♘f8!? 16 ♛g4 b4 17 ♘a2 ♛a5
18 ♚b1 0-0-0 19 g6 hg 20 hg
⬜xh1 21 ⬜xh1 f5; or 15 ... b4 16
♘a2! ♛a5 17 ♚b1 ♝xe4 18
f3. All of these lead to positions
where White holds the initiative
firmly. I do not think that praxis
will change the evaluation of
these three variations, and therefore one should recognize that
14 ... ♝b7 does not force White to
make one superfluous, that is,
defensive, move, and is therefore
a "blank shot".

Now we can embark on our
analysis of the immediate advance
of the b-pawn.

14   ...   b4

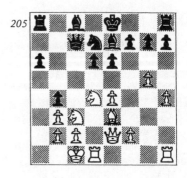

205

15   ♘a2!

For some reason 15 ♘a4 is seen
more frequently, but it is hard to
explain why that move is, in principle, better than the withdrawal
to a2.

Is the control of c5 significant?
It has been proven that after 15 ...
♘c5, 16 ♘xc5 is the least promising
continuation since the ♘d4 is thereby robbed of its beautiful square:
16 ... dc 17 ♘f3 a5 18 ♘d2 a4
19 ba ⬜xa4 20 ♘c4 0-0 21 ♛g4
♝a6 ∓ Cox–Netskarzh, 1974.

What about the blockade of the
Pa6? To that it must be said that
the position of the knight on a4 is
unstable, i.e. 15 ... ♘c5 16 f3 ♝d7!
17 h5 ♘xb3+ 18 ♘xb3 ♝xa4 and
Black stands no worse. It is true
that White can forget about his
central pawn and play more strongly
with 16 h5, in which case Black's
defensive task is more difficult, but
the position can be held. In a number of games White won rapidly,
but in each case analysis has shown
that the positions could have been
defended by Black, and now there
are several ways out of the woods:

a) **16 ... ♘xe4!?** 17 g6 ♝d8 18 h6

fg 19 hg ♕xg7.

b) **16** ... ♗d7 17 g6 ♘xb3+ (but not 17 ... ♗f6? 18 e5! ♗xe5 19 ♕f3! 0-0 20 gf+ ♔h8 21 ♗g5 △ h6 ± ± Razuvayev) 18 ♘xb3 ♗xa4 19 gf+ ♔xf7.

c) **16** ... ♗d7 17 ♔b1 ♗xa4 (But why not 17 ... ♘xe4 18 g6 f5 or even 17 ... ♘xa4 18 ba g6?) 18 ba ♘xa4 19 g6! with a sharp game, Planinc–Belyavsky, 1975: 19 ... ♗f6 20 gf+ ♕xf7 21 ♕c4 0-0!

The transfer of the knight to a2 cannot really be called a retreat, since it threatens the b-pawn.

     15   ...   ♗b7

Other continuations have not been tried out in praxis, but are worth analysing:

a) **15** ... a5!? 16 ♘b5 (Black intends to play ... ♗a6 and ... 0-0-0) 16 ... ♕c6 17 ♕c4! (17 ♘a7 ♕xe4 or ♕b7 =) 17 ... ♘c5! 18 ♘xd6+ ♗xd6 19 ♖xd6 ♕xd6 20 ♗xc5 ♕c7! 21 ♖d1 e5! and there does not seem to be any way to continue the attack.

b) **15** ... ♘c5 16 ♘xb4 ♘xe4 with sharp play.

     16   h5!   ♕a5
     17   ♔b1   ♗xe4
     18   f3

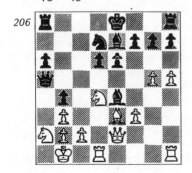

206

We now have a critical position for the evaluation of the defence with 15 ... ♗b7.

     18   ...   ♗d5

18 ... ♗f5 allowed a beautiful attack in Ljubojević–Khaman, 1975 19 ♘xb4! ♕xb4 20 ♘xf5 ef 21 ♗d4! ♘c5 22 h6 ♘e6 23 hg ♖g8 24 ♗f6! ♔d7! 25 ♖xh7 ♖ae8 26 ♖h8 ♗xf6 27 ♖xg8 ♗xg7 28 ♖xe8 ♔xe8 29 g6!. 19 ♘c6! is also good.

After the text move White can play 19 g6, to which Black should reply not 19 ... 0-0 20 h6!, but 19 ... ♗f6! 20 gf+ ♔xf7. The situation is double-edged, and the Black bishops work well in the defence.

B

     14   ♘f5!? *(207)*

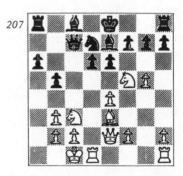

207

Grandmaster Velimirović's patented sacrifice, where White receives compensation in the form of pressure along the open files in the centre and a good target – the Black king which has been tarrying in the centre.

There is no longer any point in declining the sacrifice since the game Zaichik–Korsunsky, 1975, showed a way for White to obtain a very strong attack: 14 ... b4 15 ♘xg7+ ♔f8 16 ♕h5 ♔xg7 17 ♗d4+ ♘e5 18 f4 bc 19 fe cb+ 20 ♗xb2 d5 21 ed ♗c5 22 ♕h6+ ♔g8 23 ♖bf1. Analysis by Boleslavsky also gives White an excellent game: 15 ♘xe7 bc 16 ♘xc8 cb+ 17 ♔xb2 ♖xc8 18 ♖d2 ±.

The acceptance of the sacrifices follows logically from the position. Black has not committed such great sins that he should expect to be punished by a mating attack.

14   ...   ef
15   ♘d5   ♕d8
16   ef   ♗b7

The knight on d5 must be destroyed immediately. After the natural 16 ... 0-0 Black loses quickly: 17 f6! gf (17 ... ♘xf6 18 ♗b6! ±) 18 ♗d4 ♘e5 19 gf ♗xf6 20 ♖hg1+ ♗g7 21 ♗xe5, over-running the Black position, Velimirović–Sofrevsky, 1965.

17   f6!   gf
18   ♖he1

18 gf ♗xd5 19 fe is inferior because of 19 ... ♕a5! 20 ♗d4 ♖g8, and it is hard for White to demonstrate how his attack is worth a piece.

White adopts the clear and correct strategy, he optimally concentrates his firepower in the area in which the future battle will take place.

18   ...   ♗xd5

One still cannot castle, as 18 ... 0-0 is met by 19 gf ♘xf6 20 ♘xe7+ ♕xe7 21 ♖h1+ ♔h8 22 ♗d4! ± or 19 ... ♗xf6 20 ♕g4+ ♔h8 21 ♘xf6 ♘xf6 22 ♗d4 ♖g8 23 ♖e8!! ♖xe8 24 ♕g5 ♖e6 25 ♖g1 winning,

according to analysis by Velimirović.

19   ♖xd5   ♖g8

In the end, Black must fore-swear castling for ever. If 19 ... 0-0 20 gf ♗xf6 21 ♖g1+ ♔h8 22 ♖h5! ♗g7 (If 22 ... ♖g8, then 23 ♖xh7+) 23 ♖xg7 ♔xg7 24 ♕g4+ ♔h8 25 ♕f5, mating. No better is 20 ... ♘xf6 21 ♖g5+ ♔h8 22 ♗d4 ♖g8 (or 22 ... ♖e8) 23 ♕xe7 ±. Therefore the rook takes the place of the king at g8.

The situation is quite interesting, and the evaluation of 14 ♘f5 hangs in the balance.

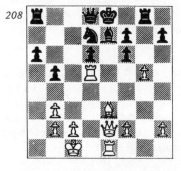

208

Black's position looks dangerous, since his pieces are paralysed and his king is caught in the centre. Grandmaster Bronstein considers that it is not necessary for White to force matters here, but can continue to place his opponent in critical positions. In our opinion, one should not underestimate Black's defensive resources, and even praxis has not yet proven an advantage for White in this position. We examine a number of continuations:

a) 20 ♗f4 seems the most dangerous

move, giving White an initiative after 20 ... ♔f8. Gheorghiu proposes that White can now take a draw by playing 21 ♕h5 ♕a5 (but not 21 ... ♖g7 22 ♖xe7 ♔xe7 23 ♗xd6+ ♔e6 24 c4! bc 25 bc ♖xg5 26 ♕h3+ f5 27 f4! ±± Matanović-Musil, 1973) 22 ♕e2 ♕d8 etc., but this conclusion can only be accepted if one can show an advantage for White after 22 ... ♘e5 (instead of 22 ... ♕d8), 23 gf ♗xf6, i.e. 24 ♖xd6 ♖e8 (△25 ... ♘d3+), or 24 ♔b1 ♕b4 25 ♗h6+ ♗g7 26 ♕e3 ♕h4. Black has more difficult problems to solve after 21 ♗xd6 ♗xd6 22 ♖xd6, where the knight is practically under a death sentence. If 22 ... fg 23 ♕d2 ♖a7 24 ♔b4! a5! (24 ... ♔g7? 25 ♕d4+) 25 ♖xd7+ ab 26 ♖xd8+ ♔g7 27 ♖xg8+ ♔xg8 28 ♖e5 f6 29 ♖xb5 ♖a1+ 30 ♔d2 Black is fighting for a draw. 22 ... ♖a7 23 gf ♖g6 24 ♕e3 ♖c7 25 ♕h3 is apparently in White's favour. But Black's position is defensible if he plays actively. The natural continuation 22 ... ♖xg5 allows Black to beat back the attack most simply, i.e. 23 f4 ♖g6 24 f5 ♖g5 25 h4 ♖xf5! 26 ♕e4 ♖e5 27 ♖xd7 ♖xe4 28 ♖xd8+ ♖xd8 etc. There is another acceptable route: 22 ... ♖c8!? 23 gf (23 ♕d2 fg! 24 ♖xd7 ♕f6 ∞) 23 ... ♖g6 24 ♕d2 (24 ♕d3 ♕a5! ∓) 24 ... ♖c7 25 ♖d1 ♖xf6 26 ♖xd7 ♖xd7 27 ♕xd7 ♕b6

b) 20 ♗d2 is quite insidious, creating the threat of 21 ♗a5. All the same Black must play 20 ... ♔f8, after which 21 ♗a5 is countered by 21 ... ♕xa5 22 ♕xe7+ ♔g7 23 ♖e3 ♖ae8 24 gf+ ♔h8 25 ♕xe8 ♘xf6!

∓. White can only continue his attack by playing 21 ♕h5, in order to meet 12 ... ♔g7 with 22 ♖e3 △ ♗c3, but 21 ... ♖g7 frees the g8 square for the king and creates problems for White in trying to fortify his position.

c) White can, of course, try to improve his position straight away with 20 h4, supporting his bridgehead at g5. But even here Black has a solid position: 20 ... ♖c8 21 ♗f4 ♔f8 22 gf (22 ♕h5 ♕a5 23 ♕e2 ♘e5 etc.) 22 ... ♘xf6 23 ♖f5 ♖c5! and now not 24 ♗h6+ ♔e8 25 ♖xf6 ♖e5! ∓.

d) The plan of attack with 20 gf ♘xf6 21 ♖f5 is more dangerous for Black. White slightly modifies his attack front. Forgetting about the d-pawn, he creates strong pressure on the d- and f-files. The bishop becomes quite strong, cutting off the king's escape via f8, (♗h6) and threatening the queen (♗b6). At the same time it can harrass the knight (♗d4). The queen at f3 creates unpleasantries for the ♘f6 and also menaces the long diagonal.

The natural defensive measures: 21 ... ♖g6 22 ♗b6! ♕d7 23 ♕f3 ♖b8 24 ♖xf6 ♖xb6, lead to an endgame which is worse for Black after 25 ♕a8+ ♕d8 26 ♖xe7+ ♔xe7 27 ♖xf7+ ♔xf7 28 ♕xd8 ±, Kupreichik-Belyavsky, 1974. White managed to repulse the attack after 21 ... ♖b8 22 ♗a7?! ♖b7 23 ♗d4 ♘g4 24 ♕f3 ♖c8! (24 ... ♖d7? 25 ♕h3! ♘e5 26 f4 ±) 25 ♕d5 ♘h6 26 ♖h5 ♖g6 27 f4 ♖c7 ∓, Taborov-Korsunsky, 1976, although White can improve, perhaps, with 22 ♗g5!

Black can seek new defences, for example 21 ... ♘g4!? 22 ♗g5 ♘e5, or 21 ... ♘d7, and it is probably worthwhile for him to do so.

Thus we return to the central question of this chapter: should Black risk undertaking operations on the queenside right away with 7 ... a6!? The foregoing analysis will, we hope, put that question in its proper perspective.

Now when you have finally reached the centre of the labyrinth of the Velimirović Attack, having seen many beautiful variations along the way, you might understand the principal, and rather tragic, drawback of the variation. Matters come to a head too quickly,

leading to forced play with clearly defined objectives. Sometimes long analysis, reaching to the 25th–40th move, is required for its explanation. It may soon come to pass that theoreticians and analysts will have worked out the position to about 35 moves, and then there will be few who wish to embark upon these monster-variations, and in the theoretical manuals of 1990, they may write: "The plan with 8 ♕e2 and 9 0-0-0 has disappeared from tournament play, since after (here they will insert a 25 move variation) White's attack is not dangerous, and the game moves into an endgame which is favourable for Black".

Index of Variations